CLOUD COMPUTING AND AWS INTRODUCTION

MASTERING AWS FUNDAMENTALS AND CORE SERVICES (HANDS-ON)

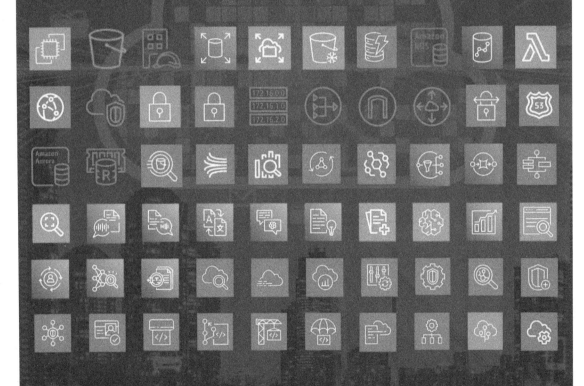

SK Singh

KnoDAX

Acknowledgments

I would like to express my heartfelt gratitude to **Adi Bhandaru** (Cloud Migration, Global Program Delivery Portfolio Lead), **Anjaiah Methuku, Anubhav Srivastava** (Lead Engineer, AOL, Author of Java 9 Regular Expressions), **Ashok Pandey, Dmitry Doronin** (Sr. Software Engineer, Dataminr), **Dr. Vimal Mishra** (Director, IERT Allahabad, India), **Jack Greene** (Project Manager for a state government in the US Northeast), **Kumar Rajesh** (Director, Regulatory Services, ArisGlobal), **Nick Sandru** (DevOps Engineer, Apple), **Nick Selya** (JPMC), **Roberto Dockery** (VP, Morgan Stanley), **Saurabh Banerjee** (Director, Data Engineering, Publicis Sapient), **Shailendra Dixit** (Tech Manager), **Sharad Sharma** (VP, JPMC), **SooBok Shin** (Software Engineer, Google), **Sushim Dalbehera** (Sr. Data Analytics Practitioner), **Vishal Tandon** (VP, JPMC), and **Vinod Kumar** (Executive Director, JPMC). Your support, thoughtful feedback, and encouragement helped make the publication of this book possible.

Table of Contents

Introduction

Cloud computing has revolutionized how businesses and individuals interact with technology, providing on-demand access to scalable and flexible resources. This book offers a comprehensive guide to mastering AWS fundamentals and core services, starting with foundational cloud computing concepts and seamlessly transitioning into AWS, the world's leading cloud services provider.

The content is divided into two sections. The first section, Cloud Computing, builds a solid understanding of core cloud concepts, including virtualization, security essentials, and service management. The second section focuses on AWS Fundamentals and explores popular AWS services, equipping readers with the skills to implement, manage, and optimize AWS cloud solutions effectively. The following provides a high-level overview of each chapter.

In Chapter 1, we lay the foundation with an exploration of cloud computing fundamentals. Readers will understand traditional IT infrastructure, the evolution of cloud computing, service models (IaaS, PaaS, SaaS), deployment types, and essential characteristics of the cloud.

Chapter 2 dives into cloud computing architecture, covering its layered structure and design principles like scalability, elasticity, and cost optimization, while introducing NIST's cloud reference model.

Chapter 3 focuses on service management in the cloud, including SLAs, cost optimization, billing models, and data management strategies to ensure efficient resource usage and scaling decisions.

In Chapter 4, we address billing and accounting, discussing financial models like CapEx, OpEx, Total Cost of Ownership (TCO), pricing schemes, and cost-benefit analysis when moving to the cloud.

Chapter 5 explains cloud virtualization, a cornerstone of cloud computing. It covers virtualization types, hypervisors, virtual networking, and storage virtualization, detailing how resources are abstracted for greater efficiency.

Security remains critical in the cloud, and Chapter 6 introduces cloud security essentials, focusing on trust, compliance, security tools, and contractual models for safeguarding data and services.

From Chapter 7, the book shifts focus to AWS, the leading cloud services provider. Readers are introduced to AWS's history and core services, setting the stage for hands-on exploration.

Chapter 8 guides readers through getting started with AWS, including account setup, access management, and cost optimization through AWS billing tools and Free Tier usage.

Chapter 9 explores AWS global infrastructure, breaking down regions, availability zones, edge locations, and local zones that power AWS's scalability and reliability.

In Chapter 10, readers gain an overview of AWS core services across compute, storage, database, and networking, including practical exercises.

Chapter 11 covers AWS Identity and Access Management (IAM), introducing users, groups, roles, and policies that secure cloud resources with best practices for access control.

Networking fundamentals take center stage in Chapter 12, which introduces Amazon VPC, CIDR addressing, subnets, security groups, and VPN configurations for secure and scalable network design.

Chapter 13 delves into AWS compute services, including EC2, AWS Lambda, and serverless models, while Chapter 14 introduces AWS storage services such as Amazon S3, EBS, Glacier, and EFS for managing data.

Chapter 15 focuses on AWS database services, covering managed relational databases (RDS), NoSQL options like DynamoDB, and warehousing with Redshift.

Data-driven insights are explored in Chapter 16, which introduces AWS analytics services, including Athena, Kinesis for real-time streaming, and OpenSearch for search and analytics.

In Chapter 17, readers explore application integration services such as SNS, SQS, EventBridge, and Step Functions to build event-driven and integrated applications.

Chapter 18 highlights AWS DevOps services, including tools like CodePipeline, CodeBuild, and Elastic Beanstalk to automate and streamline deployments.

For observability, Chapter 19 focuses on monitoring and logging services with CloudWatch, CloudTrail, AWS X-Ray, and Config to manage and troubleshoot cloud resources.

Security takes a deeper dive in Chapter 20, which details AWS security services, compliance tools, and automation strategies for securing workloads.

Finally, Chapter 21 introduces AWS AI/ML services, covering tools like Rekognition, SageMaker, Polly, and Comprehend to integrate AI-driven capabilities into applications.

By following this book, readers will gain both theoretical and practical knowledge to confidently leverage cloud computing and AWS services for modern IT and business solutions.

Chapter 1. Cloud Computing

This chapter introduces to the foundational concepts and evolution of cloud technology, starting with traditional IT infrastructure and its limitations. The chapter provides an overview of various computing paradigms—such as distributed, cluster, grid, and utility computing—that have paved the way for cloud computing. It explores the evolution of cloud computing, identifying the key business drivers that encourage organizations to adopt cloud solutions. The chapter defines cloud computing, including the widely accepted NIST definition, and outlines cloud service models like Infrastructure as a Service (IaaS), Platform as a Service (PaaS), and Software as a Service (SaaS).

Additionally, the chapter discusses extended models like Function-as-a-Service (FaaS) and cloud storage, along with various cloud deployment models, such as public, private, hybrid, community, and multi-cloud. Readers will gain insights into the essential characteristics of cloud computing, its advantages and disadvantages, and critical topics like software quality attributes, scope of responsibility, and multitenancy. By the end of the chapter, readers will have a comprehensive understanding of cloud computing, its diverse models, and its role in modern IT infrastructure.

1.1 Traditional IT Infrastructure

AWS, a leading cloud provider with over a million customers across 200 countries, operates on a robust cloud computing architecture. For a cloud practitioner, having a solid understanding of cloud computing concepts is fundamental. To appreciate the evolution of cloud computing, it's essential to explore traditional IT infrastructure, its challenges, and the need for innovation.

In the late 90s, during the dot-com boom, startups like Amazon and Google emerged, often beginning in garages with a few servers. As user bases grew, businesses faced scalability challenges, prompting a move from garages to server rooms in offices. These rooms addressed issues like bandwidth, power supply, and cooling. However, as demand increased further, businesses transitioned to data centers—facilities offering 24/7 power, cooling, security, and scalability to support hundreds or thousands of servers.

Despite their advantages, data centers posed challenges: high operational costs, limited space, maintenance complexity, and vulnerability to natural disasters, creating a single point of failure. These issues led to the question: Is there a better solution? The answer is cloud computing.

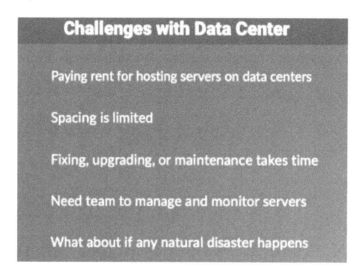

Cloud computing revolutionized IT infrastructure, providing on-demand resources via the Internet. It powers the tools and platforms we use daily—Facebook, Gmail, Zoom, and more. Unlike traditional systems, cloud computing eliminates the need for physical infrastructure management, offering scalability, flexibility, and cost-efficiency. The term "cloud" in cloud computing serves as a metaphor for the Internet, symbolizing the delivery of IT resources seamlessly and on demand. This innovation marks a significant shift from conventional IT practices to modern, Internet-based solutions.

1.2 Computing Paradigm Overview

The term computing paradigm means a set of practices to compute any task. The technology community consortium has proposed, from time to time, various computing techniques based on current technology and practices. It's essential to know about computing paradigms, i.e., shifting computing technology from one practice to another.

Client-Server Computing: Resources are centrally stored on a server and shared with clients via an integrated operating system. This architecture forms the backbone of modern systems like supercomputers and data centers.

Parallel Computing: Multiple processors work together, sharing centralized memory, to execute tasks simultaneously. This is known as parallel processing, requiring specialized parallel programming.

Distributed Computing: Independent computers, with private memory, are connected via a network to exchange data through message passing. Distributed systems appear as a single system to users through distributed programming.

Cloud Computing: An internet-based system that combines centralized and distributed resources using parallel and distributed concepts. Cloud computing leverages virtualized infrastructure and is often seen as a utility service.

Quantum Computing: Quantum computers use qubits instead of classical bits, enabling calculations far faster than traditional systems. Though in its infancy, quantum computing has the potential to revolutionize computational power.

Nano Computing: Nano computing employs nanoscale components like nanowires and transistors for faster, energy-efficient computing. Research continues in molecular and DNA-based nano computing architectures.

The development of distributed and parallel computing has led to advancements like fog and edge computing and ubiquitous computing through the Internet of Things (IoT). IoT integrates networks, sensors, and analytics to achieve edge computing, enabling real-time communication anywhere, anytime. Internet computing unifies all paradigms over the internet for advanced connectivity and computing.

1.3 Recent Trends in Computing

The overview of the computing paradigm gives a clear idea that computing technology is evolving continuously. Every day [figuratively], we are witnessing improvement in computing performance with the help of advanced research and development. Companies are launching new products and services regularly to meet consumer requirements and preferences. Let's discuss the current trends that are popular in computing.

1.3.1 Distributed Computing

Distributed Computing refers to a computing paradigm where multiple independent machines, connected over a network, coordinate tasks through message passing. Unlike centralized systems, distributed computing divides and processes tasks simultaneously across multiple nodes, enabling efficient resource use and faster results.

Key characteristics include Parallel Processing, where tasks are broken into subtasks and processed concurrently across machines, and Inter-process Communication (IPC), which ensures effective coordination and synchronization between nodes. Resource Sharing allows the distribution of computing power, memory, and storage among nodes, leading to better resource utilization and cost reduction.

Fault Tolerance ensures the system continues functioning even if some nodes fail, through redundancy and error recovery mechanisms. Data Distribution allows data to be partitioned or replicated across nodes to enhance access speed and resilience. Lastly, Scalability enables distributed systems to handle growing workloads by adding or removing nodes as needed.

Distributed computing is widely used in applications such as big data processing, scientific simulations, and web services. While it offers benefits like improved performance and resource efficiency, it also introduces challenges such as managing network communication, data consistency, and node coordination, which require careful design and implementation.

1.3.2 Cluster Computing

Cluster Computing is an advanced form of distributed computing where a group of interconnected computers, called nodes, work together as a single unit to perform tasks. These nodes are tightly coupled through a Local Area Network (LAN) and share resources like processing power, memory, and storage to handle computational workloads efficiently.

The main characteristics of cluster computing include High Performance, achieved by distributing tasks across multiple nodes for efficient execution, and Parallel Processing, where complex tasks are divided into subtasks that run concurrently on different nodes. Load Balancing ensures the even distribution of tasks across nodes, optimizing their contribution.

Resource Sharing enhances cost efficiency and hardware utilization by sharing CPU, memory, and storage among nodes. Fault Tolerance mechanisms, like redundancy and failover strategies, ensure system reliability during node failures. Lastly, Scalability allows clusters to adapt to increased workloads by adding or removing nodes.

Cluster computing is widely used for applications requiring high-performance computing (HPC), such as scientific research, financial modeling, weather forecasting, and extensive data analysis. It is also integral to supercomputing, where interconnected high-performance clusters simulate complex phenomena like nuclear reactions, climate patterns, and massive data processing tasks.

1.3.3 Grid Computing

Grid Computing is a distributed computing paradigm where multiple computers, often called nodes or resources, collaborate as an interconnected network to solve large-scale computational problems or tasks requiring significant computing power. It harnesses the combined processing, storage, and data-sharing capabilities of geographically dispersed and heterogeneous resources to achieve a common goal.

Key features of grid computing include Resource Sharing, where resources like processing power, memory, and storage are shared across nodes, often from different organizations or locations. Parallel Processing enables complex tasks to be divided into subtasks and processed simultaneously across multiple nodes, improving efficiency. Distributed Data Management ensures data is stored across various nodes, with replication or partitioning for better performance.

Grid computing embraces Heterogeneity, supporting diverse hardware, software, and networks using interoperability standards and middleware for smooth coordination. It is Scalable, allowing resources to be added or removed dynamically to meet variable workloads. High Availability is ensured through fault tolerance and redundancy mechanisms, keeping the system operational despite node failures. Additionally, Collaborative and Virtual Organizations are facilitated, enabling shared infrastructure for organizations and individuals to manage grid resources effectively.

Grid computing is widely used in scientific research, engineering simulations, weather forecasting, and large-scale data analysis. Initiatives like the European Grid Infrastructure (EGI) and Open Science Grid (OSG) exemplify its role in supporting scientific and academic projects. Unlike cluster and cloud computing, grid computing emphasizes leveraging geographically dispersed, heterogeneous resources to form a dynamic and interconnected computing environment.

1.3.4 Utility Computing

Utility Computing is a computing model where users pay for resources like processing power, storage, and networking on a pay-as-you-go or metered basis, similar to utility services such as electricity or water. Users can access these resources without owning or maintaining the underlying hardware and infrastructure.

Key characteristics of utility computing include On-Demand Provisioning, where users can scale resources up or down as needed, and Metered Billing, where costs are calculated based on actual resource usage. Managed Services are often provided, such as security, databases, and monitoring, to simplify infrastructure management. It leverages Resource Sharing by virtualizing the infrastructure, enabling efficient resource utilization. The model ensures Scalability to meet changing demands and offers Accessibility for users to connect from anywhere via the internet.

Utility computing aligns closely with cloud computing models like Infrastructure as a Service (IaaS) and Platform as a Service (PaaS), offering businesses cost-effectiveness, flexibility, and scalability. It allows organizations to focus on core operations while outsourcing IT resource management. However, users must monitor resource usage to avoid unexpected costs and address security and data privacy concerns when dealing with sensitive data.

1.4 Evolution of Cloud Computing

Cloud computing evolved over decades, starting with mainframe computing in the 1950s-1960s, where centralized systems processed data for multiple users. In the 1970s, virtualization emerged with IBM's technology, allowing multiple virtual machines to run on a single mainframe, enabling resource sharing. By the 1980s, client-server computing distributed processing power, marking a shift toward decentralized systems.

In the 1990s, the growth of the Internet and web services allowed remote access to applications through browsers, with companies like Amazon, Google, and Salesforce offering online services. The 2000s introduced utility computing, where resources were provided on a pay-as-you-go model, similar to utilities like water or electricity.

The launch of AWS in 2006 marked the modern cloud era, pioneering Infrastructure as a Service (IaaS) with services like EC2 and S3. In 2008, Google introduced Google App Engine as a Platform as a Service (PaaS) for web applications. By 2010, cloud computing diversified with providers like Azure, IBM Cloud, and Google Cloud Platform, offering databases, machine learning, and serverless computing.

In 2014, AWS Lambda introduced serverless computing, allowing developers to focus on code while AWS managed infrastructure and auto-scaling. Organizations then adopted hybrid and edge computing, combining public and private clouds and processing IoT data closer to its source to reduce latency.

Today, cloud computing continues to integrate advanced technologies like AI, containerization (Kubernetes), and quantum computing. It has democratized access to IT infrastructure, enabling scalability, cost-effectiveness, and innovation, and remains pivotal for businesses and digital transformation.

1.5 Business Drivers for Adopting Cloud Computing

Adopting cloud computing technology in business offers several significant benefits driven by cost efficiency, scalability, and operational agility. One major advantage is cost reduction, as organizations can avoid heavy upfront investments in hardware and data centers. Cloud services help reduce both Capital Expenditures (CapEx), like purchasing equipment, and Operating Expenses (OpEx), such as salaries and utilities, by offering a pay-as-you-go pricing model. This model allows businesses to scale resources up or down based on demand, enhancing agility and optimizing costs.

Cloud computing also supports business continuity and disaster recovery by backing up data across multiple geographically distributed data centers. This ensures uninterrupted business operations and quick recovery during disruptions, minimizing risks and data loss.

The convenience of cloud computing is another key driver. Unlike physical storage devices (e.g., CDs, USBs), cloud storage guarantees accessibility to files from any internet-connected device, providing reliability and ease of use. Combined with its cost-effectiveness and scalability, cloud computing has become essential for modern business operations.

1.6 Defining Cloud Computing

Cloud computing is one of the most important technologies that has become a part of our lives. Cloud computing means storing and retrieving data and software applications through the Internet. In the conventional method, we store data and run a program from the local computer's hard drives.

This practice has been referred to as local computing. At the same time, cloud computing refers to internet-based computing in which all IT resources are delivered over the Internet, similar to the pay-as-you-go pricing model.

It is clear here that the term cloud in cloud computing refers to the Internet. Conventionally, we represent the Internet pictorially with a cloud symbol. That's why internet-based computing is referred to as cloud computing. There is no relation between cloud computing and the physical cloud.

Let's see the formal definition of cloud computing according to the NIST (National Institute of Standard and Technology, United States)

1.6.1 NIST Definition

The formal definition of cloud computing is given by the National Institute of Standards and Technology (NIST): *"Cloud computing is a model for enabling ubiquitous, convenient, on-demand network access to a shared pool of configurable computing resources (e.g., networks, servers, storage, applications, and services) that can be rapidly provisioned and released with minimal management effort or service provider interaction. This cloud model is composed of three service models, four deployment models and five essential characteristics."*

This NIST definition of cloud computing would be easily understandable if the meaning of the following terminology is clear: ubiquitous, on-demand network access, shared pool of configurable computing resources, rapidly provisioned and released service provider.

Ubiquitous

Cloud computing allows users to access any resources from anywhere over the internet. According to the definition, the users can interact with any resources seamlessly, regardless of their physical location.

On-Demand Network Access

In traditional IT infrastructure, we initially require a huge investment in infra setup and a lot of effort to procure of this setup. Practically, It has been observed that optimum utilization of the resources is rare, and often, resources remain idle. Contrary to this, cloud computing provides on-demand network access, meaning cloud services are typically available on-demand, and users can request and start using any resources when needed.

Service Provider

Service providers deliver cloud services, and users interact with these providers to access and manage their resources. This interaction can be done through the Internet. A few popular service providers are Amazon, Microsoft, Rackspace, Google, etc.

Shared Pool of Configurable Computing Resources

The infrastructure and resources required for cloud computing are shared among multiple users and organizations. Instead of each user or organization having their dedicated hardware and infrastructure, they can access and utilize the resources provided by the cloud service provider.

Rapidly provisioned and released: One of the most important advantages of cloud computing is its capability to rapidly provision and release resources. Users can scale their required resources up or down to meet fluctuations in demand.

3-4-5 Principles of Cloud Computing

The 3-4-5 principles of cloud computing describe the three (3) essential and fundamental service offering models of cloud computing. Four (4) deployment models are used to describe the cloud computing architectural models, and five (5) essential char-acteristic features of cloud computing define cloud computing.

1.7 Cloud Computing Models

The three main kinds of services with which the cloud-based computing resources are available to end customers are as follows: Infrastructure as a Service (IaaS), Platform as a Service (PaaS), and Software as a Service (SaaS).

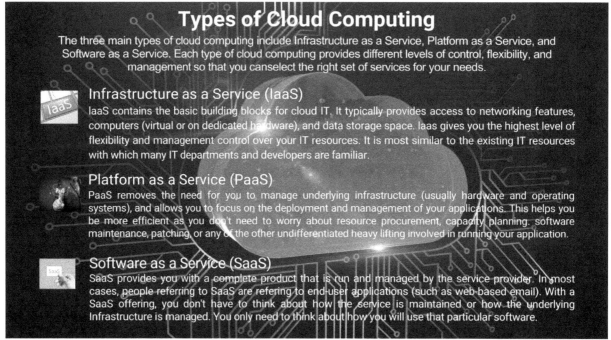

Screenshot Reference: https://aws.amazon.com/types-of-cloud-computing/

1.7.1 Infrastructure as a Service (IaaS)

The acronym IaaS denotes "Infrastructure as a Service". A cloud service provider offers virtualized computing resources via the internet under the IaaS model. This consists of storage, networks, virtual machines, and other essential components related to the computing infrastructure.

These resources are accessible and manageable remotely, eliminating the necessity for users to make investments in and maintain their own physical infrastructure. IaaS provides consumers with increased flexibility and control over their computing environment. They have the ability to provision and configure virtual machines, manage and deploy applications and operating systems.

This enables organizations to regulate the scalability of their infrastructure in accordance with their infrastructure up or down based on their needs, and pay solely for the resources they employ.

The following is the definition of IaaS from the NIST:

The capability provided to the consumer is to provision processing, storage, networks, and other fundamental computing resources where the consumer is able to deploy and run arbitrary software, which can include operating systems and applications. The consumer does not manage or control the underlying cloud infrastructure but has control over operating systems, storage, and deployed applications; and possibly limited control of selected networking components (e.g., host firewalls).

Let's understand virtual servers in IaaS with a practical use case. Suppose we need three Linux machines to work on a proof-of-concept (POC) project, such as building a homegrown load balancer. We know that once the POC is complete, these machines will no longer be required. Additionally, as students with a tight budget, purchasing physical servers isn't feasible. In this situation, Infrastructure as a Service (IaaS) is an ideal solution. Using the IaaS offering from a cloud provider, we can launch virtual servers to work on our POC. Once the POC is complete, we can terminate the servers, ensuring we only pay for what we used without incurring additional costs.

Similarly, IaaS offers virtual storage as a cost-effective and flexible alternative to physical storage. Let's explore this with another use case. Suppose we need temporary storage of 5 TB to store media files for about a month to share with our friends. We've decided not to use other video hosting services for personal reasons. In this scenario, leveraging virtual storage from a cloud provider becomes the most viable and economical choice compared to purchasing physical storage. Once we no longer need the storage, we can delete the media files, and the cloud provider will stop charging us.

This flexibility in provisioning and de-provisioning resources, whether servers or storage, highlights the cost-efficiency and scalability of IaaS. It is especially useful for short-term or temporary needs, making it a perfect solution for students, startups, or organizations operating on limited budgets.

Key Features and Advantages of IaaS

We got an understanding about what IaaS is. Let's try to understand IaaS fruitfulness. Some of the advantages listed here are common across all cloud computing delivery models.

Eliminate On-premises Data Center's Expense: One of the advantages of the IaaS type of cloud computing platform is that it could eliminate an on-premises data center's buying, setup, and maintenance expense. It's an obvious advantage. When using IaaS -- to procure servers, storage, and network – depending on how much infrastructure you procure, you would be able to cut down huge on your on-premises data-center expenses.

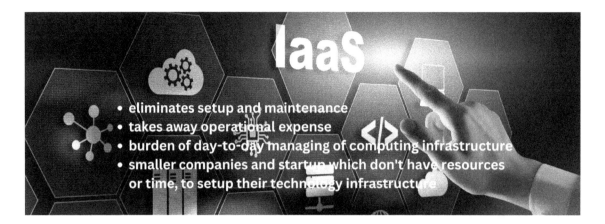

Since IaaS helps reduce data-center expenses significantly, IaaS could be an excellent choice for smaller companies and startups that don't have the resources or time to set up their technology infrastructure. Not only does IaaS help reduce the setup cost of technology infrastructure, but IaaS also takes away the operational expense and the burden of day-to-day managing of computing infrastructure. For example, you can outsource day-to-day tasks such as taking backup, applying patches, ensuring that the system is secured (not a security risk) to the IaaS provider.

Metered Billing: This is a common benefit which customers get in all cloud computing delivery models. In IaaS, cloud customers get bills based on what IaaS type of resources has been used and what was the duration usage – this is very typical how metered billing generally works. With this are many good practical advantages of metered billing, just to mention one here is there is no need to buy and maintain some special high-end servers only for some special need, day, or hour.

Choice of Server Hardware: With IaaS it's much easier get different types of servers. For example, AWS offers not only traditional Intel-based processers, but also offers AMD, GPU, and ARM processor options.

Scalability: IaaS helps in making system scalable. IaaS system can easily provision additional resources to meet the unexpected or planned demand. The reason is IaaS utilizes very large pool of resources.

High Availability: High availability is a general feature of cloud irrespective of a delivery model. With respect to IaaS, since IaaS utilizes very large pool of resources along with redundancy, it is easier to manage high availability by quickly provisioning additional resources or just failover to other available resources.

Security: Cloud providers take responsibility of physical security of servers. In addition, there is network security. In IaaS default no inbound traffic is allowed, and additionally there is security at user level as well, for example, the user has access to the resource or not.

1.7.2 Platform as a Service (PaaS)

The acronym PaaS denotes "Platform as a Service." A cloud service provider provides a platform comprising the required infrastructure, development tools, and runtime environment for building, deploying, and managing applications under the PaaS model.

The following is the definition of PaaS from the NIST:

The capability provided to the customer is to deploy onto the cloud infrastructure consumer-created or acquired applications created using programming languages, libraries, services, and tools supported by the provider. The customer does not manage or control the underlying cloud infrastructure including network, servers, operating systems, or storage, but has control over the deployed applications and possibly configuration settings for the application-hosting environment.

Users can concentrate on application development and operation without having to be concerned with the underlying infrastructure. PaaS offers a complete environment for deployment and development, comprising application hosting, database administration, middleware, and development tools, among other components.

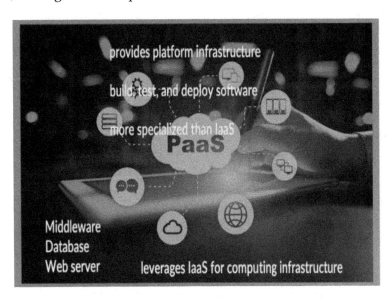

It allows developers to efficiently build, validate, and distribute applications by utilizing the preconfigured elements and services of the platform. PaaS enables developers to concentrate on application development and code creation, while the cloud provider manages the infrastructure underlying the platform, such as storage, networking, and servers. This facilitates rapid development cycles, scalability, and seamless project collaboration.

To understand how PaaS relates to IaaS, let's visit the cloud computing pyramid diagram as you can notice that PaaS is above IaaS. What it means is that PaaS can utilize IaaS for its infrastructure-related needs. In other words, PaaS can fulfill its virtual servers, storage, and network-related needs from IaaS.

We now understand that Platform as a Service (PaaS) provides cloud-based development and deployment environments. Let's illustrate PaaS with a practical use case. Suppose you are the VP of Engineering at a startup with a global team, and you want to offer your team the flexibility of remote work, including local team members. You've heard that PaaS is a cloud computing model that delivers a complete development and deployment environment. The key question is: What tools, services, or platforms can you procure using PaaS to fulfill your team's software development needs?

In a PaaS environment, you can access a wide range of tools and services required to set up a comprehensive application development ecosystem. For instance, PaaS offers an Integrated Development Environment (IDE) for coding, source code management tools for version control, and build tools for compiling and deploying applications. Additionally, PaaS provides services like databases, integration tools, web servers, and ETL (Extract-Transform-Load) tools for managing and transforming data. You can also access analytics tools for insights and reporting. These services are readily available on cloud platforms like AWS, Azure, and Google Cloud.

To summarize, PaaS simplifies software development by providing a complete suite of development and deployment tools on the cloud. It allows teams to collaborate seamlessly, focus on coding and innovation, and eliminates the need for managing underlying infrastructure, enabling greater efficiency and flexibility.

Key Features and Advantages of PaaS

Following are the key features and the advantages of PaaS. You may find that some of the features are overlapping with the cloud service models, that is because all cloud service models inherit general features of cloud computing, in-addition to having specific features for the particular service model.

Multiple Environments: PaaS makes it easier to setup and test applications on multiple environments as it if much easier and quicker to provision different types of environments. Let's take an example, if you were test to an application on Windows, Linux and MacOS operating system, you can launch these environments much quickly and you pay only based on metered billing. You can also create Sandbox environment and provide access to a few developers to try out services to build proof of concept. Sandbox environments are very good to test out applications which are build using AWS services in a separate environment before deploying to production.

Ease of Upgrades: Since cloud providers take care of upgrades of PaaS, it becomes much easier of customer. Let's say, for example, you are a data engineer on the AWS platform, and if you are using Jupyter Notebook, or EMR (Elastic Map Reduce) to build data analytic application, if any of these need to be upgraded, it will be incumbent upon the cloud provider.

Cost Effective: Since PaaS or any cloud service model used metered billing, customers only pay for the services they are using. If you ran EMR service to run some analytic job for 2 hours, you only for using EMR for the duration you used the service.

Licensing: Licensing is another feature of PaaS. In cloud environment, cloud providers are assumed to be handling and managing licensing of operating systems and platforms as opposed to the organization taking care of this important task to maintain compliance and security of system. Within PaaS cloud service model, the licensing cost are assumed to a part of the metered cost. What it means the cloud provider is responsible for coordinating with vendors to manage licensing aspect of PaaS – not the customer.

To summarize, PaaS provides complete development and deployment-related tools and services in the cloud. Moreover, these services can be accessed anytime on-demand from anywhere over the Internet. Thus, it eliminates in-house buying and setup of databases, web servers, development, and deployment-related tools and services. PaaS can help in setting up multiple environments quickly, upgrade and licensing of PaaS incumbent upon cloud provider, and cost effective.

1.7.3 Software as a Service (SaaS)

The acronym SaaS denotes Software as a Service. The Software-as-a-Service (SaaS) paradigm entails the provision of software applications by a cloud service provider, who has the responsibility of hosting and delivering these software to users through the internet. Instead of installing, and executing software on personal computers or servers, individuals have the option to utilize software via a web browser.

Software as a Service (SaaS) alleviates concerns regarding software installation, maintenance, and infrastructure management for users. The cloud provider has responsibility for various backend operations, software updates, security measures, and scalability. Typically, users pay a membership price in order to obtain access and utilize the program on a pay-as-you-go model.

The following is the definition of SaaS from NIST.

The capability provided to the customer is to use the provider's applications running on a cloud infrastructure. The applications are accessible from various client devices through either a thin client interface, such as a web browser (e.g., web-based email), or a program interface. The consumer does not manage or control the underlying cloud infrastructure including network, servers, operating systems, storage, or even individual application capabilities, with the possible exception of limited user-specific application settings.

SaaS is a very well-known type of cloud computing platform. The reason is SaaS is very visible to the common public usage wise. For example, as we know SaaS software such as Facebook, Netflix, Zoom, Microsoft Office 365 are very popular and have a global reach to millions of users. Additionally, with cloud computing, building SaaS applications have become relatively much faster, which further helps increase its popularity in the developer community.

Comparing SaaS with other main cloud computing types, if you look at the cloud computing pyramid diagram, SaaS is at the top. It means that if you are building SaaS solutions, you can use PaaS for platform-related needs and IaaS for infrastructure-related needs.

Key Features and Advantages of SaaS

The following are the key features and advantages of SaaS. As you have earlier for IaaS and PaaS, some features are general in nature inherited from cloud computing, however some of them are unique to SaaS.

Support Costs and Efforts: In SaaS, we do not need to install any special software. SaaS software can be up and running quickly and can scale as needed. There is a substantial cost benefits for smaller or startup organizations in using SaaS.

Licensing: With respect to cost, SaaS software is typically licensed on a subscription basis. SaaS providers manage all the aspects of software, such as delivery and management, ensuring that service level agreement (SLA) is maintained. Thus, the software is available whenever or wherever the customer needs it, and it performs as per the service level agreement.

Ease of Use: Since SaaS is delivered over the Internet, we don't need to deploy or install any software on your local computer -- we can start using SaaS software as soon as we establish the connection using a web URL. In other words, it can be quickly up and running.

Scalability: Furthermore, SaaS software can be easily scaled as needed. What it means, we wouldn't notice any performance degradation if traffic or the number of users increases.

Standardization: This is very important feature if we compare it with software of 90s. In other words, software which are not of SaaS type. Compare SaaS with the software of 90s where engineers would have visit to different geographical location for the installation of new release or a patch for large software that were installed on multiple locations such as ERP, Manufacturing, and Financials. Since software is deployed centrally, all users get the same screen, same version; and new feature release and patch management are much easier because of centralization. In other words, SaaS helps in having software more standardized in many key aspects.

In the late 90s, before cloud computing dominance, buying, and setting up enterprise software such as ERP, CRM, HR was very expensive. However, SaaS has made a significant difference in pricing, particularly for smaller or startup organizations, which could not afford to buy and set up expensive software such as ERP, CRM, HR, and many. In other words, the subscription-based pricing model of SaaS has made it much easier for smaller or startup organizations to use or subscribe to costly SaaS software to help grow their business.

1.8 Cloud Computing Service Models (XaaS)

Cloud Computing Service Model (XaaS) refers to a broad concept where users access products, tools, technologies, and services "as a service." This means that today, almost everything can be offered and consumed as a service. Users can subscribe to various services, tools, or technologies by paying a nominal subscription fee. The three primary cloud computing service models are:

- Software as a Service (SaaS)
- Platform as a Service (PaaS)
- Infrastructure as a Service (IaaS)

Cloud computing is continuously evolving, introducing new service models to meet diverse user needs. Many providers are now offering specialized services, including:
- Network as a Service (NaaS)
- Desktop as a Service (DaaS)
- Database as a Service (DBaaS)
- Storage as a Service (STaaS)

Looking ahead, we can expect further innovations, such as Testing as a Service (TaaS), Backup as a Service (BaaS), and Firewall as a Service (FWaaS). In essence, the concept of XaaS (Everything as a Service) signifies that virtually anything can be delivered as a service to end users, ensuring greater flexibility, scalability, and cost-efficiency in managing IT solutions.

1.8.1 Function-as-a-Service (FaaS) or Serverless Computing

Function-as-a-Service (FaaS), synonymous with serverless computing, is another modern cloud computing platform or cloud computing type.

- **synonymous term for serverless computing**
- **infrastructure and computing resources**
- **focus on the code**
- **scales up or down automatically**
- **pay by the function call**

So, what does FaaS do? In FaaS, users only need to focus on the code (write a Java class, for example), not on the infrastructure (no need to set up JVM, for example). Users deploy the code having a function (Java class, for example), and the FaaS provider executes the code. The runtime environment is provided by the providers and managed as well.

Advantages

FaaS providers provide infrastructure and computing resources to functions without users setting up the infrastructure and computing resources to execute the process.

Additionally, the execution environment scales up or down automatically. Because of the automatic theoretical unlimited scalability feature of FaaS, it is an excellent solution for method or function calls, which have a dynamic workload that fluctuates a lot. Moreover, one distinct advantage of FaaS is that we only pay for the computing resources used by function calls – essentially a pay-as-you-go-pricing model.

One of the main drawbacks of function-as-a-service is the execution time. Since the process needs to have resources provisioned each time they run, some performance lag is possible.

Examples

One of the examples of function-as-service is AWS Lambda. For example, we have an image processing function for generating thumbnail images. We can write the process in the language choices, such as Java, Python, and other supported languages by the cloud provider, and let AWS Lambda execute the function.

In this use case, we only need to write a function for image processing and configure the computing resource requirement on AWS Lambda. Then, AWS Lambda will take care of the allocation of computing resources and run the image processing function.

1.8.2 Cloud Storage

We know the various storage technologies like floppy disc, CD, DVD, Hard disc flash drive, Solid State Drive (SSD), etc. As technology grows, the need for different devices evolves. Nowadays, we need cloud-based storage for huge amounts of data such as high-definition imaging data, video stream-ing data, surveillance camera data, etc.

Cloud Storage is a cloud computing model in which we store the data on the cloud with the help of the internet. Many cloud storage providers provide the storage facility as a service.

Advantages of Cloud Storage

Reduced Storage Cost: Cloud storage operates on a subscription or rental model, which is more cost-effective than traditional systems. Users pay only for the storage they use without needing to maintain physical hardware.

Disaster Recovery: Cloud storage ensures robust disaster recovery with data backups stored off-site across multiple data centers. This makes it less vulnerable to natural disasters like fires, floods, or earthquakes compared to on-premises storage.

Scalability: Cloud storage offers flexibility to scale storage space up or down based on user or organizational needs, providing on-demand adjustment without additional infrastructure.

Syncing: Cloud services feature automatic data syncing, ensuring data backups arc regularly updated. Any changes to connected devices reflect automatically on the cloud server, reducing the risk of data loss.

Security: Cloud storage providers use advanced security measures such as end-to-end encryption, secure authentication protocols, and two-factor authentication. Data is often distributed across geographically separated servers to enhance security.

Popular Cloud Storage Providers: Examples include Amazon S3, Google Cloud, Oracle Cloud, Dell EMC, HPE, and Microsoft Azure.

Cloud Deployment Models

The cloud deployment model describes how cloud services can be deployed or made available to their customers, depending on the organizational structure and the provisioning location. It describes how cloud computing platforms are implemented and hosted and who can access it.

For instance, what is the accessibility of computing resources? Are all computing resources available to the public? Or not all -- only some of them are available to the public, and some computing resources are protected. How are computing resources accessed, managed, audited, or governed? How is the security of computing resources managed? Understanding computing resources in terms of cloud computing comes under the term cloud computing deployment model (or cloud deployment model).

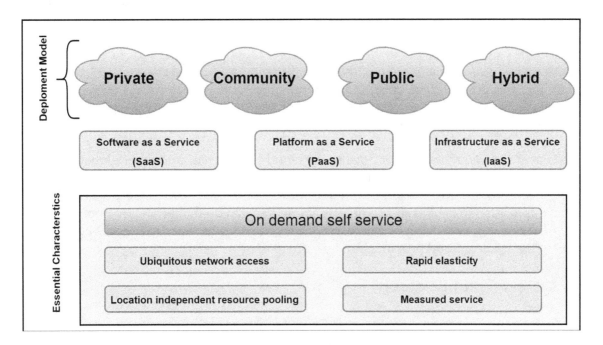

In simple words, Internet-based computing resources can be deployed in various forms depending on the locations where data and services are acquired and provisioned to its users. Four deployment models are usually used to deploy cloud services: public, private, hybrid, and community.

1.8.3 Public Cloud
The public cloud deployment model refers to a cloud infrastructure made available for use by the general public. This cloud environment can be owned, overseen, and operated by a business, educational institution, government organization, or a collaborative effort involving these entities. It is typically hosted at the cloud provider's facilities.

A public cloud deployment model (or public cloud) provides on-demand availability of all kinds (for example, IaaS, PaaS, SaaS) of cloud services worldwide. A public cloud generally has a massive amount of -- computing resources and storage, is easily available, and is easily scalable.

A public cloud has easy accessibility compared to any other type of cloud. This is because public clouds, by nature of the public, are generally available to everyone. So, for example, if you would like to launch a virtual server on AWS (a public cloud provider), you just need to have an account with AWS, and you can easily and quickly launch a virtual server on AWS. Similarly, you can quickly get storage on a public cloud like AWS.

The main point to understand as it relates to accessibility is that getting cloud services from public cloud providers is relatively much more straightforward than getting cloud services in any other type of cloud deployment model (private, hybrid). The reason is that accessibility limits or permission issues are much more lenient in the public cloud than in any other cloud deployment model.

Public cloud providers generally provide cloud platforms for all main cloud computing types: Infrastructure-as-a-Service (IaaS), Platform-as-a-Service (PaaS), and Software-as-a-Service (SaaS). For example, they provide infrastructure-as-a-service (IaaS), which means you can launch virtual servers on the cloud, such as Linux virtual servers, Windows virtual servers, or even macOS-type virtual servers on AWS. Furthermore, they provide platform-as-a-service (PaaS), which means, for example, you can get development and deployment software and tools on the cloud. Also, they provide software-as-a-service (SaaS), which means you can get application software solutions delivered over the Internet.

A public cloud is recommended for developing cloud-based applications for globally distributed teams because the public cloud helps in team collaboration regarding cloud resources. Moreover, once the application development is complete, if you would like to move the final application to a more secure private cloud, you can do that easily. Examples of public cloud providers are AWS, Google, Microsoft, IBM, Oracle, Salesforce, SAP, and Microsoft, which are the leading cloud providers.

Pros & Cons of Public Cloud

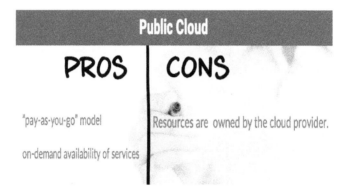

A public cloud provides most of the advantages of cloud computing, such as the pay-as-you-go pricing model and on-demand availability of all cloud services worldwide.The one main drawback of a public cloud is that the cloud provider owns the computing resources. In that sense, there is a single point of failure if something goes wrong at the provider's end, for example, if the provider goes out of business.

1.8.4 Private Cloud

The private cloud deployment model refers to a cloud infrastructure designed exclusively for a single organization, which may consist of various consumers like different business units. This cloud environment can be owned, overseen, and run by the organization, a third-party service provider, or a collaboration between them. Furthermore, it can be situated either on the organization's premises or at an external location.

It is like a public cloud, but a private cloud is the most restrictive. A private cloud is sometimes called an on-premises cloud solution if the cloud resources are within the organization's data center.

With respect to how a private cloud is like a public cloud, in a private cloud, you can get all the public cloud features, such as the on-demand availability of all kinds of cloud services from across the world. Additionally, like a public cloud, a private cloud also has massive computing resources and storage available, making it easily scalable -- but relatively less compared with a public cloud.

As we discussed, though a private cloud is like a public cloud, a private cloud is more restrictive and has tighter controls -- typically protected by firewalls.

Because of stricter control and firewall protection, usually, a single organization utilizes a private cloud. Organizations with solid security and regulatory requirements, such as banks and healthcare providers, prefer private cloud – particularly total on-premises cloud solutions.

There is an emerging trend of using colocation providers, in which an organization's private cloud is set up inside a third-party data center. Thus, instead of having its own on-premises data center, the organization is outsourcing to a third-party data center.

Pros & Cons of Private Cloud

Security and control are the main advantages of a private cloud. For example, since a private cloud is behind a firewall, the private cloud makes it easier to restrict access to valuable assets.

Concerning the control advantage of the private cloud, since an outside public cloud provider does not control a private cloud, there is no risk or a single point of failure if something goes wrong with the public cloud provider. This is a real plus, as in a private cloud, essentially, there is no dependency on public cloud providers -- the private cloud controls all computing resources. Another point about the controlling advantage of a private cloud is that a private cloud is recommended if regulatory needs are critical to controlling the environment.

Regarding its disadvantages, one of the disadvantages of the private cloud is cost. The company that owns a private cloud must bear the cost of the IT infrastructure of data centers and software. This cost factor makes private clouds less attractive compared to public clouds. Another disadvantage is that increasing scalability in the private cloud is not as quick as in the public cloud because, in the private cloud, resources are in a limited capacity.

1.8.5 Hybrid Cloud

A hybrid cloud refers to a cloud infrastructure created by combining two or more separate cloud deployment models (such as private, public, or community). These individual cloud setups retain distinct identities but are interconnected using standardized or proprietary technology. This connection allows for the smooth movement of data and applications, enabling capabilities like cloud bursting and load balancing between different cloud instances.

In simple words, it combines both public and private clouds. The main point to remember about a hybrid cloud is that it is a cloud solution that allows seamless interaction between public and private clouds. For example, a public cloud can access data and applications of a private cloud, and the converse is also possible.

Therefore, it is an excellent solution for organizations that need the flexibility, cost-saving, and quick scalability features of a public cloud and better security and control features.

Types of Hybrid Clouds

There are two types of hybrid clouds: cloud bursting hybrid cloud and the other one is classic hybrid cloud. In the bursting hybrid cloud, organizations use private clouds to securely store their data and proprietary applications.

However, when more resources are needed due to increased service needs, and if their private cloud infrastructure is improved, look for public clouds and tap into public cloud resources to fulfill their increased service demands. In a classic hybrid cloud, organizations store their data and proprietary applications on the private clouds. However, they outsource their non-critical applications to public clouds -- such as Microsoft Office 365, or CRM solutions such as Salesforce. Also, organizations can leverage multi-cloud architecture in a hybrid cloud to use different cloud providers for the needs of their various cloud services.

Pros & Cons of Hybrid Cloud

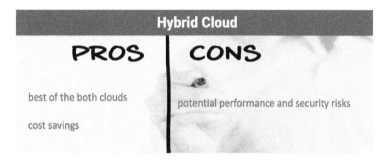

A hybrid cloud's main advantage is that we can leverage the best features of both types of clouds. For example, organizations can use private clouds to secure and regulate their data tightly. Furthermore, they can securely move them to public clouds such as AWS, for example, to leverage their analytical machine learning services to build actionable insight solutions with cost and time efficiency.

Additionally, a hybrid cloud saves overall IT infrastructure costs because a public cloud can be used when scalability is needed. In addition to cost savings, many services are readily available on public cloud providers, which can be leveraged instead of developing your in-house solutions, for example, analytical services. With regards to cons, since there is integration involved between private and public clouds. This integration can cause potential performance issues because of -- network latency and security risks -- as data are shared between public and private clouds.

1.8.6 Community Cloud

Community cloud refers to a cloud infrastructure that is utilized by multiple organizations, catering to a particular community with common interests, such as shared missions, security needs, policies, and compliance requirements. Management responsibilities for this cloud environment can rest with the participating organizations or be delegated to a third party. Additionally, the community cloud can be located either on the premises of the organizations or externally.

Essentially, a community cloud is a private cloud. However, it functions as a public cloud. Community clouds are collaborative and multi-tenant in nature and usually cater to the same type of businesses or industries that share the exact requirements regarding security and compliance. Though community clouds are not commonly used, they are typically used by government, healthcare, financial, and other organizations.

Pros & Cons of Community Cloud

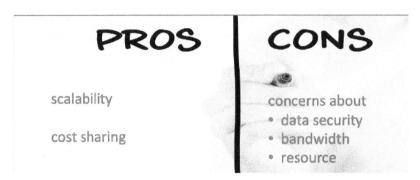

The community cloud's advantages are scalability and cost. They are more scalable compared to private clouds. Also, costs could be shared among the organizations using the community clouds. Besides advantages, community clouds have some significant drawbacks because of the sharing nature of this type of cloud. These concerns data security, bandwidth, and resource usage utilization and prioritizations.

1.8.7 Multi-Cloud

In some cases, just one private, public, or hybrid doesn't fulfill all the cloud computing needs of organizations, and they resort to a multi-cloud model. The multi-cloud model involves private clouds and many public clouds. Though multi-clouds exist, all the clouds can be accessed from a single network.

A multi-cloud model use case generally fits into a larger organization, where one department's cloud needs and budgets may not be aligned with the other departments. For example, the engineering department needs cloud resources for its development and deployment needs. However, the marketing and HR departments cannot use the cloud setup or resources of the engineering department because marketing and HR departments may have additional requirements.

In these scenarios, organizations sometimes choose from the available public cloud providers that best fit their computing and budget needs rather than using the one-size-fits-all solution. Because of the utilization of multi-cloud providers, organizations not only avoid their dependency on a single provider, but multi-cloud can also help them decrease cost and increase flexibility in the long run.

1.9 Essential Characteristics of Cloud Computing

The cloud computing system has the following essential characteristics. It is important to note that if any of these characteristics still need to be included, it is not an actual cloud computing system.

Cloud Computing Essential Characteristics

On-Demand Self-Service

The concept of on-demand self-service allows consumers to acquire computing resources independently and automatically, such as server time and network storage, without the need for direct human interaction with the service provider. This means that consumers can provision these capabilities as required without relying on manual intervention from the provider.

Broad Network Access

The capabilities provided by the system are accessible through the network and can be utilized using standard mechanisms. These mechanisms are designed to facilitate usage across a wide range of client platforms, whether they are thin or thick clients. Examples of such platforms include mobile phones, laptops, and personal digital assistants.

Resource Pooling

The provider's computing resources are combined into a shared pool to cater to the needs of multiple consumers. This is done through a multitenant model, where different physical and virtual resources are allocated and reallocated based on consumer demand. While the exact location of the resources is typically unknown to the customer, there is a sense of location independence. These resources include storage, processing power, memory, and network bandwidth.

Rapid Elasticity

The system allows for the fast and flexible provisioning of capabilities, which can be rapidly scaled up or down as needed. In some cases, this provisioning can even happen automatically. From the consumer's perspective, the available capabilities for provisioning may seem limitless and can be purchased in any desired quantity at any given time. Additionally, these capabilities can be quickly released when no longer needed, enabling efficient scaling down.

Measured Service

Cloud systems have built-in mechanisms to automatically manage and optimize the utilization of resources. This is achieved by utilizing a metering capability that operates at a suitable level of abstraction for the specific service, such as storage, processing, bandwidth, or active user accounts. The usage of resources can be continuously monitored, controlled, and reported, ensuring transparency for both the provider and the consumer of the service.

1.10 Cloud Computing Services Requirements

Based on the above cloud computing principles, specific attributes must be present for cloud services. The following are the essential prerequisites for any entity to become a service in the cloud environment.

Multitenancy: Multitenancy is one of the most essential characteristics of cloud computing, which maximizes resource sharing in the cloud system. Multitenancy is a functionality that enables the concurrent satisfaction of multiple users (tenants) with a single instance of resource. This is a mandatory requirement for any entity to become the service.

Scalability: The internet-based services face considerable fluctuations in demand, and a good cloud service should be able to adjust the resources in response. This feature is known as Scalability, which guarantees that users are provided with uninterrupted access to the resources whenever they require.

Data Security and Backup: Data security is one of the most essential requirements for a cloud service. The cloud service uses comprehensive security measures like encryption, access controls, and data protection to safeguard user information. A systematic backup and recovery system should be present to restore the data in case of accidental loss.

Data Portability: Cloud service users should be able to move their data in and out of the system without being bound to a specific vendor. Also, cloud services should be able to port their workload (virtual machine portability) with limited service disruption.

Billing and charging: A cloud service should be capable of supporting transparent billing and charging policies. There should be a clear price for every individual service and provision for cost control.

1.11 Advantages and Disadvantages of Cloud Computing Systems

The following is the list of consolidated points describing the advantages of cloud computing.

Cost Efficient: Cloud computing provides services based on the pay-as-you-go model, which is very cost-efficient. Any user or organization can access the infra resources as per their needs. So, there is no need to spend vast amounts of money on hardware, software, or licensing fees; instead, they can pay for cloud services with nominal subscription charges.

Accessibility: Cloud services are accessible anytime from anywhere. We can access any services 24/7 from anywhere; the only thing required is an active internet connection.

Environment Supportive: Cloud computing has the potential to be advantageous for the environment. Since it enables more effective use of available resources, cloud providers can maximize the use of their servers and reduce their energy usage.

Improved Flexibility: Cloud service providers offer cloud services at competitive prices. The competitive prices help cloud users to choose the best one that meets their needs. This flexibility allows instant changes in our cloud system without serious issues.

Optimum Resource Utilization: The cloud service provider uses various tools for monitoring and utilizing resources. This way, the cloud service provider ensures optimum utilization of resources and minimizes the computing resources and energy. In comparison to the individual users, cloud service providers achieve better performance.

Unlimited storage capacity: Another advantage of the cloud computing system is its almost unlimited storage capacity. Every coin has two faces. Similarly, every technology has both positive and negative aspects. It is essential; we have to consider all factors before implementing it. The points above highlight the benefits of using cloud technology. The following discussion will outline the potential disadvantages of cloud computing.

Vulnerability to Attacks: Nowadays, most of the company's data is stored online. This data storage in cloud-based systems presents a severe challenge to keeping information safe from leaks. Even the most reputable organizations have had security breaches. Despite implementing sophisticated security protocols in cloud systems, storing sensitive information remains a potentially precarious endeavor. Consequently, it is imperative to acknowledge the susceptibility to security breaches.

Network Dependency: Cloud computing systems have a tight dependency on the Internet. This strong dependency on the Internet means that organizations leveraging cloud computing must have reliable and consistent Internet service, a fast connection, and proper bandwidth to capitalize on the benefits of cloud computing.

Vendor Lock-in: When a company or user wants to migrate from one cloud platform to another, the engineering team might face different challenges because of the strong coupling with vendor platforms -- that has been chiefly observed. As a result, hosting and running the applications from the current cloud platform to some other platform may cause support issues, configuration complexities, and additional expenses.

Limited Control: Cloud customers often encounter a situation where they have restricted control over their deployments. Since the cloud services are hosted on remote servers owned and overseen by service providers, organizations can configure and manage their hardware and software resources according to their precise specifications in the traditional on-premises model.

However, in the cloud, these elements are abstracted away from the user's physical location and entrusted to the cloud service provider. As a result, the customers have limited control over their underlying IT infrastructure.

1.12 Software Quality Attributes in Cloud Computing

Understanding software quality attributes is crucial, especially in distributed computing environments like cloud computing. The complexity arises due to multiple variables, such as fluctuating load requests, network downtimes, bandwidth limitations, latency issues, or failures of cloud resources. These factors significantly impact the software's performance: if managed well, performance improves; if neglected, performance degrades.

What are software quality attributes?

Software quality attributes are measurable characteristics of software that determine its performance and effectiveness. These attributes include how reliable, available, or scalable the software is. Some of the key quality attributes are usability, maintainability, modifiability, extensibility, portability, testability, flexibility, reusability, reliability, availability, and scalability. The importance of these attributes varies depending on the nature of the software and the Service Level Agreements (SLA).

In cloud computing, the most critical quality attributes are:

Scalability: The ability to handle increasing loads or adapt to fluctuating demands.
Availability: Ensuring the system is operational and accessible when needed.
Reliability: The software's ability to consistently perform as expected without failure.

Addressing these attributes effectively is key to overcoming performance-related challenges in cloud computing environments.

Availability, Reliability

Let's begin by understanding availability and reliability in the context of system performance.

Availability is defined as the percentage of time a system or service remains operational and accessible. Cloud platforms ensure high availability due to their vast resources and well-structured infrastructure. In virtualized environments, cloud providers can seamlessly move virtual machines, provision new ones, and manage infrastructure components to minimize downtime. This ensures that virtual machines, storage, and network systems operate with little to no disruption.

Reliability, also referred to as **resiliency**, focuses on a system's ability to continue functioning even when certain components fail. The key difference between availability and reliability is that reliability emphasizes the system's capacity to recover or failover gracefully. For example, if a system reboots quickly without significant downtime, it achieves high availability. However, if it transitions to a redundant backup system without interruption, it is considered reliable. Redundancy is a primary mechanism used to enhance reliability, ensuring that failures do not affect system operations.

In summary, **availability** measures the percentage of time a system remains operational, while reliability measures how long the system can perform its intended function without failure.

To illustrate this with an example:
If a machine operates for an hour but shuts down for 6 minutes before restarting, its availability is calculated as: $(60-6)/60=90$

Here, the reliability of the system is 1 hour, as it fails once during that period. If the machine restarts quickly without extended downtime, it achieves high availability.

In cloud environments, the combination of vast resources, redundancy mechanisms, and rapid recovery processes enables both high availability and reliability for deployed applications.

Just keep this in mind. A reliable system has high availability, but an available system may not be reliable.

Scalability

Scalability is a vital quality attribute in cloud computing, particularly when managing unpredictable and fluctuating request loads. It refers to a system's ability to maintain optimal performance as workload or traffic increases. Essentially, scalability ensures that software can handle growth without any degradation in performance, as outlined in its service-level agreements (SLAs). A system that can sustain performance under higher loads is considered scalable, while one that fails or slows down is labeled non-scalable.

For instance, imagine an e-commerce web application deployed on a server with 2 CPUs and 8 GB of RAM, capable of handling 100 concurrent requests per second. If a sudden traffic surge occurs due to a promotional event, exceeding the server's capacity, performance will degrade unless scalability measures are in place. High CPU, RAM, or I/O utilization can lead to slow response times or even system failure.

To manage scalability effectively, two key approaches are used:
Horizontal Scalability (Scaling Out): Adding more servers or machines to distribute the workload efficiently across multiple resources.
Vertical Scalability (Scaling Up): Upgrading the existing server hardware, such as increasing CPU, memory (RAM), or storage capacity.

Cloud environments excel in scalability, allowing businesses to dynamically adapt to varying workloads. By leveraging cloud resources, organizations can scale horizontally or vertically based on demand without requiring significant infrastructure changes. This flexibility ensures that applications remain responsive, reliable, and efficient even during peak usage periods.

Vertical Scalability

A system can be considered constrained on CPU, RAM, and storage resources and thus can negatively impact overall performance. Therefore, to improve this system's performance by the "vertical scalable" mechanism means adding more resources such as CPU, RAM, and storage.

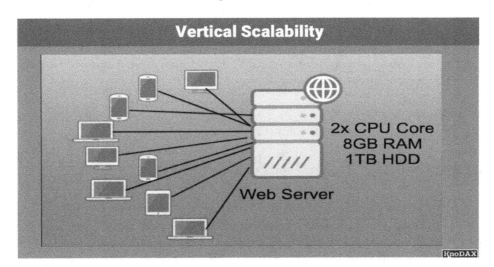

However, since when making the system vertically scalable, there is no addition of a machine or node, making the system vertically scalable doesn't improve the fault tolerance of the overall system.

Making the system scalable by applying the vertical scalability technique was a typical pattern before the inclusion of stateless web services in modern software architecture.

Horizontal Scalability

Horizontal scalability enhances a system's capacity by adding more nodes or machines to distribute workloads efficiently. Compared to vertical scalability, where resources like CPU and RAM are increased on a single machine, horizontal scalability is generally preferred. This is because it improves fault tolerance by allowing tasks to run on parallel machines, ensuring workload distribution and high availability. If one machine fails, other machines in the system can seamlessly take over its workload, reducing downtime and improving system resilience.

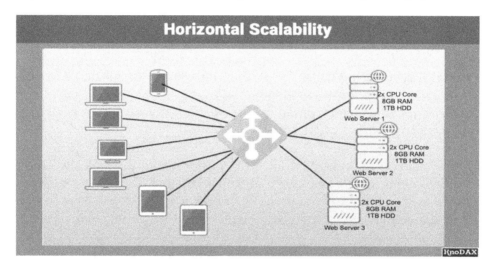

Performance: Cloud providers like AWS optimize application performance using features such as auto-scaling, caching, and latency management tools. These mechanisms ensure efficient handling of varying workloads, minimize latency, and maintain smooth operations even during traffic spikes.

Portability: Portability reduces dependency on specific platforms, frameworks, or operating systems, allowing applications to move seamlessly between cloud providers. If issues like SLA breaches, pricing concerns, or provider unavailability occur, organizations can easily migrate workloads to alternative platforms.

Service Level Agreements (SLAs): SLAs are critical for ensuring reliability and customer satisfaction. Cloud providers like AWS define clear commitments around availability, support, security, and reporting. Failure to meet SLAs may result in penalties or credits, helping businesses maintain consistent services and earn customer trust.

Regulatory Requirements: Businesses must comply with regulations like HIPAA (healthcare), FISMA (federal agencies), and PCI DSS (finance). AWS and other cloud providers are certified for many of these standards, simplifying compliance for organizations. This ensures smooth cloud transitions while adhering to legal and regulatory frameworks.

Security: Security remains a top priority, especially for regulated industries. AWS offers baseline security by default, such as blocking inbound traffic and permitting outbound connections. Organizations can enhance security further using services like AWS SSL certificates to protect web traffic. This layered approach helps safeguard assets and meet specific security needs.

Privacy: Managing data privacy in the cloud is complex due to varying regional laws and data usage regulations. Cloud providers like AWS address this by ensuring data remains within specified geographic regions based on customer requirements, reducing privacy risks and unauthorized data movement.

Auditability: In distributed cloud environments, auditability enables organizations to monitor and track system activities, events, and changes. AWS tools like CloudWatch provide visibility and control by tracking application performance, ensuring compliance, and enhancing operational transparency.

By leveraging horizontal scalability alongside these quality attributes, cloud systems ensure high performance, fault tolerance, and operational efficiency. This makes them ideal for businesses aiming to scale dynamically while maintaining reliability and security.

1.13 Scope of Responsibility

Software does not operate in isolation; it relies on components such as servers, storage, operating systems, virtualization (when using virtual machines), networking, and databases (if required by the application). Managing the software involves addressing performance aspects like scalability while ensuring appropriate security measures based on the application's needs.

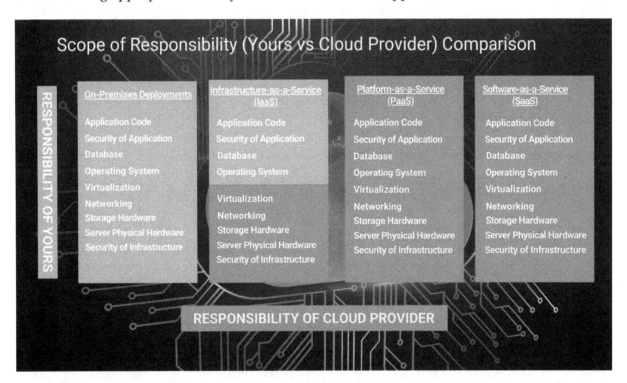

The allocation of responsibilities for managing these runtime aspects depends on the deployment model. In on-premises deployments, the software owner is entirely responsible for managing and controlling all components, including hardware, networking, security, and application performance. However, in cloud deployments, this responsibility shifts and becomes shared between the cloud provider and the application owner, depending on the cloud service model being used — IaaS, PaaS, or SaaS.

For on-premises deployments, every aspect, from physical hardware to application security, is managed by the software owner. In contrast, with SaaS (Software-as-a-Service), the cloud provider assumes full responsibility for all components, including hardware, operating systems, networking, databases, and security, allowing the application owner to focus solely on using the software.

In the IaaS (Infrastructure-as-a-Service) model, responsibilities are divided. The cloud provider manages physical hardware, storage, networking, and virtualization, while the application owner is responsible for the operating system, database, application code, and application-level security. For PaaS (Platform-as-a-Service), the cloud provider takes on additional responsibilities, managing the operating system, database, and platform infrastructure. The application owner is responsible only for the application code and its security.

In summary, as you move from on-premises to SaaS, the responsibility gradually shifts from the application owner to the cloud provider. Understanding this division helps application owners leverage cloud models effectively based on their needs for control, flexibility, and resource management.

1.14 Multitenancy

Multitenancy is a software architecture where a single instance of a software application serves multiple end-users or user groups, known as tenants. Each tenant operates in a logically isolated environment while sharing the underlying infrastructure, such as servers, storage, and computing resources. Popular examples of multi-tenant SaaS applications include Salesforce, Google Gmail, Microsoft Office 365, and TurboTax's cloud version.

Single Tenancy

In contrast, single tenancy provides each end-user or group with their own dedicated software instance. For example, TurboTax offers a classic desktop version, which a single user can purchase, install, and use independently. Similarly, desktop typing software provides a single-tenant solution, unlike its SaaS alternatives.

Advantages of Multitenancy

Cost Savings: In a multitenant architecture, computing resources are shared among multiple users, significantly reducing costs for individual tenants. For instance, using TurboTax's SaaS version for tax filing is much cheaper than purchasing its single-tenant desktop version.

Flexibility: Multitenancy eliminates the challenges of resource provisioning. Users only pay for what they consume, avoiding the risks of over-provisioning (higher costs) or under-provisioning (reduced performance). Additionally, resource management tasks like patching, updates, and security are handled by the provider, allowing users to focus on their operations.

Overall, multitenancy combines cost efficiency with operational flexibility, making it an ideal solution for businesses seeking scalable and affordable software solutions.

1.15 Cloud Computing Related Terms

Below some other cloud computing related terms and their definitions are given. These definitions are based on ISO/IEC 17788, "Cloud Computing – Overview and Vocabulary."

Availability: Property of being accessible and usable upon demand by an authorized entity.

Confidentiality: Property that information is not made available or disclosed to unauthorized individuals, entities, or processes

Integrity: Property of accuracy and completeness.

Information Security: Preservation of confidentiality, integrity, and availability of information. In addition, other properties, such as authenticity, accountability, non-repudiation, and reliability can also be involved.

Service Level Agreement (SLA): Documented agreement between the service provider and customer that identifies services and service targets. A service level agreement can also be established between the service provider and a supplier, an internal group or a customer acting as a supplier. A service level agreement can be included in a contract or another type of documented agreement.

Cloud Application: An application that does not reside or run on a user's device, but rather is accessible via a network.

Cloud Service Provider: Party (Natural person or legal person, whether or not incorporated, or a group of either) which makes cloud services available.

Cloud Service Customer: Party (Natural person or legal person, whether or not incorporated, or a group of either) which is in a business relationship for the purpose of using cloud services

Cloud Service User: Natural person, or entity acting on their behalf, associated with a cloud service customer that uses cloud services. Examples of such entities include devices and applications.

Measured service: Metered delivery of cloud services such that usage can be monitored, controlled, reported and billed.

Tenant: One or more cloud customers sharing access to a pool of resources.

Multi-tenancy: Allocation of physical or virtual resources such that multiple tenants and their computations and data are isolated from and inaccessible to one another.

On-demand Self-service: Feature where a cloud service customer can provision computing capabilities, as needed, automatically or with minimal interaction with the cloud service provider.

Resource pooling: Aggregation of a cloud service provider's physical or virtual resources to serve one or more cloud service customers.

1.16 Related YouTube Videos

- Cloud Computing Simplified- Part 1: https://youtu.be/pAtWw-Ve8d8
- Cloud Computing Simplified- Part 2: https://youtu.be/ifMEqxK64SU
- Cloud Computing: Key Features: https://youtu.be/qSZu5U-y5kU
- Cloud Computing Types Introduction: https://youtu.be/P21FAXsGBQc
- Introduction to Infrastructure-as-a-Service (IaaS): https://youtu.be/rDCVHwWgz0g
- Introduction to Platform-as-a-Service (PaaS): https://youtu.be/oW9PU6l-ZsE
- Introduction to Software-as-a-Service (SaaS): https://youtu.be/8jThZfBnerM
- Introduction to Data-as-a-Service (DaaS): https://youtu.be/psO1NZ2bNIE
- Introduction to Desktop-as-a-Service: https://youtu.be/5Em7GEso1x0
- Introduction to Function-as-a-Service (FaaS): https://youtu.be/P0o_y1KFgPg
- Public Cloud: https://youtu.be/2aQE6J1o6-4
- Private Cloud: https://youtu.be/5BA2IID_0Uw
- Hybrid Cloud: https://youtu.be/TlzGS54gtWE
- Multi-Cloud: https://youtu.be/ZM-JtSoPdiU
- Community Cloud: https://youtu.be/9B1ZnACZr9Q
- Multi-Tenancy: https://youtu.be/y_ocQKEbLGQ
- Cloud Computing Advantages: https://youtu.be/pFdnV9FB3u8

1.17 Chapter Review Questions

Question 1:
Which of the following is an example of a traditional IT infrastructure?
- A. Virtual Machines
- B. Physical On-Premise Servers
- C. Cloud Storage
- D. Multi-Cloud Deployment

Question 2:
What is the primary characteristic of distributed computing?
- A. It centralizes all computing resources in a single location.
- B. It uses interconnected systems to share computing tasks.
- C. It eliminates the need for internet access.
- D. It focuses only on data storage.

Question 3:
What type of computing paradigm is known for leveraging quantum phenomena?
- A. Parallel Computing
- B. Nano Computing
- C. Quantum Computing
- D. Grid Computing

Question 4:
Which of the following is NOT a recent trend in computing?
- A. Distributed Computing

Cloud Computing and AWS Introduction

B. Cluster Computing
C. Cloud Firewalls
D. Utility Computing

Question 5:
According to NIST, which characteristic of cloud computing ensures resource pooling?
    A. Ubiquitous Access
    B. On-Demand Self-Service
    C. Shared Pool of Configurable Resources
    D. Service Provider Monitoring

Question 6:
Which of these is NOT part of the 3-4-5 principles of cloud computing?
    A. Three types of cloud deployment models
    B. Four essential characteristics
    C. Five cloud service delivery models
    D. Three types of cloud service models

Question 7:
What is the primary benefit of Infrastructure as a Service (IaaS)?
    A. Simplified development environments
    B. Elastic computing resources
    C. Prebuilt applications for end-users
    D. Reduced data storage needs

Question 8:
Platform as a Service (PaaS) is best suited for:
    A. End-users accessing ready-made applications
    B. Developers building and deploying applications
    C. System administrators managing VMs
    D. Data storage and backup solutions

Question 9:
Which cloud computing model is described as "Function-as-a-Service (FaaS)"?
    A. Infrastructure-as-a-Service (IaaS)
    B. Platform-as-a-Service (PaaS)
    C. Serverless Computing
    D. Desktop-as-a-Service (DaaS)

Question 10:
What is a key advantage of public cloud deployment models?
    A. Higher level of data privacy
    B. Cost-effectiveness and scalability
    C. Customization for specific organizational needs
    D. Limited internet dependency

Question 11:
Which of the following best defines a hybrid cloud?

A. A combination of multiple public cloud providers

B. A mix of public and private cloud environments

C. On-premises deployment with local servers

D. A community-based cloud system

Question 12:

What is a defining feature of multi-cloud deployments?

    A. Using services from multiple cloud providers

    B. Hosting everything on a private cloud

    C. Dependency on a single cloud provider

    D. Limited scalability

Question 13:

Which deployment type keeps all resources within an organization's premises?

    A. Public Cloud Deployment

    B. On-Premises Deployment

    C. Hybrid Deployment

    D. Multi-Cloud Deployment

Question 14:

What is one essential characteristic of cloud computing?

    A. Fixed resource allocation

    B. Limited network access

    C. Broad network access

    D. Manual provisioning of services

Question 15:

Which term is used to describe the capability of supporting multiple tenants on the same infrastructure?

    A. Single Tenancy

    B. Multi-Tenancy

    C. Timesharing

    D. SaaS

1.18 Answers to Chapter Review Questions

1. B. Physical On-Premise Servers

Explanation: Traditional IT infrastructure relies on physical servers housed within an organization's premises, contrasting with modern cloud-based or virtual solutions.

2. B. It uses interconnected systems to share computing tasks.

Explanation: Distributed computing involves multiple systems working together to perform tasks, increasing efficiency and scalability.

3. C. Quantum Computing

Explanation: Quantum computing leverages quantum mechanics principles to perform computations that are significantly faster for certain tasks compared to classical computing.

4. C. Cloud Firewalls

Explanation: While distributed computing, cluster computing, and utility computing are established trends, cloud firewalls are specific tools, not general trends.

5. C. Shared Pool of Configurable Resources
Explanation: NIST defines resource pooling as the ability of cloud systems to serve multiple clients using a shared pool of computing resources, dynamically allocated as needed.

6. C. Five cloud service delivery models
Explanation: The 3-4-5 principle refers to three deployment models, four essential characteristics, and three service models (IaaS, PaaS, SaaS). "Five cloud service delivery models" is not included.

7. B. Elastic computing resources
Explanation: IaaS provides scalable and flexible computing resources, allowing organizations to provision and release resources based on demand.

8. B. Developers building and deploying applications
Explanation: PaaS provides a platform and tools for developers to build, test, and deploy applications without managing the underlying infrastructure.

9. C. Serverless Computing
Explanation: Function-as-a-Service (FaaS) refers to serverless computing, where developers deploy functions or services that run without managing servers.

10. B. Cost-effectiveness and scalability
Explanation: Public clouds offer economies of scale, making them more affordable and allowing users to scale resources as needed.

11. B. A mix of public and private cloud environments
Explanation: Hybrid clouds combine private and public cloud resources, enabling flexibility and optimization of workloads.

12. A. Using services from multiple cloud providers
Explanation: Multi-cloud deployments involve using cloud services from more than one provider to avoid vendor lock-in and enhance reliability.

13. B. On-Premises Deployment
Explanation: On-premises deployments keep all IT resources and data within the organization's physical location, offering greater control but less flexibility.

14. C. Broad network access
Explanation: An essential characteristic of cloud computing is that services are accessible over the network via standard mechanisms, enabling widespread access.

15. B. Multi-Tenancy
Explanation: Multi-tenancy refers to a single infrastructure hosting multiple clients (tenants) while ensuring data and configuration isolation.

Chapter 2. Cloud Computing Architecture

In this chapter, we explore the foundational structure of cloud computing systems, focusing on their architecture and design principles. Cloud computing architecture provides a clear framework for delivering services efficiently while ensuring performance, scalability, and cost-effectiveness.

We begin with an overview of cloud architecture, offering insights into its purpose and significance in modern IT environments. This leads to the layered architecture of cloud computing, which breaks down the system into four distinct layers: the User Layer, Network Layer, Cloud Management Layer, and Hardware Resource Layer, each serving a critical function in delivering cloud services.

Next, we delve into the widely accepted NIST Cloud Computing Reference Architecture, which provides a standardized model for understanding cloud actors, their roles, and responsibilities.

The chapter also highlights the key design principles essential for building robust and efficient cloud architectures. These principles include scalability for handling increasing workloads, elasticity for adapting to demand fluctuations, and automation for minimizing manual intervention. We explore the importance of loose coupling to reduce interdependencies, security to protect data and systems, and caching to enhance performance. Additionally, we discuss strategies like cost optimization to manage resources efficiently, the importance of parallel processing for improved throughput, and how to design for failure to ensure system reliability and resilience.

By the end of this chapter, readers will have a comprehensive understanding of cloud architecture, its layered structure, and the key principles that guide the design of scalable, secure, and efficient cloud-based systems.

2.1 Overview of Cloud Architecture

Cloud architecture describes the overall operational mechanism of cloud systems, highlighting the components involved and their dependencies on the internet. It is typically represented as a layered architecture, which provides a structured approach to understanding, managing, and scaling cloud infrastructure and applications.

The cloud's layered architecture depends on both cloud service models (IaaS, PaaS, SaaS) and cloud deployment models (Private, Public, Hybrid, Multi-Cloud). For instance, in a private cloud, organizations retain full control over the entire stack, including data center services. In a public cloud, the cloud provider manages the entire infrastructure. Hybrid and multi-cloud models combine layers from multiple providers, offering greater flexibility.

This layered structure simplifies service delivery by segmenting cloud architecture into well-defined levels, ensuring organizations can securely manage their resources. It enables better implementation of security and compliance measures by creating secure boundaries and controlling access to data and resources. This helps organizations meet regulatory requirements and reduces the time and effort required to develop and deploy applications and services.

Cloud providers further streamline operations by offering a wide range of pre-configured services such as storage, networking, and compute resources, which can be quickly provisioned and managed.

The cloud architecture can be broadly divided into four layers:

User Layer: Interfaces where users access cloud services.
Network Layer: Facilitates connectivity and communication within the cloud.
Cloud Management Layer: Handles resource provisioning, monitoring, and management.
Hardware Resource Layer: Provides underlying physical infrastructure, including servers, storage, and networking hardware.

These layers work together to deliver essential infrastructure and services, forming the foundation for cloud computing systems.

2.2 Layered Architecture of Cloud Computing

The layered architecture of cloud computing is a multi-tier architecture model that can be used to define the different components of a cloud computing system and help us see how it all works together.

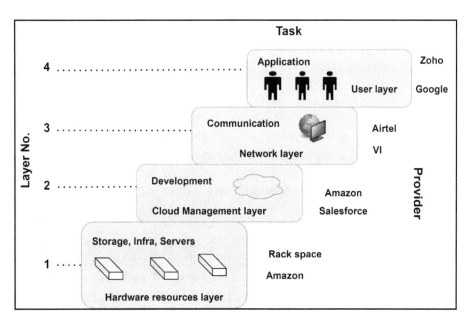

The cloud architecture has four layers, which act as different user access levels. We can think of them as different floors in the cloud building, each with its purpose. **Let's look into all** the four layers of cloud architecture.

2.2.1 User Layer

The user layer is the first or bottom layer in cloud architecture. All the people or customers are part of this layer. This is where clients/users start connecting to the cloud. The client can be any device, such as a thin client, thick client, mobile device, or anything else that can basically access a web app.

A thin client is entirely dependent on another system to work at all. Simply put, they only have a little processing power. Thick clients, conversely, are regular computers that can handle things themselves. They've got enough energy for independent work. Usually, a cloud app can be accessed just like a website. But behind the scenes, cloud apps are quite different. This layer includes web applications, mobile applications, and enterprise applications.

2.2.2 Network Layer

The second layer is the network layer, facilitating user connectivity to the cloud computing infrastructure. The entire cloud architecture depends on the network through which clients provide services. When discussing a public cloud, the subject under consideration pertains mainly to the Internet. The public cloud often manifests in a designated geographical setting, with its location being abstract and undisclosed to the user.

Moreover, the public cloud can be accessible globally. In the context of a private cloud, the provision of connectivity is typically facilitated through a local area network (LAN). In this scenario, the functionality of the cloud is entirely contingent upon the network infrastructure being utilized. Typically, when customers access the public or private cloud, they demand minimal bandwidth, as determined by the cloud providers. This layer mainly provides the service to manage the cloud environment and applications. It includes security, management, monitoring, and deployment services.

2.2.3 Cloud Management Layer

The third layer is cloud management, which consists of software applications used to effectively manage cloud computing environments. A cloud platform is provided to develop, deploy, and manage applications. It includes cloud hosting, virtualization, cloud software, and databases.

Cloud operating systems are intermediaries between the user and the data center or management programs facilitating resource management. These software applications typically facilitate resource management, such as scheduling and provisioning, as well as optimization tasks, such as server consolidation and storage workload consolidation. Additionally, they support internal cloud governance.

This layer is within the scope of service level agreements (SLAs), meaning that the activities occurring in this layer have the potential to impact the SLAs negotiated between users and service providers. The occurrence of any delay in the processing of tasks or any inconsistency in the supply of services has the potential to result in a breach of the Service Level Agreement (SLA).

According to the stipulated regulations, the occurrence of any breach in the Service Level Agreement (SLA) would entail the imposition of a penalty by the service provider. The Service Level Agreements (SLAs) encompass private and public cloud environments. Amazon Web Services (AWS) and Microsoft Azure are widely recognized as prominent service providers in the public cloud domain. Similarly, both OpenStack and Eucalyptus can create, deploy, and administer private cloud environments.

2.2.4 Hardware Resource Layer

Layer four is the hardware resource layer, with tangible hardware resource provisions. Typically, a data center is employed in the backend of a public cloud. Likewise, within a private cloud, a data center might serve as a substantial assemblage of networked hardware resources situated in a designated place or a system characterized by advanced configurations.

This particular layer falls within the Service Level Agreements (SLAs) scope. The layer in question holds significant importance in the governance of Service Level Agreements (SLAs). The impact of this layer on Service Level Agreements (SLAs) is particularly significant within the context of data centers. The prompt emphasizes the need to ensure prompt customer access to the cloud, adhering to the specific timeframes outlined in the Service Level Agreements (SLAs).

As previously stated, in the event of any inconsistencies in the allocation of resources or applications, the service provider is obligated to incur a penalty. Therefore, the data center comprises a network connection with high-speed capabilities and an efficient algorithm for transferring data from the data center to the management. Multiple data centers can be utilized for cloud infrastructure, and conversely, a data center can be shared by multiple clouds.

Therefore, the following is an overview of the architectural framework of a cloud computing system. Strict layering is a fundamental principle in the design and implementation of cloud applications. The degree of separation between Layer 3 and Layer 4 may vary based on the specific deployment of the cloud infrastructure.

2.3 NIST Cloud Computing Reference Architecture

The NIST Cloud Computing Reference Architecture provides a widely accepted, high-level conceptual model for understanding cloud computing. It extends the NIST cloud computing definition and serves as a common framework for discussing the requirements, roles, and operations of cloud systems. Importantly, it is vendor-neutral, focusing on cloud services' requirements rather than specific implementations or solutions.

The architecture highlights five key actors with defined roles and responsibilities:
- Cloud Consumer – Uses cloud services.
- Cloud Provider – Delivers cloud services.
- Cloud Auditor – Assesses security, compliance, and performance.
- Cloud Broker – Manages relationships between providers and consumers.
- Cloud Carrier – Facilitates connectivity and transport of cloud services.

This model helps organizations understand cloud operations, compare services, and evaluate technical standards like security, interoperability, and portability. It is a tool for designing and developing cloud architectures while ensuring clarity, flexibility, and innovation.

Cloud Consumer

The end-user or organization that uses cloud services. Consumers interact with cloud providers to request services, set up contracts, and use provisioned services. They are billed based on service usage, which may vary depending on their needs (e.g., SaaS, PaaS, or IaaS).

Cloud Provider

Responsible for delivering cloud services. Providers manage infrastructure, platforms, or software, depending on the service model:

SaaS: Providers deploy and manage software applications, leaving minimal control to consumers. PaaS: Providers manage the infrastructure while consumers control application development and hosting settings.
IaaS: Providers deliver core computing resources, while consumers manage applications and environments but not the underlying infrastructure.

Cloud Auditor

An independent entity that assesses the security, performance, and compliance of cloud services. Auditors evaluate controls, privacy impact, and adherence to service contracts, ensuring proper implementation and security compliance.

Cloud Broker

Acts as an intermediary between cloud consumers and providers, managing service access, performance, and delivery. Roles include:
- Intermediation: Enhancing services, such as access and security.
- Aggregation: Integrating multiple services into a unified offering.
- Arbitrage: Selecting services from multiple providers based on consumer needs.

Cloud Carrier

The intermediary that connects cloud consumers and providers through networks, telecommunications, and access devices (e.g., computers, laptops, or mobile phones), enabling seamless delivery of cloud services.

This framework simplifies understanding cloud roles and their responsibilities, ensuring efficient operation and collaboration within cloud ecosystems.

2.4 Key Design Principles in Building Cloud Architecture

Let's look into crucial design principles that help build well-architected cloud solutions. The design principles are Scalability and elasticity, automation, loose coupling, security, caching, cost optimization, think parallel, and design for failure. First, we will start with Scalability and elasticity, as these two are the most compelling reasons for cloud adoption besides cost and other features.

2.4.1 Scalability

Scalability is the ability of a system to scale without changing the design as input or workload increases. Cloud infrastructure and applications are designed with the premise that the load on the application can grow. In this scenario, if proper mechanisms are not in place in the design, the system will suffer – either the system will stop functioning or underperform. We need to design the system to allow components to be added when demand increases on the system – without changing the design.

Additional components can be added to manage the extra load to drive seasonal traffic. However, automatic Scalability is considered a much better design, where the additional system components are added automatically based on the runtime metrics such as CPU, memory, or storage utilization.

Design horizontally scalable cloud applications. There are two ways to manage Scalability: horizontal and vertical.

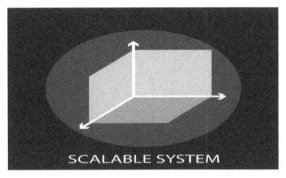

A "vertical scalable" system is considered constrained on CPU, RAM, and storage resources, negatively impacting the overall system's performance. Therefore, to improve this system's implementation by the "vertical scalable" mechanism means adding more resources such as CPU, RAM, and storage. However, since there is still no addition of a machine or node, making the system vertically scalable doesn't improve the fault tolerance of the overall design.

A "horizontally scalable" system increases its resource capacity by adding more nodes or machines. If we compare a horizontally scalable system with a scalable vertical design, the horizontally scalable system is preferred over vertically scalable systems. The reason is that a horizontally scalable system helps increase the degree of fault tolerance of the overall strategy and helps improve performance by enabling parallel execution of the workload and distributing that workload across multiple machines.

Horizontal Scalability helps increase the system's horizontal Scalability. In a horizontally scalable system, since more machines are added to increase the pool of resources, thus if one machine goes down, the other machine is allocated to process the workload of the failed machine. Thus helping to increase the degree of fault tolerance in the overall system.

Vertical Scalability is an old style in which the application is ported to a new server with more CPU, memory, or storage. It could lead to some downtime. The other one, horizontal Scalability, is a more modern and common approach to handling Scalability. In horizontally scalable systems, additional resources such as servers are added automatically to maintain the same performance as the load increases — design horizontally scalable cloud applications.

To summarize, scalable architecture is critical to use a scalable infrastructure. Increasing resources results in a proportional increase in the system's performance. A scalable service can handle heterogeneity, is operationally efficient, and is resilient, and it becomes more cost-effective when it grows.

2.4.2 Elasticity

Let's talk about elasticity as a design principle in architecting cloud applications. Elasticity and scalability are generally considered together when architecting solutions on the cloud application. Elasticity is the ability of a system to use resources in a dynamic and efficient way to maintain the SLA as the workload on the system increases and release them as the workload on the system decreases. The dynamic distribution or release of resources when they are not needed is the key aspect of elasticity, as it avoids the cost of over-provisioned resources such as servers, power, space, and maintenance.

Don't assume that components will always be in good health. Don't assume the fixed location of components. Use designs to re-launch and bootstrap your instances. Enable dynamic configuration to help answer instances on boot question: Who am I & what is my role?

2.4.3 Automation

DevOps, in which automation is one of the key features, has become an essential role in many software engineering organizations. Automation is one of the key design principles for architecting applications on a cloud platform. The reason is it avoids human intervention – particularly if it relates to repetitive tasks, integrating systems, or batch jobs.

Thus, many operations become more automated and efficient, and organizations save time on staff – particularly maintenance staff. This frees up some staff time. Time saved from the automation could be utilized on some other high-priority tasks in line with the organization's business objectives.   Moreover, with automation with thoroughly tested scripts, we not only automate start, stop, and terminate operations, but we also minimize failures by handling failures in codes.

As the system throws an error, we look up the error and fix the script so that next time, we don't need to handle it manually. These automated processes, over time, make the system resilient -- running with very little human intervention.

AWS has an extensive set of APIs to automate its services. For example, you can easily write a Python script (AWS Python SDK is called boto 3) to automate launching EC2.

2.4.4 Loose Coupling

Enterprise systems have many modules or services (terms used in modern micro-services architecture) encapsulating unique business features such as shopping cart service, checkout service, billing service, warehouse service, and support service. These modules are loosely coupled in well-architected systems – typically using web services or messaging frameworks (for example, JMS in Java).

Design everything as a Black Box.

Loose coupling is a key design principle in building any kind of system – even in monolith systems. Loose coupling becomes critically important in building distributed and cloud applications. The reasons are many. We can replace, modify, maintain, or test part of the application in isolation as a separate module or as a separate component by not taking down the entire application, as the price of taking down the entire system could be huge. Imagine if Google, CNN, BBC, Amazon, or any critical applications are going down even for a few seconds for maintenance, to add a new release feature, or to fix some bugs.

2.4.5 Security
Security is paramount for any organization, startup, small, medium-sized, or large enterprise. It is even critical for organizations that are handling data related to public health and money. These organizations are also bound to many security and compliance regulations.

Design security in mind. Design security in every layer.

When designing systems, security must be thought of from the very beginning as opposed to thinking and implementing security in bits and pieces when the application is deployed on production. It could be catastrophic if any security-related incident happens.

Broadly speaking, we can divide security into three aspects: physical security, platform security on which applications run, such as operating systems and web servers, and application security. When it comes to designing the security of data, data should be secured at transit and at rest. In other words, data should be stored in encrypted form both at rest and in transit.

With the cloud, you lose some part of physical control but not your own. A few guidelines related to cloud security. Restrict external access to specified IP ranges. Encrypt data "at rest" and encrypt data "at transit" (SSL). Consider an encrypted file system. Rotate your credentials. When passing arguments, pass the arguments as encrypted. Use Multi-factor factor authentication.

2.4.6 Caching

The basis of cloud computing's architecture is distributed computing. Distributed computing, on the one hand, by using the basic computing science technique divide-and-conquer, helps to improve processing workload, and loose coupling improves modifiability, maintainability, and scalability. There are extremely important features for enterprise systems.

However, distributed computing adds some challenges, for example, more indirection and more layers to communicate to get the final result. This increases latency and thus impacts how fact an output will be retrieved by the end-user.

Not all information in the system needs to be fetched or calculated each time to process a request. There is information that changes almost very little, for example, country names, city names, persons' demographics, and such – in fact, master data or look-up values in database terms. By the same token, many contents, such as images, videos, or documents in general, don't frequently change in production systems.

Since this information is of a mostly static nature, we can leverage the caching design principle of cloud architecture to not only improve request processing time but also help reduce operational costs. Data movement from the bottom layer to the top layer is reduced by a few layers, reducing data transfer costs. Also, computing resource usage is reduced due to caching.

As we discussed above, caching improves request processing time, saves costs on data transfer, and saves costs on computing resource utilization. Let's understand the type of caching. There are two types of caching: application data caching and edge caching.

In application data caching, essentially, data that is mostly of a static nature, such as master data, are cached in the in-memory cache. There are many products you can leverage to manage application data caching, such as Amazon ElasticCache (managed Memcache), Redis (in-memory database), and Hibernate Ehcache. You can also implement your custom application data caching for problems smaller in scope.

The other type of caching mechanism, which is, by and large, very common in cloud architecture, is edge caching. Essentially, for content management, the common caching solution is edge caching. In cache caching, content is served by the infrastructure's edge node server (AWS Edge Locations), which is closer to the user, thus improving latency and overall system performance. Amazon CloudFront is a typical example of edge caching.

2.4.7 Cost Optimization

Cost optimization is the most important design principle. The reason is that cloud costs, to a large part – particularly in the public cloud- are based on the OpEx (operating expenditure) model. Cost optimization essentially becomes an extremely important consideration.

Some principles are common: utilizing the right services for the right duration. For example, if an EC2 medium-size instance provides the required performance, then utilizing large or z-large will cost more. If services are being utilized, terminate them or stop them if you are using on-demand instances. You can also consider reserved instances and spot instances as opposed to on-demand instances for EC2 instances to optimize costs.

Auto-scaling is also a very good feature to optimize the cost. Using Auto-scaling, you can not only scale by adding more instances horizontally to maintain performance if the workload increases, but you can also scale down to terminate the resources automatically if they are needed by adding some configuration using the CloudWatch service.

The main points here are the right service for the right job, not using more resources, and for more time if you don't need it. Look into various cost options and their pros and cons (for example, on-demand instances, reserved instances, and spot instances) provided by the cloud provider, and select the best option for your use case to optimize the cost.

2.4.8 Think Parallel

Many software engineering problems can be solved in less time if the concept of parallel processing is used. For example, a data processing job can be divided into many parts, and each part can be processed in parallel. Map-Reduce job is a good example of parallel processing. Extending on parallel processing, when you are designing applications to run on a cloud platform, parallel thinking becomes even more important and valuable as the cloud has massive resources. Parallel processing helps solve large problems in less time.

There are two main reasons for using parallel computing. Parallel computing saves time (wall clock time), and it helps solve large problems. Some guidelines for parallel thinking: experiment with different architectures for multi-threading and concurrent requests. Run parallel MapReduce jobs. Use Elastic Load Balancing with Auto-Scaling to distribute loads across multiple machines.

2.4.9 Design for Failure

"Everything fails, all the time," Werner Vogels, CTO, Amazon.com. Design for failure and nothing will really fail! A few guidelines: *Avoid single points of failure -- assume everything fails*. Design with a backward goal as applications should continue to function even if the underlying physical hardware fails is removed or is replaced.

2.5 Chapter Review Questions

Question 1:
Which of the following layers in the cloud computing architecture interacts directly with end-users?
   A. Cloud Management Layer
   B. Network Layer
   C. User Layer
   D. Hardware Resource Layer

Question 2:
What is the primary role of the Network Layer in cloud computing architecture?
   A. Managing user authentication and access
   B. Facilitating communication between users and cloud resources
   C. Handling physical server infrastructure
   D. Monitoring cloud resource usage

Question 3:
Which layer in the cloud architecture is responsible for managing physical servers, storage, and networking?
   A. Cloud Management Layer
   B. Hardware Resource Layer
   C. User Layer
   D. Application Layer

Question 4:
According to the NIST Cloud Computing Reference Architecture, which of the following is a key principle?
   A. Fixed resource allocation
   B. Broad network access and resource pooling
   C. Manual provisioning of resources
   D. Centralized server-only deployments

Question 5:

What is scalability in the context of cloud computing architecture?
- A. The ability to handle increasing workloads by adding resources
- B. Automating resource provisioning
- C. Encrypting data across the cloud
- D. Isolating different user environments

Question 6:
Elasticity in cloud computing refers to:
- A. Providing fixed computing resources
- B. The ability to scale resources up or down based on demand
- C. Ensuring data security across cloud layers
- D. Automating routine cloud operations

Question 7:
What does the principle of "Loose Coupling" in cloud architecture emphasize?
- A. Strong dependency between cloud services
- B. Building components with minimal interdependencies
- C. Fixed resource allocation
- D. Strict isolation of cloud services

Question 8:
Which design principle focuses on building systems to recover gracefully from failures?
- A. Think Parallel
- B. Elasticity
- C. Design for Failure
- D. Caching

Question 9:
What is the role of caching in cloud computing architecture?
- A. Encrypting data for security
- B. Storing frequently accessed data for improved performance
- C. Scaling workloads across different regions
- D. Managing user access to cloud resources

Question 10:
Which principle in cloud computing architecture helps minimize costs while ensuring efficient use of resources?
- A. Automation
- B. Cost Optimization
- C. Scalability
- D. Loose Coupling

2.6 Answers to Chapter Review Questions

1. C. User Layer
Explanation: The User Layer in the cloud computing architecture directly interacts with end-users, providing the interface through which they access cloud services.

2. B. Facilitating communication between users and cloud resources

Explanation: The Network Layer manages the transmission of data and facilitates communication between users and cloud resources, ensuring smooth data flow.

3. B. Hardware Resource Layer
Explanation: The Hardware Resource Layer is responsible for managing physical components such as servers, storage, and networking in cloud computing architecture.

4. B. Broad network access and resource pooling
Explanation: According to NIST Cloud Computing Reference Architecture, broad network access and resource pooling are essential characteristics, enabling flexible resource sharing and remote access.

5. A. The ability to handle increasing workloads by adding resources
Explanation: Scalability allows cloud systems to handle increasing workloads by dynamically adding resources, ensuring performance consistency.

6. B. The ability to scale resources up or down based on demand
Explanation: Elasticity refers to the ability to adjust resources dynamically, scaling them up or down to match workload requirements in real time.

7. B. Building components with minimal interdependencies
Explanation: Loose Coupling emphasizes designing system components with minimal dependencies, enabling independent updates, scaling, and maintenance.

8. C. Design for Failure
Explanation: The "Design for Failure" principle focuses on building fault-tolerant systems that anticipate and gracefully recover from failures, ensuring system reliability.

9. B. Storing frequently accessed data for improved performance
Explanation: Caching involves storing frequently accessed data temporarily to improve performance and reduce latency in cloud services.

10. B. Cost Optimization
Explanation: Cost Optimization ensures that cloud resources are used efficiently to minimize costs while maintaining performance and scalability.

Chapter 3. Service Management

In today's cloud-driven world, Service Management plays a critical role in delivering efficient, reliable, and cost-effective cloud solutions. This chapter explores the foundational elements of managing services in cloud environments, ensuring performance, scalability, and cost optimization.

We begin with an introduction to Service Level Agreements (SLAs), the cornerstone of service delivery, highlighting their importance, components, and role in building trust between providers and customers. Effective SLA management, monitoring, and reporting ensure services meet agreed performance standards, with billing and cost optimization strategies enhancing financial efficiency.

The chapter further examines the scaling of hardware, comparing traditional on-premises approaches to cloud-based solutions, along with the factors influencing these decisions and their economic impact. Key concepts like cost efficiency, ROI (Return on Investment), and TCO (Total Cost of Ownership) are explored to help organizations achieve sustainable growth and leverage economies of scale.

Finally, the chapter dives into data management strategies, focusing on best practices, security, and lifecycle management. It concludes with a discussion on data scalability and cloud-based solutions, emphasizing how scalability concepts ensure organizations can adapt and thrive in dynamic cloud environments. Together, these topics provide a comprehensive understanding of service management essentials for achieving business success in the cloud.

3.1 SLA Introduction

A Service Level Agreement (SLA) is a critical document that defines the expectations, responsibilities, and consequences for service delivery between a service provider and a client. Commonly used in industries like IT, telecommunications, and cloud computing, an SLA ensures services are delivered consistently and satisfactorily by outlining key parameters such as uptime guarantees, issue resolution times, and support availability.

SLAs benefit both parties by providing transparency, accountability, and a structured approach for resolving service-related issues, fostering trust and reliability. For example, an IT company providing support services may guarantee 24/7 availability with a one-hour response time for critical issues and 99.9% server uptime. Penalties for failing to meet these thresholds or escalation procedures for unresolved problems are also included.

By setting clear expectations and roles, SLAs minimize disputes, ensure performance standards are met, and strengthen business relationships between providers and clients.

Purpose of SLAs

The purpose of Service Level Agreements (SLAs) is to set clear expectations between service providers and customers by defining the scope, quality, and responsibilities of both parties. SLAs help prevent misunderstandings and disputes while enabling service performance measurement through key metrics and KPIs. They establish remedies and penalties for unmet service levels, motivating providers to prioritize reliability and quality by outlining corrective actions or compensation. Additionally, SLAs improve communication through regular reporting and reviews, fostering transparency, collaboration, and continuous improvement in service delivery.

Types of SLAs

Customer-based SLA: Tailored to meet the needs and expectations of a specific customer or group of customers.

Service-based SLA: Standardized SLAs that apply to all customers using a particular service.

Multilevel SLA: Contains multiple layers of SLAs, often with different levels of detail and specific objectives.

Underpinning SLA (USLA): An internal SLA is used by a service provider to define its internal processes and commitments.

SLAs are not static documents. They should be discussed and updated regularly to reflect changing business needs, technology advancements, and customer feedback.

3.2 Importance of SLAs in Service Delivery

Service Level Agreements (SLAs) are vital in service delivery as they build trust by establishing clear expectations and transparency between service providers and customers. They help ensure compliance with legal and regulatory standards by demonstrating adherence to service quality and availability requirements. SLAs also act as a foundation for dispute resolution by defining breaches and failures in service levels. Additionally, they provide a framework for monitoring and improving service quality, allowing providers to track performance against agreed metrics and implement corrective actions when needed.

3.3 Components of SLAs

Service Description: A detailed service description, including its features, functions, and scope.
Service Level Objectives (SLOs): Specific, measurable goals or performance targets include uptime percentages, response times, and resolution times.
Responsibilities: Clearly defined roles and responsibilities for both the service provider and the customer.
Performance Metrics: The key performance indicators (KPIs) will be used to measure the service's performance.

Penalties and Rewards: Consequences for failing to meet the agreed-upon performance standards (penalties) and rewards for exceeding them (bonuses).

Service Hours: The hours during which the service will be available and supported.

Escalation Procedures: The process for escalating issues or disputes within the organization or between the parties involved.

Termination Clause: Conditions under which either party can terminate the agreement.

3.4 SLA Management and Monitoring

SLA management and monitoring are essential to ensure service providers deliver on their commitments and maintain high service quality. It begins with well-defined SLAs that specify service metrics (e.g., response times, uptime), desired performance levels, responsibilities of both parties, and penalties or remedies for SLA breaches. Continuous monitoring plays a crucial role, involving real-time tracking of performance metrics, alerting mechanisms to address potential issues promptly, and performance dashboards for a visual representation of service performance. These tools enable proactive management, ensuring SLAs are consistently met and service quality remains high.

3.5 Reporting and Analysis

Regular reporting and analysis are crucial for monitoring trends, identifying improvements, and ensuring compliance with SLAs. This includes generating regular performance reports, analyzing root causes of SLA breaches to address core issues, and maintaining a feedback loop for suggestions. When SLAs are not met, prompt issue resolution and continuous improvement are necessary, such as implementing fixes or service credits. Insights gathered help improve service delivery, and periodic SLA reviews ensure they align with evolving business needs. Effective SLA management fosters collaboration, ensures service quality, and strengthens the provider-customer relationship.

3.6 Billing & Accounting in Cloud Services

Billing and accounting in cloud services involve tracking, measuring, and managing the costs of cloud resources to optimize expenditures. This process includes monitoring real-time resource usage (CPU, memory, storage, and bandwidth), allocating costs accurately across teams or projects for transparency, and understanding various pricing models such as on-demand, reserved, or spot instances.

Organizations use cost estimation tools to predict expenses and budget effectively, while cost optimization strategies—like rightsizing resources, auto-scaling, and reserved instances—help reduce spending. Third-party tools further enhance cost management by offering advanced analytics and reporting, ensuring organizations maximize the value of their cloud investments.

3.6.1 Cloud Service Billing Models

Cloud providers offer various billing models to meet customer needs, ensuring flexibility and cost optimization. **Pay-as-You-Go** charges users based on actual usage, making it ideal for variable workloads or testing scenarios. Reserved Instances (RIs) provide discounted pricing for pre-purchased resources over fixed terms (1-3 years), suitable for predictable workloads. **On-Demand Instances** offer resources without commitments, billing users at standard rates, ideal for fluctuating workloads.

Data Transfer Pricing charges for moving data between services, regions, or the internet, which must be carefully considered for architecture planning. **Serverless Billing** charges based on execution count and compute time, making it perfect for event-driven and microservice-based applications. By understanding and choosing the appropriate billing model, businesses can optimize cloud costs while maintaining efficiency.

3.7 Cost Management and Optimization

Cost management in cloud computing is essential to ensure efficient use of resources and avoid overspending. While cloud environments offer flexibility to scale infrastructure based on demand, unmanaged usage can lead to cost inefficiencies. Organizations can optimize costs by using cost-effective instance types, auto-scaling resources to match actual usage, and leveraging serverless computing for granular billing.

Key strategies include using **cost monitoring tools** like AWS Cost Explorer, Azure Cost Management, and Google Cloud Cost Management, which provide insights into spending. Setting **budgets and alerts** helps track expenses and prevent unexpected overages. Cloud providers also offer solutions like pricing calculators, reserved instances, and spot instances for cost optimization. By continuously monitoring and analyzing resource usage, businesses can balance performance and cost-effectiveness to maximize the value of their cloud investments.

3.7.1 Tracking and Reporting Costs

Tracking and reporting costs are essential for effective cloud cost management. By monitoring cloud-related expenses and generating detailed reports, organizations gain visibility into resource utilization and spending patterns. These reports, which break down costs by service, resource, department, or project, enable informed decisions on budget allocation and resource optimization.

Cost tracking helps identify trends, forecast future expenses, and ensure budgets remain on track. Proper tagging and cost allocation practices ensure transparency, allowing expenses to be attributed accurately to specific projects or teams. This process supports financial planning, accountability, and resource optimization.

Overall, tracking and reporting costs are critical for cost control, budget planning, and maximizing the value of cloud investments through data-driven decisions.

3.7.2 Budgeting for Cloud Services

Budgeting for cloud services is essential for financial planning and cost management. Organizations should begin by analyzing historical cloud usage and spending patterns to estimate future expenses. Collaborating with teams to define objectives and project future demand is critical, especially for upcoming projects that may impact usage.

Organizations must carefully select suitable billing models, such as pay-as-you-go, reserved instances, or spot instances, based on workload characteristics. Setting spending limits and implementing cost controls, including monitoring tools and alerts, helps prevent budget overruns. Cost allocation using tags ensures transparency and accountability by attributing expenses to specific projects or teams.

Regular reviews and adjustments are necessary to align budgets with evolving usage patterns and business needs. A dynamic budgeting approach combining data analysis, cost controls, and ongoing optimization ensures efficient cloud utilization while achieving business objectives.

3.8 Scaling Hardware: Traditional vs. Cloud

Scaling hardware in a traditional on-premises setup and a cloud-based environment presents distinct advantages and considerations. In a conventional hardware scaling model, organizations invest in and maintain their physical servers and infrastructure within their data centers. This approach provides control over the hardware but entails significant upfront capital expenditure and ongoing operational costs for maintenance, upgrades, and expansion.

On the other hand, the cloud-based model allows for rapid and flexible scaling up or down based on actual demand, eliminating the need for substantial upfront investments. Cloud providers offer various services and configurations, enabling businesses to match resources precisely to their requirements, thus optimizing cost efficiency—additionally, cloud-based scaling benefits from geographically distributed data centers, enhancing redundancy and disaster recovery capabilities.

3.8.1 Traditional Hardware Scaling

Traditional hardware scaling involves organizations managing their physical servers and infrastructure within data centers, offering control over security, compliance, and performance. However, this approach requires significant upfront capital investment to purchase servers, storage, and networking equipment, along with ongoing operational costs for power, cooling, and maintenance.

Scalability can be slow and expensive, as adding resources requires provisioning new hardware. Unlike cloud environments, on-premises setups lack built-in geographic distribution and redundancy, requiring additional investments in secondary data centers for high availability and disaster recovery.

While traditional scaling provides control, it comes with high costs, limited agility, and challenges in scalability. Organizations must weigh their requirements and budget constraints before opting for this approach over cloud alternatives.

3.8.2 Cloud Hardware Scaling

Cloud-based hardware scaling offers significant advantages over traditional approaches:

Cost-effectiveness: Cloud computing eliminates large upfront investments with pay-as-you-go pricing, allowing resources to scale up or down based on demand, reducing waste and underutilization.

Flexibility and Agility: Cloud providers offer various configurations and services, enabling rapid scaling through automated processes or minimal effort.

Global Reach: Cloud providers operate global data centers, allowing organizations to deploy resources closer to users, reducing latency, and improving performance.

High Availability and Redundancy: Robust failover and redundancy mechanisms ensure minimal downtime and enhanced system resilience.

While traditional hardware offers control for legacy or sensitive systems, cloud scaling provides unmatched scalability, flexibility, and cost efficiency, making it ideal for dynamic and modern business needs.

3.8.3 Pros and Cons of Each Approach

The choice between traditional IT and cloud infrastructure depends on an organization's specific needs, budget, scalability requirements, and risk tolerance. Many organizations today adopt a hybrid or multi-cloud strategy to combine the advantages of both approaches.

Aspect	Traditional IT	Cloud Infrastructure
Cost	High upfront hardware costs	Pay-As-You-Go
Scalability	Limited scalability, Hardware constraints	Easily scalable because of on-demand availability of resources
Security	Depends on in-house security management	Security measures provided by the cloud provider
Maintenance	Manual maintenance and updates	Availability of Managed services helps to get automatic updates
Flexibility	Limited flexibility, longer provisioning times because of limited resources	High flexibility with rapid provisioning
Downtime	More susceptible to downtime	High availability because of redundancy
Location	On-premises data centers	Geographically distributed data centers help reduce latency and availability

3.8.4 Factors Influencing Scaling Decisions

Scaling decisions in organizations are driven by technical, operational, financial, and strategic factors. Key considerations include **workload and demand patterns**, where organizations must align resources with current and projected workloads, accounting for seasonal or cyclical variations. **Technical factors** like system architecture, compatibility, and performance requirements influence whether systems scale horizontally or vertically while ensuring high availability and fault tolerance.

Cost and budget constraints play a critical role, requiring a balance between performance and financial resources. Decisions on **infrastructure type** — on-premises or cloud — depend on costs, benefits, and strategic goals. Cloud solutions, with **elastic scalability** and pay-as-you-go pricing, are attractive for organizations seeking flexibility. Ultimately, scalability solutions involve choosing between vertical and horizontal scaling to meet evolving operational needs efficiently.

3.9 Economics of Scaling: Benefiting Enormously

The economics of scaling enables organizations to optimize costs, resource allocation, and performance as they grow. By achieving economies of scale, fixed costs like infrastructure and maintenance are spread across a larger output, reducing per-unit costs and improving profit margins.

Scalability allows resources to be dynamically adjusted based on demand, minimizing over-provisioning and underutilization. Cloud-based scaling, often built on a pay-as-you-go model, eliminates large upfront investments, ensuring cost efficiency and flexibility.

Additionally, scaling improves application performance, ensuring high availability and a better user experience during peak demand, which enhances customer satisfaction and loyalty. Overall, the economics of scaling empowers organizations to achieve sustainable growth, remain competitive, and respond efficiently to evolving market demands while maintaining financial discipline.

3.9.1 Cost Efficiency in Scaling

Cost efficiency in scaling focuses on optimizing resource allocation and minimizing costs as operations grow. Key aspects include economies of scale, where increased cloud operations lower average costs by spreading fixed expenses. Resource optimization ensures resources align with demand, avoiding over-provisioning or underutilization. The pay-as-you-go model eliminates large upfront investments, as organizations only pay for what they use.

Cost-efficient scaling reduces per-unit costs, enabling competitive pricing and improved profit margins. It promotes financial prudence by allowing strategic resource allocation and avoiding unnecessary expenses. Additionally, scaling enhances performance by meeting increased demand, improving user satisfaction, and driving revenue growth. Finally, optimized infrastructure ensures resources are efficiently utilized, maximizing return on investment while avoiding waste.

3.9.2 ROI and TCO Considerations

ROI measures the return generated by an investment relative to its cost, while TCO encompasses the full spectrum of costs associated with an asset or solution. Both metrics are essential for making financially sound and strategically aligned investment decisions.

ROI measures the return generated by an investment relative to its cost, while TCO encompasses the full spectrum of costs associated with an asset or solution. Both metrics are essential for making financially sound and strategically aligned investment decisions. ROI measures the return or gain an organization receives from an investment relative to the cost of that investment.

ROI is calculated as (Net Gain from Investment / Cost of Investment) x 100%. A positive ROI indicates that the investment generated more value than its cost.

TCO represents the total costs associated with acquiring, deploying, operating, and maintaining a particular asset or technology solution over its entire lifecycle. TCO includes not only the initial purchase price but also ongoing costs such as maintenance, upgrades, support, and operational expenses.

3.9.3 Balancing ROI and TCO

Striking a balance between ROI and TCO is critical when transitioning to a cloud computing platform from on-prem or starting a brand new cloud computing environment for development and deployment.

The following are the brief key points about balancing ROI and TCO.

Strategic Alignment: Organizations should align investments with their strategic objectives, considering both short-term ROI and long-term TCO to ensure they meet business goals.

Risk vs. Reward: High ROI projects may come with higher TCO, so it's crucial to evaluate risk and reward when making investment decisions.

Lifecycle Considerations: TCO analysis emphasizes the importance of evaluating costs over the entire lifecycle, helping organizations make informed decisions about maintenance, upgrades, and replacements.

3.9.4 Leveraging Economies of Scale

Leveraging economies of scale allows organizations to improve efficiency and reduce costs as they grow. By **bulk purchasing**, companies can lower per-unit costs through larger orders and better supplier negotiations. **Production efficiency** increases with higher volumes through automation, labor specialization, and streamlined workflows.

Standardization of products and processes simplifies operations, minimizing complexity and resource waste. In **distribution and logistics**, consolidating shipping, centralizing warehouses, and optimizing routes reduce transportation costs. Lastly, investing in **technology** like ERP systems enhances productivity, streamlining operations and supporting cost-effective scaling.

3.10 Managing Data

Managing data in cloud computing involves efficiently handling storage, security, compliance, backup, integration, analytics, and costs. **Data storage** relies on organizing data using object, block, or file storage services with clear classifications and lifecycle policies. **Security and compliance** are critical, requiring encryption, access controls, and adherence to regulations. Robust **backup and disaster recovery** strategies ensure resilience and mitigate downtime risks.

Data integration tools connect cloud-based and on-premises systems for consistency, while analytics enable organizations to leverage big data for insights. Lastly, effective **cost management** through monitoring and governance ensures resource optimization and cost-efficiency. A holistic strategy allows organizations to fully benefit from cloud computing while ensuring data integrity and security.

3.10.1 Data Management Best Practices

Ensuring data quality, security, and accessibility is crucial for effective data management. High-quality data requires regular validation, cleansing, and profiling to eliminate errors. Robust data security measures, such as encryption, access controls, and audits, protect sensitive data from breaches. Accessibility ensures authorized users can access data when needed, facilitated by cloud solutions and well-structured architectures.

Maintaining thorough data documentation, including metadata and lineage, helps users understand data origins and meaning. Reliable backup and recovery strategies, such as regular backups and disaster recovery plans, ensure data resilience against failures or disasters.

Organizations must also implement strong data governance frameworks to define stewardship, compliance, and quality standards, while data integration unifies information from diverse sources for better decision-making. By monitoring and improving these processes, organizations can unlock data's full potential for enhanced decision-making and competitive advantage.

3.10.2 Data Security and Privacy

Data security and privacy are interrelated. Robust data security measures help ensure data privacy by preventing unauthorized access, while data privacy regulations drive the need for stringent data security practices. They work together to build trust for individuals, organizations, and societies in an increasingly data-driven world, balancing the benefits of data utilization with the need to protect personal information and keep sensitive data secure.

Data Security is a top priority for organizations and individuals, as data breaches can have severe consequences. Implementing a robust data security strategy is essential to safeguard sensitive information and maintain the trust of customers and stakeholders. Your summary effectively highlights the key elements of data security.

Data privacy, often referred to as information privacy, pertains to the protection of an individual's personal information and their right to control the collection, use, and sharing of that information. It involves a range of principles, practices, and regulations designed to safeguard sensitive data and respect an individual's privacy rights.

3.10.3 Data Lifecycle Management

Data Lifecycle Management (DLM) is a structured approach to managing data from its creation to disposal. It consists of key stages:

Data Creation/Acquisition: Data is generated or acquired through sources like customer interactions, sensors, or partners.
Data Ingestion: Captured data is securely stored in systems like databases or data lakes.
Data Processing: Data is cleansed, transformed, and enriched to ensure quality and usability.
Data Storage: Data is stored in scalable and cost-effective systems for accessibility.
Data Usage/Analysis: Data is analyzed for reporting, decision-making, and insights.
Data Sharing: Data is shared securely with stakeholders, adhering to privacy policies.
Data Archiving: Infrequently used data is moved to cost-effective long-term storage for compliance or historical use.
Data Deletion/Destruction: Data is securely deleted when no longer needed to comply with regulations and reduce risks.

Effective DLM optimizes storage costs, enhances compliance, improves governance, and ensures data security while enabling efficient retrieval for business needs.

3.11 Looking at Data Scalability & Cloud Services

Data scalability describes the ability to handle and manage increasing amounts of data without sacrificing throughput. It's like a rubber band that stretches when more data is added. It's like a rubber band that stretches when more data is added.

Cloud Services are like renting computer resources and software over the internet. It's like using a shared, remote computer to store and process your data instead of having your own physical computer. This is more adaptable and cost-effective.

Cloud services are like renting space on someone else's computer over the internet. Instead of owning and maintaining your own servers, you use a cloud service provider's resource. The services like AWS and Microsoft Azure are simply scalable to meet your expanding data requirements. As a result, if your company expands and you accumulate more data, you can quickly expand your storage and processing capacity in the cloud without purchasing additional gear.

Data scalability has multiple aspects:

Vertical Scalability: Vertical scalability is the process of extending the capacity of a single server or system by adding extra resources such as CPU, RAM, or storage. This technology, however, has limitations and may become excessively expensive.

Horizontal Scaling: Horizontal scaling, also known as "scale-out," is adding extra machines or nodes to the system to distribute the workload. It's a more adaptable and cost-effective method of dealing with data growth.

Elastic Scalability: This combines vertical and horizontal scalability and allows a system's resources to be dynamically adjusted dependent on workload. Elastic scalability is frequently related with cloud services.

3.11.1 Scalability Concepts

Data scalability refers to a system's or infrastructure's ability to manage rising amounts of data without sacrificing performance, dependability, or functionality. It is an important factor in data system design since data quantities are always increasing, and the ability to handle this expansion is key for businesses and organizations.

Cloud services provide various benefits for data scalability:

Scalability: Cloud services can scale resources up and down to meet changing data requirements.

High Availability: High availability and data redundancy are provided by cloud services, lowering the risk of data loss.

Cost: Because users pay for the resources they use, it is cost-effective, particularly for enterprises with variable workloads.

Global Reach: Because cloud providers operate data centers in numerous areas, data may be stored and accessed from anywhere in the world.

3.11.2 Cloud-Based Scalability Solutions

Cloud-based scalability solutions are an essential component of modern computing, allowing businesses to adapt to shifting demands while maintaining performance and lowering infrastructure costs. These points emphasize the most important features of cloud scalability.

Here are some key points regarding cloud-based scalability solutions:

Elastic Resources: Cloud platforms allow you to easily scale resources up or down based on your needs. This elasticity is a fundamental aspect of cloud scalability.

Pay-as-You-Go: Cloud services often operate on a pay-as-you-go model, meaning you only pay for the resources you use. This cost-efficiency is beneficial for businesses with variable workloads.

Virtualization: Virtualization technology enables the creation of virtual instances of servers, storage, and other resources, making it easier to scale and manage them in the cloud.

Load Balancing: Cloud platforms provide load balancing services to distribute incoming traffic across multiple servers or instances, ensuring even resource utilization and high availability.

Global Reach: Cloud providers have data centers in various regions worldwide, allowing you to store and access data closer to your users, reducing latency and improving performance.

Serverless Computing: Serverless computing technologies, such as AWS Lambda and Azure Functions, enable you to run code without having to manage the underlying infrastructure. They scale automatically in response to incoming demands.

Cost Optimization: Cloud platforms offer tools for optimizing costs, such as resource tagging and budget monitoring, helping you manage expenses as you scale.

3.12 Chapter Review Questions

Question 1:
What is the primary role of a Service Level Agreement (SLA) in cloud computing?
A. To manage cloud provider pricing models
B. To define the terms, responsibilities, and performance metrics between providers and customers
C. To describe data lifecycle management strategies
D. To implement security policies for cloud environments

Question 2:
Which of the following is NOT a type of SLA?
A. Customer-based SLA
B. Service-based SLA
C. Security-based SLA
D. Multi-level SLA

Question 3:
What is a critical component of SLA monitoring?
A. Calculating the total cost of ownership (TCO)
B. Tracking performance metrics such as uptime and response time

C. Implementing hardware scaling strategies
D. Encrypting all customer data

Question 4:
Which billing model is commonly used in cloud services?
A. Flat-rate billing
B. Pay-as-you-go billing
C. Monthly subscription with fixed resources
D. Hardware-based billing

Question 5:
What is the main advantage of cloud hardware scaling over traditional hardware scaling?
A. Reduced reliance on service providers
B. Fixed costs for resource usage
C. On-demand scalability without upfront investment
D. Complete control over physical hardware

Question 6:
How does tracking and reporting costs help in cloud cost management?
A. It eliminates the need for budgeting
B. It ensures all resources are used continuously
C. It identifies areas where resources are underutilized or wasted
D. It standardizes all cloud resources

Question 7:
Which of the following is a factor influencing hardware scaling decisions?
A. Geographic location of data centers
B. Budget constraints and workload requirements
C. Predefined network protocols
D. Encryption algorithms

Question 8:
What is the primary focus of ROI and TCO considerations in cloud services?
A. Maximizing initial investment in infrastructure
B. Balancing the cost of ownership with returns on investment
C. Eliminating the need for scalability
D. Using physical hardware instead of virtual machines

Question 9:
Which concept is emphasized by data lifecycle management?
A. Unlimited storage of all data
B. Managing data from creation through archival and deletion
C. Real-time data sharing between multiple providers
D. Implementing hardware-based encryption

Question 10:
What is a primary characteristic of cloud-based scalability solutions?
A. Fixed resource allocation for users

B. Inability to handle unpredictable workloads

C. Automatic adjustment of resources based on demand

D. High dependency on traditional hardware setups

3.13 Answers to Chapter Review Questions

1. B. To define the terms, responsibilities, and performance metrics between providers and customers

Explanation: The primary role of an SLA is to outline the agreed-upon expectations, responsibilities, and performance standards for both cloud providers and customers to ensure reliable service delivery.

2. C. Security-based SLA

Explanation: While customer-based, service-based, and multi-level SLAs are standard types, "security-based SLA" is not a recognized category, as security is typically a component of an SLA rather than its type.

3. B. Tracking performance metrics such as uptime and response time

Explanation: SLA monitoring focuses on tracking key performance metrics, such as availability and response times, to ensure the cloud provider meets the agreed-upon standards.

4. B. Pay-as-you-go billing

Explanation: Pay-as-you-go is the most common billing model in cloud services, allowing customers to pay only for the resources they consume without long-term commitments.

5. C. On-demand scalability without upfront investment

Explanation: Cloud hardware scaling allows users to scale resources dynamically as needed, eliminating the need for upfront investment in physical hardware.

6. C. It identifies areas where resources are underutilized or wasted

Explanation: Tracking and reporting costs provide visibility into resource utilization, helping organizations optimize spending and eliminate waste.

7. B. Budget constraints and workload requirements

Explanation: Factors like cost limitations and the nature of workloads are critical when deciding between traditional and cloud-based scaling options.

8. B. Balancing the cost of ownership with returns on investment

Explanation: ROI (Return on Investment) and TCO (Total Cost of Ownership) considerations aim to maximize value while managing costs effectively in cloud services.

9. B. Managing data from creation through archival and deletion

Explanation: Data lifecycle management focuses on handling data throughout its lifecycle, ensuring compliance, security, and cost-effectiveness.

10. C. Automatic adjustment of resources based on demand

Explanation: Cloud-based scalability solutions dynamically allocate or reduce resources to meet workload demands efficiently, a key advantage of cloud environments.

Chapter 4. Billing & Accounting

Understanding and managing costs is a critical part of any organization's journey toward financial efficiency, especially when adopting cloud computing. This chapter explores key financial models like Capital Expenses (CapEx) and Operational Expenses (OpEx), providing clarity on how organizations can optimize spending based on their infrastructure and business needs.

We will delve into the Total Cost of Ownership (TCO) framework, which evaluates both direct and indirect costs to help businesses make informed decisions regarding on-premises and cloud environments. Additionally, the chapter covers cost-benefit analysis, highlighting practical scenarios such as cyclical demands, shifts in focus, and cost predictability in cloud adoption.

From pricing schemes to strategies for reducing costs in the cloud, this chapter equips organizations with insights to balance expenses, optimize resources, and enhance financial control while ensuring scalability and operational flexibility.

4.1 Capital Expenses (CapEx)

Capital Expenditure (CapEx) refers to business expenses incurred to acquire long-term assets, such as buildings, equipment, and IT infrastructure, that provide benefits over several years. Examples include office buildings, data centers, physical servers, desktops, laptops, storage, software, and related equipment like printers and generators.

Capital Expenditure

CapEx also covers maintenance costs that extend the asset's lifespan or usefulness. From an accounting perspective, CapEx is considered a long-term investment and is spread across multiple years through amortization or depreciation. While these expenses add long-term value to the company, they are not straightforward tax deductions, making it more complex to evaluate their direct and indirect returns over time.

4.2 Operational Expenses (OpEx)

Operational Expenses (OpEx) are the costs required for day-to-day business operations, such as services and consumables that are regularly needed. Examples include stationery, printer cartridges, utility bills, office rent, domain name renewals, and website maintenance. Unlike CapEx, these expenses are not long-term investments.

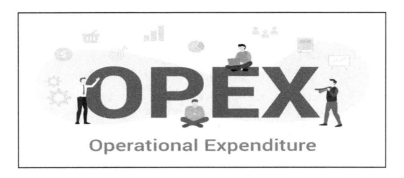

From an accounting perspective, OpEx is deductible from revenue, reducing tax liability and increasing profit. A key advantage of OpEx is flexibility; if something is not working as intended, it can be stopped or replaced easily, unlike CapEx. However, its short-term nature, typically within a year, can make it harder to measure its value proposition accurately.

4.3 CapEx, OpEx and the Cloud

CapEx and OpEx represent distinct financial models for IT expenditures, each with its use cases. If quick deployment and low upfront investment are priorities, the public cloud's pay-as-you-go model (OpEx) is ideal. It allows flexibility without significant capital expenditure. On the other hand, organizations seeking full control over IT resources may opt for a private cloud (CapEx), where they bear all infrastructure costs.

While the public cloud offers multi-faceted advantages and is a popular choice, organizations with strict security and regulatory requirements often prefer a hybrid cloud approach. Non-critical applications are migrated to the public cloud, while essential, sensitive workloads remain on a private cloud or on-premises infrastructure. This balanced strategy combines flexibility with control.

4.4 CapEx Approach to Spending

The CapEx approach provides financial stability with predictable expenses through amortization and depreciation. However, it comes with notable risks, particularly in the fast-changing technology landscape.

Upfront Investment for the Future: Purchasing resources now for future needs poses risks as technologies may evolve quickly, making current investments irrelevant.
Obsolete Resources: Technology changes may render hardware, software, or trained staff redundant, resulting in wasted investments.

Long-Term Contracts: Organizations risk being locked into long-term vendor agreements even when requirements or technologies shift.

Maintenance Costs: Paying staff to manage underutilized or redundant equipment can lead to unnecessary expenditures.

Long Setup Times: Projects requiring extended completion times may fail to deliver value if business or technology needs change before completion.

In summary, while CapEx provides control, it requires careful planning to mitigate risks of obsolescence, long-term contracts, and unutilized resources in a rapidly evolving tech environment.

4.5 OpEx Approach to Spending

The OpEx approach offers a flexible, low-risk financial model for IT expenditures, particularly in cloud-based environments.

Temporary Purchases: Resources and services are temporary, reducing risks of vendor lock-in, technology changes, or shifting business needs.

Reduced Maintenance Overhead: IT staff oversee resources rather than maintain them, freeing time for more strategic work.

Faster Resource Availability: Cloud-based solutions ensure quick access to resources, improving lead times and enabling faster project deployment.

Agility and Flexibility: Businesses can experiment with new ideas or POCs quickly. If unsuccessful, resources can be terminated with minimal loss, thanks to the pay-as-you-go model.

In summary, the OpEx approach provides flexibility, cost-efficiency, and agility, making it ideal for dynamic and rapidly changing business needs.

4.6 Total Cost of Ownership (TCO)

Cloud computing has transformed organizations of all sizes, with startups benefiting the most compared to businesses from the 90s or earlier. Startups, lacking internal IT setups, leverage cloud services to meet their infrastructure needs, reducing capital expenditures (CapEx) significantly.

The Total Cost of Ownership (TCO) evaluates the total costs associated with purchasing, operating, and maintaining an asset throughout its lifecycle. In the cloud computing context, TCO analysis assesses both direct and indirect costs, helping businesses identify hidden expenses and mitigate risks like vendor lock-in.

TCO encompasses CapEx (initial investments) and OpEx (ongoing operational costs), offering a holistic view of IT investments' long-term value. It helps organizations compare cloud and on-premises solutions while factoring in benefits such as faster time-to-market, increased productivity, and elasticity.

While TCO simplifies complex real-world scenarios, assumptions—like existing infrastructure availability and service provider transitions—help streamline the analysis. By offering clear insights into the lifecycle costs of IT investments, TCO enables businesses to make informed, strategic decisions.

4.7 Cost Types Included in TCO

These are some examples of cost types included in TCO.

- The cost related to the strategic decision on sourcing a cloud computing service which includes as-is analysis of IT infrastructure and business applications, analysis of performance indicators, selection of cloud computing services (IaaS, PaaS, SaaS), and cloud types (public, private, or hybrid cloud)
- The cost related to evaluation and selection of service provider, for example, if the provider provides the services defined in the requirements, evaluations of the provider's offerings with respect to SLA, and identification of the best alternative.
- Implementation of cloud services includes user and group creation, access control, and configuration.
- Support-related costs such as phone, email, ticket, or support via chat and messaging
- The training-related cost which includes internal training by own employees, training by an external vendor for using and operating cloud computing services
- Maintenance and modification-related costs which include testing of service operability, performance, monitoring, and reporting
- System failure related costs which include lost working time, possible cost penalty for non-delivery of services, loss of reputation

4.8 Pricing Scheme

Now let's see the general pricing scheme for IaaS, PaaS, and SaaS in TCO. Since this book is for AWS for the brevity and focus, and understanding of concepts, we have included the AWS pricing scheme in TCO.

AWS IaaS Pricing Scheme for EC2
- Price per hour for on-demand instances depends on the virtual machine's RAM, CPU cloud speed and storage, and platform (32-bit / 64-bit)
- Price of data transfers outside of AWS
- Price of reserved instances

AWS IaaS Pricing Scheme for S3
- Price per GB
- Price per transferred GB (outbound); inbound data transfer is free within the same region.
- Price per 1000 queries for PUT, POST, COPY, or LIST operations.

Most providers charge hourly – usage dependent. Some may charge less than others, but then there is room for an increase in the cost for inbound / outbound data transfer or even charging for internal data transfer.

PaaS Pricing Scheme
There are three types of pricing schemes that are used in PaaS: free of charge, complete package, usage dependent pricing. On AWS, most of the pricing for PaaS is usage dependent if you look at EMR, AWS Glue, or other PaaS type of services such as AWS Elastic Beanstalk.

SaaS Pricing Scheme

SaaS pricing schema is also used-based but simple compared to IaaS and PaaS. You may find it "free of charge" with non-binding and obligatory registration, or monthly charge based on the scope of services, the number of API calls, and the number of users.

4.9 Calculating TCO in Cloud Computing

Calculating the Total Cost of Ownership (TCO) in cloud computing involves evaluating all costs associated with current IT infrastructure, cloud migration, and ongoing operations. First, organizations analyze on-premises expenses, including server workloads, databases, and network usage.

Cloud migration costs are influenced by migration methods, such as rehosting, refactoring, or rebuilding applications, each with varying cost implications. Monthly cloud costs depend on services consumed (e.g., commodity vs. advanced services) and pricing models like on-demand, reserved, or spot instances. Pricing calculators from cloud providers, like AWS, help estimate these costs.

Additional factors include training or consultation fees for cloud migration, labor savings from outsourcing maintenance and operations to the cloud provider, and software licensing adjustments. Software licensing models often differ in the cloud, ranging from subscription-based services (e.g., Salesforce) to "Bring Your Own License" (BYOSL) programs from vendors like Oracle, IBM, and Microsoft. Key considerations for licensing include the number of users, processor usage, and virtualization rights.

By carefully evaluating migration costs, monthly expenses, labor, and licensing, organizations can accurately calculate TCO, optimize costs, and make informed cloud adoption decisions.

4.10 Cost-Benefit Analysis

Before migrating to the cloud, organizations must conduct a thorough cost-benefit analysis to determine its suitability. Cloud platforms offer significant cost advantages, particularly for startups or organizations aiming to reduce infrastructure costs. However, cloud migration may not be ideal for organizations under strict regulatory constraints or with legacy applications tightly coupled to on-premises architectures.

In such cases, alternatives like hybrid or private cloud solutions can provide a middle ground. The focus of this analysis is primarily on the benefits of public cloud adoption, as its cost-effectiveness is a key factor driving the popularity of cloud computing. By evaluating costs, constraints, and organizational readiness, businesses can make well-informed decisions on their cloud journey.

4.10.1 Cyclical or Seasoned Demand

Organizations with cyclical or unpredictable traffic, like e-commerce during holidays or news/media platforms during major events, face scalability challenges in on-premises environments. To manage load peaks, they must buy and maintain additional servers, incurring upfront Capital Expenditure (CapEx) costs. However, this comes with risks: idle servers during off-peak times, difficulty predicting future demand, and potential budget constraints.

From an Operational Expenditure (OpEx) perspective, managing extra servers increases maintenance costs and staffing requirements, adding further operational overhead.

The cloud offers a cost-effective solution by addressing these challenges. With unlimited resources and a pay-as-you-go model, organizations can scale seamlessly to meet unexpected or seasonal traffic while only paying for what they use (OpEx). Unlike on-premises setups, cloud providers handle the infrastructure's setup, maintenance, and operations, eliminating CapEx and reducing the burden of scalability management.

4.10.2 Change in Focus

Migrating to the cloud brings a shift in focus for organizations with long-standing on-premises environments. While there may not be an immediate cost-benefit, the transition can cause unease among employees who are used to directly managing systems. Their roles shift to overseeing operations, which may disrupt productivity or cause internal resistance if rushed. However, some employees may embrace the transition as an opportunity to learn new technologies and skills.

The most significant advantage is the increased creativity and agility for employees. Teams can focus on proof-of-concept projects or innovative new initiatives, as cloud platforms enable quick resource provisioning. For project managers, cloud migration accelerates development timelines, with IT resources available almost instantly, allowing faster project execution.

4.10.3 Ownership and Control

Organizations in an on-prem data center scenario have complete control of everything -- hardware, operating system, software, and data. This control is very advantageous with the freedom to manage every aspect of IT. However, in the case of cloud migration, the ownership and control parts are shared with the cloud provider.

Nonetheless, cloud providers such as AWS provide lots of flexibility in controlling the system and handling baseline security, which is better than data centers – which is, for the most part, about just renting rack space for servers.

4.10.4 Cost Predictability

In an on-premises data center environment, not only does the organization has in control of hardware, software, and data, but the organization has a predictable cost – the cost of physical IT infrastructure cost of running and maintaining the IT infrastructure. This predictability is changed totally in the cloud environment.

In general, the cloud is known for variable pricing – metered cost. This is because organizations pay based on the usage of resources. This variable or unpredictably type of cost may not be a right for some finance or budget departments of some organizations. Nonetheless, cloud providers have different pricing options, such as reserved instances that can bring more predictability to the cloud expenditure cost (OpEx).

4.11 How Does Cloud Help Reduce Cost?

Right-Sized Infrastructure

On-premises environments often face overprovisioning, with research showing more than 80% of workloads use excess resources. Organizations typically overbuy server infrastructure to meet current and anticipated demands, leading to wasted capital if workloads don't grow.

Migrating to the cloud eliminates overprovisioning through its flexibility and on-demand provisioning. Resources can be scaled up or down as needed, either manually or automatically, using features like auto-scaling and elasticity. This ensures workloads run on right-sized infrastructure, optimizing resource use and cutting costs.

Utilizing Automation Strategies

Cloud migration reduces IT infrastructure costs by leveraging automation. Tasks like backup, storage, code deployment, and configurations can be scripted, reducing human intervention and allowing IT staff to focus on critical priorities. Automation also ensures dynamic provisioning and de-provisioning of resources, further optimizing costs. AWS, for example, offers extensive APIs to automate most services without manual console management.

Reduced Security and Compliance Scope

AWS's Shared Responsibility Model reduces the organization's security and compliance burden. AWS manages physical security, while customers focus on data storage and encryption. This shared responsibility simplifies compliance and reduces operational overhead.

Managed Services

AWS managed services, such as RDS, analytics, and logging, deliver significant cost savings. With a pay-as-you-go model, these services offer flexibility and eliminate the need for expensive licenses or operational management. For instance, storing simple data tables in AWS RDS is far more cost-effective than purchasing and managing an Oracle database license.

By leveraging right-sizing, automation, shared responsibility, and managed services, organizations achieve cost efficiency, flexibility, and streamlined operations in the cloud.

4.12 Related YouTube Videos

- Cloud Computing Financials: https://www.youtube.com/playlist?list=PLxLENG-zbPwFIiQKvNEL8H40ss76FztKW

4.13 Chapter Review Questions

Question 1:
What is the primary characteristic of Capital Expenses (CapEx)?
- A. Ongoing operational costs
- B. Upfront investments in physical assets
- C. Subscription-based payment models
- D. Pay-as-you-go pricing

Question 2:
How does the Operational Expenses (OpEx) approach differ from CapEx?
- A. It focuses on upfront costs for hardware and infrastructure
- B. It spreads costs over time through ongoing operational spending
- C. It eliminates the need for budgeting entirely
- D. It prioritizes fixed resource allocation

Question 3:
What does the Total Cost of Ownership (TCO) primarily include?
- A. Only direct infrastructure costs
- B. Both direct and indirect costs associated with cloud adoption
- C. Marketing expenses for cloud services
- D. Only operational costs for cloud services

Question 4:
Which of the following cost types is NOT included in TCO?
- A. Infrastructure costs
- B. Software license costs

C. Marketing and branding costs

D. Maintenance and support costs

Question 5:

What is a key benefit of cloud computing for cost reduction?

    A. Fixed and predictable hardware maintenance costs

    B. Pay-as-you-go pricing model and scalability

    C. Elimination of all IT-related expenses

    D. Higher initial investment with long-term savings

Question 6:

What is the primary focus of a cost-benefit analysis in cloud computing?

    A. Evaluating only the financial investment in cloud hardware

    B. Assessing the trade-offs between cost and performance for cloud adoption

    C. Prioritizing fixed costs over flexible pricing models

    D. Analyzing marketing strategies for cloud services

Question 7:

How does the cyclical or seasoned demand concept affect cloud cost management?

    A. It prioritizes continuous resource usage

    B. It allows for flexible scaling during peak demand periods

    C. It eliminates the need for resource monitoring

    D. It focuses on maintaining fixed resources year-round

Question 8:

Which factor contributes to cost predictability in cloud computing?

    A. Pay-as-you-go pricing models

    B. Fixed monthly subscription fees

    C. Eliminating scalability options

    D. Using only private cloud deployments

Question 9:

What is one challenge of the ownership and control aspect of cloud cost management?

    A. Reduced flexibility for scaling workloads

    B. Loss of control over resource allocation and security

    C. Increased need for capital investment

    D. Inability to monitor cloud usage effectively

Question 10:

Which pricing scheme is commonly used in cloud services?

    A. Flat-rate billing for unlimited resources

    B. Tiered pricing based on resource consumption

    C. Annual subscriptions only

    D. Hardware maintenance-based pricing

4.14 Answers to Chapter Review Questions

1. B. Upfront investments in physical assets

Explanation: Capital Expenses (CapEx) refers to one-time, upfront investments in physical infrastructure, such as servers, data centers, and other IT equipment.

2. B. It spreads costs over time through ongoing operational spending
Explanation: Operational Expenses (OpEx) involve recurring costs for operational activities, such as cloud services and subscriptions, rather than upfront investments.

3. B. Both direct and indirect costs associated with cloud adoption
Explanation: Total Cost of Ownership (TCO) includes both direct costs (hardware, software) and indirect costs (maintenance, support) involved in cloud adoption.

4. C. Marketing and branding costs
Explanation: TCO accounts for infrastructure, software licenses, and maintenance costs but does not typically include marketing and branding expenses.

5. B. Pay-as-you-go pricing model and scalability
Explanation: Cloud computing reduces costs through its flexible pay-as-you-go pricing and scalability, which eliminates the need for large upfront investments.

6. B. Assessing the trade-offs between cost and performance for cloud adoption
Explanation: Cost-benefit analysis evaluates the balance between the cost of cloud adoption and its benefits, such as scalability and improved performance.

7. B. It allows for flexible scaling during peak demand periods
Explanation: Cyclical or seasonal demand in cloud computing refers to the ability to scale resources up or down during peak or low-demand periods, reducing costs.

8. A. Pay-as-you-go pricing models
Explanation: Pay-as-you-go pricing contributes to cost predictability by allowing users to pay only for the resources they consume, avoiding fixed costs.

9. B. Loss of control over resource allocation and security
Explanation: One challenge in cloud cost management is the reduced control over resource allocation and security, as these are often managed by the cloud provider.

10. B. Tiered pricing based on resource consumption
Explanation: Cloud services often use tiered pricing models, where costs vary depending on the level of resources consumed, enabling flexibility for users.

Chapter 5. Cloud Virtualization

Virtualization is the cornerstone of cloud computing, enabling organizations to optimize resources, enhance flexibility, and reduce costs. By decoupling physical hardware from software, virtualization allows multiple virtual environments to run on a single physical infrastructure, revolutionizing IT operations and scalability.

In this chapter, we will explore the key concepts, components, and technologies of virtualization in cloud computing. We begin by understanding the fundamentals of virtualization, its types, and its critical components. The chapter then delves into the role of hypervisors, their types, and their significance in enabling virtual machines (VMs) and containerization.

We will also discuss virtual networking and storage virtualization, which are essential for managing data and connectivity in virtualized environments. By the end of this chapter, you will have a comprehensive understanding of how virtualization powers cloud infrastructure, delivering efficiency, scalability, and innovation.

5.1 Virtualization

Cloud computing is built on key foundational technologies, with virtualization being the most critical enabler. Virtualization allows multiple operating systems to run simultaneously on a single physical machine, maximizing resource efficiency and enabling cloud platforms to function seamlessly.

In computer science, the divide-and-conquer principle breaks complex problems into smaller tasks. Similarly, virtualization takes this idea further by abstracting physical resources—such as servers, storage, and networks—into virtual instances. This abstraction allows applications to execute independently while securely sharing infrastructure resources among multiple users (tenants).

Virtualization enhances resource utilization through dynamic scaling and efficient resource allocation, ensuring optimal performance. It also improves agility by reducing downtime for maintenance, enabling quick scaling to meet demand, and cutting costs associated with purchasing and maintaining additional hardware.

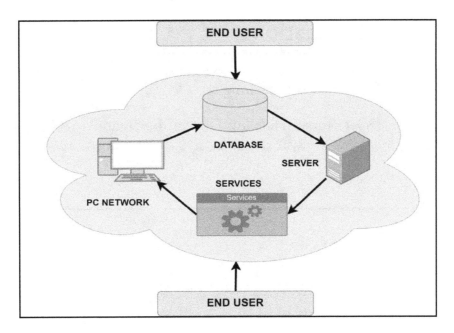

By enabling organizations to run multiple operating systems or applications on a single physical server, virtualization minimizes resource inefficiencies, supports cost-effective scalability, and forms the cornerstone of modern cloud computing environments.

Why Virtualization? In traditional setups, servers are often underutilized. Virtualization solves this by consolidating resources, running multiple virtual machines (VMs) or containers on a single server, each in an isolated environment. This ensures better resource optimization and consistent Service Level Agreements (SLAs), as applications no longer compete for resources.

What Can Be Virtualized?
Servers: Multiple virtual servers (VMs) can run different OS environments (e.g., Windows and Linux) on the same hardware.
Storage: Combining physical disks into virtual storage (e.g., RAID, Logical Volumes) for efficient use.
Networks: Physical networks can be shared across isolated containers, emulating separate networks for each environment.
Desktops: Desktop virtualization (Desktop-as-a-Service) allows multiple virtual desktops to run on one physical server.

Advantages of Virtualization:
Resource Efficiency: Optimizes underutilized resources by consolidating workloads.
Cost Savings: Reduces capital expenses (CapEx) on physical servers and lowers operating costs like power, space, and maintenance.
Flexibility: Enables running multiple operating systems and applications securely on fewer servers.

Virtualization is a game-changer, providing organizations with optimized resource utilization, reduced costs, and enhanced scalability.

5.2 Types of Virtualizations

There are several types of virtualizations used in cloud computing to abstract and manage resources, each with its own specific use cases and advantages. The following are the primary types of virtualizations used in cloud computing.

Server Virtualization: Server virtualization involves creating multiple virtual instances (virtual machines or VMs) on a single physical server. It allows multiple operating systems and applications to run independently on the same hardware.

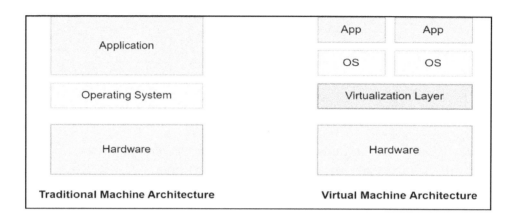

Network Virtualization: Network virtualization abstracts and partitions physical network resources into multiple virtual networks. It enables the creation of isolated, software-defined networks that can be customized for specific purposes or tenants.

Storage Virtualization: Storage virtualization abstracts physical storage resources, such as disks and arrays, to create a single, virtualized storage pool. It allows for the efficient allocation of storage to virtual machines and applications.

Desktop Virtualization (VDI): Virtual Desktop Infrastructure (VDI) virtualizes desktop environments, enabling remote access to virtualized desktops. It is commonly used for remote working, BYOD (Bring Your Own Device), and centralized desktop management.

Application Virtualization: Application virtualization decouples applications from the underlying operating system and hardware, making them more portable and compatible. It simplifies application management, deployment, and version control.

Hardware Virtualization: Hardware virtualization refers to the virtualization of physical hardware components, such as CPUs and GPUs. It allows for the efficient sharing of hardware resources among virtual machines or containers.

Storage Area Network (SAN) Virtualization: SAN virtualization abstracts and pools physical storage devices into a virtualized storage area network. It enhances storage resource utilization, simplifies management, and provides features like data migration and replication.

Operating System Virtualization: This type of virtualization involves running applications and their dependencies within isolated containers on a shared operating system kernel.

Data Virtualization: Data virtualization abstracts data from various sources, making it accessible as a unified, virtualized data layer. It simplifies data access and integration for applications and analytics.

These various types of virtualizations in cloud computing offer flexibility, resource optimization, and isolation, making them essential components of modern cloud infrastructure and services. The type of virtualization used is determined by the applications, workloads, and individual requirements for the cloud environment.

5.3 Component of Virtualization

Virtualization is a critical component of cloud computing that allows for the efficient distribution of computer resources to multiple virtual instances by abstracting and controlling the underlying hardware resources.

Virtual Machine	Virtual Machine	Virtual Machine
APP A	**APP B**	**APP C**
Guest OS	Guest OS	Guest OS
Hypervisor		
Infrastructure		

Hypervisor (Virtual Machine Monitor): A hypervisor is software or hardware that runs on real servers to build and maintain virtual machines (VMs). It enables several VMs to function on a single physical host while remaining isolated from one another. Hypervisors include VMware vSphere/ESXi, Microsoft Hyper-V, and open-source alternatives like as KVM and Xen.

Virtual Machines (VMs): VMs are the virtual instances created and managed by the hypervisor. They mimic the behavior of physical computers and can run various operating systems and applications.

Containers: Containers are a lightweight, portable, and efficient alternative to VMs for packaging and running software. Containerization is often accomplished using technologies such as Docker and Kubernetes.

Virtual Networks: In cloud computing, virtual networks are used to connect and isolate VMs or containers. Software-defined networking (SDN) technologies help manage these virtual networks efficiently.

Storage Virtualization: This technology abstracts physical storage devices to create virtual storage resources that can be dynamically allocated to VMs. It enhances storage efficiency and scalability.

These virtualization components collectively enable cloud service providers and users to abstract and pool physical resources, allocate them on-demand, and provide the flexibility, scalability, and resource isolation required for cloud computing.

5.4 Benefits of Virtualization in Cloud Computing

Virtualization enables the efficient use of physical resources, such as servers, storage, and network infrastructure, by running multiple virtual instances on a single server. This eliminates hardware underutilization and reduces infrastructure costs.

Key Benefits of Virtualization:
- Resource Optimization: Maximizes resource utilization, allowing organizations to scale resources up or down as needed for cost savings.
- Flexibility and Agility: Virtual instances can be easily customized and configured, enabling quick deployment of applications and services.
- Cost Reduction: Consolidating workloads reduces hardware, energy consumption, and data center expenses, supporting environmental sustainability.
- Disaster Recovery: Simplifies backup, recovery, and disaster planning with centralized management tools and dashboards for easier administration.
- Testing and Security: Provides isolated testing and sandbox environments essential for development, security, and quality assurance.
- Multitenancy: Supports secure resource sharing in cloud environments by isolating tenants through virtualization.

Overall, virtualization drives efficiency, flexibility, and cost-effectiveness, making it a cornerstone technology for modern IT and cloud infrastructure.

5.5 Virtualization Technologies in the Cloud

Cloud providers often combine multiple virtualization technologies to create comprehensive cloud platforms that meet various customer needs. These virtualization technologies are the building blocks of cloud computing, enabling cloud providers to deliver scalable, flexible, and cost-effective services to their customers.

Hypervisors and Virtual Machines (VMs) are closely related technologies, but they play different purposes and distinct roles in virtualization and cloud computing.

Let's try to understand Hypervisors and Virtual Machines in a brief.

5.5.1 Virtual Machine (VM)

As we talked about, one of the advantages of virtualization is that we can run multiple instances of operating systems -- also called virtual servers or VM – on single physical hardware. The virtualization technique used to create virtual servers, such as Windows or Linux servers, is called a virtual machine.

The virtual machine is also called virtual computer system, or VM, which is the more popular term for virtual machines. We can think of a virtual machine or VM as a separate isolated container having its own operating system and applications. VMs are discrete, separate, and isolated, self-contained, and completely independent.

Because they are self-contained and completely independent, we can launch multiple VMs on a single physical server. For example, we can have a Linux virtual machine and a Windows virtual machine, both of which can be run on a single physical server in their separate isolated environment. Not just two -- this is just an example.

We can run many instances of operating systems on the same physical server. Having multiple VMs on single physical servers enables various operating systems and applications to run on one physical server. This physical server is also called host as it hosts multiple VMs.

Key Benefits
- **Isolation:** VMs are isolated from each other, meaning that issues in one VM typically do not affect others. This isolation enhances security and stability.
- **Resource Allocation:** Hypervisors allocate physical resources like CPU, memory, and storage to VMs as needed, ensuring efficient resource utilization.
- **Migration and High Availability:** VMs can be migrated between physical hosts for load balancing or failover purposes. This is crucial for ensuring high availability of services.
- **Hardware Consolidation:** Hypervisors enable multiple workloads to run on a single physical server, reducing hardware and power costs.
- **Support for Legacy Systems:** Legacy applications and operating systems can be run on virtual machines, preserving the functionality of older software.

Key Points about VMs
Definition: A virtual machine is an isolated, self-contained software instance that emulates a physical computer. It operates like a separate physical system with its operating system and applications.

Placement: VMs run within the virtualized environment created by the hypervisor. They share the physical resources of the host machine but are isolated from one another. Each VM can run a different operating system, and multiple VMs can coexist on the same physical server.

Operating Systems: VMs can run different operating systems from one another and the host system. For example, a single physical server can host VMs running Windows, Linux, and other operating systems simultaneously.

Isolation: VMs are highly isolated from each other. Failures or issues in one VM generally do not affect other VMs. This isolation enhances security and stability in multi-tenant or multi-workload environments.

5.5.2 Hypervisor
A hypervisor acts as a decoupled layer between the host machine and virtual machines (VMs), enabling the allocation and sharing of host resources such as CPU, memory, and storage. It allows multiple guest VMs to operate on a single physical machine by efficiently managing resource

distribution. For instance, when hypervisor software is installed and multiple VMs are set up, the hypervisor handles resource allocation seamlessly, ensuring each VM functions independently.

Key Points about Hypervisors

Definition: A hypervisor is a software or firmware layer that creates and manages virtual environments. It directly interacts with the underlying hardware and allocates physical resources to virtual machines.

Placement: Hypervisors are typically installed directly on the physical server or host machine, and they control the hardware resources, including CPU, memory, storage, and networking.

Resource Management: Hypervisors allocate and manage physical resources among the VMs they host. They provide isolation and security features to ensure that VMs do not interfere with each other.

5.6 Hypervisors in Virtualization

A hypervisor is a decoupled software layer that allows multiple guest virtual machines (VMs) to share host resources such as CPU, memory, and storage. It allocates and manages these resources, enabling VMs to operate independently on a single physical machine. For instance, when hypervisor software is installed, it efficiently manages resource distribution among multiple VMs.

Hypervisors are essential in virtualization technology as they isolate and control VMs, allowing different operating systems and applications to run simultaneously on a single host.

Key Considerations for Choosing a Hypervisor:
- Type of workload
- Performance requirements
- Management capabilities
- Licensing costs

Types of Hypervisors:
Type 1 (Bare-Metal): Runs directly on physical hardware for better performance and efficiency.
Type 2 (Hosted): Runs on an existing operating system, suitable for smaller-scale virtualization needs.

Hypervisors form the backbone of modern virtualization, optimizing resource utilization and enabling flexible, efficient IT operations.

5.6.1 Hypervisor Types

There are two main types of hypervisors: one is referred to as Type 1 or Bare Metal Hypervisor. The other one is referred to as Type 2 or Hosted Hypervisor.

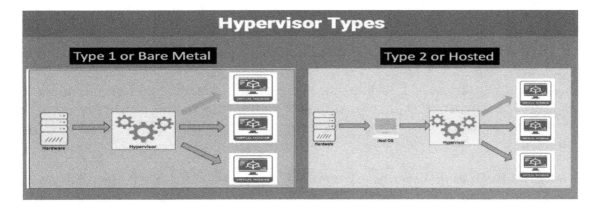

A Type-1 hypervisor runs directly on top of bare metal hardware -- without the need for an underlying operating system -- acting as a lightweight OS. They provide high performance and efficiency because they have direct access to the physical hardware.

On the other hand, a Type-2 hypervisor runs on the OS. Since a Type-1 hypervisor runs straight on the hardware, it is also referred to as "Bare Metal," and a Type-2 hypervisor runs on the OS, that's why it is also called "Hosted." They are often used for development, testing, or educational purposes and may not offer the same level of performance as Type 1 hypervisors.

5.6.2 Type-1 or Bare-Metal Hypervisor

Let's talk further about Type-1 or Bare Metal hypervisor. It is installed directly on the hardware. In other words, Type-1 replaces the operating system. In place of the operating system, we install a Type-1 hypervisor.

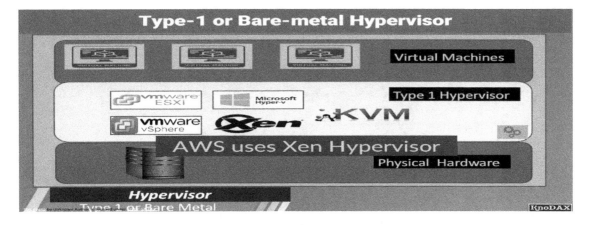

Typically, a Type-1 or Bare Metal hypervisor is deployed most. There are some genuine reasons why this type of hypervisor is deployed most. Since it is directly installed on the hardware instead of on the OS, it is more secure than Type-2. And the other reason is that since no OS layer is involved, it performs better and more efficiently than Type-2 or hosted hypervisor. Because of security and performance reasons, Type-1 hypervisors are usually preferred for enterprises when deploying hypervisors on their data centers.

The following are the key characteristics and features of a Type-1 or Bare Metal hypervisor.

Direct Hardware Access: Bare Metal hypervisors have direct access to the host machine's physical hardware. They operate without the overhead of a host operating system, allowing for better performance and resource utilization.

Efficiency and Performance: By eliminating the need for an additional layer of an operating system, Bare Metal hypervisors can provide higher performance than Type 2 hypervisors. This is especially critical in enterprise environments where optimal resource utilization and performance are paramount.

Dedicated Virtualization Layer: The hypervisor serves as a dedicated virtualization layer, managing the allocation of resources and facilitating the creation and operation of multiple virtual machines (VMs) directly on the hardware.

Isolation and Security: Bare Metal hypervisors enhance isolation and security by running VMs in an environment separate from the host operating system. This isolation helps prevent security vulnerabilities and ensures that failures within one VM do not affect others.

Commonly Used in Data Centers: Bare Metal hypervisors are commonly used in data centers and enterprise environments where performance, scalability, and resource efficiency are critical. Examples of Bare Metal hypervisors include VMware ESXi, Microsoft Hyper-V Server, and Xen.

5.6.3 Type-2 or Hosted Hypervisor

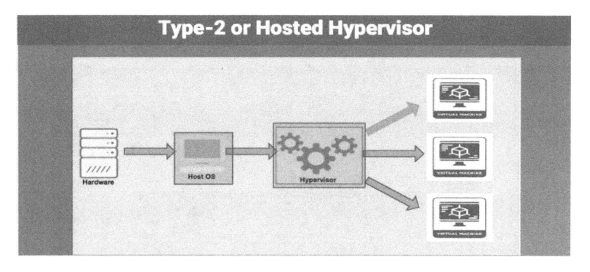

As you can see in the diagram, Type-2 or Hosted hypervisor runs on the host operating system.

This is another diagram of a Type-2 hypervisor or Hosted hypervisor. In the diagram as you can see that at the bottom layer, we have the physical hardware, then the OS is installed. Since this is a Type-2 hypervisor diagram, first a hypervisor is installed on the OS, then virtual machines are installed. Examples of Type-2 hypervisors that run on host operating systems are Oracle Virtual Box, VMware Workstation, Microsoft Virtual PC.

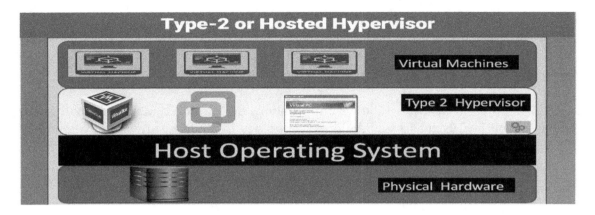

The main difference between Type-1 and Type-2 is that Type-1 hypervisors are installed on bare metal and Type-2 hypervisors are installed on an operating system.

The following are the key characteristics and features of Hosted Hypervisors:

Dependence on Host Operating System: Hosted Hypervisors run as applications on a host operating system. This means an additional layer exists between the hypervisor and the physical hardware.

Installation as an Application: Users typically install a Hosted Hypervisor as a software application within an existing operating system. Once installed, it allows users to create and run multiple virtual machines on the host system.

Resource Utilization: Since Hosted Hypervisors operate within a host operating system, they may have slightly higher resource overhead than Bare Metal hypervisors. This can impact performance, especially in resource-intensive scenarios.

5.7 Role of Hypervisors in Cloud Computing

Hypervisors play a critical role in cloud computing by enabling the virtualization of physical resources, serving as the backbone for creating and managing virtual machines (VMs). They abstract and virtualize hardware resources like CPU, memory, storage, and networking, allowing efficient allocation to multiple VMs. Hypervisors ensure strong isolation between VMs, which is essential for secure and stable multi-tenant cloud environments, where different users or tenants can run workloads on shared hardware without interference.

Additionally, hypervisors facilitate multi-tenancy, enabling cloud providers to host VMs for multiple customers on the same physical infrastructure while maintaining operational independence. They also support scalability and elasticity by dynamically provisioning and scaling VMs to meet fluctuating workload demands, making them a cornerstone of modern cloud services.

5.7.1 Containerization

Containerization is a technology and method used in software development and deployment to package an application and its dependencies into a standardized unit called a container.

It is a lightweight form of virtualization that allows you to package and run applications and their dependencies in isolated environments called containers. Containers are portable, consistent, and can be easily deployed across different platforms. They can run consistently in various computer contexts, including development, testing, and production.

Containerization has transformed the way applications are produced, deployed, and managed, and it has established itself as a foundational technology in modern software development and DevOps practices.

Docker is the most popular containerization platform, but alternatives such as Podman and Containerd exist.

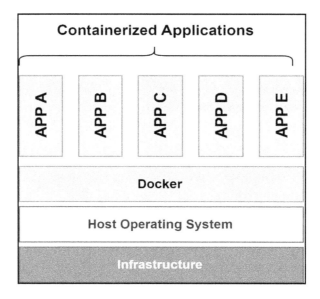

Docker: Docker is a platform designed to help developers build, share, and run container applications. We handle the tedious setup so you can focus on the code. (ref: docker.com)

Podman: Podman is a daemonless, open source, Linux native tool designed to make it easy to find, run, build, share, and deploy applications using Open Containers Initiative (OCI) Containers and Container Images (Ref: podman.io).

Containerd: **Containerd** is available as a daemon for Linux and Windows. It manages the complete container lifecycle of its host system, from image transfer and storage to container execution and supervision to low-level storage to network attachments and beyond. (Ref: containerd.io)

Key Concepts and Components

Container Image: A container image is a standalone package that includes the application code, runtime, libraries, and dependencies. It is a read-only file that forms the basis of a container. Images are created from instructions defined in a Dockerfile or similar specification.

Dockerfile: A Dockerfile is a text file containing instructions for creating a container image. These instructions include selecting a base image, copying files, installing packages, and configuring the container.

Container Engine: The container engine is the software responsible for running and managing containers. Docker is the most well-known container engine, but alternatives like containerd [https://containerd.io/] and Podman [https://podman.io/] are also available.

Container Registry: A container registry is a repository where container images are stored and can be accessed by developers and deployment systems. Docker Hub is a popular public container registry, and organizations often use private registries to store their proprietary container images.

Orchestration: Container orchestration tools like Kubernetes are used to manage containers' deployment, scaling, and networking in a cluster of servers. They help automate the deployment and scaling of containers in a production environment.

Benefits of containerization

Containerization offers several key benefits: Isolation ensures applications and their dependencies run consistently without conflicts by encapsulating them. Portability allows containers to run seamlessly across different operating systems (Windows, Linux, Mac OS) and cloud platforms like AWS, Azure, or Google Cloud. Containers provide efficiency by being lightweight and sharing the host OS kernel, enabling better resource utilization.

They support scalability, as containers can be quickly scaled up or down to meet demand, which is ideal for microservices architectures. For development and testing, containers create consistent environments, minimizing the "it works on my machine" problem. Lastly, version control enables tracking container images in registries, allowing easy rollbacks to previous versions when needed.

5.8 Virtual Networking

Virtual networking plays a critical role in virtualization technologies by enabling multiple virtual machines (VMs) or containers to connect to external networks while maintaining isolation and security. A hypervisor manages VMs and features a virtual switch to simulate physical network switches. VLANs segment traffic into logical networks, enhancing performance and security, while virtual network adapters (vNICs) allow VMs to connect and communicate.

Advanced platforms, like VMware NSX or OpenStack Neutron, leverage Software-Defined Networking (SDN) to automate and centralize network management through software controllers and APIs. Virtual networking supports load balancing and traffic shaping to optimize performance and resource allocation.

Key benefits include abstraction of network resources from physical hardware, flexibility to configure networks on demand, automation to streamline provisioning and reduce errors, and scalability to adapt to changing workloads. Virtual networks also ensure isolation, enabling multiple logical networks to coexist securely on shared infrastructure. Overall, virtual networking simplifies network management, improves agility, and enhances scalability in modern IT and cloud environments.

5.9 Storage Virtualization

Storage virtualization abstracts and centralizes storage resources by creating a virtual layer that separates the logical view of storage from physical hardware. It enables administrators to pool diverse storage devices, such as disks and arrays, into unified and easily manageable units. Key benefits include simplified management through centralized control, dynamic provisioning for efficient resource allocation, and seamless data migration without disruption.

Storage virtualization also supports load balancing, ensuring optimal performance by distributing I/O requests across devices, and enhances fault tolerance and redundancy for robust data protection. By offering scalability, flexibility, and improved operational efficiency, storage virtualization simplifies managing complex storage environments while maximizing resource utilization.

5.10 Chapter Review Questions

Question 1:

What is virtualization in cloud computing?
- A. A technique to create holographic displays.
- B. The process of creating virtual instances of hardware or software resources
- C. A method for encrypting data in the cloud.
- D. A method for reducing network latency.

Question 2:

Which type of virtualization allows multiple virtual machines (VMs) to run on a single physical server?
- A. Network virtualization
- B. Storage virtualization
- C. Server virtualization
- D. Application virtualization

Question 3:

What is the purpose of hypervisors in virtualization?
- A. To manage network connections in the cloud
- B. To control physical servers
- C. To create and manage virtual machines
- D. To compress and store virtual machine images

Question 4:

Which of the following is not a popular hypervisor for virtualization in cloud computing?
- A. VMware vSphere
- B. Microsoft Hyper-V
- C. Docker
- D. KVM

Question 5:

What is containerization in the context of virtualization?
- A. A method for storing virtual machines
- B. A technique for encapsulating and running applications and their dependencies
- C. A way to manage network connections in a virtual environment

D. A process for encrypting data in the cloud

Question 6:
Which virtualization technology provides isolation at the operating system level and shares the kernel among instances?
- A. Hardware virtualization
- B. Application virtualization
- C. Containerization
- D. Server virtualization

Question 7:
What is live migration in virtualization?
- A. A technique for moving physical servers to different data centers
- B. The process of moving a running virtual machine from one physical host to another with minimal downtime
- C. A way to migrate data between cloud storage providers
- D. A method for dynamically scaling virtual machines

Question 8:
In cloud computing, what does the term "Elasticity" mean in the context of virtualization?
- A. The ability to stretch virtual machines across multiple physical servers
- B. The ability to dynamically adjust resources to match workload demands
- C. The ability to create secure virtual networks
- D. The ability to migrate virtual machines between data centers

Question 9:
What is a virtual private cloud (VPC) in cloud computing?
- A. A cloud service that provides virtual machines for free
- B. A cloud environment that is isolated from other tenants, providing network and resource privacy
- C. A virtual reality-based cloud platform
- D. A cloud service for managing virtual desktops

Question 10:
What is the primary benefit of virtualization in cloud computing?
- A. Enhanced security
- B. Reduced hardware costs
- C. Improved internet speed
- D. Better user experience

5.11 Answers to Chapter Review Questions
1. B. The process of creating virtual instances of hardware or software resources
Explanation: Virtualization in cloud computing refers to creating virtual versions of hardware, software, or storage resources, enabling efficient resource utilization and scalability.

2. C. Server virtualization
Explanation: Server virtualization allows multiple virtual machines (VMs) to run on a single physical server by abstracting the underlying hardware.

3. C. To create and manage virtual machines
Explanation: Hypervisors are responsible for creating, managing, and allocating resources to virtual machines on a physical server.

4. C. Docker
Explanation: Docker is not a hypervisor; it is a containerization platform. Popular hypervisors include VMware vSphere, Microsoft Hyper-V, and KVM.

5. B. A technique for encapsulating and running applications and their dependencies
Explanation: Containerization isolates applications and their dependencies into containers, providing lightweight, portable, and efficient virtualization.

6. C. Containerization
Explanation: Containerization provides isolation at the operating system level, where containers share the host OS kernel but remain isolated from one another.

7. B. The process of moving a running virtual machine from one physical host to another with minimal downtime
Explanation: Live migration enables the transfer of a running VM between hosts without significant interruption, ensuring continuity of service.

8. B. The ability to dynamically adjust resources to match workload demands
Explanation: Elasticity in virtualization refers to scaling resources up or down based on demand, optimizing performance and cost-efficiency.

9. B. A cloud environment that is isolated from other tenants, providing network and resource privacy
Explanation: A Virtual Private Cloud (VPC) is an isolated section of a cloud provider's infrastructure, offering enhanced privacy and control over resources.

10. B. Reduced hardware costs
Explanation: Virtualization reduces the need for physical hardware by allowing multiple virtual instances to share a single physical resource, significantly lowering costs.

Chapter 6. Cloud Security Essentials

In today's digital landscape, cloud security is a cornerstone of cloud adoption, ensuring the protection of data, applications, and infrastructure in virtual environments. This chapter explores the critical elements of cloud security that organizations must address to build trust, manage risks, and ensure seamless access for users.

We begin by understanding client access mechanisms in cloud computing and their role in enabling secure and efficient connections. The chapter then highlights commercial and business considerations, emphasizing how security impacts organizational trust and decision-making.

Next, we delve into the concepts of trust and reputation in cloud computing, two essential factors that influence the success of cloud providers and adoption by businesses. The importance of security is examined in detail, demonstrating why robust security measures are vital for protecting sensitive assets in cloud environments.

Further, we introduce key cloud security tools and technologies that help secure infrastructure and data while enhancing compliance. Finally, we explore the cloud contracting model, outlining its role in establishing clear agreements, service-level expectations, and accountability between cloud providers and clients.

This chapter provides a comprehensive foundation for understanding cloud security essentials and their significance in achieving a secure, reliable, and trustworthy cloud environment.

6.1 Client Access in Cloud Computing

Client access in cloud computing caters to diverse users, including end-users and developers, through multiple interfaces. Web browsers provide a user-friendly way to access cloud applications without local installations, simplifying usage and updates. APIs enable programmatic access, allowing developers to integrate cloud services for automation and custom solutions, such as mobile apps using cloud storage.

Dedicated client software like desktop and mobile applications offers specialized access with enhanced functionality and tailored experiences. Command-Line Interfaces (CLIs) support advanced users and administrators, enabling efficient resource management and automation.

IoT devices communicate with cloud services using protocols and APIs to transfer data seamlessly. In hybrid cloud environments, clients access both on-premises and cloud resources, balancing data control with scalability. VPNs ensure secure and private access to cloud resources by establishing encrypted communication channels. Finally, mobile applications allow users to manage cloud services conveniently from smartphones and tablets.

These access methods collectively provide flexibility, security, and efficiency for interacting with cloud platforms.

6.2 Commercial and Business Considerations

Commercial and business considerations are integral components of cloud computing, as they influence decisions related to adopting, implementing, and managing cloud services. These considerations play a significant role in shaping an organization's cloud strategy.

Here are some key commercial and business aspects to consider in cloud computing:

Cost Analysis: One of the primary considerations is the cost-effectiveness of cloud services. Organizations need to assess their current IT infrastructure costs compared to the potential savings and scalability offered by the cloud. This analysis should include the upfront costs and ongoing operational expenses.

Return on Investment (ROI): Businesses should evaluate the expected ROI when transitioning to the cloud. This includes considering how cloud services will impact productivity, revenue generation, and cost reduction over time.

Scalability: Scalability is a crucial factor for businesses. Cloud services allow organizations to scale resources up or down as needed. Assessing the ease and cost of scalability is essential for accommodating changing business requirements.

Compliance and Security: Compliance with industry regulations and data security are paramount in cloud computing. Businesses must ensure that their cloud provider complies with relevant standards and offers robust security measures to protect sensitive data.

6.3 Trust in Cloud Computing

Effective and secure use of cloud services hinges on trust between users and cloud providers. Trust is established through robust security measures like encryption, access controls, and monitoring to safeguard data. Providers must comply with regulations (e.g., GDPR, HIPAA) and ensure transparency regarding operations, SLAs, and data handling policies.

Key trust factors include reliability through high availability and disaster recovery mechanisms, strong customer support, and clear data ownership policies that enable data portability. A provider's reputation, demonstrated performance, and user reviews significantly influence trust.

Data privacy, transparency about data center locations, and contractual agreements are also crucial. Additionally, providers that focus on continuous improvement by enhancing features and security stay ahead of emerging risks and earn long-term trust.

Ultimately, trust is built through consistent technology, policies, and practices ensuring confidentiality, integrity, and availability of data and services in the cloud.

6.4 Reputation in Cloud Computing

Reputation in cloud computing is a critical factor that influences organizations' decisions when selecting cloud providers and services. Organizations must continuously work to build and maintain a positive reputation through reliability, security, and transparency.

Here's a more detailed explanation of reputation in cloud computing.

Importance of Reputation: Organizations consider a cloud provider's reputation when choosing where to host their applications and data. A positive reputation can give businesses a sense of trust and security, reducing the perceived risks associated with migrating to or using cloud services. Cloud providers often compete based on their reputation, aiming to differentiate themselves in a crowded market. A good reputation can be a significant competitive advantage.

Provider Reputation: A cloud provider's reputation is often associated with its reliability and uptime. Providers with frequent service disruptions or outages may have a poor reputation. A cloud provider's security practices and track record play a significant role in its reputation. Providers that are transparent about their pricing, terms of service, and data handling practices tend to build trust and a better reputation among customers. A cloud provider's reputation may also be linked to its ability to scale resources rapidly, allowing businesses to grow without service degradation.

Service Reputation: Within a cloud environment, individual services and applications may have their reputations. This can be influenced by performance, uptime, and user satisfaction. Cloud services often come with SLAs that specify guaranteed uptime and performance levels. Meeting or exceeding these SLAs can enhance a service's reputation.

6.5 Importance of Security in Cloud Environments

In our contemporary digital landscape, characterized by the dominance of data and the widespread adoption of remote work, the significance of security within cloud environments is undeniable. The cloud has revolutionized the storage, accessibility, and administration of data and applications. However, this transformation carries substantial responsibilities. Safeguarding cloud environments is now essential for individuals, businesses, and organizations across various sizes.

Let's explore why prioritizing security in cloud environments is of utmost importance.

Regulatory Compliance: Governments and industries have introduced stringent regulations to protect data privacy and security. Cloud security ensures organizations comply with GDPR, HIPAA, and PCI DSS laws, reducing legal risks.

Cyber Threats Evolve: Cybercriminals are becoming increasingly difficult in their tactics. Cloud environments are attractive targets, and without robust security measures, they become vulnerable to attacks such as ransomware, phishing, and distributed denial-of-service (DDoS) attacks. Staying ahead of these threats is a continuous challenge.

Cost-Efficiency: Investing in cloud security upfront can prevent costly data breaches, legal actions, and recovery efforts. Proactively preventing security incidents is often more security incidents than responding to them after the fact.

Competitive Edge: Organizations prioritizing cloud security can differentiate themselves from competitors. Customers, partners, and investors are likelier to engage with companies that take data security seriously.

6.6 Cloud Security Tools and Technologies

Identity and Access Management (IAM):AWS Identity and Access Management (IAM): Provides centralized control over AWS resource access, including user management, role-based access control (RBAC), and multifactor authentication (MFA).

Firewalls and Network Security

Firewalls and network security solutions play a crucial role in safeguarding cloud environments. Cloud firewalls, such as AWS Network Security Groups (NSGs) and Azure Network Security Groups, enable the control of inbound and outbound traffic to virtual machines (VMs) and other resources. Additionally, Web Application Firewalls (WAF) protect web applications from common exploits and attacks. Examples of WAF solutions include AWS WAF and Azure Application Gateway.

Encryption and Key Management

Encryption and key management are essential for securing data in cloud environments. AWS Key Management Service (KMS) manages encryption keys to protect data at rest and in transit within AWS services. Similarly, Azure Key Vault safeguards cryptographic keys and secrets used by cloud applications and services. For security information and event management (SIEM), AWS offers tools like CloudWatch Logs and CloudTrail, which collect and monitor logs and events for AWS resources. In Azure, tools like Azure Monitor and Azure Security Center provide monitoring, threat detection, and incident response capabilities, ensuring robust security management.

Cloud Security Posture Management (CSPM)

Cloud Security Posture Management (CSPM) tools are critical for maintaining security and compliance in cloud environments. AWS Security Hub provides a centralized platform to manage security alerts and automate compliance checks across multiple AWS accounts. Similarly, Azure offers tools like Azure Policy and Azure Blueprints, which enable users to define, assign, and enforce policies and compliance standards for Azure resources.

Data Loss Prevention (DLP)

Data Loss Prevention (DLP) tools are essential for safeguarding sensitive data in the cloud. Microsoft Azure Information Protection classifies and protects sensitive data across Azure services, ensuring compliance and security. Similarly, AWS Macie automatically discovers, classifies, and protects sensitive data stored in AWS, providing robust data protection capabilities.

Cloud Access Security Brokers (CASB)

Netskope, McAfee Cloud Security, or Microsoft Cloud App Security (Provide visibility, control, and security for cloud applications and data)

Cloud Computing and AWS Introduction

6.7 Cloud Contracting Model

Ch The cloud contracting model is crucial for defining the terms, conditions, and responsibilities between organizations and cloud providers. It covers key elements such as Service-Level Agreements (SLAs), pricing structures, data security, compliance, and exit strategies.

- SLAs outline performance expectations, uptime guarantees, and penalties for non-compliance, ensuring accountability.
- Data Security and Privacy provisions address data handling, access control, and compliance with regulations like GDPR.
- Pricing Structures clarify subscription fees, usage-based costs, and billing terms, helping organizations manage budgets effectively.
- Exit Strategies ensure a smooth data migration and service transition when switching providers or discontinuing services.
- Compliance specifies adherence to legal obligations and industry standards (e.g., HIPAA for healthcare).

Contracts also cover intellectual property ownership, disaster recovery, and risk management, addressing concerns like service outages or data breaches. As cloud computing evolves, contracting models adapt to trends like multi-cloud, serverless computing, and edge computing. Overall, cloud contracts provide a legal and operational framework to foster trust, mitigate risks, and enable organizations to leverage cloud technology efficiently.

6.8 Chapter Review Questions

Question 1:
What is IAM in the context of cloud computing?
- A. Internet Application Management
- B. Identity and Access Management
- C. Integrated Authentication Module
- D. Internal Authorization Mechanism

Question 2:
Which of the following is a key component of Access Control in cloud security?
- A. Virtual Private Network (VPN)
- B. Firewall
- C. Encryption
- D. Role-Based Access Control (RBA

Question 3:
What does Risk in cloud computing refer to?
- A. Probability of system failure
- B. Likelihood of data loss
- C. Potential for harm or loss
- D. Server response time

Question 4:
Which authentication method is commonly used in cloud computing to verify the identity of users?
- A. Single Sign-On (SSO)

  B. Biometric authentication
  C. Username and password
  D. All of the above

Question 5:
What is the purpose of Trust in cloud security?
  A. Ensuring data confidentiality
  B. Establishing reliability and confidence
  C. Controlling access permissions
  D. Detecting security breaches

Question 6:
What does the term "Reputation" refer to in cloud computing?
  A. User feedback on cloud services
  B. Server response time
  C. Data encryption level
  D. Network bandwidth

Question 7:
In Cloud Contracting Models, which model involves paying based on actual usage?
  A. Infrastructure as a Service (IaaS)
  B. Platform as a Service (PaaS)
  C. Software as a Service (SaaS)
  D. Function as a Service (FaaS)

Question 8:
What are Commercial and Business Considerations in cloud security primarily concerned with?
  A. Technical specifications of cloud services
  B. Cost, compliance, and strategic alignment
  C. Data encryption methods
  D. Network latency

Question 9:
What is a common method for Client Access in cloud computing?
  A. Remote Desktop Protocol (RDP)
  B. Virtual LAN (VLAN)
  C. File Transfer Protocol (FTP)
  D. Secure Shell (SSH)

Question 10:
Which of the following is an example of an Authentication Factor?
  A. Something you know
  B. Something you see
  C. Something you hear
  D. Something you taste

6.9 Answers to Chapter Review Questions

1. B. Identity and Access Management
Explanation: IAM in cloud computing stands for Identity and Access Management, which involves defining and managing roles, permissions, and access controls for users in a cloud environment.

2. D. Role-Based Access Control (RBAC)
Explanation: Role-Based Access Control (RBAC) is a key component of access control in cloud security, enabling permissions to be assigned based on roles rather than individual users.

3. C. Potential for harm or loss
Explanation: Risk in cloud computing refers to the potential for harm or loss, such as data breaches, downtime, or unauthorized access.

4. D. All of the above
Explanation: Common authentication methods in cloud computing include Single Sign-On (SSO), biometric authentication, and traditional username and password combinations.

5. B. Establishing reliability and confidence
Explanation: Trust in cloud security involves establishing reliability and confidence in the cloud provider's ability to secure data and services.

6. A. User feedback on cloud services
Explanation: In cloud computing, reputation refers to the perception of a cloud provider based on user feedback and service reliability.

7. D. Function as a Service (FaaS)
Explanation: FaaS, or Function as a Service, uses a pay-as-you-go model where users are charged based on actual usage of functions.

8. B. Cost, compliance, and strategic alignment
Explanation: Commercial and business considerations in cloud security focus on ensuring cost-effectiveness, regulatory compliance, and alignment with business strategies.

9. A. Remote Desktop Protocol (RDP)
Explanation: RDP is a common method for client access in cloud computing, enabling users to connect remotely to cloud-hosted systems.

10. A. Something you know
Explanation: Authentication factors include "something you know" (e.g., a password), which is a knowledge-based factor used to verify identity.

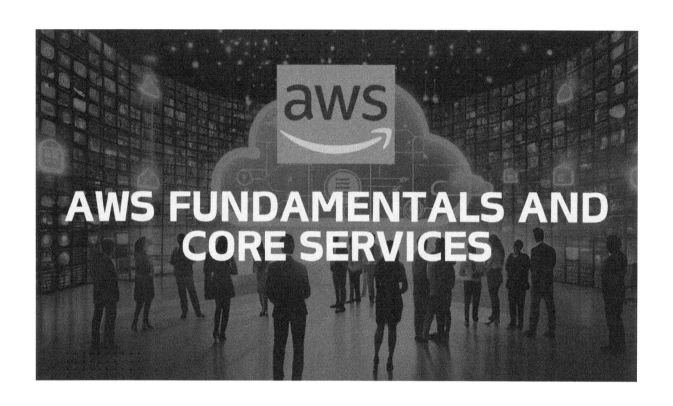

Chapter 7. What is AWS?

In the previous chapters, you gained a solid understanding of cloud computing. Now, let's dive into AWS by exploring the fundamental question: What is AWS?

7.1 Cloud Services Provider

What is AWS? AWS is a public cloud service provider, and its architectural underpinning is based on cloud computing. AWS provides almost all kinds of cloud services such as infrastructure, platform, software, analytics, machine learning, and many other types of services over the Internet. These cloud services are highly reliable, scalable, and low-cost. AWS is an evolving cloud computing platform, and new services of different types are continuously getting added. It is a cloud computing platform to procure, deploy, and manage IT Infrastructure. Additionally, AWS is a secure modern platform to build, deploy, and run almost all kinds of software applications. Most importantly, it does it with time and cost-efficiency.

7.2 Different Types of Services

AWS (Amazon Web Services) offers a wide range of services across various categories to meet diverse business and technical needs. These include compute services like Amazon EC2 for scalable virtual servers and AWS Lambda for serverless computing. Storage solutions such as Amazon S3 provide secure, scalable object storage, while Amazon EBS and Glacier cater to block storage and archival needs. AWS also excels in databases, offering managed solutions like Amazon RDS for relational databases, DynamoDB for NoSQL databases, and Redshift for data warehousing. For networking and content delivery, AWS provides services like Amazon VPC, Route 53, and CloudFront.

Its machine learning and AI offerings, including Amazon SageMaker and Rekognition, enable businesses to integrate intelligent features into applications. In the developer tools category, services like AWS CodePipeline and CodeBuild streamline DevOps processes. AWS also supports IoT with IoT Core and analytics with tools like Athena and Elastic MapReduce. Additionally, AWS offers security services like AWS Identity and Access Management (IAM) and Shield for DDoS protection, ensuring robust protection for cloud resources. This breadth of services, paired with scalability and global reach, makes AWS a one-stop solution for businesses across industries.

As a result, AWS has over a million customers in around 190 countries. It has customers from organizations of all types, such as large, medium, and startups in various industries.

7.3 AWS Cloud History

AWS genesis came in early 2000 as Amazon started building SOA-based architecture to scale their platform. Around that time, Amazon was launching its e-commerce platform for third-party retailers to make a web store for their retail store. This effort of launching an e-commerce platform for third-party retailers led to the demand for a more scalable system.

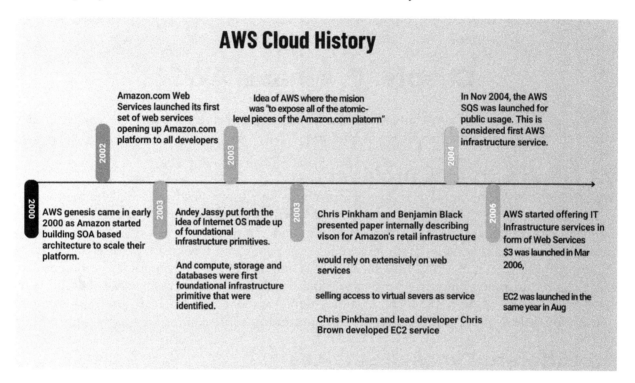

Then in 2002, Amazon.com Web Services launched its first set of web services, opening the Amazon.com platform to all developers. The most exciting story is that Amazon was caught by surprise by its developers' unexpected interest in web service API.

Then in 2003, Andy Jassy, who is CEO now, put forth the idea of Internet OS made up of foundational infrastructure primitives. The first foundational infrastructure primitives -- compute, storage, and databases -- were identified. Based on this idea, Jeff Barr, Jassy, Bezos himself, and others formulated the concept of EC2 for compute, S3 for storage, and RDS for the database. These three are very famous AWS services now.

This [2003] was an essential year for AWS. In fact, according to Amazon Web Services Wiki, Jassy recalls brainstorming sessions about a week with ten of best technology minds and ten of best product management minds on about ten different internet applications, the most primitive blocks required to build them. That discussion and other related events paved the idea of AWS, where the mission was to expose all the atomic-level pieces of the Amazon.com platform.

In 2003, Chris Pinkham and Benjamin Black presented a paper internally describing the vision for Amazon's retail infrastructure that was overhauling Amazon's retail infrastructure to be completely automated and would rely extensively on web services. The paper also mentioned the possibility of selling access to virtual servers as a service and proposed that the company generate revenue from the new infrastructure investment. And after that, Chris Pinkham and lead developer Chris Brown developed the EC2 Service.

In Nov 2004, the AWS SQS was launched for public usage. This is considered the first AWS infrastructure service.

After that, in 2006, AWS started offering IT infrastructure services in Web Services. S3 was launched in Mar 2006, EC2 was launched in the same year in Aug. Over the years, many more services have been added to the AWS platform. AWS is an evolving platform – more and more features and services are continuously added to its platform.

As of this writing, AWS has over 200 products and services in almost all possible categories where AWS can offer its services.

7.4 The Popularity of AWS Explained

AWS (Amazon Web Services) is renowned for its comprehensive, scalable, and innovative cloud computing solutions. It was one of the first cloud providers, establishing itself as a market leader with a robust and diverse portfolio of services that cater to businesses of all sizes and industries. AWS offers on-demand access to a wide range of services, including compute power, storage, databases, machine learning, analytics, and IoT, all delivered with high reliability and global availability.

Its pay-as-you-go pricing model makes it cost-effective and accessible, while its continuous innovation ensures cutting-edge tools for customers. AWS's global infrastructure, spanning multiple regions and availability zones, enables low-latency and high-resilience deployments. Furthermore, its vast ecosystem of third-party integrations, extensive documentation, and active user community make it a go-to choice for developers, startups, and enterprises alike. By consistently delivering performance, flexibility, and scalability, AWS has become synonymous with cloud computing excellence.

7.5 Chapter Review Questions

Question 1:
Which of the following best describes a cloud services provider?
    A. A company offering hardware for local data storage
    B. A service delivering on-demand computing resources over the internet
    C. A software vendor providing only SaaS applications
    D. A network equipment supplier

Question 2:
Which AWS service category is primarily used for storing and retrieving data?
    A. Compute Services
    B. Storage Services
    C. Networking Services
    D. Database Services

Question 3:
What year did AWS officially launch its first set of cloud services?

A. 2000

B. 2002

C. 2006

D. 2010

Question 4:

What is one of the key reasons for AWS's popularity?

    A. Limited availability zones and regions

    B. A single pricing model for all services

    C. A wide range of scalable and reliable services

    D. Exclusive focus on large enterprises

Question 5:

Which of the following best explains AWS's role in cloud computing?

    A. It provides an on-premises infrastructure for private clouds.

    B. It offers scalable, on-demand services for compute, storage, and other IT needs.

    C. It is a software company specializing in operating systems.

    D. It is a hardware manufacturer for data centers.

7.6 Answers to Chapter Review Questions

1. B. A service delivering on-demand computing resources over the internet

Explanation: A cloud services provider offers on-demand access to computing resources such as storage, servers, and applications over the internet, eliminating the need for physical infrastructure.

2. B. Storage Services

Explanation: AWS Storage Services, such as Amazon S3 and Glacier, are designed for storing and retrieving data, providing scalable and durable solutions for various use cases.

3. C. 2006

Explanation: AWS officially launched its first cloud services, including Amazon S3 and EC2, in 2006, marking the beginning of its cloud computing offerings.

4. C. A wide range of scalable and reliable services

Explanation: AWS is popular because it provides a broad portfolio of scalable, reliable, and innovative cloud services, catering to businesses of all sizes and industries.

5. B. It offers scalable, on-demand services for compute, storage, and other IT needs

Explanation: AWS plays a central role in cloud computing by delivering a vast array of on-demand, scalable services, including compute, storage, databases, and networking.

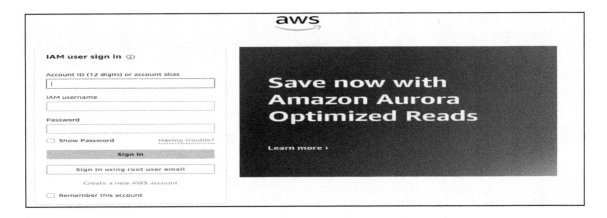

Chapter 8. Getting Started with AWS: Account Setup and Best Practices

Understanding the theory of AWS is essential to building a strong conceptual foundation. However, the real learning begins when you start using the platform hands-on. In this chapter, we will explore the practical aspects of managing an AWS account. From signing up and implementing security best practices like MFA to accessing the platform and managing costs with AWS Budgets, this chapter provides a step-by-step guide to get you started with AWS effectively and securely.

8.1 Sign Up for AWS Account

An AWS account is a unique identity that provides access to Amazon Web Services, allowing users to manage cloud resources and services. It includes tools for billing, security, and monitoring, enabling individuals or organizations to operate in the AWS cloud environment.

Let's sign up for an AWS account so that you can learn AWS services. If you already have an AWS account, then you can skip this part of the chapter.

1. Go to https://aws.amazon.com/
2. Choose to Create an AWS account.

Note: If you signed into AWS recently, you might see this option. In that case, choose Sign into the Console. Then, if Create a new AWS account still isn't visible, select Sign in to a different account and then choose Create a new one.

3. Enter your account information, and then choose Continue. Ensure you enter your account information correctly, particularly your email address. If you didn't enter your email address correctly, you won't be able to access your AWS account.

Note: Because of the critical nature of the AWS account root user of the account, it is strongly recommended that you use an email address that can be accessed by a group rather than only an individual. That way, if the person who signed up for the AWS account leaves the company, the AWS account can still be accessed and used because the email address is associated with a group.

If you lose access to the email address associated with the AWS account, you can't get access if you ever lose the password.

4. Choose Personal or Professional.

Note: There aren't any feature differences between personal and professional accounts. Both of them have the same features and functions.

5. Enter your company or personal information.

Important
For professional AWS accounts, it's a best practice to enter a company phone number rather than a personal phone number. Creating professional AWS accounts using an individual email address or a personal phone number can make your account insecure.

6. Read and accept the AWS Customer Agreement.

7. Choose Create Account and Continue.

8. On the Payment Information page, enter the payment-related information and then choose to Verify and Add.

9. Next, you must verify your phone number.

10. Enter the code displayed in the CAPTCHA, and then submit.

11. When the automated system contacts you, enter the PIN you receive and then choose Continue.
If the code is verified, it will take you to the "Select a Support Plan" page.

12. On the Select a Support Plan page, choose one of the available AWS Support plans. The "Select a Support Plan" page asks which support plans you want. Primarily for learning or trying out services for preparing for certification exams, the Basic Plan option is sufficient– as it is free. Essentially in the Basic Plan, you will leverage AWS documentation to get help if you get stuck. In my personal experience, Basic Plan is fine for learning or preparing certification exams. You will need the Developer Plan option if you need to contact someone in AWS to help solve your AWS issue. Essentially, you will create a support ticket in this option if you have any support-related questions, and the AWS support team will handle your support ticket. Finally, businesses using AWS typically use the Business Plan to get help on their AWS issue.

13. Once you select a support plan, wait for your new account to be activated. Next, you will get an email from AWS about your account setup. Then, you can log in to start using AWS. This usually takes a few minutes but can take up to 24 hours.

Check your email and spam folder for the confirmation message. After you receive this email message, you will have full access to all AWS services.

Reference: https://docs.aws.amazon.com/AWSCloudFormation/latest/UserGuide/cfn-sign-up-for-aws.html

▶ **AWS Account Sign up**: https://youtu.be/GxT1MkZJEGM

8.2 AWS Root Account Best Practices

At the time of signing up to AWS, AWS creates a root user identity for your AWS account. The root user identity you can use to sign into AWS. You can sign into the AWS Management Console using this root user identity, which is the email address and password that provided when creating the account. Your email address and password combination are also called your root user credentials.

Some of the AWS account root user security best practices are as follows:

- Do not use the AWS account root user for any task where it's not required. Instead, create a new IAM user for each person that requires administrator access. Then make those users administrators by placing the users into an "Administrators" group to which you attach the AdministratorAccess managed policy.
- If you don't already have Access Key ID and Secret Access Key for your AWS account root user, don't create one unless you need to. If you have an access key for your AWS account root user, delete it.
- Do not share your root account and password with anyone. Instead, use a strong password to help protect account-level access to the AWS Management Console.
- Secure your root account by Multi-Factor Authentication (MFA). Enable AWS MFA on your AWS account root user account.

8.3 MFA (Multi-Factor Authentication)

MFA (Multi-Factor Authentication) in AWS is an additional layer of security that requires users to provide two or more forms of verification to access AWS accounts and resources. It combines something you know (like a password or PIN) with something you have (such as a physical or virtual MFA device). AWS supports MFA through various devices, including hardware tokens, virtual MFA apps (like Google Authenticator), and even FIDO-compliant security keys. By enabling MFA, AWS significantly reduces the risk of unauthorized access, even if a user's credentials are compromised. It is an essential practice for securing the root user account and IAM users in AWS environments.

8.4 Exercise: Set up MFA Using Google Authenticator

Following are the steps for setting up Multi-Factor Authentication (MFA) using Google Authenticator:

Sign in to your AWS Management Console: Log in to your AWS account using your username and password. Once logged in, go to the IAM (Identity and Access Management) dashboard. It is under the "Security, Identity, & Compliance" section.

Access Users: In the IAM dashboard, locate and click on "Users" from the left-hand menu. Click on the username of the IAM user for whom you want to enable MFA.

Enable MFA: Under the "Security credentials" tab, find the section labeled "Assigned MFA device" and click on "Manage MFA device."

Choose MFA Device: In the "Manage MFA Device" dialog, select "Virtual MFA device" and click "Continue."

Install Google Authenticator: On your mobile device, download and install the Google Authenticator app from the App Store (for iOS) or Google Play Store (for Android).

Set Up MFA Device: In the Google Authenticator app, tap the "+" icon to add a new account. You can scan the QR code on the screen or enter the provided secret key manually.

Enter Authentication Code: Once the account is added to the Google Authenticator app, it generates six-digit codes. Enter the current authentication code displayed in the app into the "Authentication code 1" field on the AWS console.

Verify MFA Setup: After entering the authentication code, AWS will prompt you to enter another code to verify that the MFA device is set up correctly. Enter the next code generated by the Google Authenticator app.

Complete MFA Setup: Once both codes are successfully verified, click "Assign MFA" to complete the setup process.

Enable MFA on Login: After setting up MFA, the IAM user must provide authentication code from the Google Authenticator app and their username and password when logging in to the AWS Management Console.

It's important to note that MFA provides an additional layer of security to your AWS account by requiring a second form of verification, making it more difficult for unauthorized users to gain access. *Keep your mobile device secure and back up your MFA secret key safely if you need to set up MFA on a new device.*

▷ **How to Set Up MFA**: https://youtu.be/0PbkUZ52IrU

8.5 Accessing AWS Platform

AWS Management Console is a common and popular choice to access AWS as it is a compelling UI. We can perform many AWS operations on the AWS platform without programming or knowing its low-level APIs. However, AWS can be accessed in other ways as well.

Different Ways to Access AWS
- AWS Management Console (protected by password + MFA)
- AWS CLI -- AWS Command Line Interface (protected by access keys)
- AWS SDK -- AWS Software Development Kit (for code: protected by access keys)
- Integrated Development Environment (IDE)

AWS Management Console
AWS Management Console, a more formal name for AWS UI, is a prevalent choice to access AWS. You don't need to know any programming language or scripting language to access AWS if you

are using AWS its management console. You can access the AWS UI from mobile apps as well. For example, you can manage launched EC2 instances from mobile apps using AWS Management Console. It is protected by a password and optionally by MFA.

AWS CLI (Command Line Interface)

Another way to access AWS is using AWS CLI, which is AWS Command Line Interface. AWS CLI is handy for DevOps engineers who would like to access AWS from the command line to be more productive or to automate backend processes, such as launching or terminating AWS services without using its management console.

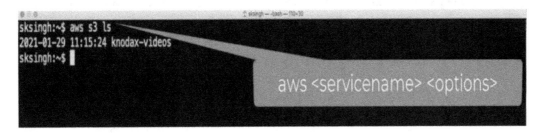

It provides direct access to the public APIs of AWS services. Using AWS CLI, you can write scripts to manage your AWS resources. It's open source: https://github.com/aws/aws-cli. **In order to access AWS Cloud using AWS CLI, you need to provide access keys.**

AWS SDK (Software Development Kit)

What if you want to perform actions on AWS directly from your application's code – without using SDK? You can use SDK -- Software Development Kit.

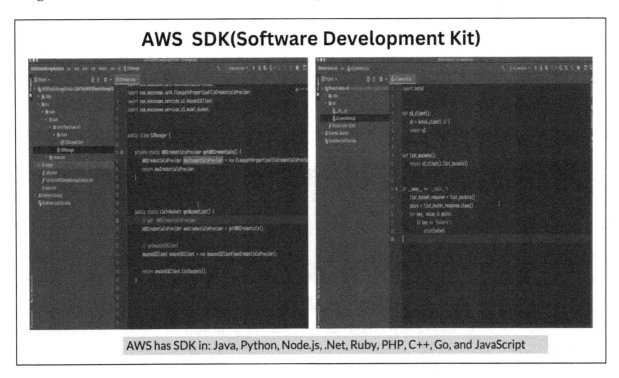

AWS SDK(Software Development Kit)

AWS has SDK in: Java, Python, Node.js, .Net, Ruby, PHP, C++, Go, and JavaScript

The AWS SDK is used mainly by AWS Developers. AWS SDK is handy for AWS developers who would like to develop programs on the AWS platform using AWS APIs. In other words, AWS

Software Development Kit (AWS SDK) is a language-specific APIs (set of libraries). It enables you to access and manage AWS services programmatically. For example, if you would like to develop a chat application on AWS. You could leverage AWS SDK in that case.

- SDKs are available for the following programming languages: **Java, Python, Node.js, .Net, Ruby, PHP, C++, Go, and JavaScript.** There are mobile SDKs (Android, iOS) and IoT device SDKs (Embedded C, Arduino) are available as well.
- We have to use AWS SDK when coding for AWS services such as DynamoDB.
- **AWS CLI uses the Python SDK (boto3).**
- If you don't specify or configure a default Region, then **us-east-1 will be used by default**.
- When using AWS SDK, you need to provide access keys.

Integrated Development Environment (IDE)
You can also use IDE. An integrated development environment (IDE) provides a set of coding productivity tools such as a source code editor, a debugger, and build tools. Cloud9 IDE is an offering from AWS under IDEs.

8.6 Access Keys
You can generate access keys through the AWS Console. Users manage their own access keys. Access Keys are secret, like user id and password. Access Key ID is like user id, and Secret Access Key is like password -- don't share them.

Other ways to understand access Keys:
Access Key ID ~= username
Secret Access Key ~= password

Please don't share access keys and make them inactive or delete them if you are not using them.

☐ **IAM Access Key and Secret Key**: https://youtu.be/R2tqNYyrDyQ

8.7 AWS Free Tier

AWS Free Tier

Gain free, hands-on experience with the AWS platform, products, and services

AWS Free Tier (https://aws.amazon.com/free) is a feature provided by AWS to try out and learn AWS services free of charge within certain usage limits, for some time, typically for one year. The AWS Free Tier is automatically activated on each new AWS account.

AWS Free Tier Offers
AWS Free Tier provides three types of offers.

Three Types of Offers

More than 100 AWS products are available on AWS Free Tier today. Three different types of free offers are available depending on the product used. Click an icon below to explore our offers.

Free Trials

Click to Learn More

12 months free

Click to Learn More

Always free

Click to Learn More

AWS Free Tier home page

Always Free

Always Free offers do not expire at the end of your 12-month AWS Free Tier term and are available to all AWS customers.

12 Months Free

You will get 12-month free with limited usage after initial signup with AWS in this type of offer. After that, you pay standard rates after your 12 months free usage term expires, or your application use exceeds the free tier limits.

Free Trials

In this type of offer, you will get short-term free trial, which starts from the date, you do first usage of a particular service. Then, once the trial period expires you simply pay standard, pay-as-you-go service rates (see each service page for full pricing details).

Free Tier Eligible label

One obvious question that comes to mind when you are new to AWS is how you would know if the service you are trying to use if it is in Free Tier or not. The next question is whether it is Always Free type, 12 Months Free type, or Trials type. Some other common questions related to AWS Free Tier are at the end of this chapter as FAQ.

In general, if you use AWS Management Console (other options are using AWS API and AWS CLI), AWS provides some label if it is in Free Tier.

Step 2: Choose an Instance Type

For example, as you can see in the screenshot above, choosing instance type when launching an EC2 instance. There is a label "Free tier eligible" on the t2.micro instance with one vCPU and 1 GiB memory. So, if you launch an EC2 example using this instance type, it is Free Tier eligible.

AWS Free Tier Details Page

Another way is: on the AWS Free Tier page https://aws.amazon.com/free, on the left side, there is a Filter by option. Using this option, you can find detail such as which services are available as Always Free, which are available as 12 Months Free, which are on Trials. So, for example, in the screenshot above, Always Free is checked, displaying the services available as Always Free. You can also filter by Product Categories such as Analytics, Database.

Summary
- AWS Free Tier enables its customers to acquire practical knowledge about AWS platform and services by reducing the cost of learning.
- They are of three types: Always Free, Short-Term Free Trial, and 12 Months Free.
- http://aws.amazon.com/free page can be used to find more details about AWS Free Tier.

☐ **AWS Free Tier:** https://youtu.be/3Ntfvx8Eu7k

8.8 AWS Billing and Cost Management

AWS Billing and Cost Management is a central, go-to place service for all billing-related aspects. The AWS Billing and Cost Management allows you to pay your AWS bill, monitor your usage, and analyze and control your costs. You cannot use this service to create data-driven business cases for transitioning your business' on-premises IT infrastructure and applications to AWS Cloud.

8.8.1 AWS Budgets

AWS Budgets give the ability to set custom budgets that alert you when your costs or usage exceed your budgeted or forecasted amount. With AWS Budgets, you can be alerted by email or SNS notification when actual or forecasted cost and usage exceed your budgeted threshold or when your actual RI and Savings Plans' utilization or coverage drops below your desired threshold.

AWS Budgets can be created at different levels, for example, the monthly, quarterly, or yearly levels, and can customize the start and end dates as well. Additionally, you can further refine your budget to track costs associated with multiple dimensions, such as AWS service, linked account, tag, and others.

8.8.2 Exercise: Budget Alert Set Up

Before using AWS, one of the critical tasks is setting up a budget alert to help keep your AWS bills within the check.

AWS has a Free Tier -- then why do I need to set up a budget alert?

Typically for preparing AWS certification exam, it's good practice to use the services given in the AWS Free Tier. AWS Free Tier is a feature provided by AWS to try out and learn AWS services free of cost for some time, typically for one year. However, the free tier may not be sufficient to learn and try out the services if you are seriously preparing for an AWS certification exam.

So, by setting up the budget alert, you make sure to get some sort of notification such as email or text, depending on what you have configured if you're exceeding the budget threshold. The budget alarm will help in keeping your AWS bills within your budget. That being said, let's go ahead to set up the budget alert.

Step 1: Billing Dashboard
In the search bar, type billing to easily find the "Billing & Cost Management Dashboard" if you have previously visited this service, it will be shown on your home page once you logged in.

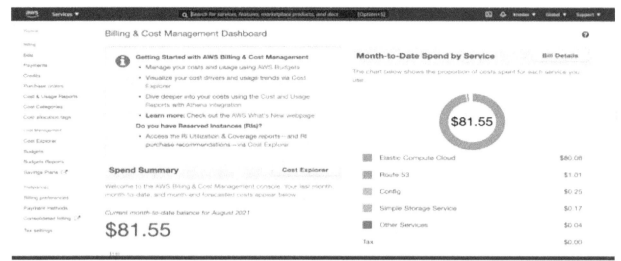

AWS billing dashboard

Step 2: Create Budget

Once you are on the "Billing & Cost Management Dashboard" page, here click on the Budget link on the left sidebar. You will get the Overview page. On the Overview page, click on the Create Budget button which is at the top right side.

It will take you to the "Choose budget type" page. Select a budget type, which is cost budget.

Step 3: Set your budget

Click next, and for the period, select monthly, and select recurring for the budget effective date. Set the starting month, and then enter the budget amount, for example, $1.00. Enter budget name, for example, "AWS Certification Preparation Budget," and then click Next.

AWS billing & dashboard -- set your budget

On the next screen, enter threshold -- 80% is typical. Next, enter the email where you would like to get the notification. Please make sure you provide the correct email address.

AWS billing & cost management -- budget amount

You can also set up $0 budget: enter $0 as the fixed budgeted amount. Next, specify the alert threshold in the "Set Alerts" section. Set the threshold to "0%" to trigger an alert as soon as any cost is incurred

📺 **How to Set Up AWS Budget Alerts:** https://youtu.be/0xIsz9veWs4

8.9 Exploring AWS Free Tier

Step 1: Sign In to the AWS Management Console
- Open your web browser and navigate to the AWS Management Console.
- Enter your email address and password, then click "Sign In."

Step 2: Access the Free Tier Page
- After signing in, go to the AWS Free Tier page.
- Here you will find information about services available under the Free Tier, including 12-month free trials, always free services, and short-term trials.

Step 3: Understand Free Tier Categories
- 12-Month Free Tier: These services are free for 12 months from the date you sign up for an AWS account. After the 12 months, standard rates apply.
- Always Free: These services are free as long as you are an AWS customer and within the limits specified.
- Short-Term Trials: These services offer limited-time free trials, usually for one month.

Step 4: Explore Popular Free Tier Services
This is just to get an idea of AWS Free Tier; we will delve deeper into launching an EC2 instance and creating an S3 bucket in their respective chapters later.

Amazon EC2:
- Under the 12-month free tier, you can use up to 750 hours of Linux and Windows t2.micro or t3.micro instances per month.
- To launch an EC2 instance, go to the EC2 Dashboard in the AWS Management Console.
- Click "Launch Instance" and follow the wizard to select a free tier eligible instance type (t2.micro or t3.micro), configure the instance, and launch it.

Amazon S3:
- Under the 12-month free tier, you can store up to 5 GB of Standard Storage in Amazon S3, 20,000 GET requests, and 2,000 PUT requests per month.
- To create an S3 bucket, go to the S3 Dashboard in the AWS Management Console.
- Click "Create Bucket," enter a unique bucket name, select the region, and click "Create."

Take advantage of the AWS Free Tier to experiment with different services and gain hands-on experience.

Note: It's always best practice to delete/remove the AWS resources if you are not using them. That being said, delete/remove any resources that you created while exploring AWS Free Tier.

AWS provides extensive documentation and tutorials to help you get started with various services. By following these steps, you can effectively explore and utilize the AWS Free Tier, allowing you to learn and experiment with AWS services without incurring costs.

8.10 Related YouTube Videos
- **AWS Account Sign Up:** https://youtu.be/GxT1MkZJEGM
- **AWS Free Tier:** https://youtu.be/3Ntfvx8Eu7k
- **AWS Budget Alert Set Up:** https://youtu.be/0xIsz9veWs4

8.11 Chapter Review Questions

Question 1:
Which of the following is a best practice for the AWS root account?
   A. Sharing the root account credentials with team members
   B. Enabling Multi-Factor Authentication (MFA) for the root account
   C. Disabling the root account after initial setup
   D. Using the root account for all day-to-day operations

Question 2:
What is the primary purpose of enabling Multi-Factor Authentication (MFA) on your AWS account?
   A. To reduce AWS service charges
   B. To enhance security by requiring an additional layer of authentication
   C. To improve account performance
   D. To enable access to the AWS Free Tier

Question 3:
What is an AWS Free Tier?
   A. A feature that provides unlimited free access to all AWS services

B. A pricing model that offers limited free usage of certain AWS services for a specified period

C. A tool for managing access keys in AWS

D. A discount program for AWS enterprise customers

Question 4:
What are AWS access keys used for?

A. To enable MFA for AWS accounts

B. To allow programmatic access to AWS services via the CLI or SDKs

C. To manage billing and cost alerts

D. To create budgets in the AWS Billing console

Question 5:
Which of the following is the primary purpose of AWS Budgets?

A. To restrict user access to certain AWS services

B. To alert users when costs exceed predefined thresholds

C. To manage access keys and API requests

D. To track service usage in real-time

8.12 Answers to Chapter Review Questions

1. B. Enabling Multi-Factor Authentication (MFA) for the root account
Explanation: Enabling MFA for the root account is a critical security best practice in AWS. It provides an additional layer of security to protect against unauthorized access.

2. B. To enhance security by requiring an additional layer of authentication
Explanation: MFA strengthens the security of an AWS account by requiring a second factor, such as a one-time code, in addition to the password.

3. B. A pricing model that offers limited free usage of certain AWS services for a specified period
Explanation: The AWS Free Tier provides limited free usage of various AWS services for up to 12 months, helping users explore AWS services without incurring costs.

4. B. To allow programmatic access to AWS services via the CLI or SDKs
Explanation: AWS access keys consist of an Access Key ID and Secret Access Key, enabling programmatic access to AWS services through the AWS CLI, SDKs, or APIs.

5. B. To alert users when costs exceed predefined thresholds
Explanation: AWS Budgets help users manage costs by sending alerts when actual or forecasted expenses exceed predefined budget thresholds, ensuring cost control.

Chapter 9. AWS Global Cloud Infrastructure

The AWS Global Cloud Infrastructure is the most secure, extensive, and reliable cloud platform, offering over 200 fully featured services from data centers globally. Whether you need to deploy your application workloads across the globe in a single click, or you want to build and deploy specific applications closer to your end-users with single-digit millisecond latency, AWS provides you the cloud infrastructure where and when you need it.

We know that AWS is a public cloud service provider and provides on-demand availability of all kinds of cloud services from across the world. How is AWS able to provide on-demand availability of all types of cloud services from across the globe?

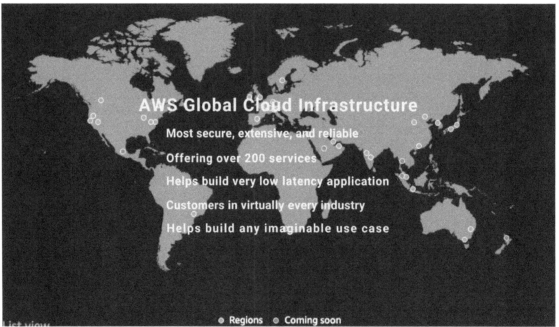

Ref: https://aws.amazon.com/about-aws/global-infrastructure/

Well, AWS has a massive amount of computing resources and storage available in data centers spread across all over the world. The AWS entire infrastructure setup of data centers across all

Cloud Computing and AWS Introduction   125

over the globe is called AWS Global Cloud Infrastructure. In this chapter, we will learn about AWS Global Cloud Infrastructure and its related concepts, such as AWS Availability Zones and AWS Regions.

AWS Global Cloud Infrastructure is the backbone of AWS. The AWS Global Cloud Infrastructure is the most secure, extensive, and reliable cloud platform, offering over 200 fully featured services from data centers globally.

It not only allows you to deploy your application across the globe with a single click, but it also allows you to build and deploy specific applications closer to your end-users with single-digit millisecond latency. It helps millions of active customers from virtually every industry build and run every imaginable use case on AWS.

This was a high-level overview of AWS Global Cloud Infrastructure. Next, we will look into AWS Regions and AWS Availability Zones, which are other important concepts related to AWS Global Cloud Infrastructure.

9.1 AWS Regions

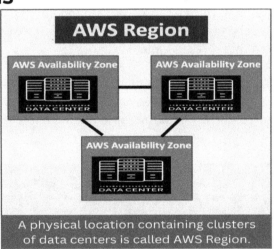

AWS has the concept of a Region, a physical location worldwide where AWS has clusters of data centers. AWS region is a physical location that has clusters of data centers. As you can see in the picture, the AWS Region has 3 three clusters of data centers. And these clusters of data centers are connected. Each AWS region is a separate geographical region. Each AWS region is completely independent having its own internal private secured network and is isolated from the other AWS regions.

AWS Regions on the Management Console

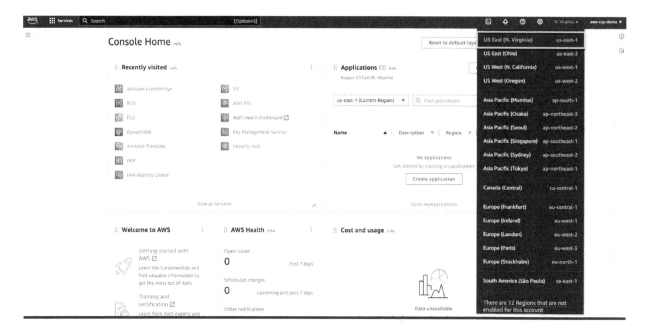

AWS region is displayed at the top right on the AWS Management Console. When you logged in to your AWS account, you will be assigned a default region. That way when you launch any AWS service, it will be served from that AWS region.

Each AWS region is assigned a region code, which is used in various configuration when using AWS services and resources. For example, US East (N. Virginia) AWS Region has a region code us-east-1. If a particular service you are looking for is not available in your default AWS region, you can change it.

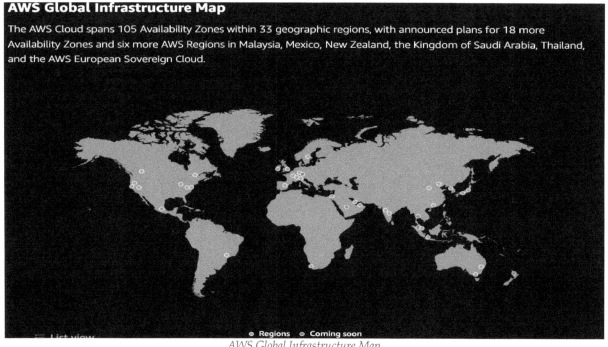

AWS Global Infrastructure Map

Let's try to understand AWS regions by looking at the AWS Global Infrastructure Map. On the AWS Global Infrastructure map above, AWS regions are represented with circles. The blue circle ones are the current AWS regions, and AWS Regions in red circles are coming soon.

As you can see, AWS has regions all over the world. The AWS Cloud spans 105 Availability Zones within 33 geographic regions around the world, with announced plans for 18 more Availability Zones and six more AWS Regions in Malaysia, Mexico, New Zealand, the Kingdom of Saudi Arabia, Thailand, and the AWS European Sovereign Cloud.

With regards to AWS regions in USA, there are 6 AWS regions in USA. Two AWS regions are on the US east coast: one is in Northern Virginia, and the other is in Ohio. Two AWS regions are on the US West Coast: one is in Oregon, and the other one is in Northern California. Additionally, there are 2 Gov cloud regions: one is on US East Coast, and other is on US West Coast. Some regions have more services than others. For example. US East (N. Virginia), US West (N. California) in America; Singapore, Sydney, Tokyo in Asia Pacific; Frankfurt, Ireland in EU offer more services in general.

AWS services are region specific. However, just to keep in mind there are some services which do not support any region. For example, AWS IAM is a global service and is not associated with any region.

Global vs. Regional AWS Services
AWS has global and regional services. AWS Global Services are IAM (Identity and Access Management), Route 53 (DNS service), CloudFront (Content Delivery Network), and WAF(Web Application Firewall). Most AWS services are Region-scoped; for example, Amazon EC2 (IaaS), Elastic Beanstalk(PaaS), AWS Lambda (FaaS), Amazon Rekognition (SaaS type), and many more.

For further details about regional services, please visit: https://aws.amazon.com/about-aws/global-infrastructure/regional-product-services

9.2 How to Select an AWS Region
Following are the guidelines for choosing AWS regions to help ensure excellent performance and resilience:

- **Proximity to customers**: To get low latency performance, choose a region closest to your location and your customers' location to get low network latency.
- **Available services within a Region**: Find out what are your most needed services. Usually, the new services start on a few main regions such as regions on us-east and us-west before being available to other regions.
- **Pricing:** Some regions will cost more than others, so use built-in AWS calculator to do rough cost estimates to get idea about your choices. SLAs usually vary by region, so be sure to be aware of what your needs are and if they're being met.
- **Compliance with data governance and legal requirements**: You may need to meet regulatory compliance such as GDPR by hosting your deployment in a specific region or regions to be compliant.

9.3 AWS Availability Zones

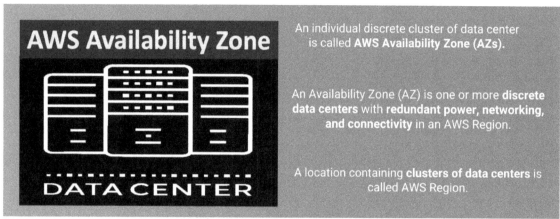

AWS Availability Zones

Another essential concept in AWS is AWS availability zone. It is also called AZ, in short. As I mentioned earlier, AWS has clusters of data centers on multiple locations worldwide, and a location containing clusters of data centers is called AWS region.

On the other hand, an individual discrete cluster of the data center is called AWS Availability Zone. Another way to way to understand is: An Availability Zone (AZ) is one or more discrete data centers with redundant power, networking, and connectivity in an AWS region.

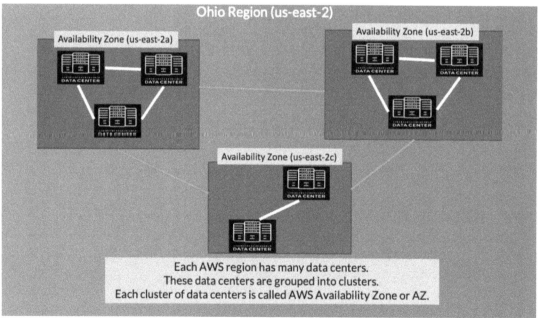

Understanding AWS Region & AZ

AWS availability zones within a Region have connectivity with one another. To strengthen the concept further, I would like to share this point:

Cloud Computing and AWS Introduction   129

More Details About AWS Availability Zones

Now you got a conceptual understanding of AWS Availability Zones. Let's go through some more details. Availability zones are separated in an AWS region. Availability zones are located away from the city and are in lower-risk flood areas to avoid the flood or any other kind of damage to the data centers. AZs are physically separated by a significant distance, many kilometers, from any other AZ.

An availability zone (AZ) is one or more discrete data centers with redundant power, networking, and connectivity in an AWS Region. All AZs in an AWS Region are interconnected with high-bandwidth and low-latency networking between AZs.

Each availability zone has its power supply and on-site backup generator. Furthermore, they are connected via different grids from independent utilities to avoid a single point of failure for any power outage.

Availability zones have code as well, like AWS regions. Availability zone code has region code + a letter added in the end. For instance, The US Ohio AWS region has region code us-east-2. And this AWS region has 3 availability zones with their code as us-east-2a, us-east-2b, and us-east-2c. If you notice, a letter has been added at the end of the region code (us-east-2+a = us-east-2a) to get the AZ code.

Availability Zones from Architectural Perspective

Let's understand Availability Zones from the solution architecture perspective. Redundancy and replication are architectural techniques to increase the high availability and fault tolerance of software applications.

To provide redundancy, AWS allows replication of resources and data in multiple availability zones, which helps avoid data loss and offers high availability for the deployed applications. All traffic between AZs is encrypted. Furthermore, you can perform synchronous replication between AZs.

However, replications across AWS regions don't happen unless organizations explicitly would like to do perform. The reason is AWS regions are separate, and they are not connected with the AWS private network, unlike AWS availability zones that are connected.

KEY POINTS

- AWS has data centers worldwide in multiple locations to help provide high availability and low latency services. These locations are divided into Regions and Availability Zones.
- Every AWS Region is divided into multiple isolated locations known as Availability Zones.

- Availability Zone is essentially an AWS Data Center with its own power supply, low-latency, and high bandwidth network setup.
- An Availability Zone (AZ) is a discrete data center with redundant power, networking, and connectivity in an AWS Region.
- Each Availability Zone has its own power supply and on-site backup generator. And, they are connected via different grids from independent utilities to avoid a single point of failure for any power outage.
- Typically, there are three Availability Zones in a Region. However, in some cases, there are more than 3. For example, N. Virginia Region has 6 Availability Zones.
- All AZs in an AWS Region are interconnected with high-bandwidth, low-latency networking between AZs.
- Availability Zones are separated in an AWS Region.
- Availability Zones are located away from the city and are in lower-risk flood areas to avoid the flood or any other damage to the data centers.
- AZ's are physically separated by a meaningful distance, many kilometers, from any other AZ.
- Availability Zones have codes as well, like Region. Availability Zone code has Region Code + a letter added in the end. For example. N. Virginia region has region code us-east-1. And this region has 6 Availability Zones with their code as us-east-1a, us-east-1b, and the rest AZs are coded in the same way.
- AWS customers focused on high availability can design their applications to run on multiple AZs to achieve even greater fault tolerance.
- AZs allow customers to operate production applications and databases that are more highly available, fault-tolerant, and scalable than would be possible from a single data center.
- AZs make partitioning applications for high availability easy. If an application is partitioned across AZs, the application is better isolated and protected from power outages, tornadoes, earthquakes, etc.
- To provide redundancy, AWS allows replication of resources and data in multiple Availability Zones. This helps avoid data loss and provides high availability to the deployed applications. However, these replications don't happen across regions unless organizations explicitly decide to do so.
- All traffic between AZs is encrypted. Therefore, the network performance is sufficient to accomplish synchronous replication between AZs.
- AWS Regions are separate, and they are not connected with the AWS private network, unlike AWS Availability Zones, which are connected.

9.4 AWS Edge Locations

AWS Edge Locations are a critical component of AWS's global infrastructure, designed to enhance content delivery and reduce latency for end-users. They serve as the backbone of Amazon CloudFront, AWS's content delivery network (CDN), providing a more efficient and seamless user experience by caching content closer to users.

Role in Content Delivery

Edge Locations are strategically placed around the world to cache and deliver content, such as web pages, videos, images, and other static and dynamic assets, closer to end-users.

Key Characteristics

- Content Caching: Edge Locations cache copies of frequently accessed content. When a user requests content, CloudFront serves it from the nearest Edge Location rather than the origin server, reducing the distance data must travel.
- Dynamic Content Delivery: In addition to static content, Edge Locations can accelerate the delivery of dynamic content by using features like Lambda@Edge, which allows for serverless code execution closer to users, optimizing performance and reducing latency.

Examples

- Media Streaming: A streaming service like Netflix or Amazon Prime Video uses Edge Locations to cache and deliver video content, ensuring high-quality playback with minimal buffering for users worldwide.
- E-commerce: An online retailer can cache product images, CSS files, and JavaScript at Edge Locations, providing a faster and more responsive browsing experience for shoppers.

Reducing Latency

Latency is the delay between a user's action and the response from the server. Reducing latency is crucial for enhancing user experience, especially for applications requiring real-time interactions.

Key Characteristics

- Geographical Proximity: Edge Locations are dispersed globally, bringing content closer to users. By minimizing the distance data travels, Edge Locations significantly reduce latency.
- Fast DNS Resolution: CloudFront integrates with Route 53, AWS's scalable DNS service, to quickly resolve user requests to the nearest Edge Location, further decreasing response times.

Examples

- Global Websites: A multinational corporation hosting its website on AWS can use Edge Locations to serve content swiftly to users across different continents, ensuring quick load times and a uniform experience regardless of user location.
- Real-Time Applications: Online gaming platforms and live streaming services can utilize Edge Locations to ensure real-time data transfer and minimal latency, crucial for maintaining an interactive and immersive user experience.

Impact on Performance

By leveraging Edge Locations, AWS enables applications to achieve higher performance and reliability. The reduced latency and improved content delivery not only enhance user satisfaction but also optimize backend processes.

Key Characteristics

- High Availability: With over 200 Edge Locations, AWS ensures high availability of content, providing redundancy and failover capabilities.
- Scalability: Edge Locations can handle varying levels of traffic efficiently, scaling automatically to meet demand without compromising performance.

Examples

- Content Delivery Networks (CDNs): CDNs use Edge Locations to distribute heavy traffic loads across multiple servers, ensuring that no single server becomes a bottleneck, thus maintaining high performance.
- Data Analytics: Businesses analyzing large datasets can distribute query requests through Edge Locations, speeding up data processing and enabling quicker insights.

AWS Edge Locations play a pivotal role in enhancing content delivery and reducing latency, ensuring that users receive fast and reliable access to content and applications. By strategically caching content closer to end-users and minimizing the distance data travels, Edge Locations significantly improve performance, making them an essential component for businesses aiming to provide a seamless and efficient user experience. Leveraging AWS Edge Locations can help organizations achieve higher availability, scalability, and overall better performance for their global applications.

9.5 AWS Local Zones

AWS Local Zones are a type of AWS infrastructure deployment that places compute, storage, and other AWS services closer to large population centers, industries, and IT hubs. They are designed to enable low-latency applications by bringing AWS resources geographically closer to end users. Local Zones are ideal for workloads that require real-time processing, such as media and entertainment, gaming, healthcare, machine learning, and edge computing. They allow organizations to run latency-sensitive applications closer to their users while still seamlessly integrating with the broader AWS ecosystem. By using Local Zones, customers can reduce latency, meet strict data residency requirements, and optimize application performance without maintaining their own on-premises infrastructure.

9.6 AWS Wavelength

AWS Wavelength is a service designed to bring AWS infrastructure and services closer to the edge of 5G networks, enabling ultra-low-latency applications. It embeds AWS compute and storage capabilities within the data centers of telecommunication providers, reducing the distance data must travel to reach end-users. This is particularly beneficial for applications requiring real-time responsiveness, such as video streaming, online gaming, autonomous vehicles, and IoT deployments. By combining the power of AWS services with the speed and efficiency of 5G networks, AWS Wavelength allows developers to build and scale edge applications with minimal latency while still leveraging the broader AWS ecosystem for management, analytics, and storage.

9.7 Lab Exercise: Exploring AWS Global Infrastructure Using the AWS Management Console

The AWS Management Console provides a graphical interface to explore and manage AWS global infrastructure, including Regions, Availability Zones, and Edge Locations. This step-by-step guide will help you navigate through the console to understand AWS's global presence and its impact on latency and fault tolerance.

Step 1: Sign In to the AWS Management Console
- Open your web browser and navigate to the AWS Management Console.
- Enter your email address and password, then click "Sign In."

Step 2: Access the Global View
- After signing in, you will be directed to the AWS Management Console home page.
- Look for the "Global" view option, typically represented by a globe icon or the word "Global" in the navigation bar.

Step 3: Explore AWS Regions
- Click on the globe icon or the "Global" view to open a map of AWS Regions.
- The map will display all available AWS Regions worldwide. Each region is marked on the map with a pin.
- Click on any region pin to see detailed information about that region, including the number of Availability Zones and the services available in that region.

Step 4: View Availability Zones
- Within the region details, you can explore the Availability Zones (AZs) in that region.
- Each AZ is listed along with its unique identifier (e.g., us-east-1a, us-east-1b).
- Understand the geographic distribution of AZs within the region and their role in providing fault tolerance.

Step 5: Explore Edge Locations
- Navigate to the Amazon CloudFront service within the console.
- In the CloudFront dashboard, look for the "Edge Locations" section.
- This section lists all the Edge Locations used for caching content closer to users.
- You can see the global distribution of Edge Locations and understand how they reduce latency for content delivery.

Step 6: Check Regional Service Availability
- Return to the global view map.
- Click on different regions to compare the availability of various AWS services.
- Some services might be available in specific regions due to compliance, data residency requirements, or strategic reasons.

Step 7: Understand Service Limits and Pricing
- Access the AWS Pricing Calculator or the service-specific pricing page from the console.
- Compare the cost of deploying resources in different regions.
- Understand the service limits and constraints for each region, which can impact your architecture decisions.

Step 8: Explore Compliance and Data Residency
- Access the AWS Compliance page from the console.
- Review the compliance certifications and data residency options available for each region.
- Ensure your deployments meet the regulatory requirements specific to your industry and location.

Step 9: Use AWS CloudShell for Region-Specific Operations

- Open AWS CloudShell from the console for command-line access.
- Use AWS CLI commands to query and manage resources in specific regions.
- Example command to list all EC2 instances in a region:

```
aws ec2 describe-instances --region us-east-1
```

Step 10: Leverage AWS Well-Architected Tool
- Access the AWS Well-Architected Tool from the console.
- Use the tool to review and optimize your architecture for high availability, fault tolerance, and performance across regions and AZs.

By following these steps, you can effectively explore and understand the AWS Global Infrastructure using the AWS Management Console. This knowledge will help you make informed decisions about deploying and managing your applications on AWS, ensuring optimal performance, availability, and compliance.

9.8 Related YouTube Videos
- **AWS Global Infrastructure:** https://youtu.be/nkf4sVa0Tug
- **AWS Regions:** https://youtu.be/NQhH2kcKI5U
- **AWS Availability Zones:** https://youtu.be/UeD7O-ErGoQ

9.9 Chapter Review Questions
Question 1:
Which of the following best describes AWS Regions?
    A. A single data center located in a specific city
    B. A geographically isolated area containing multiple Availability Zones
    C. A backup service for disaster recovery
    D. A network optimization tool for global applications

Question 2:
What is a key consideration when selecting an AWS Region?
    A. The number of Edge Locations available in the region
    B. The proximity to end-users and compliance with local regulations
    C. The total number of AWS services supported globally
    D. The availability of older instance types in that region

Question 3:
What is the purpose of AWS Availability Zones within a region?
    A. To provide redundant backups for disaster recovery
    B. To enable high availability by hosting resources in separate physical locations within the same region
    C. To connect different regions for global data sharing
    D. To improve edge computing capabilities

Question 4:

Cloud Computing and AWS Introduction

Which AWS infrastructure component is specifically designed to deliver content closer to users?
    A. AWS Regions
    B. AWS Local Zones
    C. AWS Edge Locations
    D. AWS Availability Zones

Question 5:
What is an AWS Local Zone?
    A. A physical location designed to bring AWS services closer to large metropolitan areas
    B. A backup facility for disaster recovery in each AWS Region
    C. A temporary location for scaling compute resources
    D. A low-cost alternative to Edge Locations

Question 6:
What is the primary function of AWS Wavelength?
    A. Providing archival storage services
    B. Enabling ultra-low latency applications by integrating AWS infrastructure with 5G networks
    C. Delivering content globally using CloudFront
    D. Offering scalable compute capacity in remote regions

Question 7:
How do AWS Edge Locations differ from Availability Zones?
    A. Edge Locations are used for caching content closer to users, while Availability Zones provide data center redundancy within a region.
    B. Edge Locations are physical servers, while Availability Zones are virtual data centers.
    C. Edge Locations manage compute resources, while Availability Zones are for storage optimization.
    D. Edge Locations are part of AWS Wavelength, while Availability Zones are independent regions.

Question 8:
Which AWS service primarily utilizes Edge Locations for its functionality?
    A. AWS Lambda
    B. Amazon CloudFront
    C. Amazon S3 Glacier
    D. AWS Direct Connect

Question 9:
What is the benefit of deploying applications across multiple Availability Zones?
    A. Reduced application latency for global users
    B. High availability and fault tolerance in case of a zone failure
    C. Enhanced application performance for 5G devices
    D. Reduced costs for compute and storage services

Question 10:
Which AWS infrastructure component is designed to provide low-latency applications in specific metro areas?

A. AWS Edge Locations
B. AWS Local Zones
C. AWS Availability Zones
D. AWS Wavelength

9.10 Answers to Chapter Review Questions

1. B. A geographically isolated area containing multiple Availability Zones
Explanation: AWS Regions are geographically isolated areas that contain multiple Availability Zones to ensure high availability and fault tolerance.

2. B. The proximity to end-users and compliance with local regulations
Explanation: When selecting an AWS Region, factors like proximity to end-users for low latency and compliance with local regulations are critical considerations.

3. B. To enable high availability by hosting resources in separate physical locations within the same region
Explanation: AWS Availability Zones are separate physical locations within a region, designed to provide high availability by isolating faults.

4. C. AWS Edge Locations
Explanation: AWS Edge Locations are designed to deliver content closer to users, enabling low-latency delivery through services like Amazon CloudFront.

5. A. A physical location designed to bring AWS services closer to large metropolitan areas
Explanation: AWS Local Zones extend AWS infrastructure to major metropolitan areas, bringing services closer to users to reduce latency.

6. B. Enabling ultra-low latency applications by integrating AWS infrastructure with 5G networks
Explanation: AWS Wavelength integrates AWS infrastructure with 5G networks to deliver ultra-low latency applications.

7. A. Edge Locations are used for caching content closer to users, while Availability Zones provide data center redundancy within a region.
Explanation: Edge Locations focus on content delivery (e.g., CloudFront), while Availability Zones provide redundancy and high availability within a region.

8. B. Amazon CloudFront
Explanation: Amazon CloudFront uses Edge Locations to cache and deliver content globally with low latency.

9. B. High availability and fault tolerance in case of a zone failure
Explanation: Deploying applications across multiple Availability Zones ensures that if one zone fails, the application remains operational in another zone.

10. B. AWS Local Zones
Explanation: AWS Local Zones bring AWS services to specific metropolitan areas, providing low-latency solutions for local users and applications.

Chapter 10. AWS Core Services Overview

AWS Core Services form the foundation of the AWS cloud platform, providing essential building blocks for developing and deploying applications. Key compute services include Amazon EC2 for scalable virtual servers, AWS Lambda for serverless computing, and AWS Elastic Beanstalk for easy application deployment. Storage services such as Amazon S3 for object storage, Amazon EBS for block storage, and Amazon Glacier for archival storage enable robust data management solutions. Additionally, database services like Amazon RDS for relational databases, Amazon DynamoDB for NoSQL databases, and Amazon Redshift for data warehousing offer diverse options for storing and retrieving data. Networking services, including Amazon VPC for isolated networks, Amazon Route 53 for DNS management, and Amazon CloudFront for content delivery, ensure secure and efficient data transfer across the globe.

10.1 Compute Services: EC2, Lambda, and Elastic Beanstalk

Amazon EC2 (Elastic Compute Cloud)

Amazon EC2 provides scalable virtual servers in the cloud, allowing users to run applications on-demand without the need for physical hardware. EC2 offers a wide range of instance types optimized for different use cases, including compute-intensive, memory-intensive, and storage-intensive workloads. Users can choose from various pricing models, such as on-demand instances, reserved instances, and spot instances, to optimize cost and performance. EC2 enables users to have full control over their virtual machines, including the operating system, network configurations, and attached storage.

Example: A startup uses EC2 to host its web application, scaling the number of instances up during peak traffic and down during off-peak times to manage costs effectively.

AWS Lambda

AWS Lambda is a serverless compute service that allows users to run code without provisioning or managing servers. Lambda automatically scales applications by running code in response to events, such as changes in data, shifts in system state, or user actions. Users only pay for the compute time consumed by the function, which makes it a cost-effective solution for intermittent workloads. Lambda integrates with various AWS services, enabling users to build complex, event-driven architectures with minimal operational overhead.

Example: A retail company uses Lambda to process image uploads. When a new image is uploaded to an S3 bucket, Lambda automatically resizes the image and stores it in a different bucket, ensuring images are ready for website display without manual intervention.

AWS Elastic Beanstalk

AWS Elastic Beanstalk is a platform-as-a-service (PaaS) solution that simplifies the deployment and management of applications. Users can deploy applications developed in various programming languages, such as Java, .NET, PHP, Node.js, Python, Ruby, and Go, by uploading code to Elastic Beanstalk, which handles the deployment, capacity provisioning, load balancing, scaling, and monitoring. Elastic Beanstalk allows developers to focus on writing code without worrying about the underlying infrastructure.

Example: A software development team uses Elastic Beanstalk to deploy and manage a web application. By simply uploading the application code, the team benefits from automated scaling and load balancing, ensuring the application remains responsive under varying loads.

Amazon EC2, AWS Lambda, and AWS Elastic Beanstalk are integral compute services within AWS, each serving different purposes and offering distinct advantages. EC2 provides flexible, scalable virtual servers; Lambda offers a serverless environment for event-driven applications; and Elastic Beanstalk simplifies application deployment and management. These services empower developers to choose the right tool for their specific needs, enhancing efficiency and scalability while reducing operational complexity.

10.2 Storage Services: S3, EBS, and Glacier

Amazon S3 (Simple Storage Service)

Amazon S3 is an object storage service that offers industry-leading scalability, data availability, security, and performance. S3 allows users to store and retrieve any amount of data from anywhere on the web. Objects are stored in buckets, which can be configured with different storage classes to optimize costs based on access frequency and retrieval requirements. S3 provides features such as versioning, lifecycle policies, and cross-region replication, making it suitable for a wide range of use cases, from simple backups to complex data lakes.

Example: A media company uses S3 to store and distribute high-resolution video files. By leveraging S3's scalable storage and content distribution capabilities, the company ensures fast and reliable video streaming to its global audience.

Amazon EBS (Elastic Block Store)

Amazon EBS provides persistent block storage for use with Amazon EC2 instances. EBS volumes are automatically replicated within their Availability Zone to protect against hardware failures, offering high availability and durability. EBS is ideal for applications that require consistent, low-latency performance, such as databases, file systems, and boot volumes for EC2 instances. Users can choose from different volume types based on performance needs and cost considerations, including SSD-backed volumes for high performance and HDD-backed volumes for throughput-optimized storage.

Example: A database administrator uses EBS to store data for a MySQL database running on an EC2 instance. The EBS volume ensures low-latency access and reliable performance, critical for maintaining the database's responsiveness and stability.

Amazon Glacier (S3 Glacier)

Amazon Glacier, now integrated into S3 as S3 Glacier, is a secure, durable, and low-cost storage service for data archiving and long-term backup. Glacier is optimized for infrequently accessed data where retrieval times of several hours are acceptable. It provides three retrieval options: Expedited, Standard, and Bulk, allowing users to balance retrieval speed with cost. Glacier's vaults and archives enable organizations to store large amounts of data at a fraction of the cost of other storage options, with built-in compliance and audit capabilities.

Example: A research institution uses S3 Glacier to archive historical scientific data. By storing this infrequently accessed data in Glacier, the institution reduces storage costs significantly while ensuring the data remains secure and retrievable when needed.

Amazon S3, EBS, and Glacier are essential storage services within the AWS ecosystem, each tailored to specific storage needs. S3 provides scalable object storage with versatile access and management features, EBS offers high-performance block storage for EC2 instances, and Glacier delivers cost-effective archival storage for long-term data retention. Together, these services enable users to design flexible and efficient storage solutions to meet various application requirements and budget constraints.

10.3 Database Services: RDS, DynamoDB, and Redshift

Amazon RDS (Relational Database Service)

Amazon RDS is a managed relational database service that simplifies the setup, operation, and scaling of a relational database in the cloud. RDS supports several database engines, including Amazon Aurora, MySQL, PostgreSQL, MariaDB, Oracle, and Microsoft SQL Server. RDS automates common administrative tasks such as hardware provisioning, database setup, patching, and backups. It also offers high availability through Multi-AZ deployments and read replicas for scaling read operations.

Example: An e-commerce website uses Amazon RDS to manage its product catalog and customer data. By leveraging RDS's automated backup and scaling features, the website ensures data availability and performance, even during peak shopping periods.

Amazon DynamoDB

Amazon DynamoDB is a fully managed NoSQL database service that provides fast and predictable performance with seamless scalability. It is designed for applications that require consistent, single-digit millisecond latency at any scale. DynamoDB automatically handles data replication across multiple Availability Zones to ensure high availability and durability. It also supports features such as on-demand scaling, backup and restore, and in-memory caching with DynamoDB Accelerator (DAX).

Example: A mobile gaming company uses DynamoDB to store and retrieve game state data for millions of users. DynamoDB's low-latency performance and automatic scaling capabilities ensure a smooth gaming experience, regardless of user load.

Amazon Redshift

Amazon Redshift is a fully managed data warehouse service designed to handle large-scale data analytics. Redshift allows users to run complex queries against petabytes of structured data using SQL-based tools and business intelligence applications. It offers high performance through columnar storage, data compression, and parallel query execution. Redshift also integrates with various data sources and ETL tools, making it easy to ingest and analyze data from multiple sources.

Example: A financial services company uses Amazon Redshift to analyze transactional data and generate insights for risk management and fraud detection. By utilizing Redshift's scalable data warehousing capabilities, the company can process and query vast amounts of data quickly and efficiently.

Amazon RDS, DynamoDB, and Redshift are powerful database services within the AWS ecosystem, each catering to different use cases and data requirements. RDS provides managed relational databases for traditional applications, DynamoDB offers a highly scalable NoSQL solution for low-latency workloads, and Redshift delivers a robust data warehousing platform for complex analytics. Together, these services enable organizations to manage, scale, and analyze their data effectively, supporting a wide range of application needs and business goals.

10.4 Networking Services: VPC, Route 53, and CloudFront

Amazon VPC (Virtual Private Cloud)

Amazon VPC allows users to create isolated networks within the AWS cloud, providing control over network configuration, including IP address ranges, subnets, route tables, and network gateways. VPC enables users to define and launch AWS resources in a logically isolated virtual network that they control. Users can customize the network configuration, create public-facing and private-facing subnets, and use security groups and network ACLs to control inbound and outbound traffic to instances. VPC also supports features such as VPC peering, Direct Connect, and VPN connections to integrate on-premises networks with AWS.

Example: A healthcare organization uses Amazon VPC to host its sensitive patient management system in a private subnet with strict access controls, ensuring compliance with HIPAA regulations. The VPC setup includes a VPN connection to securely connect the on-premises data center with the AWS environment.

Amazon Route 53

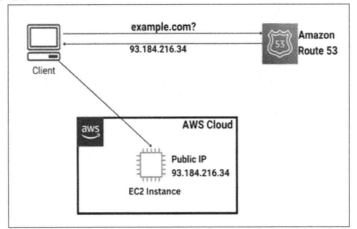

Amazon Route 53 is a highly available and scalable Domain Name System (DNS) web service designed to route end users to Internet applications by translating domain names into IP addresses. Route 53 supports various routing policies, including simple routing, weighted routing, latency-based routing, failover routing, and geolocation routing, to direct traffic based on different criteria. It also provides domain registration and DNS health checks, ensuring that traffic is directed to healthy endpoints.

Example: A global e-commerce platform uses Route 53 to manage its DNS and direct traffic based on user location. By using latency-based routing, the platform ensures that customers from different regions are routed to the nearest data center, improving website load times and user experience.

Amazon CloudFront

Amazon CloudFront is a content delivery network (CDN) service that delivers data, videos, applications, and APIs to users globally with low latency and high transfer speeds. CloudFront integrates with other AWS services such as S3, EC2, and Lambda@Edge to distribute content from edge locations close to users. It supports various content delivery methods, including live and on-demand streaming, and provides features such as geo-restriction, DDoS protection, and SSL/TLS encryption to secure content delivery.

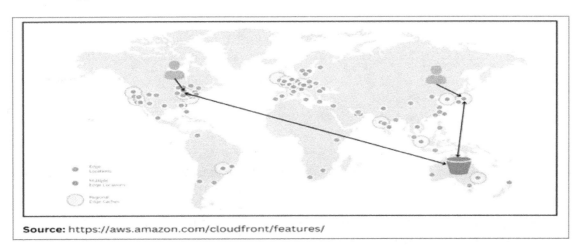

Source: https://aws.amazon.com/cloudfront/features/

Example: A media company uses CloudFront to distribute video content to a global audience. By caching video files at edge locations, CloudFront ensures fast and reliable streaming, reducing latency and buffering for viewers around the world.

Amazon VPC, Route 53, and CloudFront are essential networking services within the AWS ecosystem, each providing unique capabilities to enhance network configuration, DNS management, and content delivery. VPC offers customizable and secure virtual networks, Route 53 ensures reliable and efficient DNS routing, and CloudFront delivers content with low latency and high performance. Together, these services enable organizations to build scalable, resilient, and high-performance network architectures that meet diverse application requirements and optimize user experiences.

10.5 Lab Exercise: Launching an EC2 Instance and Connecting via SSH

Amazon EC2 (Elastic Compute Cloud) provides resizable compute capacity in the cloud, making it easy to launch and manage virtual servers. This step-by-step guide will walk you through the process of launching an EC2 instance and connecting to it via SSH.

Step 1: Sign In to the AWS Management Console
- Open your web browser and navigate to the AWS Management Console.
- Enter your email address and password, then click "Sign In."

Step 2: Navigate to the EC2 Dashboard
- In the AWS Management Console, find the "Services" menu at the top and select "EC2" under the "Compute" section.
- This will take you to the EC2 Dashboard.

Step 3: Launch an EC2 Instance

In the EC2 Dashboard, click the "Launch Instance" button.

Choose an Amazon Machine Image (AMI): Select an AMI that suits your needs. For example, you can choose the "Amazon Linux 2 AMI (HVM), SSD Volume Type."

Choose an Instance Type: Select an instance type based on your requirements. For this example, choose the "t2.micro" instance type, which is eligible for the AWS Free Tier.

Configure Instance Details:

- Click "Next: Configure Instance Details."
- Leave the default settings for this tutorial and click "Next: Add Storage."

Add Storage:

The default storage configuration is typically sufficient. Click "Next: Add Tags."

Add Tags: You can add tags to organize your instances. For this tutorial, you can skip this step by clicking "Next: Configure Security Group."

Configure Security Group:

144

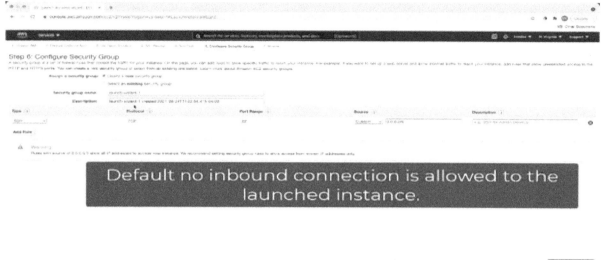

Default no inbound connection is allowed to the launched instance.

Default all outbound connections are allowed from the launched instance.

- Create a new security group or select an existing one.
- Add a rule to allow SSH access. Set the "Type" to "SSH," "Protocol" to "TCP," "Port Range" to "22," and "Source" to "My IP" to restrict access to your IP address.

Click "**Review and Launch.**"
- Review Instance Launch:
- Review your instance configuration and click "Launch."

Select or Create a Key Pair:

- In the "Select an existing key pair or create a new key pair" dialog box, select "Create a new key pair."
- Enter a key pair name and click "Download Key Pair." Save the key pair (.pem) file in a secure location on your computer.
- Click "Launch Instances."

Step 4: Connect to Your EC2 Instance via SSH

Locate Your Instance:
- In the EC2 Dashboard, click "View Instances" to see your running instances.
- Find the instance you just launched and note its "Instance ID" and "Public IPv4 address."

Open a Terminal: On your computer, open a terminal (or Command Prompt on Windows).

Change Permissions for Your Key Pair File: Ensure that your private key file (.pem) has the correct permissions. Use the following command:

```
chmod 400 /path/to/your-key-pair.pem
```

Connect to Your Instance: Use the SSH command to connect to your instance. Replace /path/to/your-key-pair.pem with the path to your key pair file and ec2-user@your-public-ip with the appropriate username and public IP address.

```
ssh -i /path/to/your-key-pair.pem ec2-user@your-public-ip
```

For Amazon Linux, the default username is ec2-user. For other AMIs, the username may vary (e.g., ubuntu for Ubuntu instances).

Example:

```
ssh -i /Users/yourusername/Downloads/my-key-pair.pem ec2-user@54.123.45.67
```

Accept the SSH Connection: The first time you connect, you may see a message asking if you want to continue connecting. Type yes and press Enter.

You have successfully launched an EC2 instance and connected to it via SSH. You can now use this instance to deploy and manage your applications in the cloud. Make sure to terminate the instance when you are finished to avoid incurring charges.

Connect to EC2 From AWS Management Console

You can also connect to an EC2 instance from the AWS Management console.

list of running EC2 instance

Amazon EC2 Instance Connect

Amazon EC2 Instance Connect provides a straightforward way to connect to your Linux instances using Secure Shell (SSH). With EC2 Instance Connect, you use AWS IAM policies to control SSH access to your instances. Thus, it removes the need to share and manage SSH keys.

EC2 User data

It is used as bootstrap script to configure EC2 instance at launch. You can specify user data to configure an instance or run a configuration script during launch. The one advantage of User Data is if you launch more than one instance at a time, the user data is available to all the instances in that reservation.

The user data to set up a web server on the EC2 instance is given below:

```
#!/bin/bash
sudo yum update -y
sudo yum install -y httpd
sudo systemctl start httpd
```

In this, the first line is about using the bash shell. The second line is to update OS – it's always good practice to update the OS. In case if there is any security patch that has been released but is not yet available in AMI, which could lead to potential security risks. The third line is about installing an HTTP web server. And the last line starts the server. Additionally, whenever this EC2 instance stops and starts again, the httpd daemon will be started, which means the webserver will be started automatically at the server startup.

KEY POINTS

- You can bootstrap EC2 instances using an EC2 User data script. Bootstrapping means launching commands when a machine starts. The script only run once at the launch of the instance.
- EC2 user data is used to automate boot tasks such as applying OS updates, installing software, downloading common files from the internet, or any other tasks you would like to perform at instance launch.
- The EC2 User Data script runs as the root user.

10.6 Related YouTube Videos
- EC2 Tutorial: https://youtu.be/3-eR1OU3dUU
- Amazon Route 53 Tutorial: https://youtu.be/Q7tZsTqo8Oc

10.7 Chapter Review Questions
Question 1:
Which of the following AWS services is best suited for deploying and managing web applications with minimal infrastructure management?
    A. Amazon EC2
    B. AWS Lambda
    C. AWS Elastic Beanstalk
    D. Amazon S3

Question 2:
Which storage service is designed for infrequent data access, offering cost-effective long-term storage?
    A. Amazon S3
    B. Amazon EBS
    C. Amazon Glacier
    D. AWS Storage Gateway

Question 3:

Which of the following is a managed relational database service provided by AWS?
- A. Amazon DynamoDB
- B. Amazon Redshift
- C. Amazon RDS
- D. Amazon ElastiCache

Question 4:
Which networking service allows you to connect securely to your AWS resources using a virtual network?
- A. Amazon Route 53
- B. Amazon CloudFront
- C. AWS Direct Connect
- D. Amazon VPC

Question 5:
What is the primary function of AWS Lambda?
- A. Hosting containerized applications
- B. Running code in response to events without provisioning servers
- C. Providing block storage for EC2 instances
- D. Managing data transfer between AWS regions

Question 6:
Which database service is designed for real-time applications requiring single-digit millisecond latency?
- A. Amazon RDS
- B. Amazon DynamoDB
- C. Amazon Redshift
- D. Amazon Aurora

Question 7:
Amazon CloudFront primarily serves what purpose?
- A. Securely connecting users to AWS services
- B. Managing domain name system (DNS) settings
- C. Delivering content to users with low latency using a global network
- D. Routing application traffic based on geographic location

Question 8:
Which AWS service is used to register domain names and manage DNS records?
- A. AWS Global Accelerator
- B. Amazon CloudFront
- C. Amazon Route 53
- D. AWS Directory Service

Question 9:
What is the key feature of Amazon EC2 that allows users to scale their applications dynamically?
- A. Elastic Load Balancing
- B. Auto Scaling
- C. Elastic Beanstalk

D. Reserved Instances

Question 10:
During the lab exercise of launching an EC2 instance, which protocol is typically used to securely connect to the instance?

    A. FTP
    B. HTTP
    C. SSH
    D. RDP

10.8 Answers to Chapter Review Questions

1. C. AWS Elastic Beanstalk
Explanation: AWS Elastic Beanstalk simplifies application deployment and management by automatically handling the infrastructure, including scaling, monitoring, and patching. It is ideal for developers looking to focus on writing code without managing resources.

2. C. Amazon Glacier
Explanation: Amazon Glacier is designed for long-term data storage and infrequent access. It offers low-cost storage for archival and backup purposes with retrieval options ranging from minutes to hours.

3. C. Amazon RDS
Explanation: Amazon Relational Database Service (RDS) is a managed service that provides scalable relational databases with automated setup, backups, and maintenance, supporting engines like MySQL, PostgreSQL, and SQL Server.

4. D. Amazon VPC
Explanation: Amazon Virtual Private Cloud (VPC) enables you to provision a logically isolated section of the AWS Cloud, allowing secure access to resources and control over networking configurations.

5. B. Running code in response to events without provisioning servers
Explanation: AWS Lambda is a serverless compute service that automatically executes your code in response to events and scales based on demand, eliminating the need to manage servers.

6. B. Amazon DynamoDB
Explanation: Amazon DynamoDB is a fully managed NoSQL database designed for applications requiring fast and predictable performance with single-digit millisecond latency.

7. C. Delivering content to users with low latency using a global network
Explanation: Amazon CloudFront is a Content Delivery Network (CDN) service that accelerates the delivery of static and dynamic content, such as web pages, videos, and APIs, to users through its global edge locations.

8. C. Amazon Route 53
Explanation: Amazon Route 53 is a scalable and highly available domain name system (DNS) web service that allows you to register domain names and manage DNS settings for routing traffic.

9. B. Auto Scaling
Explanation: Auto Scaling in Amazon EC2 dynamically adjusts the number of instances based on traffic demand, ensuring performance optimization and cost-efficiency.

10. C. SSH
Explanation: Secure Shell (SSH) is the protocol used to securely connect to an EC2 instance, allowing you to remotely manage and access your server using encrypted communication.

Chapter 11. AWS Identity and Access Management (IAM)

As organizations move to the cloud, secure access management becomes a top priority for protecting resources and data. AWS Identity and Access Management (IAM) is a fundamental service that enables organizations to securely manage access to AWS services and resources. This chapter introduces IAM and explores how to define, control, and audit user and application permissions effectively in AWS environments.

We begin with an introduction to IAM, laying the foundation for understanding how to manage identities and permissions within AWS. The chapter dives into IAM users and groups, explaining their roles, creation, and the best practices for organizing access.

Next, we explore IAM roles, which provide a mechanism for delegating permissions to applications, users, and services. Through practical labs, readers will gain hands-on experience in creating IAM roles, users, and groups for effective delegation and access control.

A key focus is on IAM policies and permissions, where we break down the structure of policies, how to write and attach them, and the difference between managed and inline policies. Real-world scenarios and lab exercises provide practical insights into policy management.

The chapter also emphasizes security best practices with IAM, including implementing the principle of least privilege, enabling Multi-Factor Authentication (MFA) for added security, and validating policies using the IAM Policy Simulator. Finally, we cover the importance of managing access keys to secure programmatic access to AWS resources.

This chapter equips readers with the knowledge and skills to implement robust identity and access management in AWS, ensuring secure, efficient, and scalable access control across cloud environments.

11.1 Introduction to IAM

AWS Identity and Access Management (IAM) is a comprehensive service that enables you to securely control access to AWS services and resources. IAM allows you to create and manage AWS users and groups and use permissions to allow and deny their access to AWS resources.

This section will provide an in-depth overview of IAM, highlighting its key components and functionalities.

Key Components of IAM

IAM Users: IAM users represent individuals or applications that need access to your AWS resources. Each user is given a unique identity within the AWS account and can be assigned specific permissions. Users can have login credentials for the AWS Management Console and access keys for programmatic access via the AWS CLI, SDKs, or APIs.

IAM Groups: IAM groups are collections of IAM users. Groups allow you to manage permissions for multiple users simultaneously. By assigning permissions to a group, all users within that group inherit those permissions, simplifying the management of user rights.

IAM Roles: IAM roles are identities that you can create in your AWS account that have specific permissions. Roles are assumed by trusted entities, such as IAM users, applications, or AWS services. Unlike IAM users, roles do not have long-term credentials. Instead, temporary security credentials are generated dynamically for role sessions.

IAM Policies: IAM policies define permissions and are written in JSON. Policies specify which actions are allowed or denied for which resources. They can be attached to users, groups, or roles, thereby granting or restricting access based on the policy's specifications.

Benefits of IAM

Fine-Grained Access Control: IAM provides detailed control over who can access your AWS resources and what actions they can perform. This fine-grained access control helps enforce the principle of least privilege, ensuring that users and applications only have the permissions necessary to perform their tasks.

Enhanced Security: By managing access through IAM, you can minimize security risks. For example, you can enforce multi-factor authentication (MFA) for added security, monitor user activities, and audit access logs to detect unauthorized access attempts.

Simplified Management: IAM simplifies the management of access permissions through its user, group, and role mechanisms. This hierarchical approach allows for efficient permission management and reduces the administrative burden of maintaining individual user permissions.

Scalability and Flexibility: IAM is designed to scale with your AWS environment. Whether you have a small team or a large enterprise, IAM can accommodate your access control needs. Additionally, IAM roles and policies provide the flexibility to integrate with various AWS services and external identity providers.

Example Scenario

A company uses IAM to manage access to its AWS resources. Developers are added as IAM users and grouped based on their roles, such as "Developers" and "Administrators." Each group is assigned appropriate permissions, such as allowing developers to deploy applications but restricting their access to billing information. The company also creates IAM roles for EC2 instances to securely grant them permissions to access S3 buckets and other services without embedding credentials in the application code.

IAM is a foundational service for managing access and securing your AWS environment. By understanding and effectively utilizing IAM, you can ensure that your resources are accessed securely and efficiently, adhering to best practices and compliance requirements.

11.2 IAM Users and Groups

IAM (Identity and Access Management) Users and Groups are essential elements of AWS's security framework, providing the foundation for managing access to AWS resources. These components help administrators efficiently organize, assign, and control permissions for individuals and applications within an AWS environment.

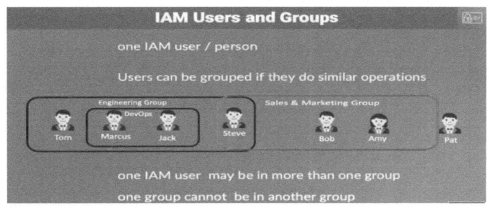

11.2.1 IAM Users

IAM users are entities created to represent individual people or applications that need access to your AWS resources. Each user has a unique set of security credentials, including a password for accessing the AWS Management Console and/or access keys for programmatic access via the AWS CLI, SDKs, or APIs.

Key Features of IAM Users
- Unique Identity: Each IAM user has a distinct identity within the AWS account, ensuring that actions taken by the user can be individually tracked and audited.
- Credential Management: IAM users can have multiple credentials, such as a password and access keys, which can be rotated or deactivated to enhance security.
- Permission Assignment: Users can be granted specific permissions through policies attached directly to the user or inherited from group memberships.

11.2.2 IAM Groups

IAM groups are collections of IAM users that simplify the management of permissions. Instead of assigning permissions to each user individually, you can assign policies to a group, and all users in the group inherit those permissions.

Key Features of IAM Groups
- Simplified Management: Groups make it easier to manage permissions for multiple users simultaneously, reducing administrative overhead.
- Consistent Permissions: Ensures that all members of a group have the same permissions, promoting consistency and reducing the risk of errors.

- Scalability: Easily scale permission management by adding users to groups based on their roles or responsibilities.

11.2.3 Best Practices

Principle of Least Privilege: Grant users and groups only the permissions they need to perform their tasks.

Use Groups for Permissions: Assign permissions to groups rather than individual users to simplify management.

Enable MFA: Implement Multi-Factor Authentication (MFA) for an additional layer of security for user access.

IAM users and groups are fundamental to managing access control in AWS. By creating users and organizing them into groups, administrators can efficiently assign and manage permissions, ensuring secure and compliant access to AWS resources. This structured approach not only enhances security but also simplifies administrative tasks, making it easier to maintain a secure and well-organized AWS environment.

11.3 IAM Roles: Understanding and Creating Roles for Delegation of Permissions

IAM Roles are a fundamental component of AWS Identity and Access Management (IAM) that allow you to delegate permissions to AWS services and applications. Unlike IAM users, roles do not have long-term credentials. Instead, they provide temporary security credentials for authentication and authorization, making them ideal for granting permissions to resources without sharing credentials.

11.3.1 Understanding IAM Roles

IAM roles are similar to IAM users in that they are AWS identities with permissions policies that determine what the identity can and cannot do in AWS. However, roles are intended to be assumable by anyone who needs them, including AWS services, applications, or users from other accounts.

Key Characteristics of IAM Roles

- **Temporary Credentials:** Roles provide temporary security credentials, reducing the risk of credential exposure.
- **Cross-Account Access:** Roles enable secure access to resources across AWS accounts.
- **Service Access:** Roles allow AWS services to interact with other AWS resources on behalf of a user or application.
- **Enhanced Security:** By using roles, you can avoid embedding long-term credentials in your application code, enhancing security.

11.3.2 Creating IAM Roles

Creating IAM roles involves defining the trusted entities that can assume the role and attaching the necessary permissions policies.

Steps to Create an IAM Role

Sign In to AWS Management Console: Access the IAM Dashboard.

Create Role: Click on "Roles" in the left navigation pane. Click the "Create role" button.

Select Trusted Entity: Choose the type of trusted entity that will assume the role. This can be an AWS service (like EC2), another AWS account, or a web identity.

Define Use Case: Select the use case for the role. For example, if you want an EC2 instance to assume the role, choose "EC2" under the AWS service.

Attach Policies: Attach permissions policies that define what the role can do. You can choose from AWS managed policies, customer managed policies, or create a custom policy.

Name and Review:
- Enter a role name, description, and tags (optional).
- Review the role configuration and click "Create role" to finalize.

Example: Creating a Role for an EC2 Instance
Scenario: You have an application running on an EC2 instance that needs to access an S3 bucket.

Steps:

Sign In to AWS Management Console: Access the IAM Dashboard.
Create Role: Click on "Roles" and then "Create role."
Select Trusted Entity: Choose "AWS service" and then select "EC2" as the use case.
Attach Policies: Attach the "AmazonS3ReadOnlyAccess" policy to allow read-only access to S3 buckets.
Name and Review:
- Name the role "EC2S3ReadOnlyRole."
- Review the configuration and click "Create role."

Assign Role to EC2 Instance:
Navigate to EC2 Dashboard: Select the EC2 instance you want to assign the role to.
Actions Menu: Click "Actions," then "Security," and select "Modify IAM Role."
Attach Role: Choose the "EC2S3ReadOnlyRole" from the list and click "Update IAM role."

IAM roles are crucial for delegating permissions securely within AWS environments. By understanding and creating IAM roles, you can enhance security, enable cross-account access, and allow AWS services to interact with each other seamlessly. This approach minimizes the risk of credential exposure and ensures that your applications and services have the necessary permissions to function effectively.

11.3.3 Lab Exercise: Creating IAM Users and Groups
This lab exercise will guide you through the process of creating IAM users and groups in the AWS Management Console. You will learn how to assign permissions and manage access to AWS resources effectively.

Step 1: Sign In to the AWS Management Console
- Open your web browser and navigate to the AWS Management Console.

- Enter your email address and password, then click "Sign In."

Step 2: Navigate to the IAM Dashboard

- In the AWS Management Console, click on "Services" in the top navigation bar.
- Under the "Security, Identity, & Compliance" section, select "IAM."

Step 3: Create an IAM Group
- In the IAM Dashboard, click on "Groups" in the left navigation pane.
- Click the "Create New Group" button.

Set Group Details:
- Enter a name for the new group (e.g., "Developers").
- Click "Next Step" to proceed.

Attach Policies:

- Select policies to attach to the group. For this exercise, choose "AmazonS3ReadOnlyAccess" to grant read-only access to S3 buckets.
- Click "Next Step."

Review and Create Group:
- Review the group details and attached policies.
- Click "Create Group."

Step 4: Create an IAM User

- In the IAM Dashboard, click on "Users" in the left navigation pane.
- Click the "Add user" button.

Set User Details:
- Enter a username (e.g., "dev-user1").
- Select the access type: choose "Programmatic access" for CLI/SDK/API access, and/or "AWS Management Console access" for console access.
- If enabling console access, set a custom password or allow AWS to generate a password.
- Click "Next: Permissions."

Set Permissions:
- Select "Add user to group."
- Choose the group you created earlier (e.g., "Developers").
- Click "Next: Tags."

Add Tags (Optional):

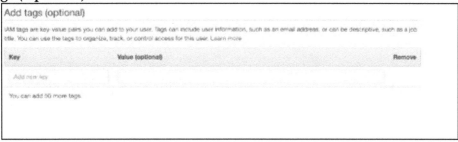

- You can add tags to organize users. This step is optional.
- Click "Next: Review."

Review and Create User:
- Review the user details and group membership.
- Click "Create user."

Step 5: Download User Credentials
- After creating the user, download the .csv file containing the user's access keys and login credentials.
- Store these credentials securely, as they will not be available for download again.

Step 6: Verify the User's Permissions
- Sign out of the AWS Management Console.
- Sign in again using the new user's credentials (username and password).
- Navigate to the S3 service to verify that the user has read-only access to S3 buckets.

Step 7: Manage the IAM User and Group
Modify Permissions: To change the permissions of the group, navigate to the "Groups" section, select the group, and modify the attached policies.
Add/Remove Users from the Group: To add or remove users from the group, navigate to the "Groups" section, select the group, and manage the group membership.

In this lab exercise, you have successfully created an IAM group and an IAM user, assigned the user to the group, and verified the permissions. This process helps in managing access control efficiently by using groups to assign permissions and users to grant individual access. This approach ensures a secure and organized AWS environment.

11.4 IAM Policies and Permissions
IAM policies and permissions are crucial components of AWS Identity and Access Management (IAM), enabling fine-grained control over access to AWS resources. Policies define permissions in a JSON document format, specifying which actions are allowed or denied for which resources. Understanding and effectively managing IAM policies and permissions is essential for maintaining a secure and compliant AWS environment.

11.4.1 IAM Policies
IAM policies are JSON documents that define permissions for actions on AWS resources. These policies can be attached to IAM users, groups, or roles to grant or restrict access based on the specified permissions.

Types of IAM Policies

Managed Policies

AWS Managed Policies: These are pre-defined policies created and managed by AWS. They provide permissions for common use cases and can be attached to multiple users, groups, or roles. Customer Managed Policies: These are policies created and managed by the AWS account owner. They offer more customization and control over permissions compared to AWS managed policies.

Inline Policies

Inline policies are embedded directly within a single user, group, or role. They offer a one-to-one relationship between the policy and the entity, providing precise control over permissions.

11.4.2 Policy Structure

IAM policies consist of one or more statements, each including:
- Effect: Specifies whether the statement allows or denies access (e.g., "Allow" or "Deny").
- Action: Lists the specific actions that are allowed or denied (e.g., "s3
- ," "ec2
- ").
- Resource: Defines the AWS resources to which the actions apply (e.g., specific S3 buckets or EC2 instances).
- Condition (Optional): Specifies conditions that must be met for the policy to take effect (e.g., IP address range, time of day).

Example Policy:

```
1.  {
2.      "Version": "2012-10-17",
3.      "Statement": [
4.          {
5.              "Effect": "Allow",
6.              "Action": [
7.                  "s3:ListBucket",
8.                  "s3:GetObject"
9.              ],
10.             "Resource": [
11.                 "arn:aws:s3:::example-bucket",
12.                 "arn:aws:s3:::example-bucket/*"
13.             ]
14.         }
15.     ]
16. }
17.
```

This policy allows the user to list objects in the specified S3 bucket and get objects from that bucket.

11.4.3 IAM Permissions

Permissions are granted to IAM entities (users, groups, and roles) through policies. These permissions determine what actions the entities can perform on specific AWS resources.

Assigning Permissions

- Attach Managed Policies: Attach AWS managed or customer managed policies to users, groups, or roles to grant predefined permissions.
- Create and Attach Inline Policies: Create inline policies for specific users, groups, or roles when more granular control is needed.
- Policy Evaluation: AWS evaluates all policies attached to the user (or the group to which the user belongs) and roles assumed by the user to determine the final set of permissions.

Best Practices
- Principle of Least Privilege: Grant only the permissions necessary for users to perform their tasks. Avoid granting excessive permissions.
- Use Groups for Permissions: Assign permissions to groups rather than individual users to simplify management.
- Monitor and Audit: Regularly review policies and permissions using AWS CloudTrail and IAM Access Analyzer to ensure compliance and security.
- Utilize AWS Managed Policies: Start with AWS managed policies for common use cases and create custom policies as needed.

11.4.4 Example Scenario
A company needs to provide developers with read-only access to S3 buckets and full access to DynamoDB tables. The company creates a group called "Developers" and attaches an AWS managed policy for read-only access to S3 and a customer managed policy for full access to DynamoDB. Developers are then added to the "Developers" group, inheriting the specified permissions.

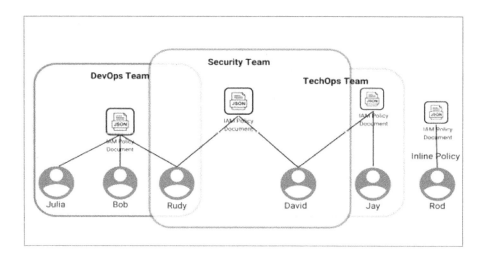

This diagram illustrates a structured approach to managing permissions in AWS Identity and Access Management (IAM) by associating policies with teams and users. It features three groups: the DevOps Team, Security Team, and TechOps Team, each of which has specific IAM managed policies attached. Members of these teams inherit permissions from the policies associated with their group. For instance, Julia and Bob, part of the DevOps Team, share permissions defined in a managed policy (depicted by the JSON document icon) that is centrally managed and reusable. Similarly, the TechOps Team, which includes David and Jay, inherits permissions from another managed policy assigned to their group.

The Security Team stands out because it overlaps with the DevOps and TechOps Teams, indicating shared responsibilities. Members like Rudy and David belong to the Security Team and inherit permissions from its managed policies while also retaining the permissions of their respective secondary groups. This overlap highlights the flexibility of IAM in allowing users to be part of multiple groups and gain permissions from all relevant policies.

On the other hand, Rod has an inline policy directly attached to his user account. Unlike managed policies, inline policies are specific to a single user and cannot be reused across multiple accounts. This is ideal for tailoring permissions to unique, non-replicable roles. Overall, this diagram showcases the importance of using group-based managed policies for scalable and consistent permissions management while leveraging inline policies for unique, custom use cases. The approach ensures secure, organized access control, particularly in environments where users belong to multiple teams or require tailored permissions.

IAM policies and permissions are fundamental to controlling access within AWS. By creating and managing policies effectively, you can ensure that users, groups, and roles have the appropriate permissions to perform their tasks securely and efficiently. Implementing best practices such as the principle of least privilege and regular auditing helps maintain a secure and compliant AWS environment.

11.4.5 IAM Policies: Writing and attaching policies to users, groups, and roles

IAM Policies are JSON documents that define permissions for actions on AWS resources. Writing and attaching policies to users, groups, and roles is a fundamental aspect of managing access control in AWS. This ensures that entities have the appropriate permissions to perform their tasks securely and efficiently.

11.4.5.1 Writing IAM Policies
Policy Structure
An IAM policy consists of one or more statements, each including:

- **Effect:** Specifies whether the statement allows or denies access (e.g., "Allow" or "Deny").
- **Action**: Lists the specific actions that are allowed or denied (e.g., "s3," "ec2").
- **Resource:** Defines the AWS resources to which the actions apply (e.g., specific S3 buckets or EC2 instances).
- **Condition (Optional):** Specifies conditions that must be met for the policy to take effect (e.g., IP address range, time of day).

Example Policy

```
{
  "Version": "2012-10-17",
  "Statement": [
    {
      "Effect": "Allow",
      "Action": [
        "s3:ListBucket",
        "s3:GetObject"
      ],
      "Resource": [
```

```
            "arn:aws:s3:::example-bucket",
            "arn:aws:s3:::example-bucket/*"
        ]
    }
  ]
}
```

This policy allows the user to list objects in the specified S3 bucket and get objects from the bucket.

11.4.5.2 Attaching Policies to Users, Groups, and Roles
Attaching Policies to Users
IAM users are individual identities that represent people or applications. Attaching policies directly to users is useful for granting specific permissions that are not shared by other users.

Steps to Attach Policies to Users
- Sign In to AWS Management Console: Access the IAM Dashboard.
- Select User: Navigate to "Users" and select the user to whom you want to attach a policy.
- Add Permissions: Click on the "Add permissions" button.
- Attach Policies: Choose to attach existing managed policies or create an inline policy.
- Review and Apply: Review the policy settings and apply them to the user.

Attaching Policies to Groups
IAM groups are collections of users that share the same permissions. Attaching policies to groups simplifies the management of permissions for multiple users.

Steps to Attach Policies to Groups
- Sign In to AWS Management Console: Access the IAM Dashboard.
- Select Group: Navigate to "Groups" and select the group to which you want to attach a policy.
- Add Permissions: Click on the "Attach policy" button.
- Attach Policies: Choose from existing managed policies or create a custom policy.
- Review and Apply: Review the policy settings and apply them to the group.

Attaching Policies to Roles
IAM roles are used to delegate permissions to AWS services and applications. Roles provide temporary security credentials and are assumed by trusted entities.

Steps to Attach Policies to Roles
- Sign In to AWS Management Console: Access the IAM Dashboard.
- Select Role: Navigate to "Roles" and select the role to which you want to attach a policy.
- Add Permissions: Click on the "Attach policies" button.
- Attach Policies: Choose from existing managed policies or create an inline policy.
- Review and Apply: Review the policy settings and apply them to the role.

11.4.5.3 Best Practices for Writing and Attaching Policies
- **Principle of Least Privilege:** Grant only the permissions necessary for users, groups, or roles to perform their tasks. Avoid providing excessive permissions that could be exploited.

- **Use Managed Policies:** Start with AWS managed policies for common use cases to leverage AWS's expertise in security best practices. Customize and create customer managed policies as needed.
- **Regularly Review and Update Policies:** Regularly review policies and permissions to ensure they align with current security requirements and best practices. Update policies as needed to address new security threats or changes in organizational needs.
- **Monitor and Audit:** Use AWS CloudTrail and IAM Access Analyzer to monitor and audit user activities and policy effectiveness. These tools help identify potential security issues and ensure compliance with security policies.

11.4.5.4 Example Scenario

A company needs to provide developers with read-only access to S3 buckets and full access to DynamoDB tables. The company creates a group called "Developers" and attaches an AWS managed policy for read-only access to S3 and a customer managed policy for full access to DynamoDB. Developers are then added to the "Developers" group, inheriting the specified permissions.

Writing and attaching IAM policies to users, groups, and roles is essential for managing access control in AWS. By creating and managing policies effectively, organizations can ensure that entities have the appropriate permissions to perform their tasks securely and efficiently. Implementing best practices such as the principle of least privilege and regular auditing helps maintain a secure and compliant AWS environment.

11.4.6 Managed vs. Inline Policies

IAM policies in AWS are crucial for defining and managing access permissions to various resources. They can be categorized into managed policies and inline policies, each serving distinct purposes with unique benefits.

Managed policies come in two forms: AWS managed policies and customer managed policies. AWS managed policies are pre-defined by AWS, designed for common use cases, and are automatically updated by AWS to incorporate best practices. They are ideal for quickly granting standard permissions across multiple users, groups, or roles without the need for custom policy creation. Customer managed policies, on the other hand, offer full customization and are created and maintained by AWS account owners. These policies provide granular control and can be tailored to meet specific organizational needs, making them suitable for complex environments that require precise access control.

Differences

Inline policies differ significantly as they are embedded directly within a single user, group, or role. Unlike managed policies, inline policies are not standalone and are tightly coupled with the entity they are attached to, providing fine-grained control over permissions. This one-to-one relationship makes inline policies ideal for scenarios where unique permissions are required that should not be shared with other entities. They are particularly useful for granting temporary access or for specialized roles that require specific permissions not applicable to others. However, the management of inline policies can be more time-consuming as they need to be individually managed for each entity, lacking the reusability offered by managed policies.

Use Cases

In practice, managed policies are used for consistency and ease of management, allowing permissions to be applied broadly across multiple users, groups, or roles. For example, using AWS managed policies like AmazonS3ReadOnlyAccess for read-only access to S3 buckets can simplify permission management across an organization. Customer managed policies come into play when there is a need for tailored permissions, such as granting specific access to certain resources based on organizational security policies. Inline policies are best suited for specific, often temporary, needs. For instance, granting a developer temporary full access to an S3 bucket for a project can be efficiently handled with an inline policy attached directly to the developer's user account.

Overall, understanding the differences and appropriate use cases for managed and inline policies helps in implementing effective access management strategies, ensuring that permissions are granted securely and efficiently in an AWS environment.

11.4.7 Lab Exercise: Creating and Attaching IAM Policies

This lab exercise will guide you through the process of creating and attaching IAM policies to users, groups, and roles in the AWS Management Console. You will learn how to define permissions and apply them to entities for controlled access to AWS resources.

Step 1: Sign In to the AWS Management Console
- Open your web browser and navigate to the AWS Management Console.
- Enter your email address and password, then click "Sign In."

Step 2: Navigate to the IAM Dashboard
- In the AWS Management Console, click on "Services" in the top navigation bar.
- Under the "Security, Identity, & Compliance" section, select "IAM."

Step 3: Create a Customer Managed Policy
- In the IAM Dashboard, click on "Policies" in the left navigation pane.
- Click the "Create policy" button.

Step 4: Define the Policy
- Choose a Service: Click on the "Choose a service" link and select a service for the policy. For example, select "S3" for Amazon S3.
- Specify Actions: Under the "Actions" section, choose the actions you want to allow. For example, select "ListBucket" and "GetObject" for read-only access to S3.
- Specify Resources: Under the "Resources" section, specify the resources to which the actions apply. For example, click "Add ARN" and enter the ARN of the S3 bucket.
- Add Conditions (Optional): You can add conditions to the policy if needed. This step is optional and can be used to further restrict access based on specific criteria.

Step 5: Review and Create the Policy
- Click the "Review policy" button.
- Name and Description:
    - Enter a name for the policy (e.g., "ReadOnlyAccessToS3").
    - Provide a description for the policy.
- Review the policy summary to ensure it meets your requirements.

- Click the "Create policy" button to finalize.

Step 6: Attach the Policy to a User
- Navigate to the "Users" section in the IAM Dashboard.
- Select the user to whom you want to attach the policy.
- Click on the "Add permissions" button.
- Attach Policies:
    - Choose "Attach policies directly."
    - Search for the policy you created (e.g., "ReadOnlyAccessToS3") and select it.
- Click the "Next: Review" button and then the "Add permissions" button to attach the policy.

Step 7: Attach the Policy to a Group
- Navigate to the "Groups" section in the IAM Dashboard.
- Select the group to which you want to attach the policy.
- Click the "Attach policy" button.
- Attach Policies: Search for the policy you created (e.g., "ReadOnlyAccessToS3") and select it.
- Click the "Next: Review" button and then the "Attach policy" button to apply the policy to the group.

Step 8: Attach the Policy to a Role
- Navigate to the "Roles" section in the IAM Dashboard.
- Select the role to which you want to attach the policy.
- Click the "Attach policies" button.
- Attach Policies: Search for the policy you created (e.g., "ReadOnlyAccessToS3") and select it.
- Click the "Next: Review" button and then the "Attach policy" button to apply the policy to the role.

Step 9: Verify the Policy Application
For Users:
- Sign in to the AWS Management Console using the user credentials.
- Navigate to the S3 service and verify that the user has read-only access to the specified S3 bucket.
For Groups:
- Add a user to the group and verify that the user inherits the group's permissions.
- Sign in with the user credentials and test access to the S3 bucket.
For Roles:
- Assume the role in the AWS Management Console or via the AWS CLI.
- Verify that the role has the specified permissions to access the S3 bucket.

11.5 Security Best Practices with IAM

Implementing security best practices with AWS Identity and Access Management (IAM) is essential for maintaining a secure and compliant AWS environment. By following these best practices, you can ensure that access to your AWS resources is granted appropriately and securely, minimizing the risk of unauthorized access and enhancing the overall security posture of your AWS infrastructure.

11.5.1 Principle of Least Privilege

The principle of least privilege is a fundamental security concept that involves granting users and roles only the permissions they need to perform their tasks and no more. This minimizes the risk of unauthorized access and potential damage from compromised credentials or malicious actions.

Key Concepts

Define Specific Permissions: When creating IAM policies, define specific permissions for each user and role. Avoid using broad permissions that grant access to all resources or actions within a service. Instead, specify the exact actions and resources needed. For example, rather than granting full access to S3 (s3:*), specify actions like s3:ListBucket and s3:GetObject for a particular bucket.

Use Managed Policies Wisely: While AWS managed policies can simplify permissions management, they might be broader than necessary. Evaluate these policies carefully and, when possible, create custom policies that precisely define the required permissions.

Regularly Review and Adjust Permissions: Permissions should be reviewed regularly to ensure they still align with users' job functions. Adjust or revoke permissions that are no longer necessary. This practice is particularly important when users change roles within an organization.

Implement Conditional Access: Use conditions in IAM policies to add an extra layer of security. Conditions can restrict access based on factors such as IP address, time of day, or whether the request is made through a secure connection (HTTPS).

Use IAM Groups and Roles: Organize permissions by assigning policies to IAM groups and roles rather than individual users. This approach simplifies management and ensures that users in the same role have consistent permissions.

Example Scenario

Consider an organization with developers who need access to specific S3 buckets for reading log files. Instead of granting s3:* permissions to the developers, a custom policy is created with the following actions:

```
1. {
2.     "Version": "2012-10-17",
3.     "Statement": [
4.         {
5.             "Effect": "Allow",
6.             "Action": [
7.                 "s3:ListBucket",
8.                 "s3:GetObject"
9.             ],
10.            "Resource": [
11.                "arn:aws:s3:::example-log-bucket",
12.                "arn:aws:s3:::example-log-bucket/*"
13.            ]
14.        }
15.    ]
16. }
17.
```

This policy ensures that developers can only list and get objects from the specific example-log-bucket and nothing else.

Benefits of the Principle of Least Privilege
- Reduced Attack Surface: Limiting permissions reduces the number of potential entry points for attackers.
- Minimized Damage from Compromised Accounts: If an account is compromised, the attacker will have limited access, reducing the potential impact.
- Compliance and Auditability: Ensuring that users have only necessary permissions helps meet regulatory requirements and simplifies audits.
- Enhanced Security Posture: A disciplined approach to permissions management enhances the overall security of the AWS environment.

Implementing the principle of least privilege is crucial for maintaining a secure AWS environment. By granting users and roles only the permissions they need, organizations can reduce the risk of unauthorized access, limit potential damage from compromised accounts, and ensure compliance with security policies and regulations. Regular reviews and adjustments to permissions, combined with the use of managed and custom policies, are essential practices for adhering to this principle.

11.5.2 MFA (Multi-Factor Authentication)
Multi-Factor Authentication (MFA) adds an extra layer of security to your AWS account by requiring not only a username and password but also an additional factor of authentication. This second factor can be something the user possesses, such as a mobile device or hardware token, making it significantly harder for unauthorized users to gain access to your account.

Key Concepts
Importance of MFA: MFA enhances security by combining two different types of authentication factors:
- Something You Know: Typically a password or PIN.
- Something You Have: A physical device like a mobile phone or hardware token that generates a time-based one-time password (TOTP).

Types of MFA Devices:
- Virtual MFA Devices: Applications such as Google Authenticator or Authy that generate TOTP codes.
- Hardware MFA Devices: Physical tokens like YubiKey that generate TOTP codes.
- SMS MFA: Sends a verification code via SMS to the user's mobile phone.
- Universal 2nd Factor (U2F) Security Key: Uses devices like YubiKey for U2F.

Benefits of MFA
- Enhanced Security: MFA significantly increases the security of your AWS account by requiring a second form of authentication.
- Protection Against Compromised Credentials: Even if a password is compromised, unauthorized access is unlikely without the second factor.
- Compliance: MFA helps meet regulatory requirements and security best practices, ensuring that your AWS environment adheres to industry standards.

Example Scenario

A company mandates MFA for all users with access to the AWS Management Console to enhance security. By implementing MFA, the company ensures that even if a user's password is compromised, the account remains secure due to the additional authentication step.

Setting up MFA is a critical step in enhancing the security of your AWS environment. By requiring multiple forms of authentication, you add an additional layer of protection that helps prevent unauthorized access, even if a password is compromised. Regularly reviewing and enforcing MFA policies for all users, especially those with elevated permissions, is essential for maintaining a secure AWS infrastructure.

11.5.3 IAM Policy Simulator: Testing and validating IAM policies.

The IAM Policy Simulator is a valuable tool provided by AWS that allows you to test and validate IAM policies before applying them to users, groups, or roles. This tool helps ensure that policies grant the intended permissions and do not inadvertently allow or deny access to AWS resources.

Key Features

Testing Policies: The IAM Policy Simulator enables you to simulate the effects of IAM policies to determine if they provide the necessary permissions. You can test policies attached to IAM users, groups, or roles by simulating various actions and access requests. This helps identify potential issues or gaps in the policy before it is deployed in a live environment.

Validating Permissions: The simulator allows you to validate permissions by running simulations based on real AWS actions and resources. You can input specific actions, resources, and conditions to see whether the policy permits or denies the requested access. This helps in fine-tuning policies to ensure they align with your security requirements and access control objectives.

Simulating Different Scenarios: The IAM Policy Simulator supports the simulation of various scenarios, including testing multiple policies simultaneously and checking the combined effect of policies attached to a user, group, or role. This is particularly useful for complex environments where multiple policies may interact.

Example Scenario

Suppose you have a custom policy attached to a role that grants read-only access to an S3 bucket but denies access to delete objects. You want to verify that the policy behaves as expected. Using the IAM Policy Simulator, you select the role and configure the simulation to test s3:GetObject and s3:DeleteObject actions on the specified S3 bucket. After running the simulation, the results should indicate that s3:GetObject is allowed and s3:DeleteObject is denied, confirming the policy's correctness.

Benefits of Using the IAM Policy Simulator

- Risk Reduction: By validating policies before implementation, you reduce the risk of granting excessive permissions or inadvertently restricting necessary access.
- Troubleshooting: The simulator helps troubleshoot access issues by allowing you to test and refine policies in a controlled environment.

- Policy Optimization: It enables you to optimize policies to ensure they meet security best practices and organizational requirements.
- Compliance: Regularly testing and validating policies helps maintain compliance with security standards and regulatory requirements.

The IAM Policy Simulator is an essential tool for testing and validating IAM policies in AWS. By simulating different scenarios and validating permissions, you can ensure that your policies grant the appropriate level of access without introducing security risks. This proactive approach to policy management helps maintain a secure and compliant AWS environment, supporting effective access control and governance.

11.5.4 Lab Exercises
11.5.5 Enabling MFA for IAM Users
Step 1: Sign In to the AWS Management Console
- Open your web browser and navigate to the AWS Management Console.
- Enter your email address and password, then click "Sign In."

Step 2: Navigate to the IAM Dashboard
- In the AWS Management Console, click on "Services" in the top navigation bar.
- Under the "Security, Identity, & Compliance" section, select "IAM."

Step 3: Manage Users
- In the IAM Dashboard, click on "Users" in the left navigation pane.
- Select the user for whom you want to enable MFA.

Step 4: Add MFA
- Click on the "Security credentials" tab.
- In the "Assigned MFA device" section, click "Manage MFA device."

Step 5: Choose MFA Device Type
- Select the type of MFA device you want to use. For this example, we will use a virtual MFA device.
- Click "Next Step."

Step 6: Configure MFA Device
Virtual MFA Device:
- Download and install a virtual MFA application on your mobile device (e.g., Google Authenticator, Authy).
- Use the MFA application to scan the QR code displayed in the AWS Management Console. If you cannot scan the QR code, you can manually enter the secret key provided.
- The application will generate a 6-digit authentication code.

Hardware MFA Device: Follow the instructions provided by the device manufacturer to link it with your AWS account.

Step 7: Assign MFA Device

- Enter two consecutive MFA codes generated by your MFA device into the AWS Management Console.
- Click "Assign MFA" to complete the setup.

Step 8: Verify MFA Configuration
- Log out of the AWS Management Console.
- Log in again using your username and password.
- When prompted, enter the MFA code generated by your MFA device to complete the login process.

11.5.6 Testing Policies with IAM Policy Simulator.
Step 1: Access the IAM Policy Simulator
- Sign in to the AWS Management Console.
- Navigate to the IAM Dashboard.
- In the left navigation pane, select "Policy Simulator."

Step 2: Choose a Policy to Simulate
- Select the type of entity you want to simulate (User, Group, Role, or Policy).
- Choose the specific user, group, role, or policy you want to test.

Step 3: Configure the Simulation
- Select Services: Choose the AWS services you want to include in the simulation.
- Select Actions: Select the specific actions you want to test (e.g., s3:ListBucket, ec2:StartInstances).
- Specify Resources: Input the resources you want to test the actions against, using Amazon Resource Names (ARNs).
- Add Conditions (Optional): Define any conditions you want to apply to the simulation, such as IP address or time of day.

Step 4: Run the Simulation
- Click "Run Simulation" to test the selected actions and resources against the specified policy or policies.
- Review the results to see whether each action is allowed or denied.

11.6 Access Keys
Access keys are long-term credentials for an IAM user or the AWS account root user. You can use access keys to sign programmatic requests to the AWS CLI or AWS API (directly or using the AWS SDK). Access keys consist of two parts: an access key ID (for example, AKIAIOSFODNN7EXAMPLE) and a secret access key (for example, wJalrXUtnFEMI/K7MDENG/bPxRfiCYEXAMPLEKEY). As a username and password, you must use both the access key ID and secret access key together to authenticate your requests. Access Keys are secret, just like a password. You should never share them.

Use Access Key ID and Secret Access Key to access AWS resources programmatically.
Access keys are long-term credentials for an IAM user or the AWS account root user. You can use access keys to sign programmatic requests to the AWS CLI or AWS API (directly or using the AWS SDK). Access keys consist of two parts: an access key ID and a secret access key. As a user name and password, you must use both the access key ID and secret access key together to

authenticate your requests. When you create an access key pair, save the access key ID and secret access key in a secure location. The secret access key is available only at the time you create it. If you lose your secret access key, you must delete the access key and create a new one.

Use Multi Factor Authentication to access AWS resources programmatically - For increased security, AWS recommends that you configure multi-factor authentication (MFA) to help protect your AWS resources. You can enable MFA for IAM users or the AWS account root user. MFA adds extra security because it requires users to provide unique authentication from an AWS supported MFA mechanism in addition to their regular sign-in credentials when they access AWS websites or services. MFA cannot be used for programmatic access to AWS resources.

Use IAM Groups to access AWS resources programmatically - An IAM Group is a collection of IAM users. Groups let you specify permissions for multiple users, which can make it easier to manage the permissions for those users. IAM Group is for managing users and not for programmatic access to AWS resources.

11.7 Related YouTube Videos
- **What is IAM**: https://youtu.be/yIhTUN764DE
- **IAM Users and Groups:** https://youtu.be/qRGLWOMoZGI
- **IAM Users and Groups Introduction**: https://youtu.be/qRGLWOMoZGI
- **How to Create IAM Users, IAM Groups**: https://youtu.be/fWSAikOkp8I
- **AWS IAM Policy Tutorial**: https://youtu.be/H7pGGcMWnGg
- **AWS IAM Role**: https://youtu.be/2kfb3MTJ3lk
- **IAM Access Key and Secret Key**: https://youtu.be/R2tqNYyrDyQ

11.8 Chapter Review Questions
Question 1:
Which of the following is a core component of AWS Identity and Access Management (IAM)?
- A. Elastic Load Balancer
- B. IAM Users, Groups, and Roles
- C. Amazon RDS Policies
- D. AWS Billing Dashboard

Question 2:
What is the main purpose of IAM Groups?
- A. To isolate users from accessing shared resources.
- B. To define reusable collections of permissions for multiple users.
- C. To directly attach policies to AWS resources.
- D. To enable temporary access to AWS services.

Question 3:
IAM Roles are primarily designed to:
- A. Provide persistent credentials to users for access to AWS services.
- B. Group users with similar job functions.
- C. Delegate permissions to services or entities without sharing long-term credentials.
- D. Manage external billing accounts for AWS services.

Question 4:

Which component of an IAM Policy defines the resources it applies to?
    A. Action
    B. Effect
    C. Resource
    D. Condition

Question 5:
What is a key difference between Managed Policies and Inline Policies?
    A. Managed Policies are directly attached to one user, while Inline Policies are reusable.
    B. Managed Policies can be attached to multiple entities, while Inline Policies are specific to one entity.
    C. Inline Policies support versioning, whereas Managed Policies do not.
    D. Managed Policies are more secure than Inline Policies.

Question 6:
Which of the following represents a best practice for managing IAM Policies?
    A. Attach the same inline policy to multiple users for efficiency.
    B. Use inline policies over managed policies to reduce complexity.
    C. Grant permissions based on the Principle of Least Privilege.
    D. Avoid attaching policies to groups to keep them isolated.

Question 7:
What is the primary function of the IAM Policy Simulator?
    A. To automatically apply policies to new IAM users.
    B. To test and validate the effectiveness of IAM policies without affecting actual resources.
    C. To create predefined IAM policies for use in production.
    D. To convert inline policies into managed policies.

Question 8:
Which authentication method is recommended to enhance IAM security for individual users?
    A. Use of long-lived access keys.
    B. Enable Multi-Factor Authentication (MFA).
    C. Create multiple IAM users with similar roles.
    D. Assign all users administrator privileges.

Question 9:
What is the main purpose of Access Keys in IAM?
    A. To log into the AWS Management Console.
    B. To provide programmatic access to AWS services.
    C. To define permissions for a group of users.
    D. To validate MFA credentials for IAM roles.

Question 10:
What does the Principle of Least Privilege ensure when applied to IAM users, roles, and groups?
    A. Users receive permissions for all AWS services by default.
    B. Permissions are granted only for the minimum access required to perform tasks.
    C. Policies are automatically inherited by all IAM users in an account.
    D. All actions by IAM entities are logged by default.

11.9 Answers to Chapter Review Questions

1. B. IAM Users, Groups, and Roles
Explanation: These are core components of AWS IAM that help manage identities and permissions to access AWS services securely. Elastic Load Balancer, Amazon RDS Policies, and the AWS Billing Dashboard are not part of IAM's core functionality.

2. B. To define reusable collections of permissions for multiple users.
Explanation: IAM Groups allow you to assign permissions to multiple users at once, simplifying permission management. Groups do not isolate resources or directly attach policies to resources.

3. C. Delegate permissions to services or entities without sharing long-term credentials.
Explanation: IAM Roles are designed for delegation, allowing AWS services or external entities to assume the role and gain permissions temporarily without needing long-term credentials.

4. C. Resource
Explanation: The "Resource" element in an IAM policy specifies the AWS resources the policy applies to, such as an S3 bucket or an EC2 instance.

5. B. Managed Policies can be attached to multiple entities, while Inline Policies are specific to one entity.
Explanation: Managed Policies are reusable and can be attached to multiple users, groups, or roles. Inline Policies, on the other hand, are embedded directly into a single user, group, or role.

6. C. Grant permissions based on the Principle of Least Privilege.
Explanation: Best practices in IAM include granting only the permissions required to perform specific tasks, which follows the Principle of Least Privilege. This reduces security risks by limiting unnecessary access.

7. B. To test and validate the effectiveness of IAM policies without affecting actual resources.
Explanation: The IAM Policy Simulator allows you to simulate policy behavior and verify permissions without impacting live resources or configurations.

8. B. Enable Multi-Factor Authentication (MFA).
Explanation: MFA adds an extra layer of security by requiring a second authentication factor, making it harder for unauthorized users to gain access even if credentials are compromised.

9. B. To provide programmatic access to AWS services.
Explanation: Access Keys consist of an Access Key ID and Secret Access Key, which are used for programmatic access to AWS services via the AWS CLI, SDKs, or APIs. They are not used for logging into the AWS Management Console.

10. B. Permissions are granted only for the minimum access required to perform tasks.
Explanation: The Principle of Least Privilege ensures that users, groups, and roles are granted only the permissions they need to perform their tasks, reducing the potential for security vulnerabilities.

Chapter 12. AWS Networking Fundamentals

In any cloud environment, networking serves as the backbone for communication, resource connectivity, and security. AWS Networking Fundamentals equips you with the foundational knowledge to build and manage secure, scalable, and efficient network architectures within AWS. The chapter begins with an understanding of CIDR (IPv4), a critical concept for managing IP address ranges efficiently. Through exercises, you will gain hands-on clarity on CIDR notations and their applications.

Next, we explore the differences between public and private IP addresses and their roles in AWS environments. The chapter then introduces Amazon Virtual Private Cloud (VPC), a core networking service that allows you to logically isolate your AWS resources. We break down VPC components, including subnets, route tables, Internet Gateways (IGW), and NAT Gateways.

A key focus is on securing your VPC with Security Groups (SGs) and Network ACLs (NACLs), explaining their functionality, differences, and troubleshooting techniques. Further, we explore advanced networking concepts such as VPC Peering, enabling connectivity between multiple VPCs, and VPN connections for establishing secure links between on-premises networks and AWS.

By the end of this chapter, you will have a strong grasp of AWS networking components, security mechanisms, and best practices to design and maintain reliable and secure network infrastructure on AWS.

12.1 Understanding CIDR – IPv4

CIDR (Classless Inter-Domain Routing) is a method for allocating IP addresses that improves the efficiency of address distribution in a network.

The CIDR is used in Security Groups rules and AWS networking in general.

IP version	Type	Protocol	Port range	Source	Description
IPv4	HTTPS	TCP	443	0.0.0.0/0	-
IPv4	HTTP	TCP	80	0.0.0.0/0	-
IPv4	SSH	TCP	22	73.81.154.236/32	-

They help to define an IP address range.

- For example, in **XX.YY.ZZ.WW/32**. The CIDR XX.YY.ZZ.WW/32 has an IP address range for one IP.
- In **0.0.0.0/0**. the CIDR 0.0.0.0/0 has an IP address range for all IPs.
- We can also define, for example,**192.168.0.0/27**. The CIDR 192.168.0.0/27 has an IP address range from **192.168.0.0 – 192.168.0.31**(32 IP addresses). It means if you use this CIDR, you will be able to allocate 32 different IP addresses for different machines in your network.

CIDR Components

A CIDR has two components: base IP address and subnet mask.

Base IP: Base IP represents an IP address part in the range -- similar to what would be seen in a normal IP address, such as 192.168.0.0, 10.0.0.0, etc.

Subnet Mask: CIDR notation is just shorthand for the subnet mask and represents the number of bits available to the IP address. For instance, the /24 in 192.168.0.101/24 is equivalent to the IP address 192.168.0.101 and the subnet mask 255.255.255.0

Or we can also understand it in another way, as a subnet mask defines how many bits can be changed in the CIDR.
For example:
/8 ⇔ 255.0.0.0 [last three octets can change]
/16 ⇔ 255.255.0.0 [last two octets can change]
/24 ⇔ 255.255.255.0 [last octets can change]
/32 ⇔ 255.255.255.255 [no octet can change]

Subnet Mask

The Subnet mask allows to the allocation of a range of IP addresses starting from the base IP. The concept depends on changing bits that can be changed. For example, if the subnet mask is /27, we can change 32-27 = 5 bits from 0 to 1 to get different IP addresses. The one permutation is when all 5 bits are 1s. and that will be the last IP address for the CIDR having subnet mask /27.

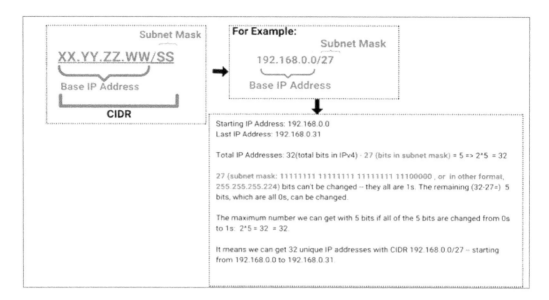

Let's see in detail to get a better understanding.

198.198.0.0 /32 => allows for *(32-32 = 0)* => 2^0 = **1** IP address => 192.168.0.0

198.198.0.0 /31 => allows for *(32-31 = 1)* => 2^1 = **2** IP addresses => 192.168.0.0 -> 192.168.0.1

198.198.0.0 /30 => allows for *(32-32 = 2)* => 2^2 = **4** IP addresses => 192.168.0.0 -> 192.168.0.3

198.198.0.0 /29 => allows for *(32-29 = 3)* => 2^3 = 8 IP addresses => 192.168.0.0 -> 192.168.0.7

198.198.0.0 /28 => allows for *(32-28 = 4)* => 2^4 = **16** IP addresses => 192.168.0.0 -> 192.168.0.15

198.198.0.0 /27 => allows for *(32-27 = 5)* => 2^5 = 32 IP addresses => 192.168.0.0 -> 192.168.0.31

198.198.0.0 /26 => allows for *(32-26 = 6)* => 2^6 = 64 IP addresses => 192.168.0.0 -> 192.168.0.63

198.198.0.0 /25 => allows for *(32-25 = 7)* => 2^7 = 128 IP addresses => 192.168.0.0 -> 192.168.0.127

198.198.0.0 /24 => allows for *(32-24 = 8)* => 2^8 = 256 IP addresses => 192.168.0.0 -> 192.168.0.255

•••

198.198.0.0 /16 => allows for *(32-16 = 16)* => 2^{16} = 65536 IP addresses => 192.168.0.0 -> 192.168.255.255

•••

198.198.0.0 / 1 => allows for *(32-1= 31)* => 2^{31} = 214,748,364,8 IP addresses => 192.168.0.0 ->255.255.255.255

12.1.1 CIDR – Review Exercise

- 192.168.0.0/24 =? => 192.168.0.0 – 192.168.0.255 (256 IPs)
- 192.168.0.0/16 = ? => 192.168.0.0 – 192.168.255.255 (65,536 IPs)
- 134.56.78.123/32 =? => just 134.56.78.123
- 0.0.0.0/0 => All IPs!

When you need a quick look-up, you can use: https://www.ipaddressguide.com/cidr

12.2 Public vs. Private IP Address

Public IP Address

- A public IP address is a unique identifier assigned to your ISP (Internet Service Provider) by your internet connection (or router) by your ISP (Internet Service Provider). Your router uses its public IP address to communicate with the rest of the internet.
- A public IP address is unique -- other devices do not use it.
- A public IP address is used to communicate with sites and servers on the internet.
- Public IP addresses are traceable by ISPs, advertisers, governments, and hackers.
- You can find your public IP address by searching for "What is my IP address" on Google.

Private IP Address

- On the other hand, the private IP address identifies different devices connected to the same local network. Once your router has received information from the global network to send it to one of the devices on your network, it needs to know which device to send it to. The private IP address helps the router identify different devices on your network to forward the response.
- Private IP addresses are not unique – different routers can reuse them.
- Private IP addresses are used to communicate between devices on a local network.
- They are traceable by other devices on the local network.
- You can find a private IP address by using system settings and preferences.

12.2.1 IP Addresses for Public and Private IP

The Internet Assigned Numbers Authority (IANA) established certain blocks of IPv4 addresses for the use of private (LAN) and public (Internet) addresses.

Private IP can only allow specific values:
- 10.0.0.0 – 10.255.255.255 (10.0.0.0/8) [Used commonly in big networks which need lots of IP addresses]
- 172.16.0.0 – 172.31.255.255 (172.16.0.0/12) [AWS default VPC range]
- 192.168.0.0 – 192.168.255.255 (192.168.0.0/16) [Used commonly in home networks]

All the rest of the IP addresses on the internet are Public IP addresses.

12.3 Introduction to VPC

Amazon Virtual Private Cloud (Amazon VPC) is a foundational service provided by AWS that enables you to launch and manage AWS resources in a logically isolated, secure virtual network environment. It gives you full control over your virtual networking environment, including selecting your own IP address ranges, configuring subnets, routing tables, internet gateways, and other network components.

Key Features of Amazon VPC

Isolation and Security: Amazon VPC isolates your resources from other customers, ensuring a private and secure environment. Security features such as security groups and network access control lists (NACLs) allow you to control inbound and outbound traffic at multiple levels.

Customizable IP Address Range: When creating a VPC, you can define an IP address range using CIDR notation (e.g., 10.0.0.0/16) to suit your network design requirements.

Subnets: VPC allows you to divide your IP address range into subnets, which can be categorized as:
- Public Subnets: Accessible from the internet.
- Private Subnets: Restricted from internet access, often used for backend services like databases.

Routing Control: You can configure route tables to control how traffic is directed between subnets, the internet, or other VPCs.

Internet Gateway (IGW): VPCs can connect to the internet through an Internet Gateway, enabling resources like EC2 instances in public subnets to communicate with the internet.

NAT Gateway: Instances in private subnets can access the internet for updates or external communication using a NAT Gateway without exposing them to incoming internet traffic.

VPN and AWS Direct Connect: VPC supports secure connectivity to on-premises environments via VPN (Virtual Private Network) or AWS Direct Connect, enabling hybrid cloud deployments.

Elastic IP Addresses: VPC supports static, public IP addresses (Elastic IPs) for resources, allowing consistent connectivity to external systems.

VPC Peering and Transit Gateway: VPC Peering allows you to connect multiple VPCs privately, while Transit Gateway facilitates large-scale VPC-to-VPC and on-premises network interconnectivity.

12.3.1 Overview Amazon VPC (High-Level) in a Diagram

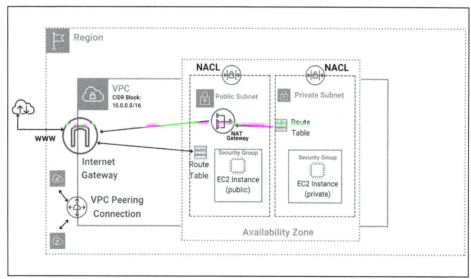

This diagram provides a detailed overview of an Amazon VPC (Virtual Private Cloud), focusing on its key components, security configurations, and flow of traffic. It highlights the integration of security controls like NACLs (Network Access Control Lists), Security Groups, and the role of networking components such as Public and Private Subnets, Internet Gateway, and NAT Gateway.

Key Components of the Diagram

VPC (Virtual Private Cloud): The entire green-bordered [in the color] rectangle represents the VPC, a logically isolated network in AWS. It is assigned a CIDR block (10.0.0.0/16) that defines the private IP address range for resources within the VPC.

Public Subnet: The Public Subnet (light green section) hosts resources that need direct internet access. An EC2 Instance resides here, which is often used for hosting web servers or public-facing applications. Traffic from the Public Subnet to the internet is routed through the Internet Gateway (IGW). The EC2 instance is protected by a Security Group (firewall rules) to allow only specific inbound and outbound traffic. The Public Subnet is protected by a Network Access Control List (NACL) to provide an additional layer of security at the subnet level.

Private Subnet: The Private Subnet (light blue section) hosts resources that should remain isolated from the public internet, such as databases or backend applications. Traffic from the Private Subnet that needs internet access (e.g., software updates) is routed through the NAT Gateway in the Public Subnet. Instances in the Private Subnet are protected by their own Security Group to control inbound and outbound access specific to their role. The Private Subnet also uses a Network Access Control List (NACL) for subnet-level security.

Route Tables:
- Public Subnet Route Table: Associated with the Public Subnet, this route table includes a route directing internet-bound traffic to the Internet Gateway (IGW).
- Private Subnet Route Table: Associated with the Private Subnet, this route table includes a route directing outbound internet traffic to the NAT Gateway.

Internet Gateway (IGW): The purple icon represents the Internet Gateway, which enables resources in the Public Subnet to communicate with the internet.
Traffic from the Public Subnet is routed through the IGW.

NAT Gateway: Located in the Public Subnet, the NAT Gateway allows resources in the Private Subnet to initiate outbound internet connections while preventing inbound connections from the internet. This is commonly used for tasks such as downloading software updates.

VPC Peering Connection: The diagram also shows a VPC Peering Connection (bottom left), which connects this VPC with another VPC, enabling private communication between resources in the two VPCs without going through the internet.

Availability Zone (AZ): The dashed blue box represents a single Availability Zone. All resources (Public and Private Subnets) are located within the same AZ in this diagram. In practice, VPCs often span multiple AZs for high availability.

How the Components Interact

Public Subnet Traffic Flow: The EC2 instance in the Public Subnet communicates directly with the internet via the Internet Gateway. Security is managed by the Security Group for instance-level rules and NACL for subnet-level rules.

Private Subnet Traffic Flow: The EC2 instance in the Private Subnet does not have direct internet access. Outbound traffic (e.g., updates) is routed through the NAT Gateway in the Public Subnet.

The Security Group and NACL provide multiple layers of access control to secure resources.

VPC Peering: The VPC Peering Connection enables secure communication between this VPC and another VPC for private applications or cross-account networking.

Security in the VPC
Security Groups: Instance-level firewalls that control inbound and outbound traffic to individual resources. Applied to EC2 instances in both Public and Private Subnets.

NACLs: Subnet-level firewalls that control traffic to and from entire subnets. Useful for setting additional security rules, such as blocking specific IP ranges or protocols.

Use Cases
Public Subnet: Hosting web servers or public-facing applications that need internet access.
Private Subnet: Hosting databases, backend servers, or applications that should remain isolated from direct internet access.
NAT Gateway: Enabling secure outbound internet access for private resources.
VPC Peering: Facilitating inter-VPC communication for distributed applications or hybrid environments.

This diagram represents a well-architected VPC setup that ensures security, scalability, and efficient resource management.

Amazon VPC forms the backbone of many AWS solutions by providing a secure, scalable, and customizable networking environment to host your cloud infrastructure. It integrates seamlessly with other AWS services like EC2, S3, RDS, and Lambda, enabling you to build secure and high-performing applications in the cloud.

12.3.2 VPC Components: Subnets, Route Tables, Internet Gateways, and NAT Gateways
Amazon Virtual Private Cloud (VPC) provides a secure and customizable virtual network environment. Each of its key components plays a specific role in networking and connectivity. Below is a detailed discussion of these components with examples:

12.3.3 Subnets
Subnets divide a VPC into smaller sections, allowing you to isolate resources and control their accessibility. Subnets are categorized into Public Subnets and Private Subnets.

Public Subnet: A public subnet has a route to an Internet Gateway and is used for resources requiring internet access, such as web servers.
Example: An EC2 instance hosting a web application is deployed in a public subnet, with an Elastic IP to allow users to access the application over the internet.

Private Subnet: A private subnet does not have a direct route to the internet and is used for resources that need to remain isolated, such as databases or backend servers.
Example: An RDS (Relational Database Service) instance is deployed in a private subnet to ensure it cannot be accessed directly from the internet.

12.3.4 Route Tables

Route tables define how traffic is directed within a VPC and beyond. Each subnet is associated with a route table, which contains routing rules.

Public Subnet Route Table: Includes a route to the Internet Gateway for internet-bound traffic. Example: A route table associated with a public subnet might have the following entry:

```
Destination: 0.0.0.0/0 (anywhere)
Target: Internet Gateway (igw-12345)
```

Private Subnet Route Table: Includes a route to the NAT Gateway for internet-bound traffic. Example: A route table for a private subnet might have:

```
Destination: 0.0.0.0/0
Target: NAT Gateway (nat-12345)
```

12.3.5 Internet Gateway (IGW)

An Internet Gateway enables resources in the public subnet to communicate with the internet. It handles two-way traffic: inbound and outbound.

Key Functionality: Allows EC2 instances in the public subnet to receive requests from the internet and send responses. Required for Elastic IPs or public IPs to function.

Example: A web server hosted in a public subnet uses an Internet Gateway to serve web pages to users globally.

12.3.6 NAT Gateway

A NAT (Network Address Translation) Gateway is used to enable resources in a private subnet to access the internet for tasks like software updates or downloading patches, without exposing them to incoming internet traffic.

Key Functionality: It routes outbound traffic from private resources to the internet while hiding the resources' private IP addresses.

Example: A private EC2 instance running a backend application requires a security patch. The NAT Gateway in the public subnet allows it to download updates from the internet without exposing the instance to incoming traffic.

12.3.7 Example Scenario

VPC Configuration
- VPC CIDR Block: 10.0.0.0/16
- Public Subnet CIDR Block: 10.0.1.0/24
- Private Subnet CIDR Block: 10.0.2.0/24

Setup

Public Subnet: Deployed an EC2 instance (10.0.1.10) with a public IP for hosting a web application. Associated the subnet with a route table containing a route to the Internet Gateway. Internet Gateway (igw-12345) is attached to the VPC.

Private Subnet: Deployed an RDS instance (10.0.2.20) for storing application data. Associated the subnet with a route table containing a route to the NAT Gateway for internet-bound traffic.

NAT Gateway: Configured a NAT Gateway in the public subnet. The NAT Gateway is associated with the route table for the private subnet to enable secure outbound internet access.

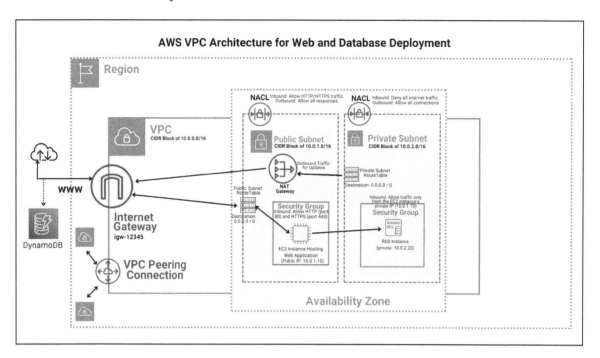

Traffic Flow

Public Subnet Traffic: Users access the web application deployed in the public subnet via its public IP. Traffic is routed through the Internet Gateway.

Private Subnet Traffic: The RDS instance in the private subnet does not accept inbound traffic from the internet. For outbound traffic (e.g., downloading security updates), the traffic is routed through the NAT Gateway in the public subnet.

Security Layers

Security Groups: Instance-level firewalls that control inbound and outbound traffic. For example, web server allows inbound HTTP (port 80) and HTTPS (port 443) traffic. RDS allows inbound traffic only from the web server's IP.

NACLs (Network Access Control Lists): Subnet-level firewalls that add another layer of protection. For example: Public subnet NACL allows inbound HTTP/HTTPS traffic and outbound responses. Private subnet NACL denies all inbound internet traffic but allows outbound connections.

This setup demonstrates a secure and scalable VPC architecture with controlled internet access for both public-facing and private resources.

12.4 Security Groups and Network ACLs

This section introduces two critical components of AWS networking security: Security Groups and Network Access Control Lists (NACLs). Both tools play distinct roles in controlling access to your AWS resources and ensuring the integrity of your applications.

12.4.1 Security Groups: Stateful firewalls for EC2 instances

Security Groups in AWS act as stateful firewalls designed to control inbound and outbound traffic for Amazon EC2 instances and other AWS resources like RDS databases, Lambda functions, and more. Unlike Network ACLs, which operate at the subnet level, Security Groups are applied at the instance level and provide highly granular control over resource access.

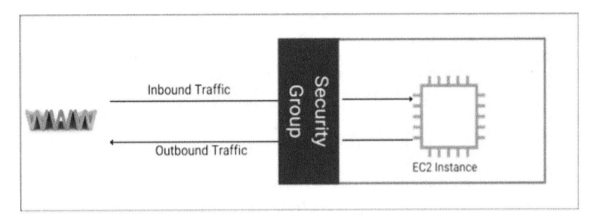

As you can notice in the above diagram, the security group is acting as a firewall for inbound and outbound traffic to the EC2 instance.

Key Characteristics of Security Groups

Stateful Nature

Security Groups automatically track the state of a connection. If an inbound rule allows traffic (e.g., HTTP on port 80), the corresponding outbound response is automatically allowed, and vice versa. There is no need to explicitly define outbound rules for allowed inbound traffic. For example, if you allow inbound HTTP traffic to your EC2 instance, the outbound response for the same connection is implicitly allowed.

Resource-Specific

Security Groups are directly attached to AWS resources, such as EC2 instances, and control traffic only for those resources.

Rules-Based Access

Security Groups define access through rules, which specify:
- **Protocol:** The type of protocol (e.g., TCP, UDP, ICMP).
- **Port Range:** The port or range of ports allowed (e.g., port 22 for SSH).
- **Source or Destination:** The IP address or CIDR block allowed for traffic (e.g., 0.0.0.0/0 for all IPs or a specific range like 192.168.1.0/24).

Rules can apply to:
- **Inbound Traffic:** Controls traffic entering the resource.

- **Outbound Traffic:** Controls traffic leaving the resource.

For example, allow inbound HTTPS traffic from the internet (0.0.0.0/0) on port 443.

Deny by Default
Security Groups operate on a "deny by default" model. Only explicitly allowed traffic (as defined in the rules) can pass through.

Multiple Security Groups
Multiple Security Groups can be attached to a single resource, and the rules are evaluated collectively. This allows flexible configurations to meet complex security needs.

Use Cases for Security Groups
Web Application Firewall: Allow inbound HTTP (port 80) and HTTPS (port 443) traffic for a public-facing web server. Restrict all other traffic.

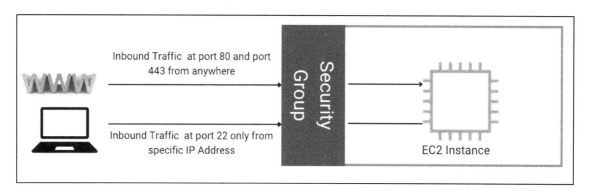

The diagram above is another way to understand the screenshot of the security group. All inbound is blocked by default. All outbound traffic is allowed. In other words, if you launch an EC2 instance and assign a default security group, all inbound traffic will be blocked and all outbound traffic will be allowed.

Secure SSH Access: Allow inbound SSH (port 22) traffic only from a specific IP address (e.g., your corporate network).
Example Rule:
- Protocol: TCP
- Port: 22
- Source: 203.0.113.0/24 (Corporate IP range).

Database Access: For a backend RDS database, allow inbound MySQL traffic (port 3306) only from the private IP of an EC2 instance hosting the application.
Example Rule:
- Protocol: TCP
- Port: 3306
- Source: 10.0.1.10 (Private IP of EC2).

Application-to-Application Communication: Allow EC2 instances within the same VPC or Security Group to communicate with each other for inter-application traffic.

Example Configuration for an EC2 Instance

Example Configuration for an EC2 Instance

Rule Type	Protocol	Port Range	Source/Destination	Purpose
Inbound	HTTP	80	0.0.0.0/0	Allow public web traffic
Inbound	HTTPS	443	0.0.0.0/0	Allow secure web traffic
Inbound	SSH	22	203.0.113.0/24	Allow SSH from corporate IP
Outbound	All	All	0.0.0.0/0	Allow all outbound connections

Examples to Explain Security Groups

Example 1: Public Web Server

Scenario: You have an EC2 instance in a public subnet hosting a web application, and you need to allow HTTP, HTTPS, and SSH access.

Security Group Rules:

Rule Type	Protocol	Port Range	Source	Purpose
Inbound	HTTP	80	0.0.0.0/0	Allow public HTTP traffic.
Inbound	HTTPS	443	0.0.0.0/0	Allow secure HTTPS traffic.
Inbound	SSH	22	203.0.113.0/24	Allow SSH from corporate IP.

Traffic Flow:
- Users access the application through HTTP or HTTPS.
- Developers access the instance via SSH only from their corporate network.

Example 2: Backend Database

Scenario: An RDS instance is deployed in a private subnet and must allow connections only from a web server hosted on an EC2 instance.

Security Group Rules:

Rule Type	Protocol	Port Range	Source	Purpose
Inbound	MySQL/Aurora	3306	10.0.1.10	Allow MySQL traffic from the EC2 server.
Outbound	All	All	0.0.0.0/0	Allow outbound connections for updates.

Traffic Flow:
- The EC2 web server communicates with the database using MySQL on port 3306.
- The RDS instance allows only traffic from the EC2 instance's private IP address (10.0.1.10).

Example 3: Application Load Balancer (ALB)

Scenario: An ALB distributes traffic to multiple EC2 instances behind it.

Security Group Rules for ALB:

Rule Type	Protocol	Port Range	Source	Purpose
Inbound	HTTP	80	0.0.0.0/0	Allow public HTTP traffic.
Inbound	HTTPS	443	0.0.0.0/0	Allow public HTTPS traffic.

Security Group Rules for EC2 Instances:

Rule Type	Protocol	Port Range	Source	Purpose
Inbound	HTTP	80	`ALB-SG` (ALB Security Group)	Allow traffic from ALB.

Traffic Flow:
- Internet users access the ALB using HTTP or HTTPS.
- The ALB forwards the requests to EC2 instances over HTTP.

Best Practices for Security Groups

Principle of Least Privilege: Configure rules to allow only the specific traffic required for the application. Avoid broad rules like allowing 0.0.0.0/0 unless absolutely necessary.

Use Descriptive Tags and Names: Clearly label Security Groups for easy identification (e.g., Web-Server-SG, DB-SG).

Review and Audit Regularly: Periodically review Security Group rules to ensure compliance with security policies.

Isolate Traffic with Multiple Security Groups: Use separate Security Groups for different tiers of an application (e.g., web servers, databases).

Avoid Using Default Security Groups: Create custom Security Groups tailored to specific resources rather than relying on default Security Groups.

Limitations of Security Groups

Cannot Deny Specific Traffic: Security Groups can only allow traffic; they cannot explicitly deny it. For subnet-level denials, use Network ACLs.

Soft Limits: AWS enforces limits on the number of Security Groups per resource and the number of rules per Security Group (e.g., 60 inbound and 60 outbound rules per group).

By using Security Groups effectively, you can enforce granular access control at the instance level, ensuring secure communication while simplifying traffic management.

12.4.2 Network ACLs: Stateless firewalls for subnets

Network Access Control Lists (NACLs) in AWS are stateless firewalls that operate at the subnet level to control inbound and outbound traffic. Unlike Security Groups, which are stateful and applied at the instance level, NACLs allow you to explicitly allow or deny traffic for entire subnets, making them a broader and more flexible layer of protection.

Key Characteristics of NACLs

Stateless Nature: NACLs are stateless, meaning that inbound and outbound rules are evaluated separately. If you allow inbound traffic, you must explicitly allow the crresponding outbound response.

Example:
- Allow inbound HTTP traffic on port 80.
- You must also allow outbound traffic on port 80 for the return response.

Applied at the Subnet Level: NACLs apply rules to all resources within a subnet, providing a layer of security that complements instance-level Security Groups.

Rules-Based Access: NACLs are composed of numbered rules that are evaluated in ascending order (lowest rule number first).

Rules can either allow or deny traffic based on:
- Protocol (e.g., TCP, UDP, ICMP).
- Port Range (e.g., 22 for SSH, 443 for HTTPS).
- Source/Destination (e.g., IP ranges in CIDR notation).

Default Deny: NACLs have a default rule (Rule *) at the bottom, which denies all traffic not explicitly allowed.

Default vs. Custom NACLs:
- Default NACL: Automatically created for each VPC and allows all inbound and outbound traffic.
- Custom NACL: User-defined, starts with no rules, and requires explicit configuration.

Multiple Rules: NACLs allow up to 20 inbound and 20 outbound rules by default (can be increased).

Examples
Example 1: Public Subnet with an Internet-Facing EC2 Instance
Scenario: A public subnet contains an EC2 instance hosting a web server. You need to allow HTTP and HTTPS traffic from the internet while denying all other traffic.

Inbound Rules:

Rule #	Protocol	Port Range	Source	Action
100	TCP	80	0.0.0.0/0	ALLOW
110	TCP	443	0.0.0.0/0	ALLOW
*	All	All	All	DENY

Outbound Rules:

Rule #	Protocol	Port Range	Destination	Action
100	TCP	80	0.0.0.0/0	ALLOW
110	TCP	443	0.0.0.0/0	ALLOW
*	All	All	All	DENY

Traffic Flow: Allows HTTP/HTTPS traffic (ports 80 and 443) from the internet to the EC2 instance. Blocks all other traffic.

Example 2: Private Subnet with a Database

Scenario: A private subnet contains an RDS database. You need to allow traffic only from a specific EC2 instance in a public subnet.

Inbound Rules:

Rule #	Protocol	Port Range	Source	Action
100	TCP	3306	10.0.1.10/32	ALLOW
*	All	All	All	DENY

Outbound Rules:

Rule #	Protocol	Port Range	Destination	Action
100	All	All	0.0.0.0/0	ALLOW
*	All	All	All	DENY

Traffic Flow: Allows inbound MySQL traffic (port 3306) only from the specific EC2 instance (10.0.1.10). Allows all outbound traffic for updates or data replication.

Example 3: Subnet-Wide Restriction on SSH

Scenario: You want to block all SSH traffic to a subnet except from a trusted IP range (e.g., corporate network).

Inbound Rules:

Rule #	Protocol	Port Range	Source	Action
100	TCP	22	203.0.113.0/24	ALLOW
*	All	All	All	DENY

Outbound Rules:

Rule #	Protocol	Port Range	Destination	Action
100	All	All	All	ALLOW
*	All	All	All	DENY

Traffic Flow: Allows SSH traffic only from the corporate network (203.0.113.0/24). Blocks all other SSH attempts.

Best Practices for Network ACLs

Use NACLs for Subnet-Wide Restrictions: Apply rules at the subnet level to enforce broad access controls.

Combine with Security Groups: Use NACLs for coarse-grained subnet rules and Security Groups for fine-grained resource-level rules.

Order Rules Carefully: Rules are evaluated in ascending order. Place specific allow/deny rules before more general rules.

Regularly Review NACL Rules: Audit NACL rules periodically to ensure they align with your security policies.

Avoid Default NACL for Sensitive Subnets: Replace the default NACL (which allows all traffic) with a custom NACL for critical subnets.

Limitations of Network ACLs

No Stateful Tracking: NACLs require explicit rules for both inbound and outbound traffic, making them less dynamic than Security Groups.

More Management Overhead: For complex applications, maintaining NACL rules for multiple subnets can become cumbersome.

12.4.3 Security Groups & NACLs Request Response Flow
Incoming Request

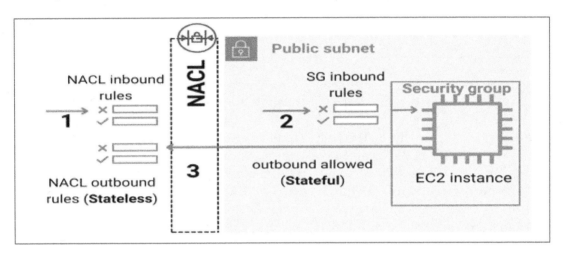

Let's understand how an incoming request is handled with NACL and Security Group. In the diagram, the request (1) is first checked by NACL rules whether the request is allowed.

Then the request (2) is checked at the instance level security group rules whether the request is allowed.

Then the outgoing response (3) is not checked by the security group as the **security groups are stateful** (if a request is allowed, its outgoing response is allowed). However, the outgoing response is evaluated at the NACL whether the outgoing response is allowed as the **NACLs are stateless** (which means both a request and its response are checked against the NACL rules).

Outgoing Request

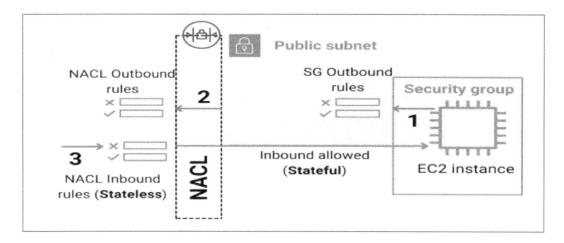

Handling of the outgoing request by Security Group and NACLs are conceptually the same – it's just the reverse of how an incoming request is handled.

From the diagram above, request (1) is first handled by the security group rules. Then the request is checked at the NACL (2). Regarding response, since NACLs are stateless, response (3) is checked against NACL rules. However, when the response goes through the security group, it is allowed as Security Groups are stateful.

Default NACL

By default, your VPC has default Network ACLs that allow all inbound and outbound traffic.

Inbound Rules

Rule#	Type	Protocol	Port Range	Source	Allow / Deny
100	All IPv4 Traffic	ALL	ALL	0.0.0.0/0	ALLOW
*	All IPv4 Traffic	ALL	ALL	0.0.0.0/0	Deny

Outboud Rules

Rule#	Type	Protocol	Port Range	Source	Allow / Deny
100	All IPv4 Traffic	ALL	ALL	0.0.0.0/0	ALLOW
*	All IPv4 Traffic	ALL	ALL	0.0.0.0/0	Deny

Though the default Network ACL can be modified, Do NOT modify the Default NACL. Instead, create custom NACLs.

- Network ACLs provide an optional layer of security for your VPC. It acts as a firewall controlling inbound and outbound traffic for one or more subnets.
- One NACL per subnet. New subnets are assigned the Default NACL.
- You can create a custom Network ACL and assign it to a subnet. By default, each custom Network denies all inbound and outbound rules until you add rules.
- Each subnet in a VPC must be assigned to a Network ACL. If the subnet is not assigned to a Network ACL, the subnet is automatically assigned to a default Network ACL.
- Network ACLs have separate inbound and outbound rules -- each rule can deny or allow traffic.
- Network ACLs are stateless, which means the response to inbound traffic is only allowed if outbound traffic is permitted and vice-versa.
- NACL rules:
    - Network ACL contains numbered rules (1 – 32766) highest number can be 32766. The order is evaluated for the lowest numbers; as soon as the lowest number rule matches, it is applied, and higher number rules are ignored.
    - Example: if you define #100 ALLOW 10.0.0.10/32 and #200 DENY 10.0.0.10/32, the IP address will be allowed because 100 has higher precedence over 200.
    - The last rule is an asterisk (*) and denies a request in case of no rule match.
    - AWS recommends adding rules by increments of 100.

- Network ACLs are different from security groups – security groups are applied at the instance level, while Network ACLs are used at the subnet level.
- NACLs are an excellent way of blocking a specific IP address at the subnet level.

12.4.4 Troubleshoot SG & NACL Related Issues

Analyze the "Action" field in flow logs.

Incoming Requests	Outgoing Requests
Inbound REJECT => NACL or SG	Outbound REJECT => NACL or SG
Inbound ACCEPT, Outbound REJECT=> NACL	Outbound ACCEPT, Inbound REJECT=> NACL

12.4.5 Ephemeral Ports

In networking, two devices must establish a connection to communicate on an endpoint and use ports. Client devices connect to a defined fixed destination port and expect a response on an ephemeral port.

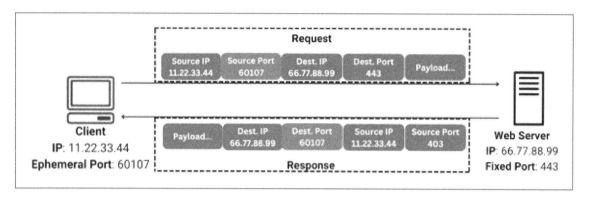

As you can see in the diagram, the client machine uses its port 60107 (ephemeral port) to connect to the web server at 443 and expects a response on its port 60107. Different operating systems use different port ranges as ephemeral ports. For example, MS Windows uses ports between 49152 and 65535, and many Linux kernels use between 32768 and 60999.

12.4.6 Security Groups vs. NACLs

Security Group	NACL
Operates at the instance level	Operates at the subnet level
Supports "allow" rules only	Supports both "allow" and "deny" rules
All rules are evaluated before deciding whether to allow traffic	Rules are evaluated in order from lowest to highest when deciding whether to allow traffic, the first match is used.
Stateful: response traffic is automatically allowed regardless of any rules.	**Stateless**: response traffic must be explicitly allowed by rules – think of ephemeral ports
Applies to an EC2 instance when specified	Automatically applies to all EC2 instances in the subnet

12.4.7 Lab Exercise: Configuring Security Groups and Network ACLs.

This lab exercise will guide you through the process of configuring Security Groups and Network ACLs in AWS to secure your resources.

Step 1: Launch the Lab Environment
Log in to the AWS Management Console. Navigate to the VPC Dashboard under the Networking & Content Delivery section. Ensure you have a VPC, subnets, and at least one EC2 instance to apply the configurations.

Step 2: Configure Security Groups
Security Groups act as stateful firewalls for your resources.

2.1 Create a Security Group for a Public Web Server
Navigate to Security Groups in the VPC Dashboard. Click on Create Security Group.
Provide a name and description:
- Name: Web-Server-SG
- Description: Security Group for public-facing web servers.

Attach the Security Group to your VPC.

2.2 Add Inbound Rules
Under the Inbound Rules section, click Edit inbound rules and add the following:
- Allow HTTP (port 80) traffic from all IPs (0.0.0.0/0 and ::/0 for IPv6).
- Allow HTTPS (port 443) traffic from all IPs (0.0.0.0/0 and ::/0 for IPv6).
- Allow SSH (port 22) traffic only from a trusted IP range (e.g., your corporate network: 203.0.113.0/24).

Save the changes.

2.3 Add Outbound Rules
By default, all outbound traffic is allowed. You can leave this as is or customize it based on your requirements. Save the Security Group.

2.4 Attach the Security Group to the EC2 Instance
Navigate to the EC2 Dashboard and select the instance running in the public subnet. Go to the Security tab and click Edit security groups. Attach the newly created Web-Server-SG to the instance.

Step 3: Configure Security Group for a Private Database
Repeat steps 2.1 through 2.4 to create a Security Group for the database instance.
Name it Database-SG and provide the following rules:
- Inbound Rules: Allow MySQL/Aurora traffic (port 3306) only from the private IP of the EC2 instance in the public subnet.
- Outbound Rules: Allow all traffic (0.0.0.0/0).

Step 4: Configure Network ACLs
Network ACLs provide subnet-wide stateless traffic control.

4.1 Create a NACL for the Public Subnet
In the VPC Dashboard, navigate to Network ACLs and click Create network ACL. Name the NACL Public-Subnet-NACL and attach it to the public subnet.

Add rules to the Inbound Rules and Outbound Rules:

Inbound Rules:

Rule #	Protocol	Port Range	Source	Action
100	TCP	80	0.0.0.0/0	ALLOW
110	TCP	443	0.0.0.0/0	ALLOW
120	TCP	22	203.0.113.0/24	ALLOW
*	All	All	All	DENY

Outbound Rules:

Rule #	Protocol	Port Range	Destination	Action
100	TCP	80	0.0.0.0/0	ALLOW
110	TCP	443	0.0.0.0/0	ALLOW
*	All	All	All	DENY

Save the NACL and ensure it is associated with the public subnet.

4.2 Create a NACL for the Private Subnet

Create a new NACL and name it Private-Subnet-NACL.

Attach it to the private subnet.

Add rules to the Inbound Rules and Outbound Rules:

Inbound Rules:

Rule #	Protocol	Port Range	Source	Action
100	TCP	3306	10.0.1.10/32	ALLOW
*	All	All	All	DENY

Outbound Rules:

Rule #	Protocol	Port Range	Destination	Action
100	All	All	All	ALLOW

Save the NACL and ensure it is associated with the private subnet.

Step 5: Validate the Configuration

Test Web Server: Access the public IP of the EC2 instance from your browser and ensure HTTP/HTTPS traffic works. Attempt SSH access only from the allowed IP range.

Test Database Access: Ensure the RDS instance allows traffic only from the EC2 instance. Attempt accessing the database directly from the internet; it should be denied.

Validate NACLs: Simulate traffic that does not match the allow rules in NACLs and confirm it is denied.

Step 6: Clean Up (Optional)

If this is a temporary lab environment, delete the created resources:

- Terminate EC2 instances and delete the RDS database.
- Remove Security Groups and Network ACLs.
- Delete the VPC if created solely for this exercise.

This lab exercise demonstrates how to configure Security Groups and Network ACLs to enforce robust security at both the resource and subnet levels in AWS.

12.5 VPC Peering and VPN

This section explores two critical networking features of AWS Virtual Private Cloud (VPC) that enable secure and efficient communication across cloud environments and on-premises networks: VPC Peering and VPN Connections. These features help establish connectivity for seamless data transfer and hybrid cloud setups.

12.5.1 VPC Peering: Connecting multiple VPCs

VPC Peering is a networking feature in AWS that allows you to connect two VPCs privately. These VPCs can be in the same AWS account or in different accounts and can be located in the same region or across different regions (referred to as inter-region VPC peering). With VPC Peering, you can route traffic between VPCs using private IP addresses, without requiring gateways, VPN connections, or the public internet.

A VPC can be understood as a data center within an on-premises environment. Since VPC is a cloud construct, it can be considered a virtual data center in a cloud. VPC Peering can be understood as a leased line or fiber cable connectivity between two data centers.

Suppose you have two VPCs. You can set up VPC Peering between two VPCs, and they can start communicating with each other.

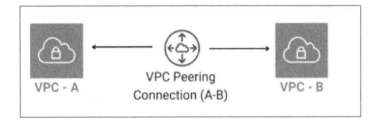

If you have another VPC, you can add one more VPC Peering to communicate with each other.

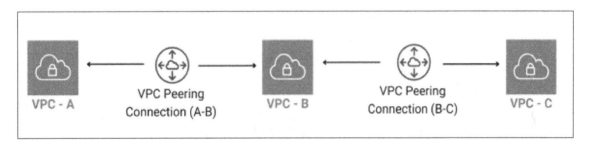

But an important point to note is that VPC Peering is a one-to-one association. So, traffic from VPC-C cannot traverse into VPC-A via VPC-B without adding VPC Peering between VPC-C and

VPC-A. If you need to set up a connection between VPC-C and VPC-A, you will have to set up another VPC Peering.

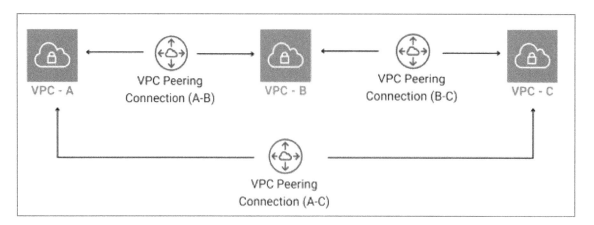

Key Features of VPC Peering

Private Connectivity: Traffic between VPCs stays within the AWS backbone network, ensuring secure communication without traversing the public internet.

Same or Different AWS Accounts: You can peer VPCs across the same AWS account or between different AWS accounts.

Inter-Region Peering: Allows VPCs in different AWS regions to communicate securely using private IP addresses.

No Single Point of Failure: VPC Peering is a fully managed, highly available service without the need for additional infrastructure or single points of failure.

Simple Routing: You use route tables to direct traffic between the VPCs. No additional hardware is required.

How VPC Peering Works

Create a Peering Connection: A peering connection is established between the two VPCs. The owner of one VPC (requester) sends a peering request. The owner of the other VPC (accepter) must accept the request.

Update Route Tables: After the connection is established, you update the route tables of both VPCs to route traffic through the peering connection.

Adjust Security Groups and NACLs: Security groups and NACLs must be updated to allow traffic between resources in the peered VPCs.

Example 1: Peering Two VPCs in the Same Region

Scenario:
You have two VPCs in the us-east-1 region:
- VPC-A: CIDR 10.0.0.0/16
- VPC-B: CIDR 192.168.0.0/16

You want instances in VPC-A to communicate with instances in VPC-B over private IP addresses.

The following are the steps:
Create a Peering Connection: In the AWS console, navigate to VPC → Peering Connections → Create Peering Connection. Select Requester VPC: VPC-A. Select Accepter VPC: VPC-B.

Accept the Peering Request: In the AWS console of the accepter account, go to VPC → Peering Connections and accept the request.

Update Route Tables:
In VPC-A's route table, add a route:
- Destination: 192.168.0.0/16
- Target: The peering connection.
In VPC-B's route table, add a route:
- Destination: 10.0.0.0/16
- Target: The peering connection.

Update Security Groups:
- For VPC-A instances, update security groups to allow inbound and outbound traffic from 192.168.0.0/16.
- For VPC-B instances, update security groups to allow inbound and outbound traffic from 10.0.0.0/16.

Traffic Flow: Instances in VPC-A can now communicate with instances in VPC-B over private IP addresses.

Example 2: Inter-Region VPC Peering
Scenario:
You have VPCs in two different regions:
- VPC-C (us-east-1): CIDR 10.0.0.0/16
- VPC-D (us-west-1): CIDR 172.16.0.0/16
You want to establish private connectivity between the VPCs for data replication.

The following are the steps:
Create a Peering Connection: In us-east-1, create a peering connection between VPC-C and VPC-D.

Accept the Peering Request: Log into the us-west-1 AWS console and accept the peering request.

Update Route Tables:
In VPC-C's route table, add a route:
- Destination: 172.16.0.0/16
- Target: The peering connection.
In VPC-D's route table, add a route:
- Destination: 10.0.0.0/16
- Target: The peering connection.

Adjust Security Groups and NACLs: Ensure the security groups and NACLs allow traffic between the CIDR blocks of the two VPCs.

Traffic Flow: Instances in VPC-C and VPC-D can now securely communicate, even though they are in different regions.

Use Cases for VPC Peering

Cross-Environment Communication: Connecting development, testing, and production environments hosted in separate VPCs.
Multi-Account Architecture: Sharing resources such as databases across multiple AWS accounts.
Inter-Region Data Transfer: Replicating data between VPCs in different regions for disaster recovery.
Hybrid Cloud Deployment: Linking on-premises environments to multiple VPCs.

Limitations of VPC Peering

No Transitive Peering: Traffic cannot flow through a third VPC. For example, if VPC-A is peered with VPC-B, and VPC-B is peered with VPC-C, VPC-A cannot communicate with VPC-C.
Manual Route Table Updates: Routes need to be manually added to enable communication.
No Overlapping CIDRs: Peering connections cannot be established between VPCs with overlapping CIDR blocks.

Best Practices

Plan IP Address Ranges: Avoid overlapping CIDRs to ensure smooth peering connections.
Use Inter-Region Peering for Latency-Sensitive Applications: AWS ensures low-latency connections between regions.
Monitor Peering Connections: Regularly review and monitor the usage of peering connections to optimize costs and performance.

By using VPC Peering, you can establish private, secure connections between VPCs, enabling efficient and scalable networking for modern cloud architectures.

12.5.2 VPN Connections: Establishing a secure connection to on-premises networks

Virtual Private Network (VPN) Connections in AWS enable you to securely connect your on-premises networks to your Amazon Virtual Private Cloud (VPC) over an encrypted Internet Protocol Security (IPSec) tunnel. This allows for a secure communication channel between your data center and AWS resources, facilitating hybrid cloud architectures where resources are spread across both environments.

Key Components of AWS VPN Connections

Customer Gateway (CGW): Represents your on-premises gateway device (e.g., a physical or software-based router). In AWS, it's a logical representation that includes information about the device (such as the public IP address).

Virtual Private Gateway (VGW): A VPN concentrator on the Amazon side of the VPN connection. It's attached to your VPC and handles VPN traffic to and from the VPC.

VPN Connection: The VPN tunnel established between the Customer Gateway and the Virtual Private Gateway. Consists of two tunnels for redundancy and high availability.

Types of AWS VPN Connections

Site-to-Site VPN: Connects your on-premises network to an AWS VPC. Uses IPSec tunnels over the public Internet.

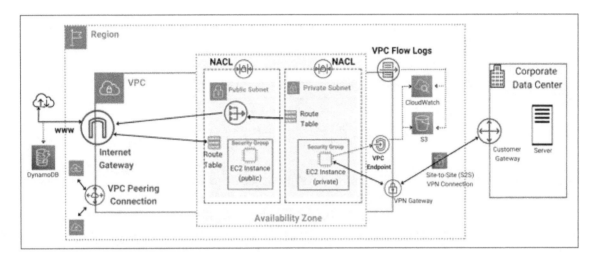

When extending an on-premises environment to the AWS Cloud, VPN is generally fast and easy to set up for many AWS customers.

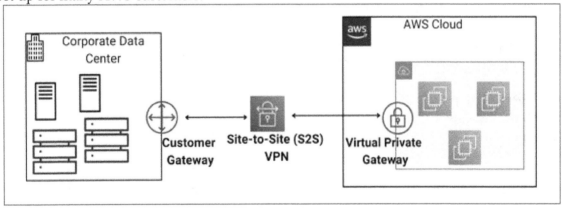

You need two things: Customer Gateway and Virtual Private Gateway. The Customer Gateway could be your Router, firewall, software application, or other things that support IPSec in your on-premises environment. The Customer Gateway resides at the on-premises end, and it is used in AWS Site-to-Site VPN connection.

AWS Direct Connect + VPN: Combines AWS Direct Connect (a dedicated network connection) with a VPN for added security. Provides consistent network performance and encryption.

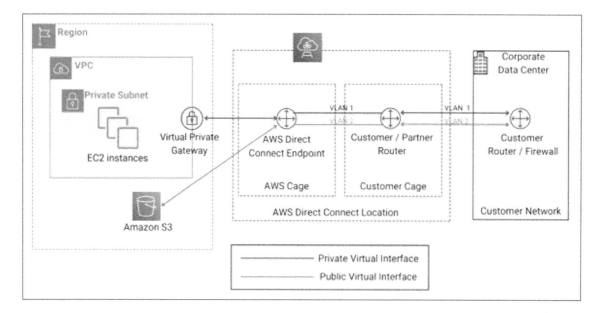

To use AWS Direct Connect, you can use the AWS Direct Connect location near your data center location. AWS has many Direct Connection locations; each of these locations has Routers managed by AWS. Then you request port on one of these Routers – maybe 1G/sec or 10 G/sec. And then, you can set up AWS connectivity either by yourself or by taking the help of an AWS Connectivity partner.

The AWS Direct Connect is a physical connection. The AWS Direct Connect provides more predictable and consistent experience for on-premises connectivity to the AWS.

Client VPN: Allows individual clients (users) to securely access AWS resources or on-premises networks.

How VPN Connections Work

Establish the Customer Gateway: Configure your on-premises gateway device to support IPSec VPN connections. Create a Customer Gateway resource in AWS, specifying the public IP address of your on-premises device.

Create a Virtual Private Gateway: In AWS, create a Virtual Private Gateway and attach it to your VPC.

Configure the VPN Connection: Create a VPN connection between the Virtual Private Gateway and the Customer Gateway. AWS provides configuration files for various vendor devices (e.g., Cisco, Juniper) to simplify setup.

Update Route Tables: Modify the route tables associated with your VPC subnets to direct traffic destined for your on-premises network through the Virtual Private Gateway.

Configure On-Premises Router: Use the provided configuration file to set up your on-premises gateway device. Establish the IPSec tunnel, which includes setting up encryption parameters, authentication methods, and tunnel endpoints.

Example Scenario

Scenario: An organization wants to securely extend its on-premises data center network (CIDR 192.168.1.0/24) to an AWS VPC (CIDR 10.0.0.0/16) to migrate applications and enable seamless communication between on-premises servers and AWS resources.

The following are the steps:

Set Up Customer Gateway: Identify the public IP address of the on-premises router (e.g., 198.51.100.10). In AWS, create a Customer Gateway resource:
- Name: OnPremises-CGW
- IP Address: 198.51.100.10
- Routing Type: Static or Dynamic (using Border Gateway Protocol - BGP).

Create Virtual Private Gateway: In AWS, create a Virtual Private Gateway:
- Name: MyVPC-VGW
- Attach the VGW to the VPC (10.0.0.0/16).

Establish VPN Connection: Create a VPN Connection:
- Name: OnPremises-VPN
- Virtual Private Gateway: MyVPC-VGW
- Customer Gateway: OnPremises-CGW
- Routing Options: Choose Static Routing and enter your on-premises network CIDR (192.168.1.0/24).

Download Configuration File: After creating the VPN connection, download the configuration file tailored for your on-premises router vendor and model.

Configure On-Premises Router: Apply the settings from the configuration file to your router. Set up the IPSec tunnels, including pre-shared keys, encryption algorithms, and authentication methods.

Update AWS Route Tables: In AWS, update the route tables associated with your VPC subnets:
- Destination: 192.168.1.0/24
- Target: MyVPC-VGW

Update On-Premises Routing: Ensure that traffic destined for the AWS VPC CIDR (10.0.0.0/16) is routed through the on-premises gateway device.

Traffic Flow

On-Premises to AWS: On-premises servers can communicate with AWS resources over the encrypted VPN tunnel, appearing as if they are on the same network.

AWS to On-Premises: AWS resources can access on-premises services, databases, or authentication systems securely.

Use Cases for VPN Connections

Hybrid Cloud Architectures: Extend your data center into the cloud, enabling seamless integration of on-premises and cloud resources.

Secure Data Transfer: Encrypt sensitive data in transit between on-premises systems and AWS.

Disaster Recovery and Backup: Replicate data to AWS for backup or set up failover systems.

Development and Testing: Use AWS resources while maintaining connectivity to on-premises development environments.

Limitations and Considerations

Internet Dependency: VPN connections over the public Internet can be subject to variability in performance and latency.

Bandwidth Constraints: Bandwidth is limited compared to dedicated connections like AWS Direct Connect.

Single Point of Failure: If the on-premises Internet connection fails, the VPN connection will be disrupted. High availability can be achieved by configuring multiple VPN connections over redundant Internet connections.

IP Address Overlaps: Ensure that there are no overlapping IP address ranges between the on-premises network and the AWS VPC.

Best Practices

Use Redundant VPN Connections: Configure multiple VPN tunnels for high availability and failover.

Monitor VPN Connections: Use AWS CloudWatch and other monitoring tools to keep track of the VPN connection's health and performance.

Consider AWS Direct Connect for High Throughput Needs: If consistent performance and higher bandwidth are required, consider using AWS Direct Connect, possibly in combination with VPN for encryption.

Implement Robust Security Measures: Use strong encryption and authentication mechanisms. Regularly update pre-shared keys and credentials.

Regularly Review Network Configurations: Ensure routing tables, security groups, and network ACLs are correctly configured to allow desired traffic.

Additional Features

AWS Transit Gateway: For complex network architectures involving multiple VPCs and on-premises networks, AWS Transit Gateway simplifies management by acting as a central hub.

Dynamic Routing with BGP: Use dynamic routing to automatically exchange routes between AWS and on-premises networks, simplifying route management.

Example with AWS Transit Gateway
Scenario:
An enterprise has multiple VPCs across different regions and wants to connect them to the on-premises network using a single VPN connection.

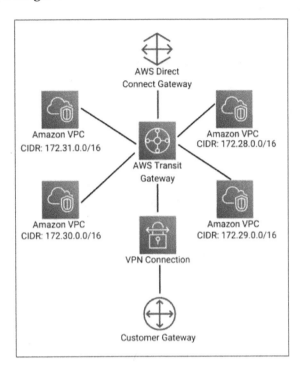

Solution:
Set Up AWS Transit Gateway: Create an AWS Transit Gateway and attach all VPCs to it.
Create a VPN Connection to Transit Gateway: Establish a VPN connection between the on-premises network and the Transit Gateway.
Configure Routing: The Transit Gateway handles routing between VPCs and the on-premises network.

Benefits:
- Simplifies network architecture by reducing the number of VPN connections.
- Centralized management of network policies and routing.

By leveraging VPN Connections in AWS, organizations can securely bridge their on-premises networks with cloud environments, enabling a cohesive, hybrid infrastructure that supports various business needs while maintaining security and compliance standards.

12.6 Chapter Review Questions
Question 1:
Which of the following is a key component of a CIDR block?
    A. Subnet mask
    B. Private IP address
    C. Elastic Load Balancer
    D. Internet Gateway

Question 2:

What does a subnet mask in CIDR notation determine?
- A. The protocol used in a VPC
- B. The division of an IP address into network and host portions
- C. The security rules applied to a subnet
- D. The route traffic takes to the internet

Question 3:
Which of the following is an example of a private IP address?
- A. 8.8.8.8
- B. 192.168.1.1
- C. 123.45.67.89
- D. 255.255.255.255

Question 4:
What is the primary role of an Internet Gateway (IGW) in a VPC?
- A. It routes traffic between public and private subnets.
- B. It enables communication between instances in the same VPC.
- C. It connects the VPC to the public internet.
- D. It encrypts data in transit.

Question 5:
Which of the following best describes a NAT Gateway?
- A. It enables resources in a private subnet to access the internet securely.
- B. It routes traffic between different Availability Zones.
- C. It provides DNS resolution for public-facing instances.
- D. It allows inbound internet traffic to private subnets.

Question 6:
What is the primary function of a Route Table in a VPC?
- A. It defines rules for allowing or denying traffic at the subnet level.
- B. It controls which subnets are public or private.
- C. It determines how traffic is routed between subnets and the internet.
- D. It attaches security groups to EC2 instances.

Question 7:
In AWS, Security Groups are best described as:
- A. Stateless firewalls applied to subnets.
- B. Stateful firewalls applied to EC2 instances.
- C. Stateless rules controlling access to VPCs.
- D. Stateful firewalls applied to NAT Gateways.

Question 8:
What is the key difference between Security Groups and Network ACLs?
- A. Security Groups operate at the subnet level, while Network ACLs operate at the instance level.
- B. Security Groups are stateful, while Network ACLs are stateless.
- C. Security Groups allow only inbound rules, while Network ACLs allow only outbound rules.

D. Security Groups allow explicit deny rules, while Network ACLs do not.

Question 9:
Which of the following is a limitation of VPC Peering?
   A. It supports only private IP communication.
   B. It cannot be used across AWS accounts.
   C. It does not allow transitive peering between VPCs.
   D. It cannot be used with instances in private subnets.

Question 10:
What is the purpose of a VPN Connection in AWS?
   A. To securely connect two VPCs within the same account.
   B. To provide public-facing access to AWS resources.
   C. To establish an encrypted connection between a VPC and an on-premises network.
   D. To route internal traffic between subnets in a VPC.

12.7 Answers to Chapter Review Questions

1. A. Subnet mask
Explanation: A CIDR block consists of an IP address and a subnet mask, which determines the division of the address into network and host portions.

2. B. The division of an IP address into network and host portions
Explanation: The subnet mask in CIDR notation specifies how many bits are used for the network portion, helping to divide the address into network and host components.

3. B. 192.168.1.1
Explanation: Private IP addresses fall within specific ranges, such as 192.168.0.0 - 192.168.255.255, which are reserved for private network use.

4. C. It connects the VPC to the public internet
Explanation: An Internet Gateway (IGW) is a component that allows resources in a VPC to communicate with the public internet using public IP addresses.

5. A. It enables resources in a private subnet to access the internet securely
Explanation: A NAT Gateway allows outbound internet access for resources in private subnets without exposing them to inbound internet traffic.

6. C. It determines how traffic is routed between subnets and the internet
Explanation: A Route Table contains rules (routes) that specify the path for traffic within a VPC and between a VPC and other networks like the internet.

7. B. Stateful firewalls applied to EC2 instances
Explanation: Security Groups are stateful, meaning they automatically allow responses to allowed inbound traffic and are attached to specific EC2 instances.

8. B. Security Groups are stateful, while Network ACLs are stateless
Explanation: Security Groups track the state of connections, whereas Network ACLs evaluate each packet independently, requiring explicit rules for both inbound and outbound traffic.

9. C. It does not allow transitive peering between VPCs
Explanation: VPC Peering connections are not transitive, meaning if VPC-A is peered with VPC-B, and VPC-B is peered with VPC-C, VPC-A cannot communicate with VPC-C.

10. C. To establish an encrypted connection between a VPC and an on-premises network
Explanation: A VPN Connection creates a secure IPSec-encrypted tunnel between an AWS VPC and an on-premises network, enabling hybrid cloud setups.

Chapter 13. AWS Compute Services

In the world of cloud computing, compute services form the foundation for running applications, processing workloads, and enabling dynamic scalability. AWS Compute Services introduces you to the powerful tools provided by Amazon Web Services (AWS) to meet diverse computing needs — whether for traditional virtual servers or cutting-edge serverless architectures.

The chapter begins with Amazon EC2 (Elastic Compute Cloud), the cornerstone of AWS compute offerings. You'll explore different EC2 instance types, their use cases, and learn how to select the right instance for your workloads. We also discuss EC2 pricing models — including On-Demand, Reserved, and Spot Instances — enabling cost-effective decision-making. The concept of EC2 Auto Scaling is introduced, highlighting its ability to maintain performance by automatically adjusting capacity. A hands-on lab exercise will walk you through launching and managing your own EC2 instance.

Next, the chapter shifts focus to AWS Lambda, a serverless compute service that eliminates infrastructure management. You'll learn about the benefits of serverless computing, how to create and deploy Lambda functions, and integrate them with other AWS services using triggers. Practical examples and a lab exercise will demonstrate Lambda's agility and scalability.

Finally, you'll be introduced to the AWS Serverless Application Model (AWS SAM), a framework for building serverless applications efficiently.

By the end of this chapter, you'll have a solid understanding of AWS compute services, from managing scalable EC2 instances to leveraging the flexibility and efficiency of serverless computing with AWS Lambda and AWS SAM.

13.1 Amazon EC2

Amazon Elastic Compute Cloud (EC2) is a core service in AWS that provides scalable and flexible compute capacity in the cloud. It allows you to launch and manage virtual servers, known as instances, to run your applications without the need to procure and maintain physical hardware.

With Amazon EC2, you can provision resources on demand, scale them up or down based on requirements, and pay only for what you use, making it an efficient solution for running workloads of all sizes.

Key Features

Amazon EC2 provides elastic and scalable compute capacity to launch and terminate virtual servers based on workload demands. It supports both horizontal scaling (adding instances) and vertical scaling (upgrading instance types).

EC2 offers a wide range of instance types optimized for various workloads:
- **General Purpose** for balanced needs (e.g., t3, m5).
- **Compute Optimized** for CPU-intensive tasks (e.g., c5, c6g).
- **Memory Optimized** for high memory applications (e.g., r5, x1).
- **Storage Optimized** for I/O performance (e.g., i3, d2).
- **Accelerated Computing** for GPU-based workloads (e.g., p4, g4ad).

The flexible pricing models include:
- **On-Demand Instances** for pay-as-you-go usage.
- **Reserved Instances** for long-term cost savings.
- **Spot Instances** for discounted, fault-tolerant workloads.
- **Savings Plans** for consistent usage with reduced pricing.

With Amazon Machine Images (AMI), users can quickly launch instances using preconfigured or custom templates. Elastic Block Store (EBS) provides durable, scalable storage with options like gp3 (General Purpose) and io2 (High IOPS).

EC2 supports Auto Scaling to dynamically adjust capacity and integrates with Elastic Load Balancer (ELB) for traffic distribution. For security and networking, it uses Security Groups (stateful firewalls), Network ACLs (stateless firewalls), and VPC integration for isolated networking.

EC2 ensures high availability and fault tolerance by deploying instances across multiple Availability Zones (AZs) and supporting Placement Groups for low-latency, high-performance workloads. It also provides Elastic IP addresses for predictable, static addressing.

Finally, monitoring and logging is achieved through integration with Amazon CloudWatch for real-time metrics and detailed activity logs.

These features make EC2 a robust, scalable, and secure compute solution for diverse workloads.

Use Cases

Amazon EC2 serves a variety of use cases across industries due to its scalability and flexibility. It is ideal for **web hosting and application servers**, supporting web applications, APIs, and backend services, such as deploying WordPress or e-commerce platforms. EC2 also powers **batch processing** for data transformation and tasks like image processing on demand. For **High-Performance Computing (HPC)**, EC2 handles computationally intensive workloads like engineering simulations and scientific research.

It enables **big data analytics** by deploying clusters with tools like Hadoop and Spark to process large-scale data. In the field of **machine learning and AI**, GPU-based instances are used to train and deploy deep learning models with frameworks like TensorFlow or PyTorch. Developers use

EC2 for **dev/test environments**, creating isolated and cost-effective setups for software testing and development. For **disaster recovery and backup**, EC2 replicates on-premises servers, ensuring failover capabilities across regions.

It is also a popular choice for **gaming servers**, providing low-latency multiplayer experiences, and for **media and content delivery**, supporting video streaming and transcoding with integration to services like S3 and CloudFront. Finally, EC2 is well-suited for **e-commerce platforms**, offering a scalable and reliable infrastructure to handle variable traffic demands.

13.1.1 EC2 Instance Types: Overview of different instance types and their use cases

Amazon EC2 offers a wide range of instance types optimized for different workloads, providing flexibility to match compute, memory, storage, and GPU resources with application requirements. Each instance type caters to specific use cases, enabling efficient resource utilization and cost optimization.

General Purpose instances provide a balanced mix of compute, memory, and networking resources, making them ideal for workloads that don't require specialized hardware or intensive optimization. Examples of such instances include t3, m5, and t3a. Common use cases involve hosting web servers, small to medium databases, development and testing environments, and application servers. For example, General Purpose instances are often used to host WordPress websites or run small e-commerce platforms.

Compute Optimized instances are specifically designed for workloads requiring high CPU performance, making them suitable for compute-intensive applications. Examples include c5, c6g, and c7g. These instances excel in use cases like high-performance web servers, scientific modeling and simulations, batch processing, and machine learning inference. A typical scenario involves running High-Performance Computing (HPC) simulations for engineering or bioinformatics tasks.

Memory Optimized instances offer high memory capacity and are ideal for memory-intensive applications that require significant in-memory processing. Examples of Memory Optimized instances are r5, x1e, z1d, and u6i. They are commonly used for large in-memory databases such as Redis or SAP HANA, real-time data processing, and high-performance computing workloads that rely on large datasets. For instance, these instances are suitable for running a Redis cluster for caching or SAP HANA for enterprise applications.

Storage Optimized instances are designed for workloads requiring high, sequential read and write access to large datasets. These instances deliver low latency and high IOPS (Input/Output Operations Per Second). Examples include i3, d2, and h1. Typical use cases include high-frequency transactional systems, big data workloads (e.g., Hadoop or Spark), data warehousing, and log processing. A common scenario is deploying a Hadoop cluster to process massive log files or analytical queries.

Accelerated Computing instances leverage hardware accelerators like GPUs or FPGAs to handle compute-intensive tasks requiring parallel processing. Examples include p4, g4dn, and f1 instances. These instances are ideal for machine learning training and inference, GPU-based graphics rendering, video transcoding, and scientific computing tasks requiring high parallelism.

For example, deep learning models can be trained using frameworks like TensorFlow or PyTorch on p4 instances.

High-Performance instances, which support enhanced networking, are optimized for workloads with significant network requirements and provide high bandwidth. Examples include m6in, c6gn, and r6in. These instances are best suited for network-intensive applications, real-time streaming, distributed databases, and hybrid cloud connectivity. A typical use case is deploying a distributed database that requires high throughput and low latency for replication.

Choosing the Right Instance Type

Selecting the appropriate instance type depends on the specific requirements of your workload:

General Purpose: Balanced compute, memory, and network.
Compute Optimized: CPU-intensive tasks.
Memory Optimized: In-memory databases and large datasets.
Storage Optimized: High I/O and data processing.
Accelerated Computing: GPU/FPGA tasks like machine learning.

In conclusion, Amazon EC2 instance types provide tailored resources for a wide range of workloads. By understanding the characteristics and use cases of each instance type, businesses can optimize performance and cost while meeting the demands of their applications.

13.1.2 EC2 Pricing Models: On-demand, reserved, and spot instances

Amazon EC2 offers flexible pricing models to optimize cost efficiency for different workloads. The three primary pricing models are On-Demand, Reserved, and Spot Instances, each catering to specific use cases and budget requirements.

On-Demand Instances: On-Demand instances allow you to pay for compute capacity per hour or per second with no upfront commitment. This model is ideal for workloads that are unpredictable or short-term. Use cases include testing, development, and applications with variable or unpredictable traffic. For example, launching an EC2 instance to test a new feature or running a temporary web application.

Reserved Instances (RIs): Reserved Instances provide significant savings (up to 72%) compared to On-Demand pricing in exchange for a 1- or 3-year commitment. RIs are ideal for steady-state workloads or applications with predictable usage patterns. This model offers options for Standard RIs (greater savings) and Convertible RIs (flexibility to change instance types). For example, running a consistent database server for enterprise applications.

Spot Instances: Spot Instances allow you to use unused EC2 capacity at steep discounts (up to 90% off On-Demand prices). They are ideal for fault-tolerant workloads, batch processing, big data analytics, and applications that can tolerate interruptions. For example, Spot Instances are often used for data processing jobs, CI/CD pipelines, or running machine learning training jobs.

Summary:
  • **On-Demand:** Flexible, no long-term commitment, pay as you go.

Cloud Computing and AWS Introduction   211

- **Reserved Instances:** Cost-effective for predictable, long-term workloads.
- **Spot Instances:** Highly cost-effective for interruptible and flexible workloads.

Choosing the right EC2 pricing model depends on your workload's predictability, duration, and tolerance for interruptions, allowing you to balance cost and performance effectively.

13.1.3 EC2 Auto Scaling: Automatically adjusting capacity to maintain performance

EC2 Auto Scaling is a feature that enables automatic adjustment of Amazon EC2 instance capacity to maintain application performance and optimize costs. It monitors your workloads and dynamically scales the number of instances up or down based on demand, ensuring that your applications remain highly available and responsive.

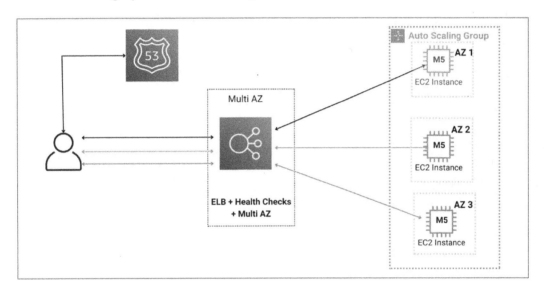

This diagram illustrates Auto Scaling in AWS with key components working together to ensure scalability, high availability, and fault tolerance. At the top, Route 53, AWS's DNS service, routes user requests to the appropriate resources. This ensures high availability and performance by directing traffic effectively. The requests are then sent to the Elastic Load Balancer (ELB), which plays a central role in distributing incoming traffic evenly across multiple EC2 instances. The ELB also performs health checks to monitor the status of each instance and ensures that traffic is routed only to healthy instances.

The Auto Scaling Group (ASG) is responsible for automatically scaling EC2 instances based on demand. In this example, instances are deployed across multiple Availability Zones (AZs), namely AZ 1, AZ 2, and AZ 3. Each AZ hosts an M5 EC2 instance, providing fault tolerance and redundancy in case of failure in one AZ. If traffic demand increases or an instance becomes unhealthy, the Auto Scaling Group can dynamically add or replace instances as needed.

The user request flow begins when a user sends a request, which Route 53 routes to the ELB. The ELB then distributes the traffic to the EC2 instances in the Auto Scaling Group across the three AZs. This architecture ensures high availability by leveraging multiple AZs, scalability through the automatic adjustment of instances, and cost efficiency by scaling resources up or down based on demand. Additionally, ELB's continuous health checks guarantee that only healthy instances serve user traffic. Overall, this design ensures the application remains reliable, scalable, and resilient to failures.

Key Features of EC2 Auto Scaling

Dynamic Scaling: Automatically adds or removes EC2 instances based on real-time metrics such as CPU utilization, memory usage, or custom-defined triggers.

Predictive Scaling: Uses machine learning to forecast future traffic patterns and proactively scale resources to handle anticipated demand.

High Availability: Ensures application uptime by distributing instances across multiple Availability Zones (AZs) for fault tolerance and redundancy.

Cost Optimization: Helps reduce costs by scaling down unused instances during low-demand periods and ensuring you only pay for the capacity you need.

Integration with Load Balancing: Works seamlessly with Elastic Load Balancer (ELB) to distribute incoming traffic across scaled instances.

Use Case Example

A web application experiencing unpredictable traffic patterns can benefit from EC2 Auto Scaling. During peak hours, Auto Scaling will automatically launch additional instances to manage increased load, ensuring performance is not impacted. As traffic decreases, it will terminate unused instances to minimize costs.

In summary, EC2 Auto Scaling ensures that applications maintain optimal performance by dynamically adjusting instance capacity in response to changing demand. It improves reliability, reduces manual intervention, and helps businesses achieve cost efficiency.

13.1.4 Lab Exercise: Launching and managing an EC2 Instance

Follow this step-by-step guide to launch and manage an Amazon EC2 instance using the AWS Management Console.

Step 1: Log in to the AWS Management Console

Open a web browser and navigate to the AWS Management Console. Log in using your AWS credentials. In the AWS console, navigate to the EC2 Dashboard by searching for EC2 in the search bar.

Step 2: Launch an EC2 Instance

From the EC2 Dashboard, click on the Launch Instance button.

Configure the following settings:

Name and Tags: Provide a meaningful name for the instance (e.g., My-Lab-Instance).
Application and OS Image (AMI): Choose an Amazon Machine Image (AMI), such as: Amazon Linux 2 (Free Tier eligible).
Instance Type: Select an instance type. For this lab, choose t2.micro (Free Tier eligible).

Key Pair (Login): Create a new Key Pair or choose an existing one. Download the key pair (.pem file) and store it securely (you will need it to connect via SSH).

Network Settings: Select the default VPC and subnet (leave defaults for simplicity). Allow SSH traffic by adding the following inbound security rule: Type: SSH, Source: My IP (or 0.0.0.0/0 for testing).

Configure Storage: For this lab, keep the default storage settings (8 GiB EBS volume). Review the settings and click Launch Instance.

Step 3: Verify the Instance

Return to the EC2 Dashboard → Instances. Locate your instance and verify its State (it should show running). Note the Public IP Address or Public DNS assigned to your instance.

Step 4: Connect to the EC2 Instance

Using SSH (Linux/Mac): Open a terminal on your local machine. Navigate to the directory where your Key Pair (.pem file) is stored. Run the following command to change the file permissions:

```
chmod 400 <key-pair-name>.pem
```

Connect to the instance using SSH:

```
ssh -i <key-pair-name>.pem ec2-user@<public-ip>
```

Replace <key-pair-name> with the name of your key pair and <public-ip> with the public IP of the instance.

Using PuTTY (Windows):

Download and open PuTTY and PuTTYgen. Use PuTTYgen to convert the .pem file to a .ppk file.

In PuTTY: Under Session, enter the Public IP address. Under SSH → Auth, browse and select the .ppk key file. Click Open to connect.

Step 5: Manage the EC2 Instance

Install Software (e.g., Apache Web Server):

Once connected via SSH, install Apache:

```
sudo yum update -y
sudo yum install -y httpd
sudo systemctl start httpd
sudo systemctl enable httpd
```

Verify the Web Server: Open a web browser and access your instance's Public IP. You should see the default Apache test page. Stop, Start, or Terminate the Instance:

Go to the EC2 Dashboard → Instances.
Select your instance and choose Actions → Instance State to Stop, Start, or Terminate the instance.

Step 6: Clean Up

If you no longer need the instance, terminate it to avoid charges: Go to EC2 Dashboard → Instances. Select your instance and choose Actions → Instance State → Terminate.

To summarize, in this lab, you successfully launched, connected to, and managed an Amazon EC2 instance. You installed a web server to demonstrate how EC2 instances can be used to host applications, and you learned how to stop or terminate instances to optimize cost.

13.2 AWS Lambda

AWS Lambda is a serverless compute service that allows you to run code without provisioning, managing, or scaling servers. You upload your code, and AWS Lambda automatically handles the execution, scaling, and availability of the infrastructure. You only pay for the compute time consumed during execution, making it a cost-effective solution for event-driven applications.

Key Features of AWS Lambda

Serverless Execution: No need to manage infrastructure or servers; Lambda handles all provisioning and scaling automatically.

Event-Driven Architecture: AWS Lambda is triggered by events from AWS services (e.g., S3, DynamoDB, API Gateway) or custom event sources.

Automatic Scaling: Lambda scales seamlessly based on the number of requests, ensuring high availability and performance.

Pay-Per-Use Pricing: You are billed only for the actual compute time (down to 1 millisecond) and the number of requests.

Support for Multiple Programming Languages: AWS Lambda supports languages like Python, Node.js, Java, Go, Ruby, .NET (C#), and custom runtimes.

Integrations with AWS Services: Easily integrates with other AWS services like Amazon S3, DynamoDB, SNS, SQS, and API Gateway.

High Availability: AWS Lambda runs your code across multiple Availability Zones for fault tolerance.

Use Cases of AWS Lambda

File Processing: Automatically process files uploaded to Amazon S3 (e.g., image resizing, log processing).

API Backends: Build RESTful APIs using Amazon API Gateway to trigger Lambda functions for handling requests.

Data Processing: Real-time stream processing with Amazon Kinesis or DynamoDB streams.

Automated Workflows: Trigger workflows for automation, such as managing AWS resources or running scheduled tasks using EventBridge.

Microservices Architecture: Build scalable and lightweight microservices where each function is triggered independently.

IoT Data Processing: Process data generated by IoT devices and perform real-time actions or analytics.

Machine Learning Inference: Run machine learning inference using trained models for applications like fraud detection or personalization.

Event-Driven Applications: Trigger actions based on events, such as notifications, database changes, or messaging systems.

In summary, AWS Lambda is a serverless compute service designed for running event-driven and on-demand workloads without managing servers. With automatic scaling, integrations with

AWS services, and a pay-per-use pricing model, Lambda is ideal for file processing, microservices, real-time data processing, and building scalable, cost-efficient applications.

13.2.1 Introduction to Serverless: Benefits and use cases of serverless computing

Serverless computing is a cloud computing model where developers can run code without managing infrastructure. With serverless services like AWS Lambda, the cloud provider handles all aspects of infrastructure management, such as provisioning, scaling, and maintenance. Developers simply upload their code, and it executes in response to events.

Benefits of Serverless Computing

No Server Management: Infrastructure is fully managed by the cloud provider, allowing developers to focus on writing code.

Automatic Scaling: Applications scale seamlessly to handle varying workloads without manual intervention.

Cost Efficiency: Pay only for the execution time and resources consumed, eliminating costs for idle infrastructure.

High Availability: Built-in fault tolerance and redundancy ensure reliability without additional configuration.

Faster Time-to-Market: Simplified infrastructure management accelerates application development and deployment.

Use Cases of Serverless Computing

Web and Mobile Backends: Build lightweight APIs and backend logic for web and mobile applications using services like AWS Lambda and API Gateway.

File and Data Processing: Process uploaded files or data streams in real time (e.g., resizing images or analyzing log data).

Event-Driven Applications: Trigger workflows based on events such as database updates, S3 uploads, or messaging queues (e.g., SNS and SQS).

Microservices: Design scalable microservices where each function handles a specific task independently.

IoT Data Processing: Process data from IoT devices in real time to trigger alerts or actions.

Automation and Scheduled Tasks: Automate tasks such as cron jobs, backups, and resource management.

Machine Learning Inference: Deploy serverless functions to run ML model inference without managing compute infrastructure.

In summary, serverless computing simplifies infrastructure management, automatically scales workloads, and optimizes costs by charging only for actual usage. It is ideal for building modern, scalable applications like APIs, event-driven workflows, and real-time data processing systems.

13.2.2 Creating Lambda Functions: Writing and deploying Lambda functions

Creating and deploying Lambda functions in AWS involves writing code, configuring triggers, and deploying it in a fully managed serverless environment. AWS Lambda allows you to execute code in response to events without managing servers.

Steps to Create and Deploy Lambda Functions
Navigate to AWS Lambda Console
Log in to the AWS Management Console. Open the Lambda service under the "Compute" section.

Create a Lambda Function
Click on Create function. Choose a method:
- Author from scratch: Write a new Lambda function.
- Use a blueprint: Start with a predefined template.
- Container image: Deploy a containerized Lambda function.

Provide the following details:
- Function Name: e.g., processS3Upload.
- Runtime: Choose a programming language (e.g., Node.js, Python, Java, C#).
- Execution Role: Assign an IAM Role with permissions for the Lambda function.

Write the Lambda Code
Use the built-in code editor in the AWS console, or upload your code as a .zip file or container image. Example of a simple Python function to process an S3 file:

```python
import boto3

def lambda_handler(event, context):
    s3 = boto3.client('s3')
    bucket = event['Records'][0]['s3']['bucket']['name']
    key = event['Records'][0]['s3']['object']['key']
    print(f"File {key} uploaded to bucket {bucket}")
    return {"statusCode": 200, "body": "File processed successfully"}
```

Configure the Trigger
Add an event source to trigger the function, such as:
- Amazon S3 (file upload)
- Amazon DynamoDB (stream changes)
- Amazon API Gateway (HTTP requests)
- CloudWatch Events (scheduled tasks).

Example: Set an S3 trigger for file upload events in a specific bucket.

Configure Memory and Timeout Settings
Specify the Memory (128 MB to 10,240 MB) and Timeout (e.g., 3 seconds to 15 minutes) based on function requirements.

Deploy the Function
Save and deploy the function. Lambda automatically packages and makes it ready for execution.

Test the Function
Use the Test tab in the AWS console to simulate an event and verify the output.

Example: Test the S3 trigger by uploading a file to the configured bucket.

Monitor and Debug

View Logs in Amazon CloudWatch to monitor function execution and troubleshoot issues. Metrics like execution duration, invocation count, and errors are available in CloudWatch.

Best Practices for Creating Lambda Functions

Optimize Code and Dependencies: Keep the package lightweight and avoid unnecessary libraries.

Use Environment Variables: Store configuration values securely without hardcoding.

Error Handling: Implement robust error handling and logging for debugging.

Set Appropriate Memory and Timeout Limits: Balance performance and cost efficiency.

Monitor Performance: Use CloudWatch for metrics and AWS X-Ray for tracing.

In summary, creating Lambda functions involves writing code, configuring triggers, and deploying it through the AWS Lambda console. Lambda integrates seamlessly with various AWS services, enabling event-driven workflows and scalable execution. By testing, monitoring, and optimizing, you can efficiently deploy serverless functions for diverse use cases.

13.2.3 Lambda Triggers and Integrations: Connecting Lambda with other AWS services

AWS Lambda seamlessly integrates with various AWS services and can be triggered by events from these services to execute serverless workflows. Lambda functions can act as event-driven processors for data, automation, and application logic, enabling scalable and efficient solutions.

Common AWS Lambda Triggers

Amazon S3: Amazon S3 triggers events such as file uploads, deletions, or updates in an S3 bucket. A common use case involves automatically processing an uploaded file, such as resizing images or extracting metadata.

Amazon API Gateway: Amazon API Gateway triggers Lambda functions through HTTP or RESTful API requests. This is ideal for building serverless web backends or microservices where Lambda processes API calls and returns responses.

Amazon DynamoDB: Amazon DynamoDB can trigger Lambda functions based on changes to tables, such as inserts, updates, or deletes. A typical use case is processing new data in real-time or replicating changes to another service.

Amazon SNS (Simple Notification Service): Amazon SNS triggers Lambda functions when messages or notifications are sent to an SNS topic. This is often used to send automated email alerts or process notifications for application events.

Amazon SQS (Simple Queue Service): Amazon SQS triggers Lambda functions when messages arrive in an SQS queue. This decouples components of an application, enabling asynchronous task processing efficiently.

Amazon Kinesis: Amazon Kinesis triggers Lambda functions in response to real-time data streaming events. This allows processing of data streams for analytics, metrics collection, or real-time monitoring.

AWS CloudWatch Events (EventBridge): AWS CloudWatch Events, or Amazon EventBridge, can trigger Lambda functions for scheduled tasks or rule-based events. Use cases include automating resource management tasks or performing scheduled backups.

AWS Step Functions: AWS Step Functions trigger Lambda workflows initiated by state transitions or events. This helps coordinate multiple Lambda functions to execute a series of interdependent tasks.

AWS IoT Core: AWS IoT Core triggers Lambda functions in response to IoT device data streams or events. A typical use case involves processing sensor data in real time and triggering specific actions based on the data.

Amazon CloudWatch Logs: Amazon CloudWatch Logs can trigger Lambda functions based on log events generated by applications or AWS resources. This is useful for automatically analyzing, filtering, or transforming logs for monitoring or debugging purposes.

How Lambda Integrates with AWS Services

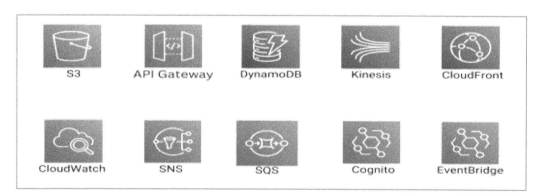

Event-Driven Architecture: AWS services generate events (e.g., S3 file upload) that invoke a Lambda function.
Seamless Integration: Lambda integrates natively with most AWS services, reducing development effort.
Chaining Services: Lambda acts as a bridge to connect services, enabling workflows like S3 → Lambda → DynamoDB or API Gateway → Lambda → RDS.
Custom Triggers: Lambda functions can also be triggered by custom events using Amazon EventBridge or API Gateway.

Example Scenarios
File Processing with S3: A Lambda function is triggered when an image is uploaded to an S3 bucket, automatically resizing and storing the processed image in another bucket.
Building an API Backend: API Gateway routes an HTTP request to a Lambda function that processes the request and returns a response, enabling serverless web APIs.

Real-Time Stream Processing: Data streams from Amazon Kinesis trigger a Lambda function that processes the data and stores it in DynamoDB.

Scheduled Tasks: A Lambda function runs on a schedule using CloudWatch Events to clean up old S3 objects every day.

Notification Automation: An SNS topic sends a message to Lambda, which processes the message and triggers additional workflows.

In summary, AWS Lambda integrates seamlessly with multiple AWS services, enabling it to act as the glue for event-driven and automated workflows. Whether triggered by S3 uploads, API Gateway requests, DynamoDB changes, or scheduled events, Lambda's flexible connectivity allows businesses to build highly scalable, cost-effective, and automated solutions.

13.2.4 Lab Exercise: Creating and Testing an AWS Lambda Function

Follow this step-by-step guide to create and test an AWS Lambda function using the AWS Management Console.

Step 1: Log in to the AWS Management Console

Open a web browser and go to the AWS Management Console. Log in with your AWS credentials. In the Search Bar, type Lambda and open the AWS Lambda service.

Step 2: Create a New Lambda Function

Click on the **Create function button**. Choose **Author from scratch**.

Provide the following details:
- **Function name:** Enter a name, such as MyFirstLambdaFunction.
- **Runtime**: Choose your preferred runtime (e.g., Python 3.9, Node.js, or Java).
- **Architecture:** Leave it as x86_64 (default).
- **Execution role:** Select Create a new role with basic Lambda permissions (for simplicity).

Click Create function.

Step 3: Write the Lambda Function Code

In the Code source section, use the built-in code editor.

For this lab, write a simple "Hello World" function:

Example Code (Python):

```
import json

def lambda_handler(event, context):
    message = "Hello, AWS Lambda!"
    print(message)
    return {
        'statusCode': 200,
        'body': json.dumps({'message': message})
    }
```

Click on Deploy to save your code changes.

Step 4: Configure a Test Event
Click on the Test tab at the top. Click on Create new event.

Provide the following details:
Event name: TestEvent1
Template: Select Hello World (or leave default JSON).
Event JSON: Use the following sample event:

```
{
  "key1": "value1",
  "key2": "value2",
  "key3": "value3"
}
```

Click Save.

Step 5: Test the Lambda Function
Click the Test button to execute your Lambda function. Check the Execution results below the code editor. Verify the Response section for output:

```
{
  "statusCode": 200,
  "body": "{\"message\": \"Hello, AWS Lambda!\"}"
}
```

Review the Log output to see the printed message.

Step 6: Monitor and Debug the Function
Go to the Monitor tab to view metrics like Invocation count, Duration, and Errors. Access detailed Logs in Amazon CloudWatch by clicking on View logs in CloudWatch.

Step 7: Clean Up Resources
To avoid unnecessary charges, delete the Lambda function:
- Return to the Lambda console.
- Select your function and click Actions → Delete.

In summary, in this lab, you created a simple AWS Lambda function, configured a test event, and executed it to verify its output. You also explored monitoring tools like CloudWatch for logs and metrics, ensuring you understand the basic workflow of creating and testing Lambda functions.

13.3 Introduction to AWS Serverless Application Model (AWS SAM)

The AWS Serverless Application Model (AWS SAM) is an open-source framework that simplifies the development, deployment, and management of serverless applications on AWS. It provides a streamlined way to define resources like Lambda functions, APIs, DynamoDB tables, and event triggers using a single, easy-to-understand template.

Key Features of AWS SAM

Simplified Resource Definition: AWS SAM uses a YAML or JSON template to define serverless resources concisely. It provides shorthand syntax to simplify the definition of AWS Lambda functions, API Gateway endpoints, and other AWS services.

Integration with AWS CloudFormation: AWS SAM builds on top of AWS CloudFormation, allowing developers to manage infrastructure as code (IaC) and benefit from CloudFormation's deployment capabilities.

Built-in Tools for Testing and Debugging:
AWS SAM CLI: A command-line tool that enables local testing, debugging, and deployment of serverless applications.
Local Simulation: You can simulate Lambda functions and API Gateway endpoints on your local machine.

Support for Standard Serverless Workloads:
AWS SAM makes it easy to define serverless resources like:
- AWS Lambda: For compute functions.
- Amazon API Gateway: To create REST APIs.
- Amazon DynamoDB: For serverless databases.
- Amazon S3: For object storage.

Simplified Deployment: Using the SAM CLI, you can package and deploy serverless applications quickly with a single command.

Common Use Cases of AWS SAM

Building RESTful APIs: Use AWS Lambda and Amazon API Gateway to create scalable, serverless APIs.
Event-Driven Applications: Trigger AWS Lambda functions using S3, SNS, DynamoDB, or EventBridge events.
CI/CD Pipelines: Integrate AWS SAM with tools like AWS CodePipeline for continuous deployment of serverless applications.
Local Development and Testing: Test Lambda functions and APIs locally before deploying to AWS.

In summary, AWS SAM provides a powerful and simplified framework for developing and managing serverless applications. By combining ease of use, integration with CloudFormation, and local development capabilities, SAM accelerates the serverless development lifecycle while enabling scalability and cost efficiency.

13.4 Related YouTube Videos
- AWS EC2 Tutorial: https://youtu.be/3-eR1OU3dUU
- EC2 Auto Scaling Tutorial: https://youtu.be/gV5dx6jSUWc
- EC2 AMI: https://youtu.be/uP7SfpymZyQ
- EC2 Instance Purchasing Options: https://youtu.be/m_0jL4LJaZs
- AWS (Amazon) Lambda Tutorial : https://youtu.be/SDnbak5Wgi8

13.5 Chapter Review Questions

Question 1:
Which of the following EC2 instance types is ideal for compute-intensive workloads?
   A. General Purpose (e.g., t3)
   B. Compute Optimized (e.g., c5)
   C. Memory Optimized (e.g., r5)
   D. Storage Optimized (e.g., i3)

Question 2:
Which EC2 pricing model is best suited for applications with predictable workloads over a long duration?
   A. On-Demand Instances
   B. Reserved Instances
   C. Spot Instances
   D. Savings Plans

Question 3:
What is the main purpose of EC2 Auto Scaling?
   A. To enable faster deployments for serverless applications
   B. To add and remove instances automatically based on traffic demand
   C. To reduce the cost of EC2 instances by selecting Spot pricing
   D. To provide high availability by deploying in multiple regions

Question 4:
AWS Lambda allows users to run code without provisioning or managing servers. What is this approach commonly known as?
   A. Virtualization
   B. Serverless computing
   C. Instance-based deployment
   D. Infrastructure as a Service

Question 5:
Which of the following can trigger an AWS Lambda function?
   A. Amazon S3 events (e.g., file upload)
   B. Manual code execution on EC2
   C. AWS CodeDeploy alone
   D. Elastic Load Balancers

Question 6:
What does AWS Serverless Application Model (AWS SAM) primarily help with?
   A. Scaling EC2 instances for heavy workloads
   B. Deploying serverless applications quickly and easily
   C. Managing Elastic Beanstalk environments
   D. Monitoring AWS compute resources

Question 7:
Which of the following EC2 pricing models provides access to spare AWS capacity at a significantly reduced cost?

A. Reserved Instances
B. On-Demand Instances
C. Spot Instances
D. Dedicated Hosts

Question 8:
What is a key benefit of using AWS Lambda for compute workloads?
  A. Ability to run operating system updates on the server
  B. Automatic scaling based on the number of incoming requests
  C. Provisioning storage volumes for large datasets
  D. Deploying on-demand GPU instances for compute-intensive tasks

Question 9:
Which AWS service can integrate directly with AWS Lambda to trigger functions when data is added to a DynamoDB table?
  A. Amazon CloudFront
  B. AWS Step Functions
  C. Amazon S3
  D. Amazon DynamoDB Streams

Question 10:
In EC2 Auto Scaling, what term refers to the metric-based policy that automatically adds instances when performance thresholds are exceeded?
  A. Elastic Load Balancing
  B. Scaling Policy
  C. Dynamic Scaling
  D. Static Scaling

13.6 Answers to Chapter Review Questions
1. B. Compute Optimized (e.g., c5)
Explanation: Compute Optimized instances are designed for workloads requiring high CPU performance, making them ideal for compute-intensive applications.

2. B. Reserved Instances
Explanation: Reserved Instances are best suited for predictable workloads as they offer significant cost savings with a commitment of 1 or 3 years.

3. B. To add and remove instances automatically based on traffic demand
Explanation: EC2 Auto Scaling automatically adjusts the number of instances to maintain performance and meet workload demands.

4. B. Serverless computing
Explanation: AWS Lambda enables serverless computing, allowing users to run code without provisioning or managing servers.

5. A. Amazon S3 events (e.g., file upload)
Explanation: AWS Lambda can be triggered by Amazon S3 events, such as file uploads, deletions, or updates.

6. B. Deploying serverless applications quickly and easily

Explanation: AWS SAM simplifies the process of building and deploying serverless applications using infrastructure-as-code.

7. C. Spot Instances

Explanation: Spot Instances provide access to spare AWS capacity at a reduced cost, making them ideal for fault-tolerant workloads.

8. B. Automatic scaling based on the number of incoming requests

Explanation: AWS Lambda scales automatically based on incoming requests, eliminating the need to manage infrastructure.

9. D. Amazon DynamoDB Streams

Explanation: Amazon DynamoDB Streams can trigger AWS Lambda functions when changes like inserts, updates, or deletes occur in a DynamoDB table.

10. C. Dynamic Scaling

Explanation: Dynamic Scaling uses metric-based policies to automatically add or remove EC2 instances when performance thresholds are exceeded.

Chapter 14. AWS Storage Services

Efficient data storage is at the heart of any modern IT infrastructure, and AWS provides a comprehensive suite of storage solutions tailored to diverse use cases. AWS Storage Services introduces you to the foundational storage offerings that empower organizations to store, manage, and protect their data seamlessly in the cloud.

The chapter begins with Amazon S3 (Simple Storage Service), a scalable object storage solution. You will learn about S3 buckets and objects, the building blocks of S3 storage, and explore various S3 storage classes like Standard, Infrequent Access, and Glacier. The chapter also covers lifecycle rules for automating data transitions between storage classes, and security controls such as permissions and encryption to safeguard your data. A hands-on lab exercise will guide you through creating and managing S3 buckets and objects.

Next, you'll dive into Amazon EBS (Elastic Block Store), which provides block-level storage for EC2 instances. You'll explore EBS volume types (SSD vs. HDD), learn about snapshots for backup and recovery, and practice attaching and detaching volumes. A lab exercise will demonstrate how to provision and manage EBS volumes effectively.

The chapter then introduces Amazon Glacier, AWS's archival storage solution for long-term data retention. You'll understand the concepts of vaults and archives, explore retrieval options, and complete a lab exercise on archiving data with Glacier.

Finally, you'll get an overview of Amazon Elastic File System (EFS), a scalable file storage service for workloads requiring shared access.

By the end of this chapter, you'll have a clear understanding of AWS's core storage services—Amazon S3, EBS, Glacier, and EFS—along with their features, use cases, and hands-on implementation.

14.1 Amazon S3

Amazon Simple Storage Service (Amazon S3) is a highly scalable, durable, and secure object storage service offered by AWS. It allows you to store and retrieve any amount of data, from anywhere on the web, making it ideal for a wide variety of use cases, such as data storage, backup, and content delivery.

Key Features of Amazon S3

Scalability and Durability: Amazon S3 automatically scales to handle large volumes of data. Data is stored with 99.999999999% (11 9's) durability across multiple Availability Zones (AZs).

Storage Classes: Offers multiple storage classes for cost optimization:
- S3 Standard: For frequently accessed data.
- S3 Infrequent Access (IA): For data accessed less frequently.
- S3 Glacier: For long-term archival storage.

Security: Data encryption (in-transit and at-rest). Fine-grained access control using AWS Identity and Access Management (IAM) policies, S3 Bucket Policies, and Access Control Lists (ACLs).

Lifecycle Management: Automatically transition data between storage classes or delete it after a specified time.

Data Management and Analytics: Integrates with AWS services like Amazon Athena and AWS Lake Formation for querying and managing large datasets.

Versioning: Enables versioning to protect against accidental deletions or overwrites.
Cross-Region Replication: Replicate data across regions for disaster recovery and latency reduction.

Common Use Cases of Amazon S3

Backup and Restore: Store backups for disaster recovery and compliance purposes.
Static Website Hosting: Host static websites (HTML, CSS, JS) directly from an S3 bucket.
Data Lakes: Centralize large datasets for analytics and machine learning applications.
Content Delivery: Store and distribute multimedia content (videos, images) efficiently.
Archival Storage: Long-term storage using S3 Glacier for cost-effective archiving.
Application Data Storage: Store application logs, user-generated content, and metadata.

In summary, Amazon S3 is a secure, durable, and scalable object storage service that supports a wide range of workloads, including backup, data lakes, content delivery, and archival storage. Its flexible storage classes, strong security features, and integration with AWS services make it a cornerstone for modern cloud-based applications.

14.1.1 S3 Buckets and Objects: Understanding the basics of S3 storage

Amazon S3 (Simple Storage Service) organizes data storage into buckets and objects, which together form the foundation of S3's object storage model. This architecture makes S3 scalable, durable, and highly reliable for storing and managing data of any size.

14.1.2 S3 Buckets

An S3 bucket is a container for storing objects. It acts as the highest-level namespace in Amazon S3. Each bucket has a globally unique name and is associated with a specific AWS region. You can create up to 100 buckets per AWS account by default (limit can be increased).

Key Characteristics of Buckets
Data Organization: A bucket can store an unlimited number of objects.
Access Control: Use Bucket Policies, Access Control Lists (ACLs), and IAM policies to manage permissions.
Static Website Hosting: Buckets can host static websites using HTML, CSS, and JavaScript.
Storage Management: Enable versioning to keep multiple versions of objects. Configure Lifecycle Policies to manage data storage transitions or expirations.
Cross-Region Replication: Replicate bucket data to another region for disaster recovery or reduced latency.

14.1.3 S3 Objects
An S3 object represents the actual data stored in the bucket. It consists of:
Key: The name or unique identifier for the object within the bucket.
Value: The actual data (file or content).
Metadata: Information about the object (e.g., size, content type, custom metadata).
Version ID (if versioning is enabled): Tracks different versions of the object.
Access Control Information: Determines who can access the object.

Key Characteristics of Objects
Storage Flexibility: Objects can range in size from 0 bytes to 5 TB.
Immutable Data: Objects are immutable—updates require replacing the entire object.
Metadata: Custom metadata can be added to describe the content or provide additional context.
Access: Objects can be accessed via the S3 API, AWS CLI, or the AWS Management Console.

Example: Creating and Managing a Bucket and Object
Create a Bucket:
Name: my-s3-bucket-12345
Region: us-east-1
Upload an Object:
- File: sample-image.jpg
- Key: images/sample-image.jpg
- Metadata: Content-Type: image/jpeg

In summary, in Amazon S3, buckets serve as containers for organizing and managing objects (files and metadata). Buckets provide access control, lifecycle management, and versioning, while objects represent the actual stored data. Together, they form the building blocks of scalable and highly reliable cloud storage for a wide range of use cases.

14.1.4 S3 Storage Classes: Standard, Infrequent Access, and Glacier
Amazon S3 offers multiple storage classes to optimize cost, performance, and access frequency for different use cases. Each storage class provides varying levels of availability, durability, and cost efficiency.

S3 Standard
The default storage class designed for frequently accessed data.

Durability: 99.999999999% (11 9's) durability across multiple Availability Zones.
Availability: 99.99% availability.

Use Case:
- Frequently accessed data.
- Websites, mobile applications, and data analytics workloads.

Cost: Higher storage cost compared to other classes but optimized for fast access.

S3 Standard-Infrequent Access (S3 Standard-IA)

Designed for data accessed less frequently but still requires quick retrieval.
Durability: 99.999999999% durability.
Availability: 99.9% availability.

Use Case:
- Backup and disaster recovery.
- Infrequently accessed files that still need low-latency retrieval.

Cost: Lower storage cost compared to S3 Standard, but with a retrieval fee.

S3 Glacier

Cost-effective solution for long-term archival storage where data retrieval is infrequent.
Durability: 99.999999999% durability.
Availability: Designed for low availability due to long retrieval times.
Retrieval Options:
- Expedited: Minutes.
- Standard: Hours.
- Bulk: Several hours.

Use Case:
- Archiving historical data.
- Compliance and regulatory backups.

Cost: Lowest storage cost but higher retrieval time and fees.

Summary

Amazon S3 storage classes provide flexibility to balance cost and access requirements:

- S3 Standard for frequently accessed data.
- S3 Standard-IA for infrequently accessed but readily retrievable data.
- S3 Glacier for cost-effective long-term archival storage.

By choosing the appropriate storage class, businesses can achieve significant cost savings while maintaining data availability based on their needs.

14.1.5 Moving Between Storage Classes

You can transition S3 objects between storage classes. The diagram shows how objects can be transitioned from one storage class to another. For objects that are accessed **infrequently**, you can move them to STANDARD_IA. For objects you don't need in the immediate or near future, you can move them to GLACIER or DEEP_ARCHIVE.

Moving objects can also be automated using a **lifecycle configuration**.

How objects automatically move between Access Tiers based on usage:
- Frequent Access tier (automatic): default tier
- Infrequent Access tier (automatic): objects not accessed for 30 days
- Archive Instant Access tier (automatic): objects not accessed for 90 days
- Archive Access tier (optional): configurable from 90 days to 700+ days
- Deep Archive Access tier (optional): configurable from 180 days to 700+ days

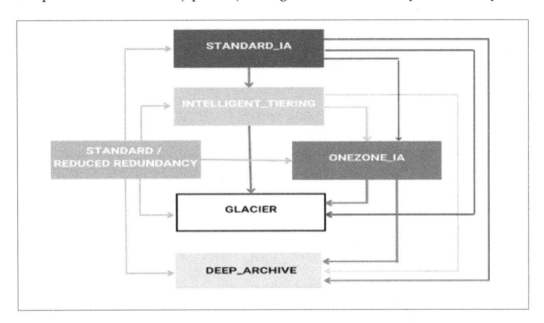

14.1.6 S3 Lifecycle Rules

To store objects cost-effectively throughout their lifecycle, you can transition them manually. You can also configure their *S3 Lifecycle* to automate transition. An *S3 Lifecycle configuration* is a set of rules that define actions that Amazon S3 applies to a group of objects.

Rules can be created for a certain prefix (for example, as s3://mybucket/mp4/*) or for a certain object tag (for example, Department: Marketing).

There are two types of S3 Lifecycle actions:

Transition Actions

It defines when objects are transitioned to another storage class. For example, you might decide to move objects to Standard IA class 60 days after creation or move to Glacier for archival six months after creating them.

Expiration Actions

It defines actions when to expire objects -- Amazon S3 deletes expired objects. For example, expiration actions can be used to delete old version files (if versioning is enabled). Expiration

Actions can be used to delete incomplete multi-part uploads. You can set Access Log files to delete after 365 days using expiration actions.

14.1.7 S3 Security and Access Control: Managing permissions and encryption

Amazon S3 provides robust security and access control mechanisms to ensure data is protected at all levels. It includes tools for managing permissions and encrypting data both at rest and in transit.

Managing Permissions

Amazon S3 uses Access Control Policies to manage who can access buckets and objects:

Bucket Policies: JSON-based policies that define access permissions for entire S3 buckets. Example: Restrict access to specific IAM users or AWS accounts.
Access Control Lists (ACLs): Grant specific permissions (e.g., read, write) to users or groups at the bucket or object level.
IAM Policies: AWS Identity and Access Management (IAM) allows fine-grained control over S3 resources by attaching policies to users, roles, or groups.
Public Access Block: Prevents accidental public exposure of S3 buckets and objects.
Pre-signed URLs: Temporary access URLs for sharing objects securely with external users.

Encryption

S3 provides encryption to protect data at rest and in transit:

Encryption at Rest

Server-Side Encryption (SSE): AWS manages the encryption keys:
- SSE-S3: Keys managed by S3.
- SSE-KMS: Keys managed by AWS KMS (Key Management Service) for enhanced control.
- SSE-C: Customer provides and manages encryption keys.
Client-Side Encryption: Data is encrypted before it is uploaded to S3, and keys are managed by the client.

Encryption in Transit

Uses HTTPS/TLS protocols to secure data while being transferred between clients and S3 buckets.

Monitoring and Auditing

AWS CloudTrail: Logs S3 API calls for auditing and tracking access.
S3 Access Logs: Record requests to buckets and objects for analysis.

In summary, Amazon S3 ensures data security through fine-grained permissions (Bucket Policies, ACLs, IAM roles) and strong encryption mechanisms for data at rest and in transit. By leveraging tools like public access blocks, pre-signed URLs, and CloudTrail logs, businesses can protect sensitive data and maintain compliance.

14.1.8 Lab Exercise: Creating and Managing S3 Buckets and Objects

Follow this step-by-step guide to create an S3 bucket, upload objects, and manage permissions in the AWS Management Console.

Step 1: Log in to AWS Management Console

Go to the AWS Management Console. Log in with your AWS credentials. Navigate to S3 by searching for it in the Services menu.

Step 2: Create a New S3 Bucket

On the S3 Dashboard, click Create bucket. Provide the following details:
* **Bucket name:** Enter a globally unique name, e.g., my-demo-bucket-123.
* **AWS Region:** Select a region, e.g., us-east-1.

Block Public Access Settings: By default, block all public access. Leave the setting enabled unless you need public access.

Bucket Versioning:
Optional: Enable versioning to keep multiple versions of objects.
Encryption:
Optional: Enable server-side encryption (SSE-S3 or SSE-KMS).

Click Create bucket.

Step 3: Upload an Object to the Bucket

Open your newly created bucket. Click Upload and follow these steps:
Add files: Click Add files and select a file from your computer (e.g., example.txt).
Optional: Click Add folder to upload an entire folder.
Permissions: Leave default settings or customize permissions as needed.

Click Upload to upload the file.

Step 4: Access and Manage the Object

In the bucket, you will see the uploaded object. Click on the object name to view its details, such as:
* **Object URL:** Use the URL to access the file (requires proper permissions).
* **Metadata:** Information such as size, type, and encryption.

Download or Delete: Use the Actions menu to download, delete, or manage the object.

Step 5: Set Object Permissions

Select the uploaded object.
Go to the Permissions tab: Modify Access Control List (ACL) to grant permissions to specific AWS accounts or the public. Update Bucket Policy for fine-grained access control using JSON policies. Click Save changes.

Step 6: Enable Versioning (Optional)

Open the bucket and navigate to the Properties tab. Under Bucket Versioning, click Edit and select Enable. Save changes. Upload the same file again with changes and observe multiple versions under Object Versions.

Step 7: Clean Up Resources

To avoid charges, delete all objects in the bucket: Select the object → Click Actions → Delete. **Delete the S3 bucket:** Go back to the S3 dashboard, select the bucket, and click Delete.

Confirm the bucket name and click Delete bucket.

Summary
In this lab, you created an Amazon S3 bucket, uploaded objects, configured permissions, and managed object versions. You also learned how to clean up resources to prevent unnecessary costs. This exercise demonstrates the basics of managing storage in S3 effectively.

14.2 Amazon EBS

Amazon Elastic Block Store (EBS) is a scalable, high-performance block storage service designed for use with Amazon EC2 instances. It provides persistent storage that can be attached to a single EC2 instance, making it ideal for applications requiring reliable and durable data storage. Amazon EBS volumes can be used as primary storage for file systems, databases, and application data.

Key Features of Amazon EBS

Persistent Storage: Data stored on EBS volumes remains intact even when the attached EC2 instance is stopped or terminated.
Scalability: EBS volumes can be dynamically resized to scale storage capacity without downtime.
High Performance: Supports high-throughput and low-latency workloads with options for SSD-backed and HDD-backed storage.
Backup and Recovery: Integrates with Amazon EBS Snapshots to back up data to Amazon S3 for disaster recovery.
Availability and Durability: EBS volumes replicate within the Availability Zone (AZ) to ensure high availability.
Flexible Volume Types: Includes General Purpose (gp3/gp2), Provisioned IOPS (io2/io1), and HDD options for different workload needs.

Common Use Cases

Database Storage: Store data for relational (e.g., MySQL, PostgreSQL) and NoSQL databases.
Enterprise Applications: Run business-critical applications that require durable, consistent storage.
Backup and Recovery: Take snapshots of EBS volumes for backup and disaster recovery.
Big Data and Analytics: Process and store large datasets with high throughput.
Boot Volumes: Use EBS as the root volume for EC2 instances to boot operating systems.

In summary, Amazon EBS provides reliable, scalable, and high-performance block storage for Amazon EC2 instances. Its flexibility, durability, and integration with other AWS services make it an essential storage solution for a variety of workloads, including databases, file systems, and critical applications.

14.2.1 EBS Volume Types: SSD vs. HDD, and use cases for each

Amazon Elastic Block Store (EBS) provides different volume types to optimize performance and cost based on workload requirements. These volumes are categorized into SSD-backed and HDD-backed types.

SSD-Backed Volumes

SSD (Solid-State Drive) volumes are optimized for low-latency and high IOPS (Input/Output Operations Per Second). They are ideal for workloads requiring fast and consistent performance.

Types of SSD Volumes

General Purpose SSD (gp3, gp2):
- Balanced cost and performance.
- Use Case: Boot volumes, small to medium databases, development environments.
- Example: Web servers, MySQL, and test environments.

Provisioned IOPS SSD (io2, io1):
- Designed for applications requiring high, predictable IOPS and low latency.
- Use Case: Mission-critical workloads, large databases (e.g., Oracle, SQL Server).
- Example: High-transaction relational databases and latency-sensitive applications.

HDD-Backed Volumes

HDD (Hard Disk Drive) volumes are optimized for throughput and cost efficiency, making them ideal for workloads requiring large sequential data transfers.

Types of HDD Volumes

Throughput Optimized HDD (st1):
- Optimized for high throughput and large sequential data workloads.
- Use Case: Big data, log processing, and data warehouses.
- Example: Streaming applications using Hadoop or Spark.

Cold HDD (sc1):
- Lowest cost per GB, designed for infrequently accessed data.
- Use Case: Archiving and workloads with low access frequency.
- Example: Backup storage and long-term archives.

Comparison: SSD vs. HDD

Feature	SSD (gp3, io2)	HDD (st1, sc1)
Performance	High IOPS, low latency	High throughput, sequential
Cost	Higher per GB	Lower per GB
Ideal Use Case	Fast, transactional workloads	Large, sequential data access
Example	Databases, boot volumes	Log processing, backups

To summarize, SSD-backed volumes are best for transactional workloads requiring fast and consistent IOPS, such as databases or boot volumes. HDD-backed volumes are ideal for cost-effective storage of large, sequential data, such as big data processing, backups, and archives. By selecting the appropriate volume type, you can optimize performance and cost for your specific workload needs.

14.2.2 EBS Snapshots: Creating and managing snapshots for backup and recovery

Amazon EBS Snapshots provide a point-in-time backup of your Amazon EBS volumes, enabling data protection and recovery. Snapshots are stored in Amazon S3 and can be used to restore volumes or create copies for redundancy.

Key Features of EBS Snapshots

Incremental Backups: EBS Snapshots only save changes (delta) since the last snapshot, optimizing storage costs and backup times.

Point-in-Time Recovery: Snapshots capture the exact state of an EBS volume at a specific moment, allowing reliable recovery.

Cross-Region Replication: Snapshots can be copied to other AWS regions for disaster recovery or geographic redundancy.

Lifecycle Management: Automate the creation, retention, and deletion of snapshots using Amazon Data Lifecycle Manager (DLM).

Fast Recovery: Snapshots allow you to quickly create a new EBS volume to restore data and minimize downtime.

Creating an EBS Snapshot

Open the EC2 Console in the AWS Management Console. Select Volumes from the left-hand menu. Choose the EBS volume you want to back up. Click on Actions → Create Snapshot. Provide a description for the snapshot and confirm creation.

Managing Snapshots

View Snapshots: Navigate to the Snapshots section in the EC2 Console to view available snapshots.

Copy Snapshots: Select a snapshot → Click Actions → Copy to replicate it to another AWS region.

Restore Volumes: Select a snapshot → Click Actions → Create Volume. Use the snapshot to create a new EBS volume for recovery.

Delete Snapshots: To save costs, delete unused snapshots after verifying their redundancy.

Use Cases

Backup and Restore: Take periodic backups of critical EBS volumes for disaster recovery.

Disaster Recovery: Copy snapshots across regions for failover and redundancy.

Volume Migration: Use snapshots to migrate data to another AWS region or account.

Data Archiving: Store long-term backups of critical data efficiently.

To summarize, EBS Snapshots are incremental, point-in-time backups that ensure reliable data recovery and protection. They enable efficient backup management, cross-region replication, and quick disaster recovery, making them a vital tool for maintaining business continuity.

14.2.3 Attaching and Detaching EBS Volumes: Practical use cases

Amazon Elastic Block Store (EBS) allows you to attach and detach volumes to Amazon EC2 instances dynamically. This capability provides flexibility in managing persistent storage for workloads that require scalability and adaptability.

Key Concepts

Attaching EBS Volumes: An EBS volume can be attached to a running EC2 instance, where it acts as a block device similar to a physical hard drive.

Detaching EBS Volumes: Volumes can be safely detached from an instance to stop access or attach to another instance.

Practical Use Cases

Dynamic Storage Expansion: When an EC2 instance requires additional storage for logs or data, a new EBS volume can be attached, formatted, and mounted to the instance. This enables on-demand storage scaling without downtime, ensuring applications can continue to operate seamlessly.

Data Persistence Across Instances: In the event of an EC2 instance failure, the data stored on the EBS volume remains intact. To recover access, the EBS volume can be detached from the failed instance and reattached to a new EC2 instance, preserving data integrity.

Backup and Recovery: For backups without downtime, the EBS volume can be detached and a snapshot can be created. This snapshot is stored for recovery, and the volume can later be reattached or restored from the snapshot as needed.

Testing and Development Environments: When developers require access to specific datasets for testing, the EBS volume can be detached from one instance and attached to a new instance. This ensures isolated testing environments without impacting production systems.

Migrating Data Between Instances: When migrating data between EC2 instances, the EBS volume can be detached from the original instance and reattached to the target instance. This allows for seamless data transfer or continued use of the volume on the new instance.

Scaling Storage Performance: For applications with high I/O workloads requiring optimized storage, the existing volume can be detached, a higher-performance volume (e.g., io2) can be provisioned, and the new volume can be reattached to the instance. This improves storage performance and application efficiency.

Workload Isolation: When multiple workloads share storage but need temporary separation, the EBS volume can be detached from one instance and reattached to another. This allows for isolated processing of workloads without interference.

Steps to Attach an EBS Volume

Open the EC2 Console. Go to Volumes and select the desired EBS volume. Click Actions → Attach Volume. Select the target Instance ID and specify the device name (e.g., /dev/sdf). Log in to the instance and: Format the volume (if new). Mount it to the desired directory.

Steps to Detach an EBS Volume

Ensure the EC2 instance is stopped or the volume is unmounted safely. In the EC2 Console, go to Volumes. Select the volume and click Actions → Detach Volume.

In summary, attaching and detaching EBS volumes allows dynamic storage management, supporting scenarios such as scaling storage, data migration, backups, and workload isolation. This flexibility ensures that EBS can meet evolving application and operational requirements.

14.2.4 Lab Exercise: Creating and Attaching EBS Volumes to EC2 Instances

Follow these step-by-step instructions to create an EBS volume and attach it to an EC2 instance in the AWS Management Console.

Step 1: Log in to AWS Management Console

Go to the AWS Management Console. Log in using your AWS credentials. Navigate to EC2 by searching for it in the Services menu.

Step 2: Launch an EC2 Instance (if not already running)

On the EC2 dashboard, click Launch Instance. Select an Amazon Machine Image (AMI) (e.g., Amazon Linux 2). Choose an Instance Type (e.g., t2.micro) and click Next. Configure instance details as needed and proceed to the Launch step. Select or create a key pair and launch the instance. Verify the instance is running in the Instances dashboard.

Step 3: Create an EBS Volume

In the EC2 Console, navigate to Volumes under the Elastic Block Store section.
Click Create Volume.
Provide the following details:
   • Volume Type: Choose a type (e.g., General Purpose SSD gp2).
   • Size: Specify the size in GiB (e.g., 10 GiB).
   • Availability Zone: Ensure it matches the Availability Zone of your EC2 instance.

Click Create Volume to finalize. Once created, verify the volume appears in the Volumes list with the Available state.

Step 4: Attach the EBS Volume to the EC2 Instance

Select the newly created EBS volume from the Volumes list. Click Actions → Attach Volume. In the Instance field, select the running EC2 instance. Specify a Device Name (e.g., /dev/sdf for Linux). Click Attach Volume. Verify the volume status changes to In-Use.

Step 5: Connect to the EC2 Instance and Mount the EBS Volume

Use SSH to connect to the EC2 instance. Example command:

```
ssh -i "your-key.pem" ec2-user@<public-IP-address>
```

List the attached block devices:
```
lsblk
```

Verify the new volume (e.g., /dev/xvdf) appears in the list.
Format the new EBS volume (if unformatted):
```
sudo mkfs -t ext4 /dev/xvdf
```

Create a mount point:
```
sudo mkdir /mnt/ebs-volume
```

Mount the EBS volume:
```
sudo mount /dev/xvdf /mnt/ebs-volume
```

Verify the mount:
```
df -h
```
The mounted volume should now be visible under /mnt/ebs-volume.

Step 6: Configure Persistent Mounting (Optional)
To ensure the EBS volume is mounted automatically on reboot:

Edit the /etc/fstab file:
```
sudo vi /etc/fstab
```

Add the following line to the file:
```
/dev/xvdf   /mnt/ebs-volume   ext4   defaults,nofail   0   2
```
Save the file and exit.

Step 7: Verify and Clean Up Resources
Verify the volume is attached and mounted correctly. To clean up, unmount the volume and detach it:

Unmount:
```
sudo umount /mnt/ebs-volume
```
Detach: Go to the Volumes section, select the volume, and click Actions → Detach Volume. Delete the volume if no longer needed: Click Actions → Delete Volume.

To summarize, In this lab exercise, you successfully created an EBS volume, attached it to an EC2 instance, and mounted it for use. This process enables persistent, flexible storage for your applications and data.

14.3 Amazon Glacier

14.3.1 Introduction to Glacier: Long-term archival storage

Amazon S3 Glacier is a low-cost, long-term archival storage solution provided by AWS for storing data that is accessed infrequently but needs to be retained for compliance, backup, or regulatory purposes. It is designed for durability, cost efficiency, and scalability.

Key Features of S3 Glacier

Cost-Effective Storage: Ideal for data that does not require immediate access, offering the lowest storage cost compared to other S3 classes.

Durability: Provides **99.999999999%** (**11 9's**) durability by replicating data across multiple Availability Zones (AZs).

Retrieval Options: Supports different retrieval speeds to balance cost and access needs:
- Expedited: Retrieve data in minutes.
- Standard: Retrieve data in hours.
- Bulk: Cost-efficient retrieval for large datasets over several hours.

Data Lifecycle Management: Easily transition data to Glacier using S3 Lifecycle Policies for automated archival.

Security and Compliance: Supports encryption (at rest and in transit) and integrates with AWS Identity and Access Management (IAM) for secure access.

Use Cases for S3 Glacier

Data Archiving: Store large datasets such as historical records, logs, and audit files.

Backup and Disaster Recovery: Retain critical backups for long-term recovery and compliance.

Regulatory Compliance: Archive sensitive or legally required data for extended retention periods.

Media Archives: Store multimedia files like video footage or images that are rarely accessed.

In summary, Amazon S3 Glacier is a highly durable, low-cost solution for long-term archival storage. With flexible retrieval options and integration with S3 Lifecycle Policies, Glacier is an excellent choice for organizations looking to retain infrequently accessed data securely and affordably.

14.3.2 Vaults and Archives: Managing Glacier storage

Amazon S3 Glacier uses Vaults and Archives to organize and manage data for long-term archival storage. These concepts allow efficient storage and retrieval while keeping costs low.

Vaults

A vault is a container where you store archived data in Amazon S3 Glacier. It serves as the top-level storage unit in Glacier.

Key Characteristics
- Each AWS region can have multiple vaults within your AWS account.
- Vaults are created, managed, and deleted using the AWS Management Console, CLI, or API.

- Access Policies: You can configure IAM policies or vault access policies to control access to data.
- Vault Inventory: Glacier maintains an inventory of all archives in a vault, which is updated daily.

Example: Create a vault named project-logs-vault in the us-east-1 region to store historical log files.

Archives

An archive is the actual unit of data stored within a vault. Archives can be any file format (e.g., documents, images, videos) and are stored as individual objects.

Key Characteristics
- Each archive is identified by a unique Archive ID (generated automatically).
- Archives can be up to 40 TB in size.
- Data is immutable: archives cannot be modified once uploaded but can be deleted.
- Upload archives using AWS CLI, SDKs, or Glacier APIs.

Example: Upload a 10 GB archive containing monthly financial data to the project-logs-vault.

Managing Vaults and Archives

Creating a Vault: Use the AWS Management Console or CLI to create a vault in the desired region.

Uploading Archives: Use the Glacier Upload Archive API or AWS CLI to store data.

Retrieving Data: Initiate retrieval requests with options like Expedited, Standard, or Bulk retrieval.

Vault Lock: Configure Vault Lock policies to enforce compliance controls, such as preventing data deletion.

Monitoring: Use AWS CloudWatch to monitor API calls and track activity in vaults.

In summary, Vaults serve as containers for organizing and securing archives, while archives are the actual data stored within the vaults. Together, these components enable efficient management of Amazon Glacier storage for archival, compliance, and backup needs.

14.3.3 Retrieving Data from Glacier: Different retrieval options

Amazon S3 Glacier provides flexible retrieval options to meet varying access needs for archived data. Each option balances speed and cost, making Glacier suitable for different use cases.

Expedited Retrieval

Speed: Data is available in 1–5 minutes.

Use Case: When immediate access to archived data is needed, such as recovering critical files during emergencies.

Cost: Higher compared to other retrieval options due to the rapid access speed.

Example: Quickly retrieving a specific document required for compliance audits.

Standard Retrieval
Speed: Data is available in 3–5 hours.
Use Case: For occasional data access where a moderate retrieval time is acceptable. Suitable for backup recovery and non-urgent workflows.
Cost: Lower than Expedited Retrieval and provides a balance between cost and retrieval time.
Example: Restoring backup files for routine maintenance or recovery processes.

Bulk Retrieval
Speed: Data is available in 5–12 hours.
Use Case: Ideal for retrieving large amounts of data (e.g., TBs or PBs) at the lowest cost. Best for infrequent, large-scale access.
Cost: Most cost-effective option but has the longest retrieval time.
Example: Restoring entire archives for historical records or long-term data analysis.

Summary
Amazon S3 Glacier offers three retrieval options — Expedited, Standard, and Bulk — to cater to different access requirements:
- Expedited for quick access within minutes.
- Standard for moderate-speed retrieval in hours.
- Bulk for cost-effective, large-scale retrieval over several hours.

By selecting the appropriate retrieval option, businesses can optimize both cost and performance for their archival storage needs.

14.3.4 Lab Exercise: Archiving Data with Amazon Glacier
Follow these step-by-step instructions to archive data using Amazon S3 Glacier and understand the process of storing, managing, and retrieving data.

Step 1: Log in to AWS Management Console
Go to the AWS Management Console. Sign in using your AWS credentials. Navigate to S3 Glacier by searching for it in the Services menu.

Step 2: Create a Glacier Vault
In the Amazon S3 Glacier Console, select the region where you want to store data. Click on Create Vault. Provide the following details:
- Vault Name: Enter a unique name, e.g., glacier-archive-demo.
- Region: Confirm the region (e.g., us-east-1).

Click Create Vault to finalize. Once created, you will see the vault listed in the console.

Step 3: Upload Data to the Glacier Vault
Amazon Glacier does not provide a direct file upload option in the console. Use the AWS CLI or SDKs: Install AWS CLI: Ensure AWS CLI is installed and configured with your credentials. Use the following command to upload a file:

```
aws glacier upload-archive --vault-name glacier-archive-demo --account-id - --body example-data.txt
```

Replace glacier-archive-demo with your vault name and example-data.txt with your file.

Note the Archive ID returned after a successful upload. This is essential for retrieving the data.

Step 4: Verify the Archive Upload

Go back to the Glacier Console and select the vault. Verify that the archive was uploaded successfully.

Note: The inventory may take up to 24 hours to update.

Step 5: Retrieve Archived Data

To retrieve the archived data, initiate a retrieval job using the AWS CLI:

```
aws glacier initiate-job --vault-name glacier-archive-demo --account-id - --job-parameters '{"Type":
"archive-retrieval", "ArchiveId": "<archive-id>"}'
```

Replace <archive-id> with the Archive ID returned during upload.
Use one of the retrieval options:
- Expedited (1–5 minutes)
- Standard (3–5 hours)
- Bulk (5–12 hours)

Step 6: Monitor Job Status

Check the status of your retrieval job:

```
aws glacier describe-job --vault-name glacier-archive-demo --account-id - --job-id <job-id>
```

Once the job is complete, download the archive using the AWS CLI:

```
aws glacier get-job-output --vault-name glacier-archive-demo --account-id - --job-id <job-id> output-
file.txt
```

Replace <job-id> with the ID of the retrieval job.

Step 7: Clean Up Resources

Delete archives you no longer need:

```
aws glacier delete-archive --vault-name glacier-archive-demo --account-id - --archive-id <archive-id>
```

To delete the vault: Ensure all archives are deleted. Use the console or AWS CLI to delete the vault.

Summary
In this lab, you created a Glacier vault, uploaded data as archives, and retrieved it using CLI commands. This hands-on exercise demonstrated the process of archiving and retrieving long-term storage data using Amazon S3 Glacier efficiently.

14.4 Overview of Amazon Elastic File System (EFS)

Amazon Elastic File System (EFS) is a fully managed, serverless file storage service designed to provide scalable, shared storage for use with Amazon EC2 instances, containers, and on-premises servers. It allows multiple resources to access a shared file system simultaneously, making it ideal for applications requiring consistent, low-latency file access.

Key Features of Amazon EFS

Fully Managed: EFS eliminates the need for infrastructure management, providing a simple setup for shared file storage.

Scalable: Automatically scales up or down based on the amount of data stored, without provisioning or management overhead.

Elastic Performance: Offers two performance modes:
- General Purpose: Low latency for general workloads.
- Max I/O: Higher throughput for large-scale workloads.

High Availability and Durability: Data is stored redundantly across multiple Availability Zones (AZs) for reliability and fault tolerance.

Multiple Access: Supports simultaneous access by thousands of instances, enabling shared access to data.

Secure: Integrated with AWS Identity and Access Management (IAM) and supports encryption in transit and at rest.

Common Use Cases

Web Serving and Content Management: Centralized file storage for websites and CMS applications.
Application Development and Testing: Shared file systems for development, testing, and CI/CD pipelines.
Big Data and Analytics: Processing large datasets requiring shared file storage.
Backup and Disaster Recovery: Store and access backup files reliably.
Container Storage: Shared storage for containers running in Amazon ECS, EKS, or Kubernetes.

In summary, Amazon EFS provides highly available, scalable, and secure file storage for a wide range of workloads. Its elasticity and ability to support multiple concurrent connections make it an ideal solution for modern applications requiring shared access to file systems.

14.5 Related YouTube Videos

- Amazon S3 Tutorial: https://youtu.be/wgFAypkUl3w
- S3 Bucket Tutorial: https://youtu.be/ZUuf7JGoI0E
- S3 Storage Classes: https://youtu.be/Nj0Htnsbq1w
- S3 Versioning: https://youtu.be/uGiBf7rI54U
- S3 Replication: https://youtu.be/Nj0Htnsbq1w
- AWS Snow Family Tutorial: https://youtu.be/oXET04W7qR4

14.6 Chapter Review Questions

Question 1:
Which of the following correctly defines an S3 bucket?
- A. A database to store structured data
- B. A container for storing objects in Amazon S3
- C. A virtual machine for storage
- D. A tool for managing file systems

Question 2:
Which Amazon S3 storage class is best for long-term archival storage at the lowest cost?
- A. S3 Standard
- B. S3 One Zone-Infrequent Access
- C. S3 Glacier
- D. S3 Intelligent-Tiering

Question 3:
What is the primary difference between S3 objects and S3 buckets?
- A. Buckets store metadata, and objects store permissions.
- B. Buckets act as containers for objects, while objects are individual data items.
- C. Objects are regions, and buckets are access policies.
- D. Buckets provide storage limits, and objects manage users.

Question 4:
Which EBS volume type is ideal for workloads requiring high IOPS performance?
- A. General Purpose SSD (gp3)
- B. Throughput Optimized HDD (st1)
- C. Provisioned IOPS SSD (io2)
- D. Cold HDD (sc1)

Question 5:
What is the purpose of creating EBS snapshots?
- A. To restore EC2 instances to a previous state
- B. To automatically scale EBS volumes
- C. To transfer instances across AWS regions
- D. To provide low-latency storage

Question 6:
Which of the following accurately describes Amazon Glacier?
- A. A managed relational database
- B. A low-latency storage solution
- C. A long-term archival storage service for infrequent access
- D. A file-sharing system for multi-instance access

Question 7:
In Amazon Glacier, what is the purpose of a vault?
- A. A temporary storage directory for frequently accessed files
- B. A container to organize archives for long-term storage
- C. A region-specific replication backup

D. A tool for monitoring storage access

Question 8:
Which AWS storage service provides shared access to file systems across multiple EC2 instances?
  A. Amazon S3
  B. Amazon Glacier
  C. Amazon Elastic File System (EFS)
  D. Amazon EBS

Question 9:
Which of the following features enhances the security of S3 objects?
  A. Subnet routing
  B. Security Groups
  C. Bucket Policies and Encryption
  D. EBS Snapshots

Question 10:
Which of the following EBS volume types is suitable for cold workloads and large sequential access?
  A. General Purpose SSD (gp2)
  B. Cold HDD (sc1)
  C. Provisioned IOPS SSD (io1)
  D. Magnetic Storage

14.7 Answers to Chapter Review Questions

1. B. A container for storing objects in Amazon S3
Explanation: An S3 bucket acts as a container to store objects (data files) in Amazon S3.

2. C. S3 Glacier
Explanation: S3 Glacier is specifically designed for long-term archival storage at the lowest cost, ideal for infrequent access.

3. B. Buckets act as containers for objects, while objects are individual data items.
Explanation: S3 buckets store and organize objects, while objects represent the individual files and their metadata.

4. C. Provisioned IOPS SSD (io2)
Explanation: Provisioned IOPS SSD (io2) volumes are optimized for workloads requiring high IOPS and low latency, such as databases.

5. A. To restore EC2 instances to a previous state
Explanation: EBS snapshots are used to back up data, allowing you to restore EC2 instances or volumes to a specific state.

6. C. A long-term archival storage service for infrequent access
Explanation: Amazon Glacier is designed for durable, low-cost, long-term archival storage for data that is rarely accessed.

7. B. A container to organize archives for long-term storage
Explanation: In Amazon Glacier, a vault is a container used to store and manage archives for long-term storage.

8. C. Amazon Elastic File System (EFS)
Explanation: Amazon EFS provides shared access to file systems across multiple EC2 instances, making it ideal for applications requiring shared storage.

9. C. Bucket Policies and Encryption
Explanation: S3 security is enhanced using bucket policies to manage permissions and encryption to protect data at rest and in transit.

10. B. Cold HDD (sc1)
Explanation: Cold HDD (sc1) volumes are cost-effective for cold workloads and optimized for large sequential access patterns.

Chapter 15. AWS Database Services

Databases form the backbone of any application, and AWS offers a robust suite of managed database services to meet the needs of diverse workloads—from relational databases to NoSQL and data warehousing solutions. In AWS Database Services, you will explore the powerful offerings that help organizations simplify database management, ensure scalability, and optimize performance.

The chapter begins with Amazon RDS (Relational Database Service), AWS's fully managed relational database solution. You'll learn about RDS database engines, including MySQL, PostgreSQL, Oracle, SQL Server, and MariaDB. Key topics such as auto-scaling storage, automated backups, and Multi-AZ deployments will be covered, ensuring high availability and durability. A lab exercise will guide you through launching and managing an RDS instance.

Next, the chapter introduces Amazon DynamoDB, a NoSQL database service designed for high performance and scalability. You'll explore the fundamentals of NoSQL, including DynamoDB's capacity modes, tables, items, and the use of indexes to optimize data retrieval. Hands-on learning through a lab exercise will teach you how to create and query DynamoDB tables.

You will then delve into Amazon Redshift, AWS's data warehousing solution for big data analytics. This section covers the architecture of Redshift clusters and nodes, techniques for optimizing queries and performance, and a step-by-step lab exercise on setting up and querying a Redshift cluster.

The chapter concludes with an overview of Amazon Aurora, Amazon ElastiCache, and Amazon MemoryDB for Redis, giving you insights into high-performance, in-memory, and advanced relational database solutions.

By the end of this chapter, you will understand how AWS's database services—RDS, DynamoDB, Redshift, Aurora, ElastiCache, and MemoryDB—empower businesses to manage data efficiently, improve scalability, and unlock powerful analytical capabilities.

15.1 Amazon RDS

15.1.1 Introduction to RDS: Managed relational database service

Amazon Relational Database Service (RDS) is a fully managed service that makes it easy to set up, operate, and scale relational databases in the cloud. RDS simplifies database administration tasks such as provisioning, patching, backups, and scaling, allowing organizations to focus on their applications instead of infrastructure management.

Key Features of Amazon RDS

Fully Managed: AWS handles database setup, maintenance, patching, and automated backups.

Database Engine Support: Supports popular relational database engines, including: Amazon Aurora, MySQL, PostgreSQL, MariaDB, Oracle, and SQL Server.

Scalability: Easily scale compute and storage resources vertically or horizontally.

Automated Backups and Snapshots: Provides automatic daily backups and point-in-time recovery.

High Availability: Multi-AZ deployments ensure high availability and fault tolerance.

Security: Integrated with AWS Identity and Access Management (IAM) and supports encryption in transit and at rest.

Performance Monitoring: Integrated with Amazon CloudWatch for monitoring metrics like CPU, memory, and throughput.

Common Use Cases

Web Applications: Hosting backend databases for web applications (e.g., MySQL or PostgreSQL).

E-commerce Platforms: Reliable and scalable database storage for shopping platforms.

Enterprise Applications: Managed solutions for Oracle and SQL Server-based workloads.

Analytics and Reporting: Using relational databases for data analytics and business intelligence.

Disaster Recovery: Multi-AZ deployments for fault tolerance and data redundancy.

In summary, Amazon RDS simplifies database management by automating maintenance tasks, improving scalability, and ensuring high availability. It supports multiple database engines and provides a secure, fully managed environment, making it ideal for modern applications that rely on relational databases.

15.1.2 RDS Database Engines: MySQL, PostgreSQL, Oracle, SQL Server, and MariaDB

Amazon RDS supports a variety of popular database engines, enabling organizations to run managed relational databases tailored to their application needs. Below is a brief overview of the supported engines:

MySQL

MySQL is an open-source relational database widely used for web applications and transactional workloads.

Features: High performance and scalability. Broad community support and integration with tools like PHP, Python, and WordPress.

Use Case: Web applications, content management systems (CMS), and e-commerce platforms.

PostgreSQL

PostgreSQL is an open-source, advanced relational database known for its extensibility and compliance with SQL standards.

Features: Supports JSON, geospatial data, and advanced queries. High performance for complex workloads and large datasets.

Use Case: Enterprise applications, analytics, and applications requiring complex queries.

Oracle

Oracle is a commercial database engine known for its robust features, scalability, and enterprise-grade reliability.

Features: Supports advanced data management features like RAC (Real Application Clusters). Suited for mission-critical, enterprise workloads.

Use Case: ERP systems, enterprise-grade applications, and large-scale business operations.

SQL Server

Microsoft SQL Server is a relational database designed for Windows-based applications with deep integration into Microsoft ecosystems.

Features: Built-in analytics and reporting tools like SSRS and SSIS. High availability options, including Multi-AZ deployments.

Use Case: Business applications, data warehousing, and Microsoft-based enterprise workloads.

MariaDB

MariaDB is an open-source database forked from MySQL, offering performance improvements and compatibility with MySQL.

Features: Optimized for high performance and scalability. Supports additional storage engines like Aria and XtraDB.

Use Case: Modern applications, web servers, and e-commerce systems requiring high throughput.

Summary

Amazon RDS supports MySQL, PostgreSQL, Oracle, SQL Server, and MariaDB to provide flexibility for different workloads and organizational needs. Whether you require high performance, advanced features, or enterprise-grade reliability, RDS makes it easy to manage and scale these engines in the cloud.

15.1.3 Database Storage Auto Scaling

Amazon RDS helps increase database storage dynamically. When RDS detects that database storage runs out of free storage, it scales automatically. That way, it avoids going through the effort of manually scaling your database storage.

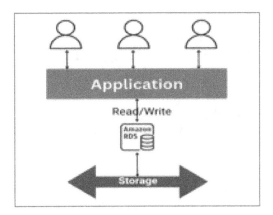

Auto-scaling of database storage is useful for applications with unpredictable workloads. Therefore, all RDS engines support auto-scaling of database storage. You have to set up a maximum storage threshold, the maximum limit for database storage. Then it automatically scales storage if free storage < 10% of allocates storage, low storage lasts at least 5 minutes, or 6 hours have elapsed since the last modification

15.1.4 RDS Backup and Restore: Automated backups, snapshots, and restores

Amazon RDS provides robust backup and restore capabilities to ensure data durability and minimize data loss. These features simplify database management by automating backups and enabling easy recovery.

Automated Backups

Amazon RDS automatically takes backups of your database during a defined backup window.
Key Features: Retains backups for a configurable period (1–35 days). Supports point-in-time recovery within the retention period. Includes transaction logs for recovering to any second within the backup window.
Use Case: Ensures regular backups for production databases without manual intervention.

Database Snapshots

Snapshots are user-initiated backups that capture the current state of the database.
Key Features: Stored until explicitly deleted by the user. Snapshots can be copied across AWS Regions for redundancy. Used to create new RDS instances (restoring data to a specific point).
Use Case: Taking ad-hoc backups before updates, migrations, or application changes.

Restoring Databases

Point-in-Time Restore: Allows recovery to any second within the automated backup retention window.
Snapshot Restore: Restores data to a new RDS instance using a previously created snapshot.
Process:
  • Choose a recovery point or snapshot.
  • Launch a new instance with the restored data.
Use Case: Recovering from accidental data deletion, corruption, or system failures.

In summary, Amazon RDS offers automated backups for continuous data protection, user-initiated snapshots for custom backup needs, and flexible restore options to ensure database reliability. These features help organizations safeguard their data and minimize downtime during recovery scenarios.

15.1.5 RDS Multi-AZ Deployments

Amazon RDS Multi-AZ deployments provide increased performance, availability, durability, and automatic failover for RDS database instances. This helps in managing database workloads.

When you provision a Multi-AZ RDS Instance, Amazon RDS automatically creates a primary DB Instance. The Amazon RDS then synchronously replicates the data to the standby instance in a different Availability Zone (AZ). In case of an infrastructure failure, Amazon RDS performs an automatic failover to the standby so that database operations can be resumed as soon as the failover is complete.

Automatic database failover can complete as quickly as 60 seconds with zero data loss and no manual intervention. Since the endpoint for your DB Instance doesn't change after a failover, the application can resume its database operation without needing manual administrative intervention.

15.1.6 RDS Multi-AZ with One Stand-By Database

Setting up multi-AZ with a stand-by database from a single AZ is a zero-downtime operation – you don't need to stop the database. Just click on "modify" for the database.

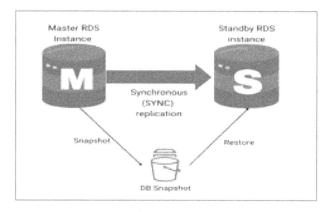

Then internally, a snapshot is taken, a new DB is restored from the snapshot in a new AZ, and synchronization is established between the two databases.

15.1.7 Lab Exercise: Launching and Managing an RDS Instance

This step-by-step guide will help you launch and manage a relational database instance using Amazon RDS.

Step 1: Log in to AWS Management Console

Go to the AWS Management Console. Log in with your AWS credentials. In the search bar, type RDS and select Amazon RDS from the services list.

Step 2: Create a New RDS Instance

On the Amazon RDS Dashboard, click Create Database. Select the Standard Create option for more customization.

Choose Engine: Select a database engine (e.g., MySQL, PostgreSQL, or MariaDB).

Specify Database Settings:
- **DB Instance Identifier:** Provide a name for your database instance (e.g., lab-rds-instance).
- **Master Username:** Set the admin username.
- **Master Password:** Enter a strong password and confirm it.

Choose Instance Type: Select the desired instance type (e.g., db.t3.micro for free-tier eligible options).

Storage Settings: Set allocated storage (e.g., 20 GB). Enable Auto Scaling if needed to automatically adjust storage.

Connectivity: Select the VPC where the RDS instance will reside. Set Public Access to Yes (if you want to connect from outside the VPC). Configure the port (default is 3306 for MySQL).

Additional Configuration: Enable Automatic Backups. Set backup retention (e.g., 7 days). Add Monitoring and Performance Insights as needed.

Click Create Database to launch the RDS instance.

Step 3: Monitor the RDS Instance

Return to the Databases section in the RDS dashboard. Verify the new instance status as Available (this might take a few minutes). View key information like endpoint, instance name, and resource usage.

Step 4: Connect to the RDS Instance

Use an SQL client like MySQL Workbench or the command line. Gather the following details from the RDS console:

Endpoint: Hostname of the RDS instance.

Port: Default is 3306 for MySQL.

Username and Password: Use the credentials you set earlier.

Connect using the following command (example for MySQL):

```
mysql -h <endpoint> -P 3306 -u <username> -p
```

Enter the password when prompted.

Step 5: Perform Database Operations

Create a sample database:

```
CREATE DATABASE lab_test;
```

Use the database:

```
USE lab_test;
```

Create a sample table:

```
CREATE TABLE employees (
```

```
    id INT AUTO_INCREMENT PRIMARY KEY,
    name VARCHAR(255) NOT NULL,
    position VARCHAR(255),
    salary INT
);
```

Insert sample data:
```
INSERT INTO employees (name, position, salary)
VALUES ('John Doe', 'Manager', 75000), ('Jane Smith', 'Engineer', 60000);
```

Query the data:
```
SELECT * FROM employees;
```

Step 6: Modify the RDS Instance

Go back to the RDS Console. Select your database instance and click Modify. Change parameters like storage, instance class, or backups. Save changes and monitor the instance for updates.

Step 7: Delete the RDS Instance (Optional Cleanup)

In the RDS Console, select your instance. Click Actions → Delete. Confirm the deletion and choose to create a final snapshot if needed. Wait until the RDS instance is deleted.

Summary
In this lab exercise, you successfully launched, connected, and managed an Amazon RDS instance. You also performed basic database operations and learned how to modify and clean up the instance. This demonstrates how Amazon RDS simplifies the management of relational databases in the cloud.

15.2 Amazon DynamoDB

15.2.1 Introduction to NoSQL: Benefits and use cases of NoSQL databases

NoSQL databases are a modern solution for handling unstructured, semi-structured, or large-scale data with flexibility and scalability. Unlike traditional relational databases, NoSQL databases do not rely on fixed schemas and support a variety of data models, including key-value, document, columnar, and graph databases. They offer several key benefits, including **scalability**, where data can be horizontally scaled across multiple servers to handle large datasets, and flexibility, which allows the storage of unstructured and semi-structured data without predefined schemas. NoSQL databases also provide **high performance** with faster read and write operations, making them ideal for real-time applications, and ensure **high availability** through built-in redundancy and distributed architectures that minimize downtime and provide fault tolerance.

The use cases for NoSQL databases are diverse. They are widely used in **real-time applications** like gaming leaderboards and IoT sensor data streams. In **content management systems**, NoSQL databases store and manage documents, images, and videos efficiently. E-commerce platforms utilize NoSQL for managing **product catalogs and customer sessions**, where data must be retrieved and updated quickly. For **big data analytics**, they process large datasets to derive actionable insights. Additionally, NoSQL databases are essential for **social media platforms**, where they manage user profiles, posts, and relationships at scale. Popular NoSQL databases like **Amazon DynamoDB, MongoDB,** and **Cassandra** excel in applications requiring speed, scalability, and agility, making them a critical component of modern, data-driven applications.

15.2.2 Amazon DynamoDB Basics

DynamoDB is a collection of tables. Each table has a Primary Key – it must be defined at the table creation time. Once a primary key is defined on the table, it cannot be changed. Each table can contain an infinite number of rows. Each table contains attributes, and additional attributes can be added over time. In addition, an item can be null. In many ways, attributes in DynamoDB tables are similar to fields or columns in other database systems. The maximum size of an item is 400 KB.

The supported data types are:
- Scalar Types – String, Number, Binary, Boolean, Null
- Set Types – String, Set, Number Set, Binary Set
- Document Types – List, Map

Partition Key	Sort Key	Attribute	Attribute
user_id	**event**	**web_page**	**duration_in_sec**
x1234	click	cart	25
y1234	purchase	checkout	45
a1234	impression	product	15
b1234	view	home	35

A Partition Key is a key that DynamoDB uses to partition your data into separate logical data shards. For example, when there is no Sort Key, then Primary Key also works as Partition Key. You can also add a Sort Key and make the primary key a composite primary key: Partition Key + Sort Key. Adding a Sort Key allows storing multiple records with the same partition key value since the partition key + sort key forms a unique pair and stores the data with the same partition key in the same data shard. DynamoDB dynamically partitions (shards) data across all of the nodes in a cluster.

15.2.3 Read/Write Capacity Modes

There are two modes to define how much read/write capacity your table needs: on-demand and provisioned (default). The read/write capacity mode controls costs for read/write throughput and how you manage capacity. You can set the capacity mode for a table when creating the table -- you can change it later.

Provisioned Mode (default)

In provisioned Mode, you need to specify the number of reads/writes per second required for your application. You need to plan the capacity. You pay for provisioned Read Capacity Units (RCU) & Write Capacity Units (WCU). You can also auto-scaling to adjust your table provisioned reads/writes capacity in response to your workload traffic change.

Provisioned Mode is a good option in the following use cases:
- You have predictable workloads
- You run applications whose workload is consistent or ramps up gradually.
- You can forecast the reads/writes capacity for your workloads.

On-Demand Mode
In On-Demand mode, read/writes are automatically scaled up/down with your workloads to maintain the throughput of single-digit millisecond latency. You don't need any capacity planning. You pay for what you use – it is more expensive.

On-Demand mode is a good option for use cases having unpredictable workloads or sudden steep spikes.

15.2.4 DynamoDB Tables and Items: Creating and managing tables and items

Amazon DynamoDB is a fully managed NoSQL database service that stores data in tables, which act as containers for items. A **table** in DynamoDB is the primary structure that organizes data, much like a table in a relational database but without a predefined schema. Instead, each table can store **items**, which are individual records consisting of **attributes**. Attributes are key-value pairs that hold the actual data, where each item must include a unique primary key (either a partition key or a composite key with a sort key) to identify it.

Creating a table in DynamoDB involves defining the table name, primary key, and optionally enabling features like on-demand capacity or provisioned throughput. Once the table is set up, you can insert items, update attributes, and delete records seamlessly. Items are highly flexible as they allow different attributes for each record, enabling you to store unstructured or semi-structured data efficiently. DynamoDB supports operations like *PutItem* for creating records, *GetItem* for retrieving specific items, and *UpdateItem* for modifying attributes without rewriting the entire record.

Managing DynamoDB tables also involves configuring indexes, such as **Global Secondary Indexes (GSI)** and **Local Secondary Indexes (LSI),** to optimize queries for different access patterns. Tables can also be integrated with **DynamoDB Streams** to capture changes in real time for further processing. For example, in an e-commerce application, a table can store customer orders, where each item represents a unique order with attributes like order ID, product details, and order status. By leveraging DynamoDB's scalability and low-latency performance, applications can efficiently manage vast amounts of data across tables and items.

15.2.5 DynamoDB Indexes and Queries: Optimizing data retrieval

Amazon DynamoDB Indexes and Queries are key features that optimize data retrieval and allow efficient access to large datasets. By default, DynamoDB uses the primary key of a table (either partition key or composite key) to retrieve items efficiently. However, when applications require querying based on attributes other than the primary key, indexes provide an optimized solution.

Indexes in DynamoDB
DynamoDB offers two types of indexes:

Local Secondary Index (LSI)
- LSI allows you to query a table using a different sort key while sharing the same partition key as the base table.
- It is created at the time of table creation, and the data in the index is always synchronized with the base table.
- Example Use Case: Querying orders in a customer table based on order date, where the partition key is CustomerID, and the sort key for LSI is OrderDate.

Global Secondary Index (GSI)
- GSI allows querying based on a completely different partition and sort key compared to the base table.
- It can be created at any time and provides flexibility for diverse query patterns.
- Example Use Case: Querying orders based on ProductID instead of CustomerID in an orders table.

Optimizing Queries
DynamoDB allows applications to retrieve data efficiently using the Query and Scan operations:
- **Query Operation:** Retrieves items based on the primary key or an index. It is highly efficient as it limits results to matching keys. For example, querying all orders by a CustomerID using the primary key or by ProductID via a GSI.
- **Scan Operation:** Reads all items in a table and filters results based on conditions. However, it is less efficient as it processes the entire table, making it suitable for small datasets.

Best Practices for Optimizing Retrieval
- **Use Global Secondary Indexes (GSI)** for flexible queries on non-key attributes.
- Leverage **Local Secondary Indexes (LSI)** when alternate sort keys are needed for queries.
- Use the **Query** operation instead of Scan to reduce read costs and improve performance.
- Design tables with **access patterns** in mind to avoid costly and inefficient retrieval.

For example, in an e-commerce application, you can design a table where the primary key is CustomerID, but a GSI allows querying all orders for a particular ProductID. By effectively using DynamoDB indexes, you can achieve low-latency data retrieval and optimize your queries for diverse access patterns.

15.2.6 Lab Exercise: Creating and Querying a DynamoDB Table
Step 1: Create a DynamoDB Table
Log in to AWS Management Console: Go to the AWS Management Console and search for "DynamoDB" in the services menu.

Navigate to DynamoDB Dashboard: Click on "Tables" in the left-hand menu, then choose Create Table.

Define Table Details:
Table Name: Provide a name (e.g., OrdersTable).
Primary Key:
- Partition Key: OrderID (String or Number).
- Sort Key (optional): CustomerID (String).

Configure Settings
- Choose **On-demand capacity** (default) for simplicity or select **Provisioned capacity** to define read and write capacity units.
- Keep other settings like encryption and backup at defaults.

Create the Table: Click Create Table and wait until the status changes to Active.

Step 2: Add Items to the Table

Navigate to the Table: In the DynamoDB console, click on your table (OrdersTable) once it's active.
Insert Data
- Go to the Items tab.
- Click Create Item.
- Add a sample record:
  - OrderID: 001
  - CustomerID: C123
  - Product: Laptop
  - Quantity: 1

Click Save. Repeat this process to add more sample items.

Step 3: Query Data in the Table

Navigate to the Table: Click on the table name from the DynamoDB dashboard.

Run a Query: Go to the Items tab and select Query from the dropdown. In the Query Builder, enter: Partition Key: OrderID = 001. Click Start Search. You should see the item with OrderID = 001.

Use Secondary Index (Optional): If you created a Global Secondary Index (GSI) with CustomerID as the partition key, query for all orders with a specific CustomerID.
In Query Builder:
- Index: Select your GSI.
- CustomerID = C123.

Run the query to see all orders for that customer.

Step 4: Scan the Table (Alternative to Query)

From the **Items** tab, choose **Scan**. A scan retrieves all items in the table and optionally filters them using conditions.

Example Filter:
- Attribute: Product
- Condition: equals
- Value: Laptop.

Run the scan to retrieve matching items.

Step 5: Clean Up Resources
After the lab, delete the table to avoid incurring unnecessary charges. Go to the DynamoDB console, select your table, and click Delete Table.

By following these steps, you created a DynamoDB table, added items, and queried the table using both the primary key and secondary index. You also explored scanning data with filters.

15.3 Amazon Redshift

15.3.1 Introduction to Data Warehousing: Benefits and use cases of data warehousing
Data warehousing is a process that involves collecting, storing, and managing large volumes of structured data from various sources to facilitate business intelligence and decision-making. A data warehouse serves as a central repository where data is consolidated, organized, and optimized for querying and analysis. Unlike operational databases, which focus on real-time transactions, data warehouses are designed for analytical workloads and historical data storage.

The key benefits of data warehousing include **improved decision-making**, as organizations can analyze historical trends and derive actionable insights. Data warehouses enable **data consolidation**, combining information from multiple sources like transactional systems, CRMs, and logs into a unified format. They also provide **performance** optimization through pre-aggregated and indexed data for faster querying. Additionally, data warehouses ensure **data integrity and consistency** by cleaning and organizing data into a standardized schema.

Common use cases for data warehousing include **business intelligence** reporting, where organizations generate dashboards and visualizations to analyze KPIs. **Customer analytics** allows companies to understand buying patterns and customer behavior, improving marketing strategies. In **financial forecasting**, data warehouses enable organizations to analyze revenue trends and predict future performance. They are also widely used in **supply chain management** to optimize inventory, logistics, and procurement processes.

Cloud-based solutions like **Amazon Redshift** offer scalable, high-performance data warehousing capabilities with cost efficiency, making it easier for businesses to analyze large datasets without extensive infrastructure.

15.3.2 Redshift Clusters and Nodes: Setting up and managing Redshift clusters
Amazon Redshift is a fully managed cloud-based data warehousing solution that uses clusters and nodes to store and process data for analytical workloads. A Redshift cluster is the core component of Amazon Redshift and consists of one or more nodes, which are individual compute

resources that manage and process data. Nodes are organized into leader nodes and compute nodes to efficiently handle data distribution and query execution.

Cluster Components

Leader Node: Manages query planning and coordination across the compute nodes. It does not store data but optimizes SQL queries and distributes work to compute nodes.

Compute Nodes: Store data and perform computations in parallel to process queries efficiently. Data is distributed across these nodes based on the chosen distribution key.

Setting up a Redshift Cluster

Log in to AWS Management Console and navigate to Amazon Redshift. Click Create Cluster and configure the following settings:

- **Cluster Identifier:** Unique name for the cluster.
- **Node Type:** Select node type based on performance needs (e.g., RA3, DC2).
- **Number of Nodes:** Choose a single-node for development/testing or multi-node for production workloads.
- **Database Configuration:** Set up the master username, password, and database name.

Configure Network and Security: Place the cluster in a VPC and set security groups to control access.

Click **Launch Cluster** and monitor the creation status until it is ready.

Managing Redshift Clusters

- Use the **Redshift Console** to monitor performance metrics, including CPU utilization and query execution times.
- Use the **resize** feature to scale the cluster by changing node types or increasing the number of nodes to handle larger datasets.
- Enable **automated backups** to ensure data recovery, or manually create snapshots of the cluster.
- Use **maintenance windows** to apply updates and patches without impacting availability.

Example Use Case

For a retail company analyzing historical sales data, a Redshift cluster with multiple nodes can store petabytes of data. By distributing data across compute nodes and using leader nodes to optimize queries, Redshift enables fast analysis of trends like customer purchases, inventory forecasts, and regional performance metrics.

By setting up and managing Redshift clusters effectively, organizations can achieve high-performance, scalable, and cost-efficient data warehousing for advanced analytics.

15.3.3 Redshift Queries and Performance: Writing queries and optimizing performance

Amazon Redshift provides a powerful, scalable data warehousing solution with tools to write and optimize queries for enhanced performance. Redshift queries are written in SQL (Structured Query Language), making it familiar for analysts and developers. However, to achieve maximum efficiency, query optimization techniques are crucial for ensuring Redshift performs effectively across massive datasets.

Writing Redshift Queries

Standard SQL Syntax: Redshift supports standard ANSI SQL for querying data. Examples include SELECT, INSERT, UPDATE, and DELETE.

Example:

```
SELECT product_name, SUM(sales)
FROM sales_data
WHERE region = 'East'
GROUP BY product_name
ORDER BY SUM(sales) DESC;
```

Joins and Aggregations: Use optimized JOIN statements to combine data across tables efficiently. Perform aggregations using GROUP BY and functions like SUM(), AVG(), etc.

Optimizing Redshift Query Performance

Use Sort and Distribution Keys: Define **a sort key** to organize data physically in a table. Queries that filter data on sort key columns run significantly faster. Select the **right distribution key** to ensure even data distribution across compute nodes, minimizing data transfer.

Analyze and Vacuum: Regularly run VACUUM to reclaim storage space and sort data after frequent inserts and deletes. Use ANALYZE to update table statistics for the query planner.
Example:

```
VACUUM sales_data;
ANALYZE sales_data;
```

Minimize Data Scans: Use SELECT specific columns instead of SELECT *. Use filters (WHERE clause) to reduce the amount of data scanned during queries.

Query Compression: Apply column-level compression to reduce the size of data stored and improve I/O performance.

Use Workload Management (WLM): Configure WLM to allocate query slots and prioritize workloads for critical queries.

Materialized Views: Use materialized views to precompute and store results of complex queries. This improves performance for frequently executed queries.

Monitoring and Tuning: Use Amazon Redshift Advisor to get recommendations for optimizing queries and workloads. Monitor query performance using Redshift Console or STL and SVL system tables.

Example Use Case

Suppose a company is analyzing sales data across regions. A query to calculate top-performing products might run slowly if the dataset is massive and unoptimized. By setting up a sort key on region and a distribution key on product_id, Redshift minimizes data shuffling and improves query performance. Additionally, using materialized views allows pre-aggregating sales data, speeding up reporting.

By writing optimized queries and applying these best practices, Redshift enables users to achieve fast, cost-effective performance for complex analytical workloads.

15.3.4 Lab Exercise: Setting Up and Querying an Amazon Redshift Cluster

Step 1: Log in to AWS Management Console
Navigate to the AWS Management Console. In the search bar, type and select Amazon Redshift.

Step 2: Launch a Redshift Cluster
Click on Create Cluster. Fill in the following details:
Cluster Identifier: Provide a unique name (e.g., redshift-lab-cluster).
Node Type: Choose an appropriate node type, such as dc2.large (ideal for small labs).
Number of Nodes: For this exercise, choose Single Node.
Database Configuration:
- Database Name: labdb
- Master Username: admin
- Master Password: Choose a secure password.

Under Network and Security, configure:
- **VPC**: Choose an existing VPC or create a new one.
- **Public Accessibility**: Select Yes to enable external access for this exercise.
- **Security Groups**: Add a security group to allow inbound access to port 5439 (Redshift default port).

Click Create Cluster and wait for the cluster to become Available.

Step 3: Connect to the Cluster Using a SQL Client
Download and install an SQL client such as SQL Workbench or DBeaver. In the SQL client, create a new connection:
- **Database Engine:** Amazon Redshift.
- **Endpoint:** Copy the cluster endpoint from the Redshift Console.
- **Port**: 5439.
- **Database Name:** labdb.
- **Username:** admin.
- **Password:** Use the password you set during creation.

Test the connection to ensure successful access.

Step 4: Create a Table in Amazon Redshift
Run the following SQL command to create a sample table:

```
CREATE TABLE sales_data (
    sale_id INT,
```

```
    product_name VARCHAR(50),
    sale_amount DECIMAL(10, 2),
    sale_date DATE
);
```

Step 5: Insert Data into the Table

Insert sample data into the table with the following SQL commands:

```
INSERT INTO sales_data VALUES
(1, 'Laptop', 1200.00, '2024-01-10'),
(2, 'Smartphone', 800.00, '2024-01-11'),
(3, 'Headphones', 150.00, '2024-01-12');
```

Step 6: Query the Table

Run basic SQL queries to fetch and analyze data:

Select all records:
```
SELECT * FROM sales_data;
```

Calculate total sales:
```
SELECT SUM(sale_amount) AS total_sales FROM sales_data;
```

Filter data by product:
```
SELECT * FROM sales_data WHERE product_name = 'Laptop';
```

Step 7: Monitor Query Performance

In the Redshift Console, navigate to Query Monitoring. Review the query execution time and performance metrics.

Step 8: Clean Up Resources

In the Redshift Console, navigate to your cluster. Select Delete Cluster to avoid unnecessary charges. Confirm the deletion and verify that the cluster is removed.

15.4 Overview of Amazon Aurora, Amazon ElastiCache, and Amazon MemoryDB for Redis.

Amazon Aurora, ElastiCache, and MemoryDB for Redis are key managed database services provided by AWS, each optimized for specific workloads.

Amazon Aurora

Amazon Aurora is a fully managed relational database engine designed for high performance and availability. It is compatible with MySQL and PostgreSQL, offering up to **five times the throughput** of standard MySQL and twice that of PostgreSQL. Aurora automatically replicates data across three Availability Zones (AZs), ensuring fault tolerance and durability. It supports auto-scaling, backups, and provides low-latency performance for modern applications. **Use cases** include enterprise-grade OLTP applications, e-commerce platforms, and SaaS solutions that require high availability.

Amazon ElastiCache

Amazon ElastiCache is a managed caching service that supports **Memcached and Redis**, enabling low-latency and high-throughput caching. By offloading frequently accessed data from databases, ElastiCache accelerates application performance, reducing response times significantly. It is commonly used for real-time applications, such as leaderboards, session storage, and caching query results.

ElastiCache – Redis Vs. Memcached
Redis

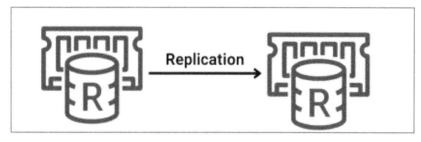

Provides Read Replicas to scale reads provides high availability using replication.Provides data durability using AOF (Append Only File) persistence. Provides backup and restore features.Provides multi-AZ with auto-failover.

Memcached

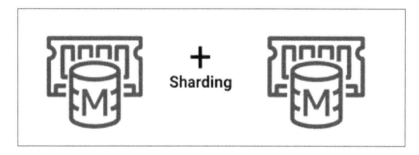

It doesn't provide persistence. It doesn't provide high availability (no replication)It doesn't provide backup and restore. It is a multi-node architecture -- uses sharding to partition data.

ElastiCache – Redis Use Case
Use cases include improving the performance of web applications, API caching, and analytics acceleration. One of the use cases of Redis is in implementing leaderboards in gaming applications. Implementing leaderboards in gaming applications is computationally complex.

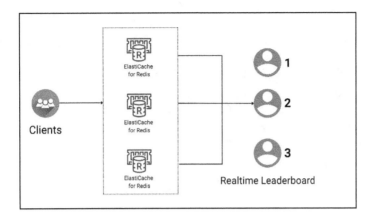

When using Redis, each time when a new participant is added, it is ranked in real-time and then added in the correct order with the help of Redis Sorted Sets that guarantee both uniqueness and element order.

Amazon MemoryDB

Amazon MemoryDB for Redis is a fully managed, **Redis-compatible** in-memory database that provides **durability** by saving data to disk. Unlike ElastiCache, which focuses on caching, MemoryDB combines the speed of Redis with the durability of a database, making it ideal for use cases requiring both high availability and persistent data. MemoryDB is optimized for real-time applications that need microsecond latency and consistency. **Use cases** include gaming, financial transactions, and event-driven applications.

In summary, **Aurora** addresses high-performance relational workloads, **ElastiCache** enhances application performance through caching, and **MemoryDB** combines in-memory speed with data durability for real-time applications. Each service is tailored to specific database needs, providing scalability, reliability, and low-latency solutions for modern workloads.

15.5 Related YouTube Videos

- Amazon DynamoDB Tutorial: https://youtu.be/J1TCIpjoIME
- RDS Tutorial: https://youtu.be/vLPM4Fyuoyg

15.6 Chapter Review Questions

Question 1:
Which of the following best describes Amazon RDS?
- A. A managed in-memory data caching service
- B. A fully managed relational database service
- C. A high-performance NoSQL database
- D. A data warehousing solution

Question 2:
Which of the following is NOT an RDS-supported database engine?
- A. MySQL
- B. PostgreSQL
- C. Cassandra
- D. Oracle

Question 3:
What is the primary benefit of using RDS automated backups?
    A. Manual intervention is required to trigger backups
    B. Backups are stored on the EC2 instance itself
    C. They allow point-in-time recovery with minimal effort
    D. Backups are performed at the database client level

Question 4:
Which AWS database service is ideal for low-latency and high-scale NoSQL workloads?
    A. Amazon RDS
    B. Amazon Redshift
    C. Amazon DynamoDB
    D. Amazon ElastiCache

Question 5:
In Amazon DynamoDB, what does an index help optimize?
    A. Data durability
    B. Data encryption at rest
    C. Data retrieval and queries
    D. Data storage size

Question 6:
Which of the following components is part of an Amazon Redshift cluster?
    A. DynamoDB tables
    B. Elastic IP addresses
    C. Leader node and compute nodes
    D. Multi-AZ deployments

Question 7:
What is the primary use case of Amazon Redshift?
    A. Real-time caching of application data
    B. Performing large-scale data warehousing and analytics
    C. Managing relational database transactions
    D. Storing unstructured NoSQL data

Question 8:
Which of the following services is Redis-compatible and offers durable, in-memory storage?
    A. Amazon DynamoDB
    B. Amazon ElastiCache
    C. Amazon Aurora
    D. Amazon MemoryDB for Redis

Question 9:
What is the key feature of Amazon Aurora compared to traditional RDS engines?
    A. It supports NoSQL workloads
    B. It provides up to 5x better performance than standard MySQL databases
    C. It integrates with Amazon Kinesis for real-time data streams

D. It is only compatible with SQL Server

Question 10:
Which AWS service would you use to store frequently accessed session data for a web application?
    A. Amazon Redshift
    B. Amazon DynamoDB
    C. Amazon ElastiCache
    D. Amazon RDS

15.7 Answers to Chapter Review Questions

1. B. A fully managed relational database service
Explanation: Amazon RDS is a managed service that allows you to set up, operate, and scale relational databases with ease.

2. C. Cassandra
Explanation: Amazon RDS supports MySQL, PostgreSQL, Oracle, SQL Server, and MariaDB, but Cassandra is not a supported RDS database engine.

3. C. They allow point-in-time recovery with minimal effort
Explanation: RDS automated backups enable point-in-time recovery, allowing you to restore databases to a specific point without manual intervention.

4. C. Amazon DynamoDB
Explanation: Amazon DynamoDB is a fully managed NoSQL database that delivers low-latency and high scalability for applications.

5. C. Data retrieval and queries
Explanation: In DynamoDB, indexes (e.g., Global Secondary Indexes) optimize queries and enable faster data retrieval by creating alternative access patterns.

6. C. Leader node and compute nodes
Explanation: Amazon Redshift clusters consist of a leader node, which manages queries, and compute nodes, which handle data storage and query execution.

7. B. Performing large-scale data warehousing and analytics
Explanation: Amazon Redshift is a fully managed data warehouse solution designed for large-scale analytics and reporting.

8. D. Amazon MemoryDB for Redis
Explanation: Amazon MemoryDB is a Redis-compatible service that provides durable, in-memory storage for high-performance workloads.

9. B. It provides up to 5x better performance than standard MySQL databases
Explanation: Amazon Aurora is a MySQL and PostgreSQL-compatible database that offers up to 5x better performance compared to traditional MySQL.

10. C. Amazon ElastiCache

Explanation: Amazon ElastiCache provides in-memory data storage, ideal for frequently accessed session data and low-latency caching.

Chapter 16. AWS Analytics Services

In today's data-driven world, analyzing vast amounts of data efficiently is critical for making informed decisions. AWS provides powerful analytics services that enable businesses to process, query, and analyze data at scale. This chapter, AWS Analytics Services, introduces you to key services like Amazon Athena, Amazon Kinesis, and Amazon OpenSearch Service that help unlock the value of data stored in the cloud.

The chapter begins with Amazon Athena, a serverless query service that allows you to run SQL queries directly on data stored in Amazon S3. You will learn how to set up and use Athena to perform ad-hoc analysis without the need for complex infrastructure.

Next, you will explore Amazon Kinesis, AWS's real-time data streaming service. This section delves into key concepts, including Kinesis Streams and Kinesis Firehose, to process and deliver real-time data. A hands-on lab exercise will guide you through creating a Kinesis stream and processing data, while understanding the architecture and workflow of Kinesis Data Streams.

The chapter concludes with Amazon OpenSearch Service, a fully managed search and analytics engine designed for log analytics, full-text search, and monitoring. You will learn how to set up and use OpenSearch to analyze large datasets effectively.

By the end of this chapter, you will have a solid understanding of AWS's analytics services and their practical applications, enabling you to process real-time data, perform queries, and extract actionable insights from your data.

16.1 Amazon Athena

16.1.1 Introduction to Athena: Querying data stored in S3

Amazon Athena is a serverless query service that allows you to analyze data directly stored in Amazon S3 using standard SQL queries. With Athena, there is no need to manage infrastructure, as it automatically scales and executes queries on demand. It is particularly cost-effective because you pay only for the queries you run. Athena works seamlessly with S3 data in formats like CSV, JSON, ORC, Parquet, and Avro, making it ideal for ad-hoc analysis of structured and semi-structured data.

Key benefits of Athena include its ease of use, as it requires no complex setup, and its integration with AWS Glue for data cataloging. Common use cases for Athena include log analysis, running ad-hoc SQL queries on large datasets stored in S3, and exploring data for business insights without setting up a traditional database or data warehouse. It is often used in big data workflows for quick analysis of data stored in S3 buckets.

16.1.2 Setting Up and Using Athena: Practical guide

To set up and use Amazon Athena, follow these steps:

Prepare Your Data in Amazon S3: Store your datasets in an Amazon S3 bucket. Athena can analyze data in common formats like CSV, JSON, ORC, Parquet, and Avro. Organize your data into folders for logical partitioning to improve query performance.

Create a Database and Table in Athena: In the AWS Management Console, open the Athena service. Start by creating a database using SQL commands:

```
CREATE DATABASE my_database;
```

Once the database is created, define a table schema to map your S3 data:

```
CREATE EXTERNAL TABLE my_table (
  column1 string,
  column2 int,
  column3 double
)
ROW FORMAT DELIMITED
FIELDS TERMINATED BY ','
LOCATION 's3://my-bucket/path/';
```

Replace my_table, column names, and my-bucket/path/ with your specific data structure and S3 path.

Run Queries: Use standard SQL queries to analyze your S3 data. For example:

```
SELECT column1, COUNT(*)
FROM my_table
GROUP BY column1;
```

Queries can be run directly in the Athena Query Editor.

Partitioning Data: To improve query performance, partition data logically (e.g., by date or region) and specify the partitions in your query:

```
ALTER TABLE my_table ADD PARTITION (date='2024-06-15') LOCATION 's3://my-bucket/2024/06/15/';
```

Integrate with AWS Glue Data Catalog: Use AWS Glue to catalog and manage metadata for your S3 data. Athena integrates with Glue to automatically query registered datasets.

Analyze Results: Query results are automatically saved in an S3 bucket. You can download, visualize, or share the results.

Use Case Example

You store application logs in S3 in JSON format. By defining a table schema in Athena, you can run SQL queries to analyze the logs, like finding error trends or user activity.

Athena simplifies querying data in S3 without requiring database management, making it ideal for ad-hoc analysis, cost-effective big data querying, and quick business insights.

16.2 Amazon Kinesis

16.2.1 Introduction to Kinesis: Real-time data streaming

Amazon Kinesis is a real-time data streaming service offered by AWS that enables you to collect, process, and analyze large volumes of streaming data efficiently. Kinesis allows applications to ingest and process data continuously, making it ideal for scenarios requiring low-latency, real-time analytics.

16.2.2 Some Key Concepts

Data Producer: It is an application that published data records in real-time as they are generated to a Kinesis data stream. The data records contain partition key the determine which shard ingests the data record.

Data Consumer: A data consumer is a distributed Kinesis application or an AWS service that retrieves data records from all shards.

Data Stream: A data stream is a logical grouping of shards – no bounds on the number of shards within a data stream. Data will be retained for 24 hours by default or optionally up to 365 days.

Shard: A unit in the stream containing an ordered sequence of records.
Capacity: 1MB/sec input or 1000 records/sec.
Output: 2MB/sec (shared) or 2MB/sec per consumer with enhanced fan-out.

Shard count can be adjusted anytime to scale ingestion and output.

Data record: It is the unit of data stored in an Amazon Kinesis stream. A record contains: a sequence number, partition key, and data blob -- the maximum size of a data blob is 1 MB.

Partition key: A partition key is typically a meaningful identifier, such as a customer ID or timestamp. The partition key is also used to segregate and route data records to different shards of a stream.

For example, assuming you have a data stream with three shards (Shard 1, Shard 2, and Shard 3) for three different customers. You can configure your data producer to use three partition keys (customer-A, customer-B, and customer-C) so that all data records with partition key customer-A key are added to Shard 1 and all data records with partition key customer-B are added to Shard 2, and all data records with partition key customer-C are added to Shard 3.

Sequence number: It is a unique identifier for each record and is assigned by Amazon Kinesis Data Streams when a data producer calls PutRecord or PutRecords API to add data to an Amazon Kinesis data stream.

Key Features

Real-Time Data Ingestion: Kinesis enables continuous data ingestion from sources like IoT devices, application logs, and social media feeds.

Multiple Components: Kinesis includes Kinesis Data Streams, Kinesis Data Firehose, Kinesis Video Streams, and Kinesis Data Analytics, each catering to specific streaming needs.

Scalability: Kinesis scales automatically to handle growing data volumes, ensuring high throughput.

Integration with AWS Services: It integrates with services like Amazon S3, DynamoDB, Redshift, and Lambda to process and store data.

Low Latency: Kinesis provides near real-time data processing with minimal delays.

Use Cases

Log and Event Monitoring: Collect and process application and server logs in real-time for monitoring and alerting.

Real-Time Analytics: Analyze customer clickstreams, user activity, and sensor data to gain instant insights.

IoT Data Processing: Stream IoT device data for predictive maintenance or automation.

Streaming Video and Media: Process and analyze live video streams efficiently.

Fraud Detection: Monitor transactions in real-time to identify fraudulent activities immediately.

Amazon Kinesis is an essential service for businesses that require timely processing and analysis of continuous data streams, enabling faster decision-making and improved operational efficiency.

16.2.3 Kinesis Streams and Firehose

Amazon Kinesis offers Kinesis Streams and Kinesis Firehose as core components to collect, process, and deliver real-time streaming data efficiently.

Kinesis Streams

Kinesis Data Streams is designed for real-time, continuous data ingestion and processing. Data is stored in shards, where each shard acts as a unit of throughput.

Use Cases: Real-time analytics, monitoring application logs, clickstream analysis, and fraud detection.

Example: Streaming sensor data from IoT devices to analyze performance metrics in real-time.

Kinesis Firehose

Kinesis Data Firehose is a fully managed service that automatically delivers streaming data to storage and analytics destinations such as Amazon S3, Redshift, or Elasticsearch. Unlike Streams, it doesn't require managing shards.

Use Cases: Batch analytics, loading data lakes, log processing, and archival storage.

Example: Delivering application logs to S3 in near real-time for later analysis using Athena or Redshift.

Key Differences

Kinesis Streams: Focuses on real-time, low-latency data processing where custom applications read and process data.

Kinesis Firehose: Simplifies data delivery by directly sending data to pre-configured storage and analytics destinations without manual intervention.

Both services enable businesses to handle continuous data streams efficiently while catering to different use cases—Streams for real-time, low-latency workloads and Firehose for automated data delivery and processing.

16.2.4 Lab Exercise: Creating a Kinesis Stream and Processing Data

Step 1: Log in to AWS Management Console

Open the AWS Management Console and navigate to the Kinesis service under "Analytics" or "Streaming Services."

Step 2: Create a Kinesis Data Stream

In the Amazon Kinesis Dashboard, click on "Create Data Stream".

Enter Stream Name: Provide a descriptive name, e.g., MyKinesisStream.

Configure Shards: Select the Number of Shards based on expected data volume. For basic setups, choose 1 shard. Each shard provides up to 1 MB/sec of input and 2 MB/sec of output.

Click "Create Stream" and wait for the stream status to show ACTIVE.

Step 3: Set Up a Data Producer

Install the AWS SDK on your local machine or use the AWS CLI. Write a Python script (or use the AWS CLI) to send sample records to the Kinesis stream.

Example Python Code (using Boto3):

```python
import boto3
import json
import time

# Kinesis client
kinesis_client = boto3.client('kinesis', region_name='us-east-1')

# Stream name
stream_name = 'MyKinesisStream'

# Send data
for i in range(10):
    data = {
        'id': i,
        'message': f"Sample message {i}"
    }
    response = kinesis_client.put_record(
        StreamName=stream_name,
        Data=json.dumps(data),
        PartitionKey="partitionKey"
    )
    print(f"Record {i} sent: {response['SequenceNumber']}")
    time.sleep(1)
```

Run the Script: Execute the script to produce records into your Kinesis stream.

Step 4: Set Up a Data Consumer

Create an AWS Lambda Function to process the data from the Kinesis stream: Go to the Lambda service and click "Create Function". Select "Author from Scratch" and provide a name, e.g., KinesisProcessorFunction. For Runtime, select Python 3.9 (or your preferred language). Create the function and open its editor.

Write a Lambda function to process incoming Kinesis records:

Example Lambda Code:

```
import json

def lambda_handler(event, context):
    for record in event['Records']:
        payload = json.loads(record['kinesis']['data'])
        print(f"Processed record: {payload}")
    return {"statusCode": 200, "body": "Records processed successfully"}
```

Add Kinesis Trigger: In the Lambda function console, add a Kinesis Trigger. Select the stream you created (MyKinesisStream) and set the Batch size (e.g., 10). Click "Add" to connect the Kinesis stream to the Lambda function.

Step 5: Monitor and Test the Setup

Re-run your producer script to send records into the stream.
Go to the CloudWatch Logs under the Lambda function to verify that data is processed.
You should see the records printed in the logs.

Step 6: Clean Up Resources

Stop any producer processes. Delete the Kinesis stream in the Kinesis console. Remove the Lambda function and any associated CloudWatch logs to avoid additional charges.

Outcome

You have successfully: Created a Kinesis Data Stream. Produced data into the stream using a producer. Processed data using an AWS Lambda function.

This exercise demonstrates real-time data streaming and processing in Amazon Kinesis.

16.2.5 Architecture and Workflow of Amazon Kinesis Data Streams

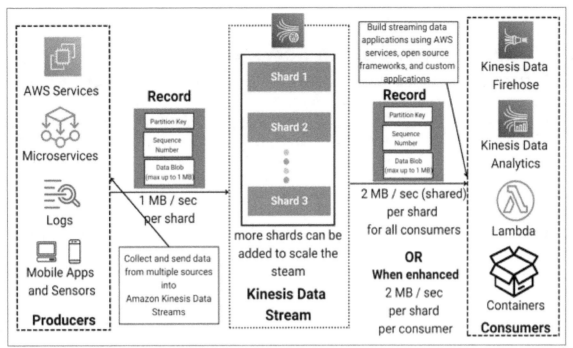

The diagram explains the architecture and workflow of Amazon Kinesis Data Streams, a fully managed service for real-time data streaming.

Producers:
Producers include AWS Services, microservices, logs, mobile apps, and sensors.
These producers collect and send data records into the Kinesis Data Stream at a rate of 1 MB/second per shard. Each record consists of a Partition Key, Sequence Number, and Data Blob (up to 1 MB).

Kinesis Data Stream:
The data is ingested into shards, which are the basic units of capacity in a Kinesis stream. Each shard can handle 1 MB/second input and 2 MB/second output. Additional shards can be added to scale the stream as needed.

Consumers:
Consumers process the records in the stream, sharing a throughput of 2 MB/second per shard, or 2 MB/second per shard per consumer when enhanced fan-out is enabled.

Examples of consumers include:
- Kinesis Data Firehose: Delivers data to destinations like S3, Redshift, or Elasticsearch.
- Kinesis Data Analytics: Provides real-time analytics and insights on the streaming data.
- AWS Lambda: Processes records using serverless compute functions.
- Containers: Applications running in containerized environments can consume and process the data.

This diagram highlights how data is collected from producers, streamed into Kinesis shards for scalability, and processed by consumers like Firehose, Analytics, and Lambda. The system supports real-time ingestion, processing, and analysis of streaming data, making it ideal for applications requiring real-time insights.

16.3 Amazon OpenSearch Service

16.3.1 Introduction to OpenSearch: Full-text search and analytics engine

Amazon OpenSearch Service is a managed service that allows users to perform full-text search, log analytics, and real-time monitoring on large datasets. It is a fully managed offering that supports OpenSearch and Elasticsearch versions, making it ideal for developers looking for search and analytics capabilities without worrying about the underlying infrastructure.

Key Features

Full-Text Search: OpenSearch enables fast and precise searches across large datasets, whether for text or structured data.

Real-Time Analytics: Supports powerful analytics on logs, metrics, and other time-series data to help identify trends or anomalies.

Scalability: Automatically scales clusters up or down based on workloads.

Integrated Dashboards: Comes with OpenSearch Dashboards for visualizing data with charts, graphs, and interactive views.

High Availability: Built-in support for multi-AZ deployments ensures redundancy and uptime.

Security: Offers encryption, fine-grained access control, and integration with AWS IAM for secure access management.

Use Cases

Application Search: Quickly index and search through documents, product catalogs, and websites.

Log Analytics: Analyze and visualize logs from applications, servers, or AWS services.

Monitoring and Observability: Monitor infrastructure performance and detect anomalies in real time.

Business Intelligence: Use dashboards to analyze business trends and operational metrics.

For example, an e-commerce platform can use OpenSearch to provide real-time product search with filters, while a DevOps team can analyze server logs to troubleshoot performance issues.

16.3.2 Setting Up and Using OpenSearch: Practical guide

Amazon OpenSearch Service is a fully managed service that enables users to deploy, operate, and scale OpenSearch clusters for full-text search, log analytics, and visualization. Here's a practical guide to setting up and using Amazon OpenSearch.

Step 1: Create an OpenSearch Domain

Log in to AWS Management Console: Go to the Amazon OpenSearch Service console.

Create Domain: Click "Create Domain" to start the process. Choose a deployment type: Production (for live workloads) or Development and testing.

Configure Domain Settings: Enter a domain name (e.g., my-opensearch-domain). Choose an OpenSearch version (latest version recommended for features and security patches).

Node Configuration: Select the instance type and number of nodes for your cluster. Use multiple nodes for high availability and data durability.

Storage Configuration:
Configure the storage type:
- EBS (Elastic Block Store) for persistent storage.
- Instance Store for temporary data.
Choose appropriate storage size.

Access Policies: Configure domain access policies to control who can access the OpenSearch domain. Use: IAM role-based access control for security. Fine-grained access control (optional) for document-level or field-level security.

Step 2: Upload Data to OpenSearch

Install OpenSearch Clients: Use curl, Postman, or the AWS SDK to interact with the OpenSearch domain.

Send Sample Data: Use the following curl command to upload a sample document to OpenSearch:

```
curl -X POST "https://your-opensearch-domain/_doc/1" -H "Content-Type: application/json" -d'
{
  "title": "Hello OpenSearch",
  "description": "This is a test document"
}'
```

Replace your-opensearch-domain with the endpoint of your OpenSearch domain.

Verify Data: Query the data using:

```
curl -X GET "https://your-opensearch-domain/_search?pretty"
```

Step 3: Visualize Data with OpenSearch Dashboards

Access OpenSearch Dashboards: Open the Dashboards URL provided in the OpenSearch domain settings. Log in using the IAM credentials or fine-grained access.

Create an Index Pattern: Go to Management > Index Patterns. Add an index pattern (e.g., * for all data or a specific index like logs-*).

Build Visualizations: Use tools like bar charts, line charts, and pie charts to create visualizations. Combine visualizations into custom dashboards to monitor and analyze data.

Step 4: Run Queries

Basic Query: Perform a search query to retrieve documents that match specific criteria:

```
GET /your-index/_search
{
  "query": {
    "match": {
      "title": "Hello"
    }
  }
}
```

Aggregation Query: Use aggregations to group data and generate analytics:

```
GET /your-index/_search
{
  "aggs": {
    "group_by_title": {
      "terms": { "field": "title.keyword" }
    }
  }
}
```

Step 5: Monitor OpenSearch Domain

CloudWatch Integration: Monitor metrics like cluster health, CPU utilization, and index performance using Amazon CloudWatch.

Set Alarms: Set CloudWatch alarms to notify administrators if resource utilization exceeds thresholds.

Scaling: If performance is impacted, scale the domain by increasing node count, upgrading instance types, or adding storage.

Use Cases for OpenSearch

Log Analysis: Aggregate and analyze log data from various AWS services like CloudWatch, Lambda, and S3.

Full-Text Search: Perform text searches on massive datasets for e-commerce, content management, and user queries.

Security Analytics: Monitor and analyze security-related data to detect anomalies and threats.

Real-Time Monitoring: Create dashboards for monitoring infrastructure, applications, and business metrics.

This guide provides a streamlined process to set up Amazon OpenSearch, upload and query data, and use OpenSearch Dashboards to gain actionable insights.

16.4 Chapter Review Questions

Question 1:
What is the primary purpose of Amazon Athena?
> A. To perform real-time data streaming
> B. To query data stored in Amazon S3 using SQL
> C. To manage data in a NoSQL database
> D. To process big data using Hadoop clusters

Question 2:
Which service is designed for real-time data streaming and analytics?
> A. Amazon OpenSearch
> B. Amazon Athena
> C. Amazon Kinesis
> D. Amazon Redshift

Question 3:
What is a key prerequisite for using Amazon Athena?
> A. Data must be stored in Amazon S3
> B. An active EC2 instance for query execution

C. A provisioned RDS instance

D. A DynamoDB table

Question 4:

Which Kinesis component delivers streaming data to storage destinations such as S3 and Redshift?

    A. Kinesis Streams

    B. Kinesis Firehose

    C. Kinesis Analytics

    D. Kinesis Data Manager

Question 5:

What type of engine powers the Amazon OpenSearch Service?

    A. Relational Database Engine

    B. Elasticsearch and OpenSearch engines

    C. NoSQL Engine

    D. Hadoop Processing Engine

Question 6:

Which query language does Amazon Athena use?

    A. SQL

    B. JSON

    C. NoSQL

    D. DynamoQL

Question 7:

Which of the following is a key use case for Amazon Kinesis Streams?

    A. Storing infrequently accessed archival data

    B. Streaming log data for real-time analytics

    C. Managing full-text search queries

    D. Querying structured data in S3

Question 8:

What is the main benefit of using Amazon OpenSearch Service?

    A. Enabling full-text search and log analytics

    B. Real-time data ingestion and delivery

    C. Running SQL queries on structured data

    D. Managing relational database workloads

Question 9:

Which Amazon Kinesis service is ideal for transforming and loading data streams in near real-time?

    A. Kinesis Data Analytics

    B. Kinesis Firehose

    C. Kinesis Streams

    D. Kinesis OpenSearch

Question 10:

What is the primary function of OpenSearch Dashboards in Amazon OpenSearch?
- A. Performing ETL on large data sets
- B. Visualizing and analyzing search results
- C. Querying S3 objects using SQL
- D. Automating data streaming workflows

16.5 Answers to Chapter Review Questions

1. B. To query data stored in Amazon S3 using SQL

Explanation: Amazon Athena is a serverless query service that allows you to analyze data stored in Amazon S3 using standard SQL queries.

2. C. Amazon Kinesis

Explanation: Amazon Kinesis is designed for real-time data streaming and analytics, enabling you to ingest, process, and analyze streaming data.

3. A. Data must be stored in Amazon S3

Explanation: Amazon Athena works directly with data stored in Amazon S3, allowing you to query it using SQL without the need for additional infrastructure.

4. B. Kinesis Firehose

Explanation: Kinesis Firehose automatically delivers streaming data to destinations like S3, Redshift, and Elasticsearch, making it ideal for real-time ingestion and delivery.

5. B. Elasticsearch and OpenSearch engines

Explanation: Amazon OpenSearch Service is powered by the Elasticsearch and OpenSearch engines to provide full-text search and log analytics capabilities.

6. A. SQL

Explanation: Amazon Athena uses SQL to query data stored in Amazon S3, making it accessible and familiar for users proficient in SQL.

7. B. Streaming log data for real-time analytics

Explanation: Amazon Kinesis Streams is primarily used for capturing and processing streaming log data and other real-time analytics workloads.

8. A. Enabling full-text search and log analytics

Explanation: Amazon OpenSearch Service enables full-text search and log analytics, allowing you to search and analyze large datasets efficiently.

9. B. Kinesis Firehose

Explanation: Kinesis Firehose is ideal for transforming and loading data streams into near real-time destinations such as S3, Redshift, and OpenSearch.

10. B. Visualizing and analyzing search results

Explanation: OpenSearch Dashboards in Amazon OpenSearch Service are used to visualize and analyze search results, providing insights into your data.

Chapter 17. AWS Application Integration Services

Modern cloud-based applications often rely on seamless communication and coordination between various services and components. AWS provides a suite of Application Integration Services designed to enable scalable, event-driven, and decoupled architectures that improve reliability and flexibility. This chapter explores key services like Amazon SNS, Amazon SQS, Amazon EventBridge, AWS AppSync, and AWS Step Functions to simplify integration and workflow management.

The chapter begins with Amazon Simple Notification Service (SNS), a fully managed messaging service that enables applications to send notifications to subscribers efficiently. You will learn to set up and use SNS for delivering notifications in a scalable manner.

Next, the focus shifts to Amazon Simple Queue Service (SQS), a messaging queue service that allows decoupling and reliable communication between distributed application components. A practical guide walks you through creating and managing SQS queues and highlights the SNS and SQS fan-out pattern.

You will then explore Amazon EventBridge, AWS's event bus for building event-driven architectures. A hands-on lab exercise demonstrates how to create event-driven applications using EventBridge. Following this, you'll learn about AWS AppSync, a powerful tool for building real-time and offline applications with GraphQL APIs, complemented by a lab exercise on real-time app creation.

The chapter concludes with AWS Step Functions, a service for orchestrating workflows by combining multiple AWS services into a cohesive application flow. Through a lab exercise, you will gain practical experience in orchestrating workflows efficiently.

By the end of this chapter, you will understand how AWS application integration services work together to simplify messaging, event handling, and workflow orchestration, enabling you to build scalable, resilient, and highly integrated cloud-native applications.

17.1 Amazon Simple Notification Service (SNS)

17.1.1 Introduction to SNS: Messaging service for sending notifications

Amazon Simple Notification Service (SNS) is a fully managed messaging service designed for sending notifications to subscribers. It enables communication between systems, applications, and users via a publish-subscribe (pub/sub) model. With SNS, messages are published to a topic, and subscribers (like email addresses, SMS, or AWS Lambda functions) receive the messages in real time.

Amazon SNS is one of the key architectural components if you want to build scalable, decoupled application architecture or integrate applications in asynchronous communication patterns.

Using Amazon SNS, you can send one message to many subscribers. It is based on pub/sub (publishers/subscribers) model.

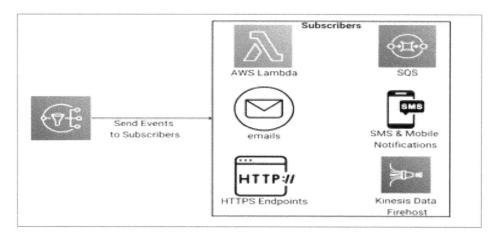

Usually the term "event" is used in case of SNS and "event producers" send messaged to one SNS topic. In other words, you could many instances of Order service (for example, deployed on multiple EC2 instances) sending order events to an SNS topic. And as many "event receivers" (or subscriptions) as we want to can subscribe to the SNS topic. Each subscriber to the topic received all the events from the topic.

Key Features of SNS

Pub/Sub Messaging: SNS supports the publish-subscribe architecture, where publishers send messages to topics, and subscribers receive notifications.

Multiple Protocol Support: SNS delivers notifications via email, SMS, mobile push notifications, and HTTP endpoints.

Scalability: SNS automatically scales to handle high message throughput.

Integration with AWS Services: SNS integrates with AWS Lambda, Amazon SQS, and other services to build event-driven architectures.

Message Filtering: Using message attributes, SNS can filter messages for specific subscribers.

Use Cases

Application Alerts: Sending critical alerts to system administrators or users.

Fanout Messaging: Distributing the same message to multiple endpoints like Lambda, SQS, and HTTP.

User Notifications: Delivering email, SMS, or push notifications for events like order updates or reminders.

Example: An e-commerce platform uses SNS to notify customers about order confirmations via email and send SMS alerts for delivery updates.

17.1.2 Setting Up and Using SNS: Practical guide

To set up and use Amazon Simple Notification Service (SNS), follow this practical step-by-step guide for creating topics, subscribing endpoints, and publishing messages:

Step 1: Create an SNS Topic

Navigate to SNS in the AWS Management Console: Go to the Amazon SNS Dashboard.
Create a Topic: Click Create topic.
Select a topic type: Standard for general-purpose messaging with high throughput. FIFO (First-In-First-Out) for ordered, deduplicated messaging. Enter a Name for your topic (e.g., OrderUpdatesTopic). Configure optional settings such as encryption, message retention, or delivery retry policies.

Click Create topic.

Step 2: Subscribe an Endpoint to the Topic

In the SNS console, select the topic you just created. Click Create subscription.
Choose a Protocol: SNS supports protocols like Email, SMS, HTTP/HTTPS, Lambda, or SQS. For example, select Email for notifications to an email address.
Enter the Endpoint: Provide the recipient's email address, phone number, or endpoint URL, depending on the protocol. Click Create subscription.
Confirm the Subscription: If you selected Email, SNS sends a confirmation link to the email address. Click the link to activate the subscription.

Step 3: Publish a Message to the Topic

In the SNS Dashboard, select your topic. Click Publish message.

Compose the Message: Enter a Subject (optional) and the Message body.
Send the Message: Click Publish message.
The message is sent to all subscribed endpoints (e.g., email, SMS, or HTTP listeners).

Step 4: Integrate SNS with Other AWS Services

Trigger SNS from Lambda: Configure an AWS Lambda function to publish messages to an SNS topic programmatically using the SDK.
Fan-out with SQS: Subscribe Amazon SQS queues to the SNS topic for parallel processing.
CloudWatch Alarms: Set up CloudWatch Alarms to publish alerts to an SNS topic when predefined thresholds are breached.

Example Use Case

E-Commerce Application:

SNS Topic: OrderUpdatesTopic.

Subscriptions: Customer's email for order confirmations, SMS for delivery updates, and an SQS queue for backend processing.

Workflow: A Lambda function publishes messages to the SNS topic when an order status changes.

With these steps, you can effectively set up, manage, and publish messages using Amazon SNS for various notification and integration needs.

17.2 Amazon Simple Queue Service (SQS)

17.2.1 Introduction to SQS: Messaging queue service

Amazon Simple Queue Service (SQS) is a fully managed message queuing service that enables decoupling of application components and facilitates reliable communication between distributed systems.

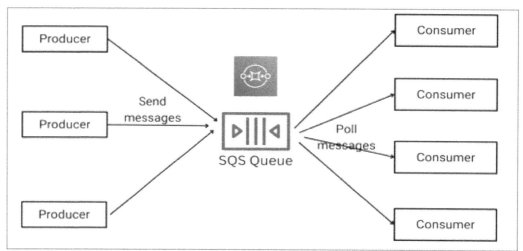

It acts as a buffer between senders and receivers, ensuring that messages are reliably stored and delivered. Using SQS, you can send, store, and receive messages between software components at any volume without losing or requiring other services to be available.

Producing Messages

You can produce messages to SQS using AWS SDK (SendMessage API). The sent message is persisted in SQS until deleted by a consumer. The default retention of messages is four days, and the maximum is 14 days.

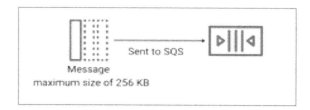

For example, an SQS producer sends an order to be processed. An order might have an order ID, customer ID, line item, etc.vSQS Standard provides unlimited throughput. For example, we can publish an unlimited number of messages in a Standard SQS queue.

Consuming Messages

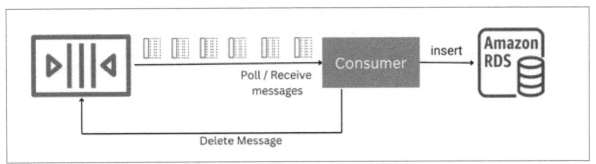

SQS consumers, which can be running on EC2 instances. You could also have SQS consumers implemented as AWS Lambda. SQS consumers poll for SQS messages on an SQS Queue. One consumer can receive up to 10 messages at a time.

After receiving the message, the consumer does some form of processing. For example, the consumer can insert the message into an RDS database or invoke another program or application to check if the credit card company processes the customer's payment information.

After processing the message, the customer deleted the message using DeleteMessage API.

Suppose the consumer throws an exception (fails) before deleting the message, and your application doesn't call the DeleteMessage action to delete the message before the visibility timeout expires. In that case, the message becomes visible to other consumers and is received and processed again. To avoid duplicate processing, you should delete the message after processing it.

Key Features of Amazon SQS
Fully Managed Service: SQS eliminates the need to manage infrastructure, making it easier to handle messaging workflows.
Decoupling Applications: SQS ensures components can communicate without being directly dependent on each other, improving fault tolerance and scalability.

Types of Queues
Standard Queue: Supports unlimited throughput, at-least-once delivery, and best-effort message ordering.
FIFO Queue: Ensures exactly-once processing and first-in-first-out message ordering for critical workloads.

Durability and Scalability: SQS ensures message durability and automatic scaling to handle variable workloads.

Security: Supports encryption using AWS KMS and access control through IAM policies.

Benefits of Amazon SQS

Decouples Distributed Systems: Applications can work independently without tight integration.
Reliability: Ensures messages are not lost, even if consumers fail temporarily.
Scalability: Handles millions of messages per second without manual intervention.
Cost-Effective: Pay only for the number of messages sent and received.
Integration: Seamlessly integrates with AWS services like Lambda, EC2, and Step Functions.

Use Cases

Task Queues: Queue tasks that need processing, such as image resizing or email notifications.
Microservices Communication: Enable communication between decoupled microservices.
Batch Processing: Collect and hold large volumes of data for batch jobs.
Workload Decoupling: Decouple web servers from backend processing systems for increased reliability.
Transactional Messaging: Use FIFO queues for payment processing or order fulfillment workflows.

Example Scenario

In an e-commerce application, a user places an order:
The order is placed in an SQS queue. A worker service retrieves the message and processes the order. If the worker service fails, the message remains in the queue until it is successfully processed.

Amazon SQS provides a robust, scalable solution for enabling asynchronous communication, improving application resilience and flexibility.

17.2.2 Setting Up and Using SQS: Practical guide

Step 1: Log in to the AWS Management Console

Sign in to your AWS account. Navigate to Amazon SQS from the Services menu under "Messaging".

Step 2: Create a New SQS Queue

Choose "Create Queue" from the dashboard.

Queue Type: Select either:
Standard Queue: Provides best-effort ordering and at-least-once delivery.
FIFO Queue: Ensures first-in, first-out message delivery with exactly-once processing.

Name Your Queue: Enter a unique queue name.
Set Queue Attributes: For a Standard Queue: Configure default settings (visibility timeout, message retention period, etc.).
For a FIFO Queue: Ensure the queue name ends with ".fifo" and enable content deduplication if needed.

Create Queue: Click "Create Queue" to finalize the setup.

Step 3: Send a Message to the Queue

Go to the newly created queue from the dashboard. Choose "Send and Receive Messages". Enter a sample message (e.g., JSON or plain text). Click "Send Message" to add it to the queue.

Step 4: Retrieve and Process Messages

Receive Messages: In the queue, click "Poll for messages" to see available messages. Messages remain hidden for a defined Visibility Timeout until they are processed.

Delete a Processed Message: After successfully processing a message, delete it from the queue to prevent reprocessing.

Step 5: Integrate SQS with an AWS Service

AWS Lambda Integration: Trigger Lambda functions whenever a new message is sent. Navigate to Lambda > Create Function. In the function trigger, select SQS Queue and attach the queue created earlier.

Decouple Microservices: Use the queue URL to let producers send messages and consumers retrieve them asynchronously.

Step 6: Monitor the Queue

View Metrics: Go to the CloudWatch Dashboard to monitor metrics like NumberOfMessagesSent or ApproximateNumberOfMessagesVisible.

Set Alarms: Configure CloudWatch Alarms for thresholds (e.g., too many messages in the queue).

Example Scenario

In a video processing application:

When a user uploads a video, a message with the video metadata is sent to the SQS queue. Worker instances retrieve messages, process videos, and delete the message after processing. If processing fails, the message stays in the queue for retries.

Amazon SQS simplifies message queuing workflows, enabling reliable and scalable communication between decoupled systems.

17.3 SNS and SQS Fan Out

You can use SNS and SQS in combination to Fan Out and make system highly scalable. Once you push an event to an SNS topic, then SQS that are subscribers to the topic receives the event. From there each SQS queue, consumer can consume their events.

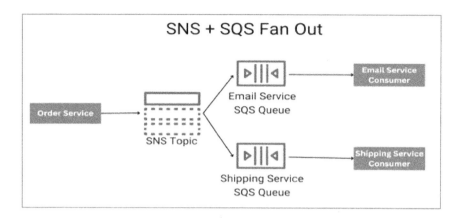

For example, Order Service publish a new order event to and SNS topic and from there Email Service SQS Service queue and Shipping Service SQS queue receive the same the order event. Then Email Service consumer reads from the event from the Email SQS Queue to sends email. Similarly, Shipping Service consumer reads from the Shipping SQS Queue to make the order ready for the shipping.

The typical Fanout scenario with SNS and SQS is when a message published to an SNS topic is pushed to multiple endpoints by replicating it, such as Amazon SQS queues, HTTP(S) endpoints, Lambda functions, Kinesis Data Firehose delivery streams. This fanout architecture allows fully decoupled parallel asynchronous processing with no data loss.

17.4 Comparison of SQS, SNS, Kinesis

SQS	SNS	Kinesis
Based on "pull"– consumers pull data from the queue	Based on "push" — data is pushed to subscribers. Up to 12,500,000 subscribers.	Standard: pull, 2 MB/shard Enhanced fan-out: push, 2 MB per shard / consumer
Data is deleted after it has been processed.	Data is not persisted – lost if it is not delivered.	Data can be replayed and deleted after X days.
Ordering is guaranteed only on FIFO queues.		Ordering is available at shard level. Data with the same Partition Key is delivered to the same shard.
No need to provision throughput	You can have up to 100,000 topics	shards to temporarily store data records -- the default is 24 hours (optionally 1 to 365 days).

17.5 Amazon EventBridge

17.5.1 Introduction to EventBridge: Event bus for building event-driven applications

Amazon EventBridge is a serverless event bus service designed for building event-driven applications by routing events between AWS services, software-as-a-service (SaaS) applications, and custom applications. It helps decouple systems, enabling real-time communication and reducing operational complexity.

Key Features
Event Routing: EventBridge allows events to flow from sources to targets in real-time. You can use rules to filter, transform, and send events to appropriate targets like Lambda, SQS, and SNS.
Fully Managed Service: EventBridge handles event ingestion, processing, and delivery without managing infrastructure.
Integration with AWS Services: Seamlessly integrates with AWS services such as AWS Lambda, Step Functions, CloudWatch, and more.
SaaS Integrations: Supports event sources from partner SaaS applications like Datadog, Zendesk, and Shopify.
Custom Event Buses: Supports custom event buses for applications that produce their own events.
Event Filtering: Rules allow you to filter specific events that meet defined criteria and route them to designated targets.

Use Cases
Real-time Application Integration: Connect microservices or distributed systems by routing events through EventBridge.
Monitoring and Automation: Automate responses to operational changes, such as EC2 instance state changes triggering a Lambda function.
SaaS Application Integration: Integrate third-party applications like Zendesk and Slack to respond to events or trigger workflows.
Data Processing Pipelines: Use EventBridge to build event-driven workflows for data processing tasks.

Example Scenario
In an e-commerce application, when a new order is placed: The event is published to EventBridge.
A rule routes the event to multiple targets: A Lambda function processes the order. An SNS topic sends a notification to the customer. An SQS queue triggers a shipping workflow.

Amazon EventBridge simplifies the development of event-driven architectures by enabling real-time, decoupled communication across services and applications.

17.5.2 Lab Exercise: Creating Event-Driven Applications with Amazon EventBridge
Step 1: Set Up the Event Source
Log in to AWS Management Console and navigate to the Amazon EventBridge service.
In the EventBridge Dashboard, select Create Rule to define an event trigger.
Name the Rule: Provide a descriptive name and optional description.
Select Event Bus: Choose Default event bus for AWS services or create a custom event bus for custom events.
Define Event Source: Choose Event Pattern for AWS services (e.g., EC2 state changes or S3 object creation). Or select Schedule if you want a periodic rule (e.g., every 5 minutes).

Step 2: Create Event Pattern

Under Event Source, choose the AWS service that will act as the event source. For example: Select EC2 as the source. Choose an event like Instance State Change. Customize the pattern (optional) to filter specific events, such as instances transitioning to "stopped" state.

Step 3: Define Event Targets

In the Targets section, add the service where the event will be sent (target). Choose one of the following targets:

AWS Lambda: To trigger a function that processes the event.
Amazon SQS: To send the event to a queue for further processing.
Amazon SNS: To send notifications to subscribers (e.g., email or SMS).
CloudWatch Log Group: To log the event data for monitoring purposes.

Configure the target details (e.g., Lambda function ARN, SQS Queue URL, or SNS Topic ARN).

Step 4: Add Permissions for Event Target

If using a Lambda function, ensure the Lambda execution role allows EventBridge to invoke the function. For SQS or SNS, verify that the appropriate access policies are in place to allow EventBridge to publish messages.

Step 5: Test the Event Rule

Trigger the event manually:
For EC2: Stop/start an instance to generate an event.
For S3: Upload an object to the configured bucket.

Verify that the target service (e.g., Lambda, SQS) receives the event.
Monitor execution using: CloudWatch Logs (for Lambda). SQS Console to see if messages are enqueued. SNS Notifications (e.g., check your email or SMS).

Step 6: Monitor and Validate

Go to the Amazon EventBridge Dashboard to view event rule metrics and logs. Check CloudWatch Logs for event details and errors. Validate that the event-triggered target performed as expected.

Example Scenario Recap

Event Source: EC2 instance transitioning states.
Event Target: AWS Lambda function to stop/start other resources.
Outcome: The Lambda function is invoked, and the event flow is verified.

By following these steps, you successfully create an event-driven application using Amazon EventBridge.

17.6 AWS AppSync

17.6.1 Introduction to AppSync: Building real-time and offline apps

Amazon AppSync is a fully managed service that simplifies the process of building real-time and offline applications by leveraging GraphQL APIs. AppSync allows you to securely access, modify, and synchronize data across multiple data sources such as Amazon DynamoDB, AWS Lambda, and Amazon RDS. It handles the complexities of real-time data updates, offline synchronization, and scalable data access, allowing developers to focus on building the application logic.

With GraphQL APIs, AppSync provides a single endpoint to query and update data with minimal network overhead. It supports real-time data subscriptions for dynamic applications such as collaborative apps, chat systems, or dashboards.

Key Benefits

Real-Time Updates: Automatically pushes updates to clients using GraphQL subscriptions.
Offline Access: Synchronizes data seamlessly when users reconnect to the internet.
Flexible Data Sources: Integrates with DynamoDB, Aurora, Elasticsearch, Lambda, and other AWS services.
Scalability and Security: Leverages AWS-managed infrastructure with fine-grained access control using AWS IAM and API keys.
Simplified Development: Enables front-end and back-end teams to collaborate efficiently using the GraphQL schema.

Use Cases

Chat Applications: Real-time message delivery using GraphQL subscriptions.
Collaboration Tools: Multi-user applications like whiteboards or project trackers.
Real-Time Dashboards: Display live updates for metrics, analytics, or IoT device data.
Offline-Capable Mobile Apps: Applications where users need access to cached data while offline.

AppSync bridges the gap between real-time data needs and backend infrastructure, making it ideal for modern, scalable, and feature-rich applications.

17.6.2 Lab Exercise: Creating a Real-time App with AWS AppSync

Objective: Build a real-time GraphQL API using AWS AppSync to handle data changes and deliver live updates to clients.

Prerequisites: An AWS account. Basic understanding of GraphQL concepts. AWS CLI and Amplify CLI installed (optional but useful for setup).

Step 1: Open AWS AppSync Console

Go to the AWS Management Console. Navigate to AppSync under Application Integration services. Click on Create API.

Step 2: Create a New GraphQL API
Choose "Create a new API". Select "Start from scratch". Provide an API name (e.g., real-time-app-demo). Click Create.

Step 3: Define the GraphQL Schema
In the API dashboard, go to Schema. Define the schema to manage real-time data updates. Here is an example schema for a simple messaging app:

```
type Message {
  id: ID!
  content: String!
  sender: String!
  createdAt: AWSDateTime!
}

type Subscription {
  onCreateMessage: Message
    @aws_subscribe(mutations: ["createMessage"])
}

type Mutation {
  createMessage(id: ID!, content: String!, sender: String!): Message
}

type Query {
  listMessages: [Message]
}
```

Save the schema.

Step 4: Attach a Data Source
Go to the Data Sources tab. Click Create Data Source. Choose Amazon DynamoDB (or other backend, like AWS Lambda). Create a DynamoDB table named Messages with id as the primary key. Attach this table as the data source.

Step 5: Set Up Resolvers
Go to the Resolvers section in the AppSync console. Attach the createMessage mutation to the DynamoDB data source. Define the resolver mappings for the mutation and query. For real-time subscriptions, AppSync automatically sets up the connection using the onCreateMessage subscription in the schema.

Step 6: Test the API
Open the Queries section in the AppSync console. Use the GraphQL Explorer to test the API. Run a sample mutation to create a new message:

```
mutation {
  createMessage(id: "1", content: "Hello World!", sender: "Alice") {
    id
    content
    sender
    createdAt
```

```
  }
}
```

Then subscribe to real-time updates:

```
subscription {
  onCreateMessage {
    id
    content
    sender
    createdAt
  }
}
```

Step 7: Deploy Front-End (Optional)

Use AWS Amplify to deploy a front-end app (React, Angular, or Vue).
Install Amplify CLI and configure it:

```
amplify init
amplify add api
amplify push
```

Connect your front end to AppSync using the GraphQL API endpoint provided.

Outcome

You have successfully created a real-time app with AWS AppSync. Clients receive live updates whenever new data is created or updated.

This lab demonstrates how AWS AppSync simplifies building real-time apps using GraphQL APIs. It enables developers to set up subscriptions for real-time data updates and seamlessly integrates with back-end data sources like DynamoDB.

17.7 AWS Step Functions

17.7.1 Introduction to Step Functions: Orchestrating AWS services

AWS Step Functions is a fully managed orchestration service that enables developers to build and run workflows by coordinating multiple AWS services into streamlined processes. It is designed to simplify the execution of complex workflows and ensures tasks are executed reliably in a sequential or parallel manner.

AWS Step Functions is a visual workflow service to build serverless distributed applications, automate processes, orchestrate microservices (or Lambda functions), and build ETL and ML pipelines. AWS Step Functions service can integrate with EC2, ECS, on-premises servers, API Gateway, SQS, and many other AWS services.

This AWS Step Functions workflow demonstrates an automated store checkout process that leverages AWS Lambda functions at each step for orchestration. The process begins with the

Check Inventory Availability and Hold Product step, where a Lambda function verifies product availability and places a temporary hold on the product for the customer.

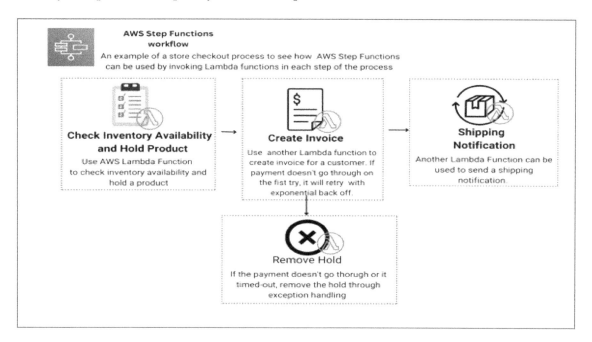

Next, in the **Create Invoice** step, another Lambda function generates the invoice. If the payment attempt fails, the function retries with exponential backoff until it succeeds or times out. Following a successful payment, the **Shipping Notification** step is triggered, where a Lambda function sends a notification to inform the customer that the product is being shipped. If the payment does not go through or the process times out, the workflow handles this exception by invoking the **Remove Hold** step, where another Lambda function releases the product hold.

This workflow highlights a robust and fault-tolerant process for automating inventory management, payment retries, and shipping notifications. AWS Step Functions efficiently orchestrates these tasks, ensuring smooth transitions between steps and managing failures through retry logic and exception handling.

The workflows (orchestration) can be sequential, parallel, or conditional. You can also add timeouts and error handling. You can also add a human approval feature in a workflow using Callback Task Pattern.

Key Features of Step Functions

Visual Workflow: Provides a visual interface to define and monitor workflows, making it easy to understand execution progress.

State Machines: Uses Amazon State Language (ASL) to define workflows, including states, transitions, and error-handling mechanisms.

Error Handling and Retries: Step Functions automatically retries failed steps and supports custom error handling to ensure reliability.

Integration with AWS Services: Seamlessly integrates with AWS Lambda, ECS, DynamoDB, SQS, and other AWS services to trigger tasks or events.

Scalable and Serverless: Automatically scales workflows to match application demands without the need for infrastructure management.

Common Use Cases

Microservices Orchestration: Coordinate multiple microservices or serverless functions in a defined sequence.

ETL Pipelines: Manage Extract, Transform, Load (ETL) processes by integrating services like S3, Lambda, and Redshift.

Business Process Automation: Automate approval workflows and other business processes with conditional logic.

Data Processing Workflows: Process large-scale data across AWS services, handling errors and retries automatically.

IT Operations Automation: Automate tasks such as backup and recovery, system monitoring, and deployment activities.

By offering a robust orchestration layer, AWS Step Functions simplifies complex application workflows while improving visibility, scalability, and fault tolerance for modern applications.

17.7.2 Lab Exercise: Orchestrating Workflows with AWS Step Functions

Learn how to create a workflow using AWS Step Functions to coordinate AWS Lambda functions. You will design, deploy, and monitor a state machine to execute a series of tasks.

Step 1: Set Up Prerequisites

Log in to the AWS Management Console. Ensure the following permissions are available for your IAM user:

Step Functions: CreateStateMachine, DescribeStateMachine, StartExecution
Lambda: CreateFunction, InvokeFunction

Navigate to the Lambda service and create two basic Lambda functions (e.g., Task1 and Task2):
Task1: Returns a message "Task 1 Completed."
Task2: Returns a message "Task 2 Completed."

Step 2: Define a State Machine in Step Functions

Go to the Step Functions console. Click Create State Machine. Choose Author with code snippets or Design with Workflow Studio:

Option 1 - Workflow Studio: Use the visual interface to drag and drop Lambda tasks into the workflow.

Option 2 - Code Snippets: Use the following Amazon States Language (ASL) definition:

```
{
  "Comment": "A simple Step Functions example to run two tasks in sequence.",
  "StartAt": "Task1",
  "States": {
    "Task1": {
      "Type": "Task",
      "Resource": "arn:aws:lambda:REGION:ACCOUNT_ID:function:Task1",
      "Next": "Task2"
    },
    "Task2": {
      "Type": "Task",
      "Resource": "arn:aws:lambda:REGION:ACCOUNT_ID:function:Task2",
      "End": true
```

```
      }
    }
  }
}
```

Replace REGION, ACCOUNT_ID, and Lambda function ARNs appropriately.

Step 3: Deploy the State Machine
Name the state machine (e.g., MyWorkflowStateMachine). Select Standard as the state machine type. Click Create State Machine.

Step 4: Start Workflow Execution
Once the state machine is created, click Start Execution. Provide a Name for the execution (e.g., Execution1). Click Start Execution to initiate the workflow.

Step 5: Monitor Execution
Observe the Execution Flow graph in the Step Functions console. Review the step-by-step execution of Task1 and Task2. Check the Lambda console to confirm both functions were invoked successfully.

Step 6: Debugging and Logs
If errors occur, review logs in Amazon CloudWatch:
Navigate to CloudWatch Logs. Check logs for Lambda functions and Step Functions executions. Fix any issues in Lambda code or the state machine definition.

Expected Outcome: Your Step Functions workflow runs Task1 and Task2 in sequence. Each Lambda function completes successfully, and execution status is Succeeded.

By completing this exercise, you've learned how to define workflows, integrate Lambda functions, and monitor execution flows using AWS Step Functions. You can now build more advanced workflows with branching, error handling, and parallel task execution.

17.8 Related YouTube Videos
- Amazon SNS Tutorial: https://youtu.be/8lb62yEN24o
- Amazon SQS Tutorial: https://youtu.be/_TyCIplCKE8
- Amazon EventBridge Tutorial: https://youtu.be/lhEhsBpdYGg

17.9 Chapter Review Questions
Question 1:
Which of the following is the primary purpose of Amazon Simple Notification Service (SNS)?
    A. To manage and process message queues
    B. To send messages or notifications to subscribers
    C. To orchestrate workflows across AWS services
    D. To query data stored in S3

Question 2:
What is a key benefit of using Amazon SNS for messaging?

A. It supports message queuing for delayed processing

B. It allows fan-out messaging to multiple subscribers

C. It stores messages in a FIFO (First-In-First-Out) format

D. It provides a real-time API for offline apps

Question 3:

Which service is best suited for decoupling application components using message queues?

A. Amazon SQS

B. Amazon SNS

C. AWS Step Functions

D. AWS AppSync

Question 4:

What is the default delivery model for Amazon SQS?

A. Pub/Sub (Publish-Subscribe)

B. Point-to-Point (Message Queuing)

C. Event-based triggering

D. Real-time message streaming

Question 5:

Which of the following AWS services allows you to build event-driven architectures?

A. Amazon SQS

B. Amazon EventBridge

C. AWS Step Functions

D. AWS AppSync

Question 6:

What does Amazon AppSync primarily facilitate?

A. Real-time data synchronization for mobile and web applications

B. Message delivery to application endpoints

C. Storage and retrieval of application data

D. Workflow orchestration across distributed systems

Question 7:

Which feature of AWS Step Functions enables the execution of tasks in a coordinated workflow?

A. Event bus integration

B. State machines

C. Real-time API connections

D. SQS message polling

Question 8:

In Amazon SQS, which queue type ensures that messages are processed exactly once and in order?

A. Standard Queue

B. Dead-letter Queue

C. FIFO Queue

D. Delayed Queue

Question 9:
Which AWS service is used to create and manage event-driven applications using an event bus?
- A. Amazon SNS
- B. Amazon SQS
- C. Amazon EventBridge
- D. AWS Step Functions

Question 10:
What is a typical use case of AWS Step Functions?
- A. Sending notifications to subscribers
- B. Decoupling components through message queues
- C. Orchestrating multiple AWS services into workflows
- D. Providing APIs for real-time applications

17.10 Answers to Chapter Review Questions

1. B. To send messages or notifications to subscribers

Explanation: Amazon SNS is a managed messaging service designed to send notifications to subscribers through various endpoints, including email, SMS, and Lambda functions.

2. B. It allows fan-out messaging to multiple subscribers

Explanation: SNS enables a publish-subscribe (pub/sub) model where a single message can be delivered to multiple subscribers simultaneously.

3. A. Amazon SQS

Explanation: Amazon SQS is a fully managed message queuing service that decouples and scales application components to improve system resilience.

4. B. Point-to-Point (Message Queuing)

Explanation: Amazon SQS follows the point-to-point messaging model where messages are sent to a queue and processed by a single consumer.

5. B. Amazon EventBridge

Explanation: Amazon EventBridge is used to build event-driven applications by routing events from sources to targets using an event bus.

6. A. Real-time data synchronization for mobile and web applications

Explanation: Amazon AppSync is a managed GraphQL service that facilitates real-time data synchronization between mobile/web clients and backend systems.

7. B. State machines

Explanation: AWS Step Functions use state machines to coordinate and execute tasks in a structured workflow, enabling orchestration of AWS services.

8. C. FIFO Queue

Explanation: Amazon SQS FIFO queues ensure that messages are processed exactly once and in the same order in which they were sent.

9. C. Amazon EventBridge

Explanation: Amazon EventBridge is designed for building event-driven architectures using an event bus to connect sources and targets.

10. C. Orchestrating multiple AWS services into workflows

Explanation: AWS Step Functions are used to coordinate and manage multiple AWS services into workflows, ensuring seamless task execution.

Chapter 18. AWS DEVOPS SERVICES

The adoption of DevOps practices has revolutionized the way organizations build, deploy, and manage applications, enabling faster delivery, improved collaboration, and streamlined operations. AWS provides a comprehensive suite of DevOps services to automate the software development lifecycle and infrastructure management. This chapter introduces the essential AWS tools that empower teams to implement DevOps principles effectively.

The chapter begins with an introduction to AWS DevOps, outlining how AWS services facilitate continuous integration, continuous delivery, and automated infrastructure management. You'll explore key services such as AWS CodePipeline, a fully managed service for automating the release pipelines, and AWS CodeCommit, a secure, scalable, and managed source control service.

Next, you'll learn about AWS CodeBuild, a managed build service that compiles source code, runs tests, and produces deployable artifacts. This is followed by AWS CodeDeploy, a service that automates software deployments to compute services like EC2, Lambda, and on-premises servers.

The chapter also delves into AWS CloudFormation, a service for defining and provisioning infrastructure as code, enabling repeatable and version controlled deployments. You'll then explore AWS OpsWorks, a configuration management service that automates operational tasks, and AWS Elastic Beanstalk, a platform-as-a-service (PaaS) offering that simplifies application deployment and scaling.

By the end of this chapter, you will have a solid understanding of AWS DevOps services and how they work together to automate, monitor, and manage the application development and deployment lifecycle, accelerating the delivery of reliable, high-quality software solutions.

18.1 Introduction to AWS DevOps

DevOps is a modern software delivery approach that emphasizes collaboration between development and operations teams to accelerate software deployment and improve reliability. AWS DevOps combines tools and practices that enhance Continuous Integration/Continuous Delivery (CI/CD), Infrastructure as Code (IaC), automation, and monitoring to streamline the software development lifecycle.

Key concepts of DevOps include CI/CD, which ensures frequent code integration and rapid deployment with minimal manual intervention. Infrastructure as Code (IaC) allows developers to manage and provision infrastructure programmatically, ensuring consistency, versioning, and scalability. Automation plays a pivotal role in reducing errors and repetitive tasks, enabling teams to focus on innovation. Monitoring ensures observability, allowing teams to detect issues early and optimize performance.

Using AWS services for DevOps brings significant benefits, such as faster deployment cycles, improved resource management, enhanced scalability, and reduced operational overhead. AWS tools like CodePipeline, CodeBuild, CloudFormation, and CloudWatch make it easier to implement DevOps practices, empowering organizations to deliver high-quality software faster and more efficiently.

18.2 AWS CodePipeline

AWS CodePipeline is a fully managed Continuous Integration and Continuous Delivery (CI/CD) service that automates the software release process, enabling fast and reliable delivery of updates. It helps streamline development workflows by allowing developers to continuously build, test, and deploy their applications, reducing manual effort and increasing deployment speed.

Features and Benefits

Automation: CodePipeline automates the entire release process, including build, test, and deployment stages, ensuring consistency across deployments.

Customizable Workflows: Developers can design and manage custom workflows for their application deployment stages, enabling flexibility based on project requirements.

Scalability: CodePipeline scales to handle any workload, making it suitable for small teams as well as enterprise-level applications.

Integration: CodePipeline integrates natively with other AWS services like CodeCommit, CodeBuild, CodeDeploy, and third-party tools like GitHub, Jenkins, and Atlassian Bitbucket.

Rapid Delivery: Continuous integration and continuous delivery ensure that code changes are tested and deployed quickly, improving time-to-market and software quality.

Setting Up a CI/CD Pipeline

To set up a CI/CD pipeline, follow these steps:

Source Stage: Start by specifying the source repository for your code. You can use AWS CodeCommit, GitHub, or Bitbucket as the source.

Build Stage: Configure CodeBuild or third-party build tools to compile the source code, run tests, and generate build artifacts.

Test Stage: Add testing processes to validate the build output before deployment, ensuring quality.

Deploy Stage: Use AWS CodeDeploy or other deployment tools to push the code to target environments such as EC2, Lambda, or on-premises servers.

Monitoring: Integrate CloudWatch and other monitoring tools to track performance and logs throughout the pipeline.

Integrations with CodeCommit, CodeBuild, and Third-Party Tools

AWS CodePipeline integrates seamlessly with AWS CodeCommit for source control, AWS CodeBuild for building applications, and AWS CodeDeploy for automated deployments.

Additionally, it supports third-party tools like Jenkins, GitHub, and Bitbucket, enabling teams to use their existing tools and workflows.

Overall, AWS CodePipeline provides a robust and scalable solution to automate software delivery, improving speed, reliability, and efficiency for modern DevOps practices.

18.3 AWS CodeCommit

AWS CodeCommit is a fully managed source control service that allows teams to host secure, scalable, and highly available Git-based repositories. It eliminates the need to manage and maintain on-premises version control systems, making it an ideal solution for modern development workflows.

Features

Git-Based Repositories: CodeCommit supports the standard Git protocol, enabling developers to use their preferred Git tools, including Git commands and clients, for version control.

Encryption: CodeCommit ensures data security by encrypting repositories at rest using AWS Key Management Service (KMS) and in transit via HTTPS and SSH.

Collaboration Tools: It facilitates team collaboration through features like pull requests, code reviews, and notifications, enabling developers to work efficiently together.

Fully Managed: As a managed service, CodeCommit removes the operational overhead of maintaining servers, backups, and software updates.

Scalability: CodeCommit can store any number of repositories and support large file sizes, making it ideal for projects of all sizes.

Integration: CodeCommit integrates seamlessly with AWS services like CodePipeline, CodeBuild, and CloudWatch for CI/CD, building, and monitoring.

Managing Code Repositories and Workflows

Create Repositories: Developers can easily create private Git repositories to store and version their source code.

Clone and Push: Use Git commands to clone, push, and pull changes from CodeCommit repositories. Developers can use HTTPS or SSH for secure access.

Pull Requests and Code Reviews: CodeCommit provides tools to initiate pull requests, review code, discuss changes, and merge code efficiently.

Notifications: Set up notifications using Amazon SNS to inform teams about repository activity, such as commits, pull requests, or merges.

Workflow Automation: Integrate CodeCommit with AWS CodePipeline for automated CI/CD workflows and CodeBuild for build automation.

Best Practices for Version Control

Branching Strategy: Implement a branching strategy (e.g., feature branches, development, and main/master branches) to organize and manage code changes effectively.

Commit Guidelines: Use meaningful and descriptive commit messages to document code changes clearly.

Regular Reviews: Perform regular code reviews using pull requests to maintain code quality and team collaboration.

Secure Access: Use IAM policies to control user access to repositories and enforce encryption for data security.

Automation: Leverage CI/CD tools like CodePipeline to automate build, test, and deployment processes for faster and more reliable releases.

AWS CodeCommit simplifies version control with a secure, scalable, and managed Git-based platform, enabling teams to collaborate effectively and integrate seamlessly with AWS DevOps tools for efficient workflows.

18.4 AWS CodeBuild

AWS CodeBuild is a fully managed build service designed for continuous integration, allowing developers to compile code, run tests, and produce deployable artifacts without managing build servers. It integrates seamlessly with other AWS services, enabling a streamlined DevOps workflow.

Features

Build Specifications: CodeBuild uses buildspec.yml, a configuration file that defines the build process, including environment variables, phases, and commands.

Parallel Builds: Run multiple builds concurrently, reducing build times and enhancing efficiency for projects with high workloads.

Custom Environments: Use pre-configured build environments or create custom environments with Docker images to meet specific requirements.

Scalability: CodeBuild automatically scales resources to handle build requests, ensuring consistent performance regardless of project size.

Security: Build artifacts and logs are encrypted in transit and at rest. IAM roles allow fine-grained access control to resources.

Pay-As-You-Go Pricing: CodeBuild charges only for the compute time used during the build process, optimizing costs for on-demand builds.

Integration: It integrates with CodePipeline, CodeCommit, and third-party tools like GitHub and Bitbucket for end-to-end CI/CD pipelines.

Monitoring: Use Amazon CloudWatch to monitor and analyze build performance, errors, and logs in real-time.

AWS CodeBuild simplifies the build process for CI/CD workflows by eliminating infrastructure management. With its scalability, flexible environments, and cost-effectiveness, developers can focus on delivering high-quality software efficiently.

18.5 AWS CodeDeploy

AWS CodeDeploy is a fully managed service that automates software deployments to compute services like Amazon EC2, AWS Lambda, and on-premises servers. By simplifying and automating the deployment process, CodeDeploy reduces downtime, minimizes errors, and ensures seamless application updates.

AWS CodeDeploy allows organizations to automate deployments in a reliable and repeatable manner. It supports a variety of environments, from the AWS Cloud to on-premises infrastructure, and integrates seamlessly into CI/CD workflows. This flexibility ensures consistent deployments while maintaining high availability and application performance.

Deployment Types

In-place Deployment: Updates application code on existing instances or servers. CodeDeploy stops the application, installs the updated code, and restarts the application. This is suitable for applications that can tolerate downtime during updates.

Blue/Green Deployment: CodeDeploy shifts traffic from the existing application environment (Blue) to a new one (Green). It allows rollback to the original environment if issues occur. This approach minimizes downtime and reduces risk during deployments.

Managing and Monitoring Deployments

Deployment Configuration: Define deployment settings, such as batch size, rollback conditions, and failure thresholds, for precise control. Use appspec.yml to specify how to deploy code and run lifecycle hooks (e.g., ApplicationStop, BeforeInstall, AfterInstall).

Monitoring Deployments: AWS CodeDeploy integrates with Amazon CloudWatch and AWS X-Ray to monitor deployment metrics, application health, and logs. You can track deployment success rates, errors, and rollback triggers in real time.

Rollback and Recovery: If a deployment fails or issues arise, CodeDeploy automatically triggers rollback mechanisms to revert to the previous version. This ensures minimal disruption and quick recovery from failures.

Deployment Strategies: Use deployment groups to organize instances or Lambda functions for targeted rollouts. Implement traffic shifting strategies in Blue/Green deployments to gradually transition traffic.

Benefits of AWS CodeDeploy

Automation: Eliminates manual intervention by automating deployments across environments.
High Availability: Blue/Green deployments ensure minimal downtime, maintaining user experience.
Scalability: Supports deployments to thousands of EC2 instances, Lambda functions, or on-premises servers.
Monitoring and Rollback: Provides detailed insights and automated recovery for failed deployments.
Cost-Effective: Integrates with existing CI/CD tools without requiring additional infrastructure management.

By streamlining the deployment process, AWS CodeDeploy empowers teams to release features faster while maintaining reliability and minimizing risks. Its flexibility to handle multiple environments and deployment strategies makes it a core component of DevOps pipelines.

18.6 AWS CloudFormation

AWS CloudFormation is a powerful Infrastructure as Code (IaC) service that allows you to provision and manage AWS resources in a declarative and automated manner. By using templates to define infrastructure, CloudFormation simplifies the process of deploying and managing complex environments, ensuring consistency and repeatability.

CloudFormation enables organizations to treat their infrastructure as code. Instead of manually provisioning resources, you define the desired state of your AWS environment using JSON or YAML templates. CloudFormation then automates the provisioning, updating, and management of AWS resources, saving time and reducing errors.

Key Components

Templates: A CloudFormation template is a text file written in JSON or YAML format that defines the desired AWS resources and configurations. Templates include sections like Resources (the core section defining AWS resources), Parameters, Outputs, and Mappings.
Example: Defining an EC2 instance, S3 bucket, or VPC with specific settings.

Stacks: A stack is a collection of AWS resources managed as a single unit. When you submit a template to CloudFormation, it creates a stack and provisions the resources specified in the template. Updates to the stack ensure the infrastructure remains consistent with the template.

Change Sets: Change Sets allow you to preview changes before applying updates to a stack. This ensures that modifications to the infrastructure do not result in unexpected issues. By reviewing the proposed changes, you can validate the impact of updates before executing them.

Creating Reusable Infrastructure Templates

Define Your Template: Use JSON or YAML to define the AWS resources and configurations in a CloudFormation template. Modularize templates using nested stacks for large or complex infrastructures.

Parameterization: Use parameters in templates to make them reusable. Parameters allow you to customize values (e.g., instance types, environment names) when creating a stack. Example: Replace hard-coded values with input parameters like InstanceType or BucketName.

Outputs and Mappings: Use outputs to display useful information, such as resource ARNs or endpoint URLs, after stack creation. Mappings help configure resource properties dynamically based on regions or conditions.

Deploying Infrastructure: Upload the template to CloudFormation, validate it, and create the stack. Use the AWS Management Console, AWS CLI, or AWS SDKs to deploy and manage stacks.

Version Control and Automation: Store templates in version control systems like Git for collaboration and versioning. Integrate CloudFormation with CI/CD pipelines to automate resource provisioning.

Benefits of AWS CloudFormation

Automation: Provision and manage infrastructure automatically using code-based templates.
Consistency: Ensure consistent deployments across environments (e.g., dev, test, prod).
Scalability: Easily scale resources or replicate infrastructure across multiple regions.
Change Management: Use Change Sets to safely review and apply updates to your infrastructure.
Reusability: Templates can be reused across projects and teams, reducing duplication of effort.

Cost Optimization: Efficiently manage resources and eliminate manual errors, leading to optimized costs.

By leveraging AWS CloudFormation, teams can achieve faster, more reliable deployments, ensure infrastructure consistency, and simplify resource management through automation. It is a foundational tool for implementing Infrastructure as Code in modern DevOps practices.

18.7 AWS OpsWorks

AWS OpsWorks is a configuration management service that uses Chef and Puppet to automate and manage infrastructure at scale. It enables DevOps teams to provision, configure, and manage servers both in the cloud and on-premises. OpsWorks simplifies the process of managing infrastructure by automating tasks such as software installation, updates, and server configuration, ensuring consistency across your environment.

Features and Use Cases

Configuration Management with Chef and Puppet: AWS OpsWorks provides support for popular configuration management tools like Chef and Puppet. These tools use declarative configurations to define and maintain the desired state of servers, applications, and infrastructure. OpsWorks for Chef Automate: Integrates Chef Automate for managing complex configurations and compliance. OpsWorks for Puppet Enterprise: Enables centralized management of resources with Puppet Enterprise.

Stacks and Layers: OpsWorks organizes infrastructure into stacks, where a stack represents a group of resources (e.g., web servers, app servers). Within a stack, layers are defined to group specific functions, such as a layer for load balancers or database servers.

Automating Server Management: OpsWorks automates the entire server lifecycle, including bootstrapping, scaling, and patch management. Users can create recipes or scripts that run during lifecycle events like setup, configure, deploy, and shutdown.

Scalability: OpsWorks supports automatic scaling of servers based on time-based or load-based triggers, ensuring resources meet workload demands. It integrates with Elastic Load Balancing (ELB) to distribute traffic efficiently across multiple servers.

Monitoring and Logging: OpsWorks integrates with Amazon CloudWatch and AWS CloudTrail to provide monitoring, logging, and auditing capabilities. CloudWatch metrics can trigger alarms, enabling proactive resource management.

Use Cases

Application Deployment: Automate the deployment and configuration of multi-tier applications using Chef or Puppet.
Server Configuration: Define and enforce configuration policies to manage large fleets of servers in AWS or on-premises.
Compliance Management: Use Chef Automate or Puppet Enterprise to ensure that servers comply with regulatory and security standards.
Auto Scaling Workloads: Use load-based or time-based scaling to dynamically scale infrastructure resources as needed.

Hybrid Infrastructure: OpsWorks supports managing resources both in AWS and on-premises environments, enabling hybrid cloud management.

Automating Server Management with OpsWorks

Define Stacks and Layers: Start by organizing infrastructure into stacks and layers for logical resource grouping.

Configuration Management: Use Chef cookbooks or Puppet manifests to define server configurations and desired states.

Lifecycle Events: Automate tasks like server setup, software deployment, and shutdown using lifecycle hooks.

Scaling Policies: Configure auto-scaling policies to optimize resource utilization and handle traffic spikes.

Monitoring: Leverage CloudWatch and CloudTrail for continuous monitoring, logging, and troubleshooting.

AWS OpsWorks simplifies infrastructure and configuration management by leveraging automation tools like Chef and Puppet. It enables efficient scaling, monitoring, and compliance enforcement while reducing manual overhead, making it ideal for large-scale deployments and hybrid cloud environments.

18.8 AWS Elastic Beanstalk

AWS Elastic Beanstalk is a Platform as a Service (PaaS) offering from AWS that simplifies the deployment and management of web applications. It allows developers to deploy applications quickly without worrying about the underlying infrastructure. Elastic Beanstalk supports a wide range of programming languages such as Java, Python, PHP, .NET, Node.js, and Ruby, making it versatile for various development needs.

One of its key features is **automatic scaling**, where Elastic Beanstalk adjusts capacity up or down based on application traffic, ensuring optimal performance and cost-efficiency. Additionally, it manages the environment, including provisioning infrastructure resources like EC2 instances, load balancers, and databases, while enabling users to focus solely on their code. Monitoring is built into the platform through integrations with Amazon CloudWatch, which provides metrics and alerts to monitor application health and performance.

The deployment process in Elastic Beanstalk is straightforward. Developers upload their application code via the AWS Management Console, CLI, or API, and Elastic Beanstalk handles the rest—such as resource allocation, environment creation, and deployment of updates. It also supports rolling updates, version management, and rollback capabilities, which help ensure smooth application transitions and minimize downtime.

AWS Elastic Beanstalk is ideal for teams seeking an efficient way to manage web applications without diving deep into infrastructure setup. Its user-friendly features and automated workflows make it a popular choice for developers looking to deploy scalable and reliable applications in the cloud.

18.9 Related YouTube Videos

📺 AWS CloudFormation Tutorial: https://youtu.be/bmYLYUW0kFQ

18.10 Chapter Review Questions

Question 1:

Which AWS service provides a fully managed continuous integration and continuous delivery (CI/CD) pipeline?

    A. AWS CodeBuild

    B. AWS CodeCommit

    C. AWS CodePipeline

    D. AWS OpsWorks

Question 2:

What is the primary purpose of AWS CodeCommit?

    A. Build and test application code

    B. Manage version control using Git-based repositories

    C. Automate deployments to EC2 instances

    D. Create and manage infrastructure as code

Question 3:

Which AWS service is used for automated build and testing of code?

    A. AWS CodePipeline

    B. AWS CodeBuild

    C. AWS CodeDeploy

    D. AWS Elastic Beanstalk

Question 4:

Which AWS service supports both in-place and blue/green deployment strategies?

    A. AWS CodePipeline

    B. AWS OpsWorks

    C. AWS CodeDeploy

    D. AWS Elastic Beanstalk

Question 5:

What does AWS CloudFormation primarily enable?

    A. Deploying applications to on-premises servers

    B. Automating infrastructure provisioning using templates

    C. Managing source code with Git repositories

    D. Scaling web applications automatically

Question 6:

Which AWS service automates server configuration management using Chef and Puppet?

    A. AWS Elastic Beanstalk

    B. AWS CloudFormation

    C. AWS OpsWorks

    D. AWS CodePipeline

Question 7:

What is AWS Elastic Beanstalk best described as?

    A. A Platform as a Service (PaaS) for deploying web applications

    B. A source control service for managing Git repositories

C. A fully managed build service for CI/CD pipelines

D. A tool for managing server configurations and deployments

Question 8:
Which AWS service enables infrastructure automation using code templates known as "stacks"?

A. AWS OpsWorks

B. AWS CloudFormation

C. AWS CodePipeline

D. AWS CodeBuild

Question 9:
What feature does AWS CodePipeline provide for DevOps workflows?

A. Version control for managing code

B. Continuous delivery through automated pipelines

C. Configuration management for EC2 instances

D. Real-time log monitoring and analysis

Question 10:
In AWS OpsWorks, what is a Layer used for?

A. Automating build processes for CI/CD workflows

B. Defining software packages and configurations for servers

C. Hosting application environments with scaling

D. Creating and deploying infrastructure as code templates

18.11 Answers to Chapter Review Questions

1. C. AWS CodePipeline
Explanation: AWS CodePipeline is a fully managed CI/CD service that automates the build, test, and deployment phases of release pipelines.

2. B. Manage version control using Git-based repositories
Explanation: AWS CodeCommit is a fully managed source control service that provides Git-based repositories to store and manage code.

3. B. AWS CodeBuild
Explanation: AWS CodeBuild is a fully managed build service for compiling, testing, and packaging application code.

4. C. AWS CodeDeploy
Explanation: AWS CodeDeploy supports both in-place and blue/green deployments for EC2, Lambda, and on-premises servers.

5. B. Automating infrastructure provisioning using templates
Explanation: AWS CloudFormation enables infrastructure as code, allowing users to provision and manage resources using templates and stacks.

6. C. AWS OpsWorks
Explanation: AWS OpsWorks is a configuration management service that uses Chef and Puppet to automate server configurations.

7. A. A Platform as a Service (PaaS) for deploying web applications

Explanation: AWS Elastic Beanstalk is a PaaS that simplifies the deployment and management of web applications.

8. B. AWS CloudFormation

Explanation: AWS CloudFormation enables infrastructure automation using code templates, which are deployed as "stacks."

9. B. Continuous delivery through automated pipelines

Explanation: AWS CodePipeline enables continuous delivery by automating the build, test, and deployment stages of workflows.

10. B. Defining software packages and configurations for servers

Explanation: In AWS OpsWorks, a Layer defines the software configurations, settings, and packages for servers in an application stack.

Chapter 19. AWS Monitoring and Logging Services

Monitoring, logging, and tracing are essential components of cloud operations, ensuring that resources and applications remain reliable, secure, and high-performing. AWS offers a suite of powerful monitoring and logging services that provide comprehensive visibility into infrastructure, application performance, and security events. This chapter introduces you to AWS Monitoring and Logging Services, which enable proactive resource management, troubleshooting, and compliance tracking.

The chapter begins with an introduction to AWS Monitoring and Logging, highlighting their significance in maintaining operational health and security. You'll first explore Amazon CloudWatch, a central service for monitoring AWS resources, tracking metrics, configuring alarms, and managing logs and events. Key features like CloudWatch Metrics, Alarms, and Logs are covered in detail, along with CloudWatch Events (Amazon EventBridge) for event-driven workflows.

Next, you will learn about AWS CloudTrail, a service that records and audits API activity across your AWS account. The section explains CloudTrail Event Types, enabling and configuring CloudTrail, and integrating it with CloudWatch for actionable insights.

The chapter then introduces AWS X-Ray, a service for tracing and debugging distributed applications. You'll gain an understanding of how X-Ray works, its key features, and its integration with AWS services to identify performance bottlenecks and troubleshoot issues.

You'll also explore AWS Config, a configuration management service that tracks resource changes, enforces compliance through rules, and provides snapshots of resource configurations.

Finally, the chapter outlines best practices for effective monitoring and logging, along with example scenarios to help you apply these tools in real-world use cases. By the end of this chapter, you'll be equipped to monitor, log, and troubleshoot AWS resources effectively, ensuring optimal performance, security, and compliance across your cloud environment.

19.1 Introduction to AWS Monitoring and Logging

Monitoring and logging are essential components in cloud environments to ensure observability, proactive issue detection, and performance optimization. AWS provides a suite of tools to address these needs, enabling businesses to monitor resources, troubleshoot issues, and manage costs effectively. **Amazon CloudWatch** is a key service that collects and tracks metrics, monitors logs, and sets alarms for resources to ensure optimal performance and availability.

AWS CloudTrail offers visibility into API calls and user activity, providing a critical audit trail for governance and compliance. **AWS X-Ray** enables distributed tracing to analyze and debug applications, making it easier to identify and resolve bottlenecks. Together, these tools deliver end-to-end visibility, facilitating proactive monitoring, rapid troubleshooting, cost management, and overall performance optimization in cloud-based applications.

19.2 Amazon CloudWatch: Monitoring AWS Resources

19.2.1 Overview of CloudWatch

Amazon CloudWatch is a vital AWS monitoring and observability service that enables organizations to collect, analyze, and act on operational data for resources running in AWS and on-premises. CloudWatch monitors metrics, logs, and events to provide a comprehensive view of system performance, resource utilization, and application health. By continuously gathering metrics and logs, CloudWatch supports observability, allowing you to detect issues, troubleshoot errors, and optimize performance.

One of CloudWatch's most important roles is improving application and infrastructure performance analysis. It achieves this by aggregating and analyzing real-time metrics from EC2 instances, databases, serverless functions, and other AWS services. Logs can also be ingested from resources, enabling users to track detailed events and workflows.

CloudWatch empowers teams to set alarms, automate responses using event triggers, and visualize trends through dashboards. This helps organizations maintain high availability, optimize costs, and identify performance bottlenecks proactively. As a key monitoring solution, CloudWatch plays a significant role in observability frameworks for modern cloud applications, supporting both reactive troubleshooting and proactive resource management.

19.2.2 CloudWatch Metrics

Amazon CloudWatch Metrics provides a powerful mechanism for collecting and monitoring performance data from AWS services and custom applications. Metrics represent time-ordered sets of data points, helping users gain real-time insights into system performance, resource utilization, and operational health. CloudWatch collects default metrics from AWS services like EC2, S3, RDS, and Lambda, while also allowing users to publish custom metrics from their applications using the AWS SDK or CLI.

Key features of CloudWatch Metrics include Dashboards, Alarms, and Real-time Monitoring. CloudWatch Dashboards offer customizable visualizations for tracking metrics across resources, enabling teams to quickly identify trends and anomalies. Alarms allow users to set thresholds for specific metrics, triggering notifications or automated actions when performance deviates from the defined parameters. For example, an alarm can be configured to notify administrators when the CPU utilization of an EC2 instance exceeds 80%, enabling proactive resource scaling or troubleshooting.

An example of CloudWatch Metrics in action is monitoring CPU utilization for EC2 instances. CloudWatch collects the CPU usage data at regular intervals, which can be visualized on a dashboard or used to trigger alarms for high CPU activity. By combining metrics with real-time monitoring and automation, CloudWatch ensures that performance issues are addressed promptly, optimizing the reliability and efficiency of AWS applications and infrastructure.

19.2.3 CloudWatch Alarms

Amazon CloudWatch Alarms allow users to monitor specific metrics and take automated actions or trigger notifications when thresholds are breached. By setting up alarms, administrators can proactively address performance issues, ensuring system reliability and availability. CloudWatch Alarms operate by continuously evaluating monitored metrics against user-defined thresholds. If a threshold is exceeded, an alarm can enter either an "ALARM" or "OK" state, initiating a predefined response.

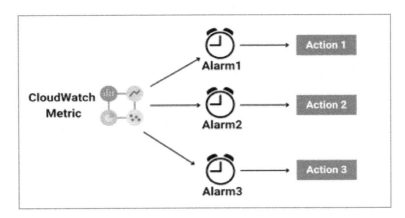

Key Features include integration with Amazon SNS (Simple Notification Service) for notifications and Auto Scaling to adjust resources dynamically. For example, when an alarm detects high memory usage on an Amazon RDS instance, it can automatically send an SNS notification to alert administrators or trigger Auto Scaling policies to add additional resources. These automated actions help maintain optimal performance without manual intervention.

A practical example of configuring a CloudWatch Alarm would involve monitoring high memory usage on RDS instances. Users can specify a memory utilization threshold, such as 80%, and define actions like sending email alerts through SNS or scaling the database resources. Once the memory usage exceeds the threshold, the alarm will activate, notifying stakeholders or initiating scaling operations to maintain system performance. This approach ensures proactive monitoring and operational efficiency across AWS services.

19.2.4 CloudWatch Logs

Amazon CloudWatch Logs is a powerful service that enables users to capture, store, and analyze logs from AWS resources, applications, and on-premises environments. It provides centralized log management, making it easier to monitor system activities, troubleshoot issues, and optimize performance across AWS workloads.

Key Features

Log Groups: Logs are logically organized into groups, which act as containers for related logs from the same AWS resource or application, such as Lambda functions, EC2 instances, or RDS databases.

Log Streams: Within each log group, log events are further organized into streams, which represent sequences of logs generated by a specific resource or process over time.

Filters: Users can apply metric filters to search for specific keywords, patterns, or numerical values in logs. These filters allow the extraction of insights and the creation of actionable CloudWatch metrics.

CloudWatch Logs for EC2

If you need to push logs from an EC2 instance to CloudWatch --- you will have to use the CloudWatch Logs agent. By default, EC2 instances don't push logs to CloudWatch.

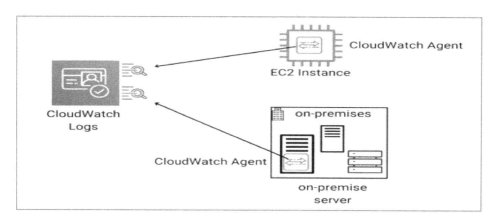

You need to run a CloudWatch agent on EC2 to push the log files you want. The CloudWatch Logs agent provides an automated way to push log data to CloudWatch from Amazon EC2 instances. The log agent includes a script that initiates the process of pushing log data and a plug-in to the AWS CLI that pushes log data.

Example: Analyzing Lambda Execution Logs

When an AWS Lambda function executes, it automatically generates logs (e.g., errors, function execution details, and output) and sends them to CloudWatch Logs. Developers can analyze these logs to:
*   Debug errors by searching for specific keywords such as "ERROR" or "FAILURE."
*   Identify performance issues, such as excessive invocation times or failed executions.
*   Visualize logs for deeper insights using CloudWatch Dashboards.

By capturing logs, applying filters, and monitoring key metrics, CloudWatch Logs improves observability and accelerates debugging, ensuring efficient management of AWS applications and infrastructure.

19.2.5 CloudWatch Events (Amazon EventBridge)

Amazon CloudWatch Events (now part of Amazon EventBridge) is a fully managed event bus service that enables automated responses to changes in AWS resources. It allows you to monitor system changes in near real-time and trigger actions based on rules you define. EventBridge simplifies automation across AWS services and integrates with both AWS and third-party SaaS applications.

Key Features

Event Sources: EventBridge captures changes from AWS services (e.g., S3, EC2, and Lambda) and external SaaS providers.

Rules: Users define event rules to match specific patterns, determining what events trigger actions.

Targets: Events are routed to targets, such as AWS Lambda functions, SQS queues, SNS topics, Step Functions, and EC2 instances.

Example: Triggering a Lambda Function on S3 Object Creation

When a new object is uploaded to an S3 bucket:

Event Source: Amazon S3 sends an event notification to CloudWatch Events.

Rule: A rule is configured to match the S3 object creation event.

Target: The rule triggers an AWS Lambda function that processes the new S3 object, such as analyzing its metadata or performing image processing.

By automating responses to changes, EventBridge improves operational efficiency, reduces manual intervention, and enables event-driven architectures for modern cloud applications.

19.3 AWS CloudTrail: Auditing and Logging API Calls

AWS CloudTrail is a service that logs and tracks API activity across your AWS accounts. It provides a detailed history of AWS service actions performed by users, roles, or AWS services, ensuring full visibility into your cloud environment. CloudTrail records all API calls made within an AWS account, including those made via the AWS Management Console, AWS CLI, SDKs, or other services. These logs are critical for monitoring activities, troubleshooting issues, and auditing access.

Key Use Cases

Security Analysis: CloudTrail helps detect unauthorized access or unusual activities by logging events like failed login attempts or modifications to security settings. Security teams can review logs to identify potential threats.

Compliance: Organizations use CloudTrail logs for compliance audits and reporting. It aligns with regulations like PCI-DSS, GDPR, and HIPAA by providing visibility into user actions.

Troubleshooting: CloudTrail simplifies diagnosing operational issues. If resources are created, modified, or deleted unexpectedly, the logs can help pinpoint the source of the change and responsible user.

How It Works

CloudTrail automatically records event history for all AWS API actions and stores the logs in Amazon S3. You can enable log delivery to CloudWatch Logs for real-time monitoring or integrate it with AWS EventBridge for automated responses. Logs include details such as the user identity, resource affected, time of action, and request parameters.

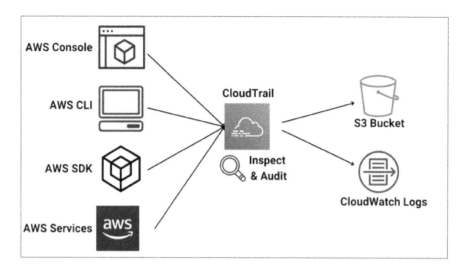

This diagram explains the AWS CloudTrail service, highlighting its role in auditing and logging activity across AWS services.

AWS CloudTrail monitors and records all API activity and events within an AWS account, providing visibility into actions taken through various interfaces. These interfaces include the AWS Console, AWS CLI, AWS SDK, and other AWS Services.

Once CloudTrail captures the API calls and activities, it allows the data to be stored and further analyzed. Specifically, the recorded logs are delivered to an S3 Bucket for long-term storage, making it easy to archive and retrieve the logs when needed. Additionally, CloudTrail logs can be sent to CloudWatch Logs to enable real-time monitoring, alerting, and further analysis of API activity. CloudWatch integration helps detect unusual activities, troubleshoot issues, and set up alarms for critical operations.

Example Scenario
If an IAM policy is modified unexpectedly, CloudTrail can log the event, showing:
- Who made the change (user or role)
- When it happened
- The API call used

This data enables quick identification and resolution of unauthorized changes. AWS CloudTrail plays a key role in ensuring transparency, security, and compliance in AWS environments.

In summary, AWS CloudTrail serves as a central tool for inspecting and auditing AWS account activities, offering both secure storage in S3 buckets and advanced monitoring capabilities through CloudWatch Logs. This ensures governance, compliance, and operational transparency across AWS services.

19.3.1 CloudTrail Event Types

AWS CloudTrail categorizes events into two primary types: Management Events and Data Events, enabling detailed tracking of API activities within an AWS environment. This classification allows users to better monitor resource changes and access patterns, ensuring visibility and control.

Management Events

Management events log high-level operations that change the configuration, state, or management of AWS resources. These events provide insights into actions like creating, modifying, or deleting resources.

Examples:
- CreateBucket (Amazon S3): Creates a new S3 bucket.
- StartInstances (EC2): Starts stopped EC2 instances.
- DeleteGroup (IAM): Deletes an IAM group.

Management events are enabled by default and typically account for critical administrative activity across AWS services.
By monitoring these events, organizations can detect unauthorized changes, audit configuration management, and ensure operational governance.

Data Events

Data events capture resource-level activity related to AWS services, such as access or changes to data stored in specific resources. These events are not logged by default due to their volume but can be enabled selectively for granular monitoring.

Examples:
- S3 Object Access: Logs operations like GetObject or PutObject for specific S3 buckets.
- DynamoDB Data Access: Tracks API calls such as GetItem or PutItem to access table records.

Data events are particularly useful for security analysis and auditing, as they provide details about who accessed sensitive data and how.

Use Case Example
- If an organization needs to monitor who is downloading files from a specific S3 bucket, enabling data events for GetObject operations will track this activity.
- To monitor EC2 instance state changes, management events such as StartInstances and StopInstances provide the required visibility.

By leveraging both management events and data events, AWS CloudTrail ensures comprehensive visibility into resource changes and data access, facilitating security, compliance, and operational monitoring.

19.3.2 Enabling and Configuring CloudTrail

AWS CloudTrail enables logging, tracking, and analyzing API activity across your AWS environment. By creating a trail, you can capture API calls and store logs securely for long-term retention in Amazon S3. This configuration improves governance, compliance, and operational monitoring.

Steps to Enable CloudTrail

Sign in to AWS Management Console: Navigate to CloudTrail under the Management & Governance services section.

Create a Trail: Select Create Trail and provide a name for the trail (e.g., organization-trail). Choose whether the trail will log events for a single account or all accounts in an AWS Organization.

Enable Log Delivery to S3: Configure the trail to deliver logs to an Amazon S3 bucket:
Specify an existing bucket or create a new one. Optionally, enable log file encryption using AWS KMS for added security. S3 buckets serve as the primary storage for CloudTrail logs, enabling long-term retention and retrieval.

Select Event Types: Specify whether to log:
Management Events (default): Captures actions that modify AWS resources, such as CreateBucket or StartInstances.
Data Events: Captures detailed access activity for resources like S3 objects (PutObject) or DynamoDB tables.

Enable CloudWatch Logs Integration (Optional): CloudTrail can send logs to Amazon CloudWatch Logs, where you can create alarms for specific API activities and analyze logs in near real-time.

Enable Multi-Region Trail: Check the option to apply the trail across all AWS regions, ensuring a unified view of activity. This simplifies compliance and auditing across your AWS infrastructure.

Configure Log File Integrity (Optional): Enable log file integrity validation to ensure that the logs have not been tampered with. CloudTrail generates a digest file for validation purposes.

Review and Create: Review the trail settings and confirm creation.

Log Storage in Amazon S3 for Long-Term Retention

CloudTrail stores logs in the configured S3 bucket with a directory structure organized by account, region, and service for easy retrieval. For long-term retention, you can configure S3 lifecycle policies to:
* Transition logs to Amazon S3 Glacier for archival.
* Define expiration rules for old logs to save storage costs.

Benefits of Enabling CloudTrail

Centralized Monitoring: Unified logging of API activity across AWS resources.
Compliance and Auditing: Meet regulatory requirements with secure, immutable logs stored in S3.
Security Analysis: Detect unauthorized activity and suspicious API usage.

Cloud Computing and AWS Introduction

Operational Insights: Troubleshoot resource changes and automate responses using log data.

Example Use Case

To monitor API activity in an AWS account, you can configure CloudTrail to:
- Log all management events across regions.
- Store logs securely in S3 for 1 year.
- Use CloudWatch alarms to trigger notifications for high-risk actions such as DeleteBucket or StopInstances.

By enabling and configuring CloudTrail, organizations gain visibility into AWS API activity, ensuring improved security, compliance, and operational efficiency.

19.3.3 CloudTrail Insights

CloudTrail Insights helps detect unusual operational activity in your AWS account by analyzing API usage patterns. It identifies anomalies, such as unexpected spikes in API requests, and generates insight events that highlight deviations from normal behavior. These events include key details like API names, user identities, and affected resources. CloudTrail Insights integrates with CloudTrail logs, storing detected anomalies in Amazon S3 for easy access.

The service is particularly useful for enhancing security posture, improving operational monitoring, and simplifying troubleshooting by providing actionable insights into unusual activity. For example, it can detect a sudden increase in TerminateInstances API calls, allowing teams to investigate and respond proactively. By enabling quick identification and resolution of anomalies, CloudTrail Insights supports better incident response, reduces downtime, and ensures operational stability.

19.3.4 Integrating CloudTrail with CloudWatch

Integrating AWS CloudTrail with Amazon CloudWatch allows real-time monitoring of API activity in your AWS environment. By sending CloudTrail events to CloudWatch Logs, you can set up alarms, monitor unusual API behavior, and track operational activities in real-time. This integration enhances observability, enabling faster detection of security breaches or abnormal activities such as unauthorized API calls or failed login attempts. CloudWatch dashboards and metrics provide visibility into CloudTrail events, while CloudWatch Alarms notify teams immediately, ensuring proactive issue resolution and improved security posture.

19.4 AWS X-Ray: Tracing and Debugging Applications
19.4.1 Overview of AWS X-Ray

AWS X-Ray is a powerful distributed tracing service designed to analyze and debug microservices and serverless applications. It enables developers to trace requests as they travel through various services, providing end-to-end visibility into the application's flow. X-Ray is particularly important for identifying bottlenecks, latency issues, and root causes of errors in complex architectures. By visualizing service interactions and performance data, teams can optimize the performance of their distributed systems and improve the reliability of applications running on AWS.

19.4.2 How AWS X-Ray Works

AWS X-Ray traces requests as they pass through different services in an application, providing detailed insights into performance and dependencies. It operates using key components such as the X-Ray daemon, which collects trace data, and segments that represent individual services involved in a request. These segments can further include subsegments, offering granular insights into smaller operations like database calls or external API interactions. Trace maps visually connect these segments, enabling developers to identify latency, errors, and bottlenecks across the application's architecture. This comprehensive tracing helps debug and optimize distributed systems effectively.

19.4.3 Key Features of AWS X-Ray

AWS X-Ray provides latency analysis to identify and address performance bottlenecks across distributed applications. It generates service maps for visualizing the flow of requests, showing interactions between different services and their dependencies. X-Ray also aids in error detection by identifying faults and failures in requests. Additionally, request sampling ensures efficient tracing by capturing only a representative subset of requests, helping reduce overhead while maintaining visibility into application behavior. These features enable developers to troubleshoot, optimize, and improve the performance of their applications effectively.

19.4.4 Integrating X-Ray with AWS Services

AWS X-Ray seamlessly integrates with various AWS services such as API Gateway, Lambda, EC2, ECS, and others. It allows developers to trace requests through these services to monitor performance and identify issues. For instance, when a Lambda function is invoked by an API Gateway endpoint, X-Ray traces the request flow, captures latency, and provides insights into execution time, errors, and bottlenecks. This enables end-to-end visibility into serverless and distributed applications, simplifying debugging and performance optimization across AWS resources.

19.5 AWS Config: Configuration Tracking and Compliance

19.5.1 Overview of AWS Config

AWS Config is a service designed to track configuration changes across AWS resources. It provides a detailed inventory of resource configurations and changes over time, helping organizations maintain governance and compliance. Use cases include auditing resource compliance with predefined rules, troubleshooting operational issues caused by misconfigurations, and enabling resource tracking for security and policy enforcement. AWS Config ensures visibility and accountability, making it a key tool for effective configuration management.

19.5.2 AWS Config Rules

AWS Config Rules allow you to define compliance rules to evaluate AWS resources for specific configurations. These rules help ensure that resources meet your organization's standards. For example, you can create a rule to check if S3 buckets have encryption enabled. If a resource becomes non-compliant, AWS Config flags it, enabling proactive monitoring and ensuring compliance with governance policies. Config Rules simplify resource auditing and operational control.

19.5.3 AWS Config Snapshots and History

AWS Config Snapshots and History allow you to capture and analyze resource configurations over time. Snapshots provide a point-in-time view of all your AWS resources, while the history tracks changes to their configurations. This enables you to identify configuration drift, troubleshoot issues, and ensure compliance by analyzing past and present configurations. These features are particularly useful for audit trails and operational troubleshooting.

19.6 Best Practices for Monitoring and Logging

Setting Up Centralized Logging: Combine CloudTrail, CloudWatch Logs, and Amazon OpenSearch to create a unified view of logs, improving operational visibility and troubleshooting.

Using CloudWatch Metrics for Cost Optimization: Monitor resource utilization with CloudWatch Metrics to optimize scaling and reduce costs.

Automating Monitoring with CloudWatch Alarms and EventBridge: Use CloudWatch Alarms to trigger automated actions through EventBridge when thresholds are breached, improving system reliability.

Monitoring and Securing API Activity: Integrate CloudTrail for continuous API activity logging to support compliance audits and identify security risks.

This approach ensures proactive monitoring, cost efficiency, and secure logging in AWS environments.

19.7 Example Scenarios

Monitoring a Web Application Using CloudWatch and X-Ray: Integrate CloudWatch to monitor metrics and set alarms while using X-Ray for distributed tracing to identify performance bottlenecks and optimize a web application.

Auditing API Activity with CloudTrail: Use CloudTrail to set up trails that log API activity, enabling detection of changes and suspicious actions for security auditing and compliance purposes.

Centralized Log Analysis Using CloudWatch and OpenSearch: Stream logs from CloudWatch Logs to Amazon OpenSearch for advanced analytics and troubleshooting, providing unified visibility for faster issue resolution.

19.8 Related YouTube Videos

- AWS CloudWatch Logs Tutorial: https://youtu.be/04GjxhXNwN4
- AWS CloudWatch Metrics Tutorial: https://youtu.be/rJoUonq7sdg
- AWS CloudTrail Tutorial: https://youtu.be/64YqQcNrnrU
- AWS CloudTrail Event History: https://youtu.be/IShAYSyDHrI

19.9 Chapter Review Questions

Question 1:

Which AWS service provides metrics and logs for monitoring AWS resources?

    A. AWS CloudTrail

    B. AWS Config

    C. Amazon CloudWatch

    D. AWS X-Ray

Question 2:

What is the primary purpose of CloudWatch Alarms?

    A. Capturing API call history

    B. Triggering notifications or automated actions based on thresholds

    C. Tracing application requests across services

    D. Configuring compliance rules for resource changes

Question 3:

Which CloudWatch feature allows you to visualize metrics and monitor system performance?

    A. CloudWatch Alarms

    B. CloudWatch Events

    C. CloudWatch Dashboards

    D. CloudTrail Insights

Question 4:

What is a key use case for AWS CloudTrail?

    A. Analyzing Lambda execution logs for debugging

    B. Auditing and tracking API activity across AWS accounts

    C. Managing application configurations using rules

    D. Visualizing latency for microservices

Question 5:

Which of the following is a Data Event in CloudTrail?

    A. Creating an S3 bucket

    B. Accessing objects in an S3 bucket

    C. Enabling EC2 instances

    D. Configuring IAM policies

Question 6:

What does AWS X-Ray primarily help with?

    A. Monitoring resource utilization in real time

    B. Tracing requests and analyzing performance in applications

    C. Storing logs for compliance

    D. Automating resource provisioning

Question 7:

In AWS X-Ray, what component represents a unit of work in a request?

    A. Trace map

    B. Subsegment

    C. Daemon

D. Log group

Question 8:
Which AWS service tracks configuration changes and ensures resource compliance?
 A. AWS CloudTrail
 B. AWS Config
 C. AWS X-Ray
 D. Amazon CloudWatch

Question 9:
What does CloudWatch Events (Amazon EventBridge) enable you to do?
 A. Automate responses to changes in AWS resources
 B. Visualize application performance issues
 C. Capture resource configuration history
 D. Audit API activity in AWS accounts

Question 10:
Which AWS service would you use to detect unusual operational activity in API calls?
 A. AWS Config Rules
 B. CloudTrail Insights
 C. Amazon CloudWatch Metrics
 D. AWS X-Ray

19.10 Answers to Chapter Review Questions

1. C. Amazon CloudWatch
Explanation: Amazon CloudWatch provides metrics and logs to monitor AWS resources and applications, helping with performance monitoring and system health.

2. B. Triggering notifications or automated actions based on thresholds
Explanation: CloudWatch Alarms notify users or trigger automated actions when specified thresholds for monitored metrics are breached.

3. C. CloudWatch Dashboards
Explanation: CloudWatch Dashboards allow you to visualize system metrics and monitor performance by creating customizable dashboards.

4. B. Auditing and tracking API activity across AWS accounts
Explanation: AWS CloudTrail records API calls, providing logs for auditing, tracking changes, and detecting security issues.

5. B. Accessing objects in an S3 bucket
Explanation: Data Events in CloudTrail include operations like accessing objects in S3 or DynamoDB table changes, capturing activity on data resources.

6. B. Tracing requests and analyzing performance in applications
Explanation: AWS X-Ray traces requests through distributed applications, helping identify performance bottlenecks and errors.

7. B. Subsegment

Explanation: In AWS X-Ray, a subsegment represents a unit of work in a request, providing granular insights into specific operations within the request.

8. B. AWS Config

Explanation: AWS Config tracks configuration changes in AWS resources, ensuring compliance and enabling operational troubleshooting.

9. A. Automate responses to changes in AWS resources

Explanation: CloudWatch Events (Amazon EventBridge) enables automation by triggering actions like Lambda functions in response to resource changes.

10. B. CloudTrail Insights

Explanation: CloudTrail Insights helps detect unusual operational activity in API calls, such as unexpected spikes in request volume.

Chapter 20. AWS Security

Security is the cornerstone of any cloud deployment, and AWS provides a comprehensive suite of tools and frameworks to ensure your applications and data are well-protected. This chapter, AWS Security, focuses on implementing robust security strategies, maintaining compliance, and automating security practices across AWS environments.

The chapter begins with an introduction to AWS security, where you'll explore the Shared Responsibility Model, highlighting the division of security responsibilities between AWS and customers. The benefits of AWS security services are also discussed, showcasing AWS's ability to safeguard infrastructure, data, and applications.

In securing data in AWS, you'll learn about critical services like AWS Secrets Manager and Parameter Store, which help manage sensitive information. A hands-on lab exercise demonstrates how to enable and verify encryption for Amazon S3 buckets, a key practice for protecting stored data.

The chapter then dives into protecting AWS resources with monitoring and logging, introducing AWS security monitoring tools and methods for detecting threats in your cloud environment.

Next, AWS application security explores protective measures like the Web Application Firewall (WAF), AWS Shield, and securing APIs against threats and vulnerabilities.

The section on compliance and governance covers AWS compliance programs such as HIPAA, PCI-DSS, and GDPR, as well as tools for managing security standards and governance.

The chapter also highlights automating security in AWS, showcasing how automation can streamline security processes and enable automated security assessments to maintain continuous protection.

Finally, advanced topics like Zero Trust Architecture, hybrid and multi-cloud security, and cross-account access management are explored to help organizations address complex security scenarios.

The chapter concludes with best practices and a security checklist, providing actionable recommendations and a structured approach to securing AWS workloads. By the end of this chapter, you will be equipped with the knowledge and tools to implement effective security measures, maintain compliance, and continually improve the security posture of your AWS environment.

20.1 Introduction to AWS Security

AWS security is a foundational component of cloud computing, ensuring that data, applications, and infrastructure remain protected. In the cloud, security is critical because organizations rely on shared responsibility with AWS. AWS secures the infrastructure, while customers are responsible for securing their applications, data, and configurations. Cloud security protects against data breaches, cyberattacks, and unauthorized access, ensuring compliance with regulations and maintaining customer trust.

20.1.1 Shared Responsibility Model

The Shared Responsibility Model defines the security roles of AWS and its customers. AWS is responsible for "**security of the cloud**", ensuring the infrastructure, including hardware, software, networking, and facilities that run AWS services, is secure. Customers are responsible for "**security in the cloud**", which includes configuring security settings, managing data, and protecting applications, operating systems, and networks. This model ensures clear accountability and collaboration for maintaining a secure cloud environment.

20.1.2 Benefits of AWS security services

AWS security services provide **enhanced protection, compliance, and control** for cloud workloads. Key benefits include scalability, allowing security measures to grow with resources, **automation** for threat detection and response (e.g., GuardDuty, Inspector), and robust data **encryption** for protection in transit and at rest. AWS also ensures compliance with industry standards (like GDPR, HIPAA) and offers tools for continuous **monitoring and logging** (e.g., CloudTrail and Security Hub). These services empower businesses to build secure, resilient applications efficiently.

20.2 Securing Data in AWS

Securing data in AWS involves encryption at rest and encryption in transit to protect sensitive information.

Encryption at Rest
- AWS Key Management Service (KMS) helps manage keys securely for encryption.
- SSE-S3: Server-Side Encryption for Amazon S3 using AWS-managed keys.
- SSE-EBS: Encryption for Elastic Block Store volumes.

Encryption in Transit
Uses protocols like SSL/TLS to secure data moving between services.

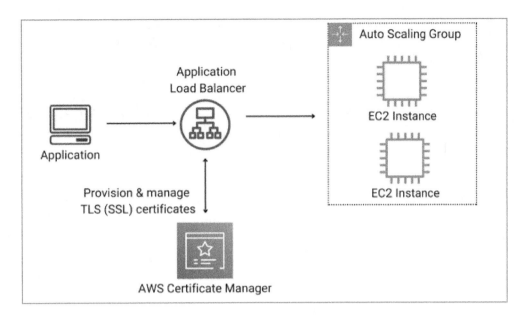

AWS Certificate Manager (ACM) simplifies the provisioning and management of SSL/TLS certificates.

These encryption methods ensure data remains confidential and secure across AWS environments.

20.2.1 AWS Secrets Manager and Parameter Store

AWS Secrets Manager and Systems Manager Parameter Store are tools designed to manage application secrets and configuration data securely.

AWS Secrets Manager: Securely stores, rotates, and retrieves secrets like database credentials, API keys, and OAuth tokens. Supports automatic secret rotation with integrated services like RDS. Simplifies secret management by securely storing encrypted values.

AWS Systems Manager Parameter Store: Manages configuration data and secrets in plain text or encrypted form. Organizes values using hierarchies and integrates with AWS services for easier access. Provides basic storage, ideal for parameters or secrets without advanced rotation needs.

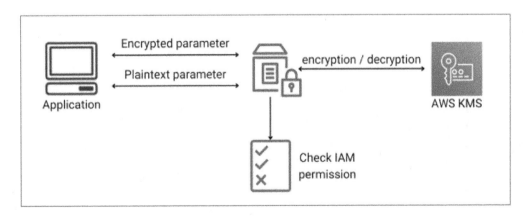

This diagram illustrates the AWS Systems Manager Parameter Store workflow with AWS KMS (Key Management Service) for securely managing and encrypting application parameters. Here's how the flow works:

The application sends a request to retrieve or store a parameter. The parameter can be either a plaintext value or an encrypted value. AWS Systems Manager Parameter Store acts as a centralized store to manage configuration data and secrets. It securely stores parameters and integrates with AWS KMS for encryption and decryption.

If the parameter is encrypted, AWS KMS performs the encryption or decryption process. When the application requests the encrypted parameter, Parameter Store retrieves it and uses KMS to decrypt the value securely before returning the plaintext parameter to the application.

AWS Identity and Access Management (IAM) verifies if the application (or the user/role) has the necessary permissions to access the parameter and perform encryption or decryption operations. If permissions are not granted, access is denied.

Encrypted parameters ensure that sensitive data like API keys, credentials, or secrets remain protected. Plaintext parameters are non-sensitive data that do not require encryption.

In summary, the AWS Systems Manager Parameter Store allows you to securely manage and retrieve configuration values and secrets. By integrating with AWS KMS, it provides encryption for sensitive parameters and ensures that only authorized entities can access or decrypt the data. IAM permissions play a crucial role in maintaining security and access control.

Both tools help improve security by removing hardcoded credentials and managing sensitive information efficiently.

20.2.2 Lab Exercise: Enabling and Verifying Encryption for S3 Buckets

This lab exercise demonstrates how to enable and verify encryption for Amazon S3 buckets using SSE-S3 (Server-Side Encryption with Amazon S3-Managed Keys) and verify that encryption is applied correctly.

Step 1: Log in to AWS Management Console

Go to the AWS Management Console. Navigate to the S3 service under "Storage" from the AWS Console dashboard.

Step 2: Create or Select an S3 Bucket

In the S3 Console, click on Create bucket or select an existing bucket where you want to enable encryption. Provide a unique Bucket name (if creating a new bucket). Select the AWS Region where the bucket will reside.

Scroll to the Default encryption section under bucket settings.

Step 3: Enable Default Encryption

In the Default encryption section: Select Enable. Choose SSE-S3 (Server-Side Encryption with S3-Managed Keys) as the encryption method.

Click on Save changes or Create bucket if it's a new bucket.

Step 4: Upload a Test Object

Open your newly created or existing S3 bucket. Click on the Upload button. Choose a file to upload as a test object. Verify that the encryption settings remain applied: Expand the "Properties" section of the uploaded file to confirm Server-Side Encryption is enabled and set to SSE-S3.

Step 5: Verify Encryption

Select the object you uploaded. Go to the Properties tab of the object. Under the Server-side encryption section, confirm the following:
Encryption key: AES-256 (this indicates SSE-S3 encryption is applied).

If no encryption is visible, revisit bucket settings and ensure encryption is enabled.

Step 6: Test with AWS CLI (Optional Verification)

To verify encryption using AWS CLI: Run the following command to retrieve the metadata of the uploaded object:

```
aws s3api head-object --bucket <BucketName> --key <ObjectKey>
```

Replace <BucketName> with your bucket name and <ObjectKey> with the file name.

Check the output: Confirm the presence of "ServerSideEncryption": "AES256", which indicates SSE-S3 encryption.

Step 7: Clean Up Resources

Delete the uploaded test object to avoid unnecessary storage charges. Optionally, delete the S3 bucket if no longer needed.

You have successfully enabled SSE-S3 encryption for an S3 bucket and verified encryption through both the AWS Console and AWS CLI. This ensures all objects stored in the bucket are automatically encrypted at rest using Amazon S3-Managed Keys.

20.3 Protecting AWS Resources with Monitoring and Logging

20.3.1 AWS Security Monitoring Tools

This section discusses key AWS services for monitoring and maintaining security in the cloud:

AWS CloudTrail: Logs all API activity in an AWS account, enabling auditing, security analysis, and troubleshooting. It helps track changes and detect suspicious actions.

Amazon CloudWatch: Monitors AWS resources and applications by collecting metrics, logs, and events. It allows real-time monitoring and alerts to detect performance or security issues.

AWS Config: Provides resource compliance checks by tracking configuration changes and assessing AWS resources against predefined rules. This helps maintain governance and security standards.

These tools collectively provide visibility, monitoring, and compliance tracking to ensure a secure AWS environment.

20.3.2 Detecting Threats

Amazon GuardDuty: GuardDuty is a managed threat detection service that continuously monitors AWS accounts, workloads, and data for malicious or unauthorized activity. It uses machine learning, anomaly detection, and integrated threat intelligence to identify potential security threats such as compromised instances or unusual API calls.

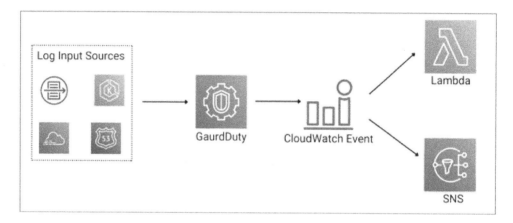

This Amazon GuardDuty diagram illustrates the workflow for detecting and responding to security threats in AWS. GuardDuty ingests data from various log input sources, including VPC Flow Logs, AWS CloudTrail, and DNS logs, to monitor network activity and detect anomalies or unauthorized actions. When a threat is identified, GuardDuty generates findings, which are sent to Amazon CloudWatch Events. CloudWatch Events acts as an event bus to trigger automated actions.

For example, AWS Lambda functions can be invoked to take corrective measures, such as isolating compromised instances or revoking permissions. Additionally, Amazon SNS sends notifications to security teams for immediate action. This integration of GuardDuty, CloudWatch Events, Lambda, and SNS ensures efficient threat detection, automation, and timely alerting to enhance security across AWS environments.

AWS Security Hub: Security Hub provides a unified view of security alerts and compliance status across AWS accounts and services. It consolidates findings from multiple AWS services like GuardDuty, CloudTrail, and Config, as well as third-party tools, allowing centralized monitoring and management of security posture.

20.4 AWS Application Security
20.4.1 Web Application Firewall (WAF)

AWS WAF is a web application firewall that helps protect web applications or APIs from common attack patterns such as SQL injection, cross-site scripting (XSS), and other vulnerabilities. It enables you to monitor, filter, and control HTTP and HTTPS traffic to applications. AWS WAF allows you to create rules to block or allow specific request patterns based on predefined conditions, helping safeguard against security threats and ensuring application availability.

20.4.2 AWS Shield

AWS Shield provides protection against Distributed Denial of Service (DDoS) attacks to ensure application availability and security. It offers two levels of protection:

AWS Shield Standard: Automatically enabled at no cost for all AWS customers. It defends against common and low-level DDoS attacks on AWS services like Amazon EC2, CloudFront, and Route 53.

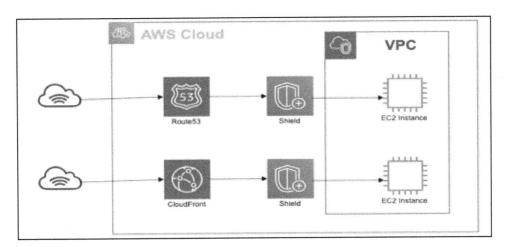

This AWS Shield diagram shows how AWS Shield protects resources from DDoS attacks. Incoming traffic flows through Route 53 or CloudFront, where AWS Shield mitigates malicious traffic before it reaches EC2 instances in a VPC. Route 53 handles DNS requests, while CloudFront provides content delivery, both safeguarded by AWS Shield. This ensures high availability and protection against DDoS threats for critical AWS resources.

AWS Shield Advanced: Offers enhanced protection for complex and large-scale DDoS attacks. It includes advanced monitoring, near real-time mitigation, cost protection for scaling, and detailed reporting. It integrates seamlessly with AWS WAF for better application layer protection.

AWS Shield helps maintain service availability, ensuring uninterrupted performance during DDoS attempts.

20.4.3 Security for APIs

API Gateway Security focuses on securing APIs and managing access to ensure reliable and authorized communication between clients and services. It includes:

Authentication with AWS Cognito:
- AWS Cognito is used to provide user authentication and authorization for APIs.
- It manages user pools for identity verification and ensures secure access through tokens.

Integration with API Gateway:
- API Gateway integrates with AWS Cognito to validate tokens and enforce access control.
- It enables fine-grained permissions, protecting endpoints from unauthorized access.

By using AWS Cognito and API Gateway, you can ensure secure, authenticated access to APIs while maintaining scalability and flexibility.

20.5 Compliance and Governance in AWS

20.5.1 AWS Compliance Programs (HIPAA, PCI-DSS, GDPR, etc.)

AWS provides a wide range of compliance programs to help customers meet regulatory and industry-specific security requirements. Key programs include:

HIPAA: Ensures secure handling of Protected Health Information (PHI) for healthcare applications. AWS supports HIPAA-eligible services to maintain data privacy.
PCI-DSS: Enables secure handling of payment card data for organizations processing, storing, or transmitting credit card information.
GDPR: AWS helps customers comply with the General Data Protection Regulation by offering tools for data protection, encryption, and privacy controls.

By aligning with these compliance frameworks, AWS allows organizations to build secure and compliant solutions across industries like healthcare, finance, and e-commerce.

20.5.2 Managing Security Standards

AWS Well-Architected Framework Security Pillar: This pillar outlines best practices to ensure data protection, access management, and threat detection in AWS environments. It provides guidance on implementing strong identity controls, enabling traceability, and automating security measures.

AWS Artifact for Compliance Reports: AWS Artifact is a central resource for accessing AWS compliance reports and certifications. It allows organizations to download audit-ready reports for programs like HIPAA, PCI-DSS, and GDPR, helping them meet security and regulatory requirements.

Together, these tools help maintain security standards and achieve compliance efficiently.

20.5.3 Governance Tools

AWS Organizations: Centralized Account Management
AWS Organizations enables centralized management of multiple AWS accounts, streamlining governance and billing. It allows for consolidated control and ensures consistent policies across accounts.

Service Control Policies (SCPs)

SCPs are a key feature of AWS Organizations, providing fine-grained control over permissions. They allow administrators to define policies that limit or restrict AWS service usage for specific accounts or organizational units (OUs), ensuring compliance and governance standards are met.

These tools help organizations efficiently manage their AWS environment while maintaining strong governance and security practices.

20.6 Automating Security in AWS
20.6.1 Security Automation with AWS
Automating Incident Response with AWS Lambda: AWS Lambda enables automated incident response by triggering actions based on predefined events. For example, when a security issue is detected (e.g., unauthorized access), Lambda can automatically remediate it by isolating affected resources, notifying administrators, or applying security patches.

Infrastructure as Code (IaC) and Security (CloudFormation, Terraform): Using IaC tools like AWS CloudFormation or Terraform allows for the consistent, repeatable deployment of secure infrastructure. Security best practices can be embedded in templates, ensuring resources meet compliance standards and reducing human error.

By leveraging automation, organizations can streamline security processes, respond to incidents quickly, and ensure robust infrastructure management.

20.6.2 Automated Security Assessments
Automating Incident Response with AWS Lambda: AWS Lambda enables automated incident response by triggering actions based on predefined events. For example, when a security issue is detected (e.g., unauthorized access), Lambda can automatically remediate it by isolating affected resources, notifying administrators, or applying security patches.

Infrastructure as Code (IaC) and Security (CloudFormation, Terraform): Using IaC tools like AWS CloudFormation or Terraform allows for the consistent, repeatable deployment of secure infrastructure. Security best practices can be embedded in templates, ensuring resources meet compliance standards and reducing human error.

By leveraging automation, organizations can streamline security processes, respond to incidents quickly, and ensure robust infrastructure management.

20.7 Advanced Security Concepts
20.7.1 Zero Trust Architecture in AWS
Zero Trust Architecture in AWS is a security model based on the principle of "never trust, always verify". It assumes that no entity, whether inside or outside the network, can be trusted by default.

Key Concepts:
- Identity and Access Management (IAM): Enforce least-privilege access for users and applications.
- Continuous Authentication: Validate identity and permissions for every access request.
- Micro-segmentation: Isolate workloads using security groups and network ACLs.

AWS Tools:
- AWS IAM for managing granular access.
- Amazon VPC and Security Groups for segmentation.
- AWS Network Firewall for inspecting and filtering network traffic.

Zero Trust in AWS improves security by limiting access, verifying identities, and reducing the attack surface, ensuring that all requests are continuously authenticated and authorized.

20.7.2 Hybrid and Multi-Cloud Security

Hybrid and Multi-Cloud Security focuses on securely integrating AWS with on-premises and other cloud environments:

- AWS Direct Connect: Provides private, dedicated network connections between on-premises data centers and AWS, reducing latency and improving security.
- VPNs: AWS VPN allows secure, encrypted connections over public internet to link on-premises networks with AWS Virtual Private Cloud (VPC).

By leveraging these tools, organizations ensure seamless, secure connectivity across hybrid and multi-cloud environments, maintaining consistent network performance and robust security.

20.7.3 Managing Cross-Account Access

AWS provides efficient tools to manage cross-account access, ensuring secure resource sharing and access control between accounts.

Resource Sharing with AWS Resource Access Manager (RAM): AWS RAM allows you to securely share AWS resources, like VPC subnets, Transit Gateways, or license configurations, across multiple accounts without needing to duplicate resources. This simplifies resource management in a multi-account environment.

Cross-Account Roles and Permissions: AWS Identity and Access Management (IAM) enables cross-account access by defining roles with specific policies. Trusted accounts can assume these roles using temporary credentials. This approach is ideal for granting secure, granular access to resources in other AWS accounts without sharing long-term credentials.

Together, AWS RAM and cross-account IAM roles help streamline collaboration while maintaining robust security.

20.8 Best Practices and Security Checklist
20.8.1 General AWS Security Best Practices

Implementing general AWS security best practices helps ensure a secure cloud environment.

Regular Audits and Penetration Testing: Regularly perform security audits and penetration tests to identify vulnerabilities in your AWS resources. Services like AWS Inspector can help automate vulnerability scans, while manual penetration testing can uncover gaps not detected by automated tools.

Patching EC2 Instances: Keeping Amazon EC2 instances up to date with the latest patches is critical for maintaining security. Use AWS Systems Manager Patch Manager to automate the process of applying security updates and patches, ensuring compliance with security standards.

By combining regular audits and patch management, organizations can reduce security risks and strengthen their cloud posture.

20.8.2 Checklist for Securing AWS Workloads

To secure AWS workloads, follow these essential practices:

IAM (Identity and Access Management)

- Implement the principle of least privilege by granting only necessary permissions to users and roles.
- Use IAM roles instead of access keys for services and applications.
- Enable Multi-Factor Authentication (MFA) for critical accounts.

VPC (Virtual Private Cloud)
- Design secure network architectures by leveraging private subnets and Network Access Control Lists (NACLs).
- Use Security Groups to restrict inbound and outbound traffic.
- Enable VPC Flow Logs for monitoring network traffic.

Data Encryption
- Encrypt data at rest using AWS KMS and service-specific encryption options (e.g., SSE-S3, EBS encryption).
- Encrypt data in transit with SSL/TLS for secure communication.
- Regularly rotate encryption keys.

Monitoring
- Use Amazon CloudWatch for monitoring logs, metrics, and alarms.
- Enable AWS CloudTrail to log API activity for auditing and compliance.
- Implement Amazon GuardDuty for threat detection and security insights.

This checklist ensures that AWS workloads are secure across identity management, networking, data protection, and monitoring.

20.8.3 Continuous improvement with AWS security services

Continuous improvement in AWS security involves leveraging AWS tools and best practices to strengthen and evolve your security posture over time.

Regular Security Audits and Monitoring: Use AWS CloudTrail and Amazon GuardDuty to continuously log, analyze, and detect suspicious activities. Implement AWS Config for tracking changes in resource configurations and maintaining compliance.

Proactive Threat Management: AWS services like AWS Shield and AWS WAF provide protection against DDoS attacks and common vulnerabilities. Use AWS Security Hub to gain a unified view of your security posture and identify gaps for remediation.

Automation for Security Best Practices: Automate incident response using AWS Lambda and Amazon EventBridge for faster resolution. Continuously scan workloads using AWS Inspector to detect vulnerabilities.

Adopt a Security Feedback Loop: Continuously review and refine security policies, IAM permissions, and encryption strategies based on insights from monitoring tools.

By integrating AWS security services into a continuous improvement strategy, organizations can proactively address security threats, ensure compliance, and maintain resilience against evolving risks.

20.9 Related YouTube Videos
- AWS Security & Compliance: https://youtu.be/9tANRNJTybY
- AWS Organizations Tutorial: https://youtu.be/7am_CWLJTTU

20.10 Chapter Review Questions

Question 1:
What is the primary principle of the Shared Responsibility Model in AWS?
   A. AWS is responsible for securing customer data entirely.
   B. AWS and customers share responsibility for cloud security.
   C. Customers are responsible for all infrastructure security.
   D. AWS ensures compliance for all customer workloads.

Question 2:
Which AWS service is used to store and manage secrets securely?
   A. AWS Key Management Service (KMS)
   B. AWS Secrets Manager
   C. Amazon CloudWatch
   D. AWS Artifact

Question 3:
Which encryption method ensures data protection at rest in Amazon S3?
   A. AWS Shield
   B. AWS WAF
   C. Server-Side Encryption (SSE-S3)
   D. AWS CloudTrail

Question 4:
What does AWS Shield primarily protect against?
   A. SQL injection attacks
   B. Unauthorized API access
   C. Distributed Denial of Service (DDoS) attacks
   D. Resource misconfigurations

Question 5:
Which AWS tool provides compliance reports to meet regulatory requirements such as HIPAA and GDPR?

    A. AWS Inspector
    B. AWS Artifact
    C. AWS Security Hub
    D. AWS Config

Question 6:
What is the main purpose of AWS Web Application Firewall (WAF)?

    A. Protect against DDoS attacks
    B. Monitor EC2 instance performance
    C. Block common attack patterns like SQL injection
    D. Encrypt data stored in S3 buckets

Question 7:
How does AWS Security Hub enhance security management?

    A. By automating incident response actions
    B. By consolidating findings from multiple security tools
    C. By scanning for infrastructure vulnerabilities
    D. By enforcing Service Control Policies

Question 8:
Which AWS service helps automate vulnerability scanning for EC2 instances?

    A. AWS Inspector
    B. AWS Secrets Manager
    C. AWS Shield
    D. AWS WAF

Question 9:
What concept focuses on verifying every user and device at each access point to ensure security?

    A. Zero Trust Architecture
    B. Shared Responsibility Model
    C. Infrastructure as Code (IaC)
    D. Security for APIs

Question 10:
What AWS feature allows centralized account management and enforcement of security policies?

    A. AWS IAM
    B. AWS RAM
    C. AWS Organizations
    D. AWS CloudTrail

20.11 Answers to Chapter Review Questions

1. B. AWS and customers share responsibility for cloud security
Explanation: The AWS Shared Responsibility Model defines that AWS is responsible for the security of the cloud (infrastructure), while customers are responsible for the security in the cloud (data, configurations, etc.).

2. B. AWS Secrets Manager

Explanation: AWS Secrets Manager is designed to securely store, manage, and retrieve secrets like API keys, database credentials, and other sensitive information.

3. C. Server-Side Encryption (SSE-S3)

Explanation: SSE-S3 ensures encryption of data at rest in Amazon S3, where AWS manages the encryption keys.

4. C. Distributed Denial of Service (DDoS) attacks

Explanation: AWS Shield provides protection against DDoS attacks, helping to maintain application availability and performance.

5. B. AWS Artifact

Explanation: AWS Artifact provides on-demand access to compliance reports and certifications, such as HIPAA, PCI-DSS, and GDPR.

6. C. Block common attack patterns like SQL injection

Explanation: AWS WAF protects applications by filtering and blocking common attack patterns, including SQL injection and cross-site scripting (XSS).

7. B. By consolidating findings from multiple security tools

Explanation: AWS Security Hub provides a unified view of security findings across AWS services, simplifying security management and compliance.

8. A. AWS Inspector

Explanation: AWS Inspector automates vulnerability assessments to identify security issues in EC2 instances and improve compliance.

9. A. Zero Trust Architecture

Explanation: Zero Trust Architecture focuses on verifying every user and device at each access point, ensuring no implicit trust in the network.

10. C. AWS Organizations

Explanation: AWS Organizations enables centralized management of multiple AWS accounts and allows enforcement of Service Control Policies (SCPs) for governance.

Chapter 21. AWS AI/ML Services

Artificial Intelligence (AI) and Machine Learning (ML) have revolutionized the way businesses operate, enabling smarter decision-making, automation, and improved user experiences. AWS AI/ML Services provides a robust suite of tools that allow organizations of all sizes to harness the power of AI and ML without deep expertise in the field.

This chapter explores the broad spectrum of AI/ML services offered by AWS. You'll dive into key services, including Amazon Rekognition, which enables image and video analysis, and Amazon Transcribe, which converts speech into text for various applications.

The chapter also covers services like Amazon Polly for text-to-speech conversion, Amazon Translate for language translation, and Amazon Lex for building conversational chatbots and voice interfaces. For customer engagement, Amazon Connect integrates seamlessly for intelligent contact centers.

You'll also learn about advanced services like Amazon Comprehend for natural language processing, Amazon SageMaker for building, training, and deploying ML models, and Amazon Forecast for time-series forecasting.

Additionally, tools like Amazon Kendra for intelligent search, Amazon Personalize for recommendation systems, and Amazon Textract for extracting text and data from documents are discussed in detail. Services like Amazon Fraud Detector and Amazon Sumerian for AR/VR applications highlight the diverse capabilities AWS provides.

The chapter concludes with an AWS ML Summary, offering a concise overview of how these services integrate to solve real-world challenges. By the end of this chapter, you'll understand how to leverage AWS AI/ML services to create powerful, scalable, and intelligent applications across various domains.

21.1 AWS AI/ML Services
The AWS AI/ML Services seamlessly integrate intelligence into applications. Amazon offers a wide range of AI and ML services -- some of the most prominent ones are listed below:
- Amazon Rekognition
- Amazon Transcribe

- Amazon Polly
- Amazon Translate
- Amazon Lex
- Amazon Comprehend
- Amazon Comprehend Medical
- Amazon SageMaker
- Amazon Forecast
- Amazon Kendra
- Amazon Personalize
- Amazon Fraud Detecto
- Amazon Textract
- Amazon Fraud Detector
- Amazon Sumerian

21.2 Amazon Rekognition

Amazon Rekognition is a fully managed computer vision service that simplifies image and video analysis using highly scalable deep learning technology. It extracts insights such as facial attributes, object and scene detection, text recognition, and inappropriate content moderation. With features like face comparison, celebrity recognition, and activity detection, Rekognition enables applications to automate content tagging, enhance user verification, and ensure content compliance.

It integrates seamlessly with services like S3, Lambda, and DynamoDB to enable serverless, event-driven workflows for storing and querying results efficiently. Rekognition can process both stored videos and streaming content using Kinesis Video Streams, supporting real-time tracking and analysis. Its use cases span media moderation, retail sentiment analysis, inventory classification, and user verification, allowing organizations to add AI-powered visual analysis to applications quickly and cost-effectively.

Image Analysis

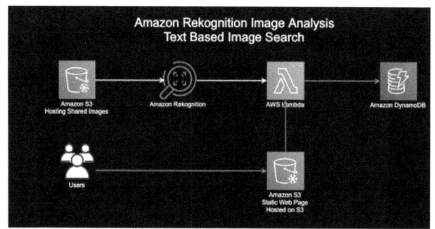

Amazon Rekognition offers a wide array of powerful features for image and video analysis. It includes **object and scene detection**, which identifies keywords like objects (e.g., vehicles) and environments (e.g., sunset). With **facial analysis**, Rekognition extracts details such as facial landmarks, emotions, and demographic information. The face recognition feature allows matching faces against pre-indexed images, returning similarity scores. It also includes **celebrity recognition**, identifying prominent figures and linking to relevant information. **Unsafe image detection** helps moderate user-generated content by flagging explicit or suggestive material.

Rekognition can also **extract text from images**, even in complex real-world scenes like license plates or street signs. For implementation, AWS provides a serverless pipeline where images uploaded to S3 trigger Lambda functions that call Rekognition APIs, process results, and store them in DynamoDB. Non-storage APIs, like DetectLabels, analyze data without storing it, while storage APIs, like IndexFaces, persist data for later use. Amazon Rekognition's scalability and cost-effectiveness make it a go-to solution for applications like content moderation, sentiment analysis, and image search automation.

Video Analysis

Amazon Rekognition extends its capabilities to video analysis, enabling innovative use cases like personal entertainment, security, and customer behavior tracking. Unlike traditional frame-by-frame video analysis, Rekognition preserves temporal context to detect **objects, activities, person tracking, facial analysis, unsafe content, celebrity recognition**, and face matching effectively. For video files stored in S3, Rekognition operates asynchronously: APIs such as **StartFaceDetection** or **StartCelebrityRecognition** analyze videos and publish results to an Amazon SNS topic. A Lambda function fetches results using APIs like **GetFaceDetection** and stores them in DynamoDB for querying through a web app via API Gateway.

Person tracking identifies individuals across video frames, even when faces are obscured, providing positional data and timestamps. Rekognition can search detected faces against pre-indexed collections using the **FaceSearch API**. It also performs **content moderation**, identifying explicit or suggestive content for filtering or compliance purposes. This powerful solution makes video analysis scalable, contextual, and cost-effective for modern applications.

Streaming Analysis

Amazon Rekognition integrates with **Amazon Kinesis Video Streams** to enable real-time video streaming analysis. Kinesis Video Stream securely ingests, stores, and indexes video data from connected devices, scaling automatically to handle millions of streams. Using **Producer SDKs** for Java or C++, developers can easily capture and stream video data to Kinesis.

To perform analysis, Rekognition connects the video stream (source) with a **Kinesis Data Stream** (destination) for processed results. By creating a Rekognition **video stream processor**, ARNs for both the input and output streams are provided. Rekognition then processes the video frames in real time using APIs like **StartPersonTracking** or **StartLabelDetection**. The analyzed results are sent to the destination Kinesis Data Stream, allowing applications to consume and process this data further.

This setup creates a **seamless, scalable, and event-driven workflow** for video streaming analysis, enabling applications to detect objects, track people, and extract actionable insights from streaming video content.

Content Moderation

Using Amazon Recognition, you can detect content that is inappropriate, unwanted or offensive in images and videos. This feature can be used in social media, broadcast media, advertising, and e-commerce to help create a safer user experience.

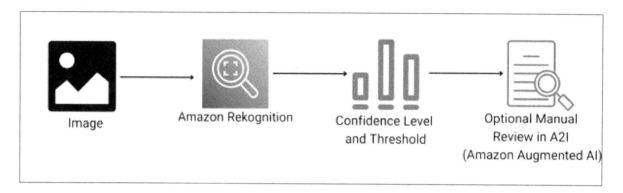

You can set a minimum confidence threshold for items that should be flagged. Flagged content can be manually reviewed in A2I (Amazon Augmented AI).

The content moderation feature also helps comply with regulations.

Use Cases

If your application or app contains user-generated or submitted content, you probably want to know if that content is free, explicit, or suggested. You can set up an automatic moderated pipeline like this.

If you upload your content on Amazon S3, you can trigger the Lambda function whenever new content is added to your storage bucket. In addition, the Lambda function can start Rekognition Detect Moderation Label's API. If it gets any label back, you can set the image to be reviewed by a human for selling to your users.

Another use case. Automatic sentiment analysis for a retail store. You can take a stream video feed from a retail store and have Rekognition perform real-time demographic and sentiment analysis on the faces of the people it sees in the store. You can keep this metadata on S3, periodically load it into RedShift, and plug it into Amazon QuickSight to quickly analyze the content and visualize trends, demographics, and customer sentiment over time.

As you can see, Amazon Rekognition lets you add the power of AI to image and video analysis capability to your application in minutes with only a few lines of code. For example, automatically extract and scene description, recognize and compare faces, detect suggestive and explicit video content, collect demographic details, track people in image and video streams, perform sentiment analysis, etc.

It's easy to get started and cost-effective too.

- Find objects, people, and text in images and videos

- Perform facial analysis and facial search for user verification
- Create a database of "familiar faces" or compare against celebrities
- Use cases: Labeling, Content Moderation, Text Detection, Face Detection and Analysis, Face Search and Verification, Celebrity Recognition

21.3 Amazon Transcribe

Amazon Transcribe service helps you quickly add high-quality speech-to-text capabilities to your applications. For example, you can quickly extract actionable insights from customer conversations.

In another use case, content producers can use this service to convert audio and video assets into fully searchable content automatically. For example, you can create subtitles for your broadcast content to increase accessibility and improve customer experience.

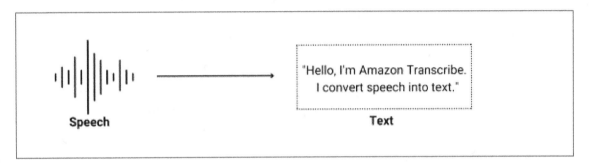

Amazon Transcribe service can be used in the medical field as well. For example, doctors and practitioners can use Amazon Transcribe Medical to quickly document clinical conversations into electronic health record (EHR) systems for analysis.

KEY POINTS

- It uses a deep learning process called Automatic Speech Recognition (ASR) for automating speech-to-text conversion.
- Automatically removes Personally Identifiable Information (PII) using Redaction.
- Use cases: transcribe customer service calls, automate closed caption and subtitle, and generate metadata for media assets to create a fully searchable archive.

21.4 Amazon Polly

Amazon Polly is a Text-to-Speech (TTS) service that turns text into lifelike speech. It uses advanced deep-learning techniques to synthesize natural-sounding human speech, which helps developers build speech-enabled products -- applications that can talk.

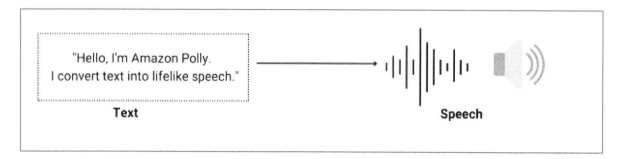

Using machine learning, Amazon Polly offers Neural Text-to-Speech (NTTS) voices, delivering advanced improvements in speech quality. Amazon Polly Brand Voice can also create a custom NTTS voice for your organization's exclusive use.

Lexicon & SSML

It can customize the pronunciation of words with pronunciation lexicons. For example, the acronym. AWS can be converted into speech as "Amazon Web Services." You need to upload lexicons

Additionally, you use generate speech from plain text or documents marked with Speech Synthesis Markup Language (SSML) – which enables more customization. For example, it can emphasize specific words or phrases and include breathing sounds and whispering.

- Turns text into lifelike speech
- Enables developers to build speech-enabled products

21.5 Amazon Translate

Amazon Translate is a natural machine translation that delivers fast, high-quality, affordable, and customizable **language translation**.

Amazon Translate differs from traditional statistical and rule-based translation algorithms. Instead, it uses natural machine translation, which uses deep learning models to provide more accurate and natural-sounding translations.

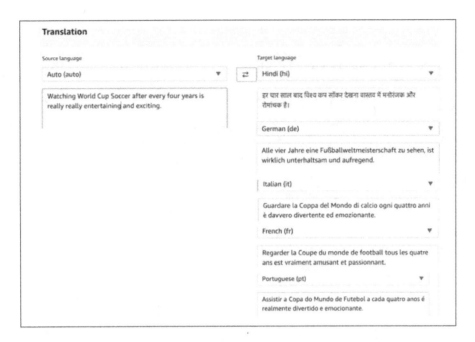

As a result, the Amazon Translate service can help you **localize content** such as websites and applications for your different types of diverse users. In addition, it can quickly translate large volumes of text for analysis and efficiently enable **cross-lingual** communication between users.

21.6 Amazon Lex

Amazon Lex is a service for building conversational interfaces into any application using voice and text. It provides the advanced deep learning functionalities of automatic speech recognition (ASR) for converting speech to text, and natural language understanding (NLU) to recognize the text's intent, enabling you to build applications with highly engaging user experiences and lifelike conversational interactions.

Amazon Lex is a service for building conversational interfaces using voice and text. Powered by the same conversational engine as Alexa, Amazon Lex provides high-quality speech recognition and language understanding capabilities, enabling the addition of sophisticated, natural language 'chatbots' to new and existing applications.

21.7 Amazon Connect

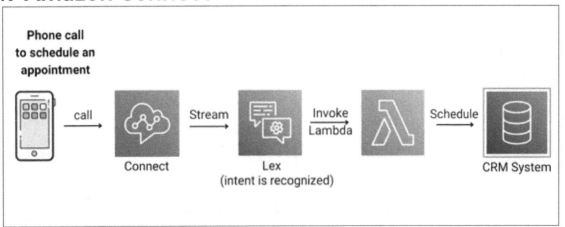

It's a cloud-based virtual contact center -- it can create contact flows. Amazon Connect can be integrated with other CRM systems or AWS. It's for free, 12 months, as part of the AWS Free Tier program. Users can get access to 90 minutes per month with the Free Tier.

21.8 Amazon Comprehend

Amazon Comprehend is a Natural-Language Processing (NLP) service used to uncover valuable insights and relationships in unstructured text. For instance, it can mine business and call center analytics to detect customer sentiment and analyze interactions to categorize inbound support requests automatically. The service also allows indexing and searching product reviews by focusing on context and sentiment rather than just keywords.

Additionally, Amazon Comprehend helps secure documents by identifying and redacting Personally Identifiable Information (PII). Expanding its capabilities, **Amazon Comprehend Medical** is designed specifically for detecting and extracting useful information in unstructured clinical text, such as physician's notes, discharge summaries, test results, and case notes. Using NLP, it can detect Protected Health Information (PHI) through the **DetectPHI API**, ensuring compliance and data protection.

21.9 Amazon SageMaker

It is a fully managed service for ML/AI engineers/data scientists to build ML models. It helps solve some pain points of building ML models by putting all the processes in one place, such as provisioning servers, preparing, building, training, tuning, and deploying high-quality machine learning models. In other words, Amazon SageMaker puts all ML processes in one place. This helps provide a faster turnaround time to build ML pipelines.

Amazon SageMaker JumpStart provides a collection of solutions for the most common use cases that can be deployed readily with just a few clicks.

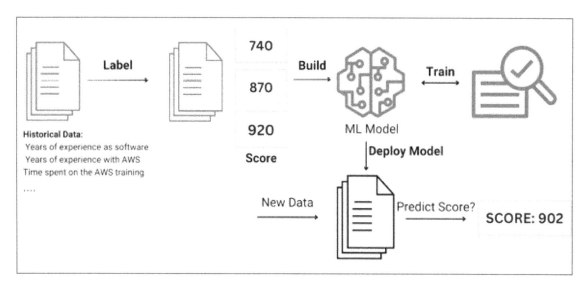

For example, as you can see in the diagram, how Amazon SageMaker ML Model predicts the exam's score by learning (train) from historical data.

21.10 Amazon Forecast

Amazon Forecast uses statistical and machine learning algorithms to deliver highly accurate time-series forecasts – without any machine learning experience. It is a fully managed service. Amazon Forecast provides automation by finding the optimal combination of machine learning algorithms for your datasets. In addition, it offers several filling methods to automatically handle missing values in your datasets.

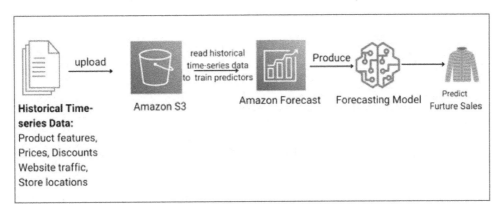

You can use this service for use cases such as retail demand planning to predict product demand, allowing you to vary inventory and pricing more accurately at different store locations. It can also be used in supply chain planning to forecast the quantity of raw goods, services, or other inputs required by manufacturing.

Another use case is a resource planning to predict staffing, advertising, energy consumption, and server capacity requirements. And finally, Amazon Forecast can be used in operational planning to predict levels of web traffic, AWS usage, and IoT sensor usage.

You can use the APIs, AWS Command Line Interface (AWS CLI), Python Software Development Kit (SDK), and Amazon Forecast Console to import time-series datasets, train predictors, and generate forecasts.

21.11 Amazon Kendra

Amazon Kendra is fully managed intelligent search service that adds natural language search capabilities. Amazon Kendra reimagines enterprise search for websites and applications so that employees and customers can easily find the right answers to questions when that they need them.

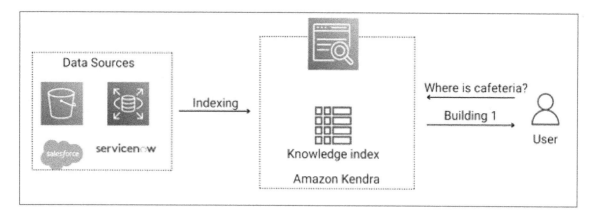

How Kendra does it -- Kendra does it by searching through troves of unstructured data to provide the right answer.

21.12 Amazon Personalize

Amazon Personalize is a fully managed ML service to build real-time personalized recommendations. For example, you can use this service for product recommendations, personalized product re-ranking, and customized direct marketing.

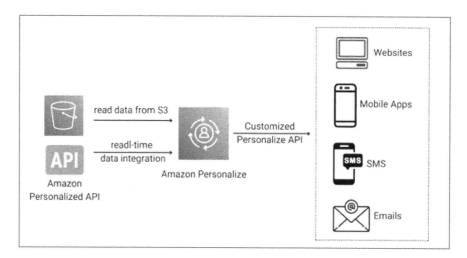

Amazon Personalize provisions the infrastructure and manages the entire ML pipeline, including pre-processing, features extraction, applying the best algorithm. It also trains, optimize, and deploy the model. You just need to call API endpoints for the deployed model. All data is encrypted, private, and secure, and is only used to create recommendations for your users.

The same technology is used by Amazon.com. It can be integrated into existing websites, applications, SMS, email marketing systems. It can be implemented in days, not months -- you don't need to build, train, and deploy ML solutions.

Amazon Personalize supports the following key use cases:
- Personalized recommendations
- Similar items
- Personalized reranking i.e. rerank a list of items for a user
- Personalized promotions/notifications

Cloud Computing and AWS Introduction   347

- To recommend personalized products for users based on their previous purchases

21.13 Amazon Textract

Amazon Textract service enables you to add document text detection and analysis to your applications easily. Using Amazon Textract, customers can automatically extract text and data from millions of scanned documents in just hours. It can read and process any type of document such as PDFs, images.

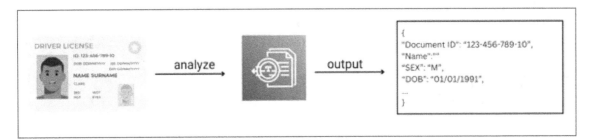

Amazon Textract has many use cases.
- Using the Amazon Textract Document Analysis API, you can extract text, forms, and tables from structured data documents.
- By using AnalyzeExpense API you can process invoices and receipts.
- By using the AnalyzeID API, you can process ID documents such as driver's licenses and passports issued by the U.S. government.

21.14 Amazon Fraud Detector

Amazon Fraud Detector is a fully managed service enabling customers to identify potentially fraudulent activities. For example, you can flag suspicious online payment transactions before processing payments and fulfilling orders. In another example, you can detect new account fraud. You can accurately distinguish between legitimate and high-risk account registrations, so that you can selectively introduce additional checks — such as phone or email verification.

21.15 Amazon Sumerian

Amazon Sumerian is a managed service that lets you create and run 3D, Augmented Reality (AR) and Virtual Reality (VR) applications. You can build immersive and interactive scenes that run on AR and VR, mobile devices, and your web browser. Whether you are non-technical, a web or mobile developer, or have years of 3D development experience, getting started with Sumerian is easy. You can design scenes directly from your browser and, because Sumerian is a web-based application, you can quickly add connections in your scenes to existing AWS services.

Amazon Sumerian leverages the power of AWS to create smarter and more engaging front-end experiences. Easily embed conversational interfaces into scenes using Amazon Lex and embed scenes in a web application using AWS Amplify. Amazon Sumerian embraces the latest WebGL and WebXR standards to create immersive experiences directly in a web browser, accessible via a simple URL in seconds, and able to run on major hardware platforms for AR/VR. Build your scene once and deploy it anywhere.

21.16 AWS ML Summary

- Amazon Rekognition: face detection, labeling, celebrity recognition
- Amazon Transcribe: speech to text

- Amazon Polly: text to speech
- Amazon Translate: translations
- Amazon Lex: build chatbots
- Amazon Connect: cloud contact center
- Amazon Comprehend: natural language processing (NLP)
- Amazon SageMaker: ML for developer/data scientist
- Amazon Forecast: build highly accurate forecasts
- Amazon Kendra: ML-powered search engine
- Amazon Personalize: real-time personalized recommendations
- Amazon Textract: detect text and data in documents

21.17 Related YouTube Videos

▶ Amazon ML Services: https://www.youtube.com/playlist?list=PLxLENG-zbPwHSvzuIXf6vx_6D70bCVMCx

21.18 Chapter Review Questions

Question 1:
Which AWS service is used for image and video analysis, including object detection and facial recognition?
- A. Amazon Polly
- B. Amazon Rekognition
- C. Amazon Comprehend
- D. Amazon Lex

Question 2:
What is the primary function of Amazon Transcribe?
- A. Convert text to speech
- B. Translate text into different languages
- C. Convert speech into text
- D. Analyze sentiment in text

Question 3:
Which AWS service allows you to generate speech from text?
- A. Amazon Polly
- B. Amazon Rekognition
- C. Amazon SageMaker
- D. Amazon Textract

Question 4:
What is the primary use case of Amazon Translate?
- A. Detecting fraudulent activity
- B. Real-time text-to-speech conversion
- C. Text translation between languages
- D. Optical character recognition

Question 5:

Which service provides natural language understanding for building chatbots and conversational interfaces?

    A. Amazon SageMaker

    B. Amazon Lex

    C. Amazon Rekognition

    D. Amazon Forecast

Question 6:

Amazon Comprehend is primarily used for which of the following tasks?

    A. Extracting insights from unstructured text

    B. Forecasting time-series data

    C. Fraud detection

    D. Optical character recognition

Question 7:

Which service helps train and deploy machine learning models quickly?

    A. Amazon Rekognition

    B. Amazon Textract

    C. Amazon SageMaker

    D. Amazon Lex

Question 8:

What is the main function of Amazon Forecast?

    A. Forecasting future trends using machine learning

    B. Detecting objects in videos

    C. Translating text between languages

    D. Extracting text and data from scanned documents

Question 9:

Which AWS service is used for document analysis and extracting text from images or PDFs?

    A. Amazon Polly

    B. Amazon Textract

    C. Amazon Kendra

    D. Amazon Rekognition

Question 10:

What is the role of Amazon Kendra in AWS AI/ML services?

    A. Providing intelligent search capabilities

    B. Detecting and preventing fraud

    C. Generating conversational interfaces

    D. Analyzing and summarizing text

21.19 Answers to Chapter Review Questions

1. B. Amazon Rekognition

Explanation: Amazon Rekognition is used for image and video analysis, including object detection, facial recognition, and content moderation.

2. C. Convert speech into text

Explanation: Amazon Transcribe is a speech-to-text service that converts audio files into accurate and readable text.

3. A. Amazon Polly
Explanation: Amazon Polly is a text-to-speech service that converts text into natural-sounding speech.

4. C. Text translation between languages
Explanation: Amazon Translate is used to translate text between different languages in real time.

5. B. Amazon Lex
Explanation: Amazon Lex is a natural language understanding service used to build chatbots and conversational interfaces.

6. A. Extracting insights from unstructured text
Explanation: Amazon Comprehend is a natural language processing service used to analyze text for insights such as sentiment, key phrases, and entities.

7. C. Amazon SageMaker
Explanation: Amazon SageMaker is a fully managed service that helps train, build, and deploy machine learning models quickly and efficiently.

8. A. Forecasting future trends using machine learning
Explanation: Amazon Forecast uses machine learning to provide accurate time-series predictions for future trends.

9. B. Amazon Textract
Explanation: Amazon Textract is used for document analysis, extracting text, and structured data from images or scanned documents like PDFs.

10. A. Providing intelligent search capabilities
Explanation: Amazon Kendra is a highly accurate enterprise search service that uses machine learning to deliver relevant search results across content sources.

Appendix - Setting Up AWS CLI and AWS SDK

The AWS Command Line Interface (CLI) and AWS Software Development Kit (SDK) are essential tools for DevOps engineers working with AWS. The AWS CLI allows you to interact with AWS services using command-line commands, while the SDKs enable programmatic access to AWS services in your applications. This chapter will cover the installation and configuration of both the AWS CLI and SDKs on macOS and Windows platforms, providing examples and best practices for each.

Setting Up AWS CLI
Installing AWS CLI on macOS
1. Homebrew Installation:
  - First, ensure that Homebrew is installed. Open Terminal and run:

```
1. /bin/bash -c "$(curl -fsSL https://raw.githubusercontent.com/Homebrew/install/HEAD/install.sh)"
```

  - Install AWS CLI using Homebrew:

```
1. brew install awscli
```

  - Verify the installation:

```
1. aws --version
```

2. Direct Download:
  - Download the installer from the AWS CLI download page.
    (https://docs.aws.amazon.com/cli/latest/userguide/install-cliv2-mac.html)
  - Open the downloaded .pkg file and follow the on-screen instructions to install.
  - Verify the installation:

```
1. aws --version
```

Installing AWS CLI on Windows
1. Direct Download:
  - Download the MSI installer for Windows from the AWS CLI download page.
  - Run the downloaded installer and follow the setup instructions.
  - Open Command Prompt (cmd) or PowerShell and verify the installation:

```
1. aws --version
```

2. Windows Package Manager (winget):
  - Open Command Prompt or PowerShell and run:

```
1. winget install awscli
```

  - Verify the installation:

```
1. aws --version
```

Configuring AWS CLI
1. Configuration Command:
  - Run the configuration command to set up access keys, default region, and output format:

```
1. aws configure
```

- You will be prompted to enter:
  - AWS Access Key ID
  - AWS Secret Access Key
  - Default region name (e.g., us-west-2)
  - Default output format (e.g., json)

2. Configuration File:
- Configuration details are saved in ~/.aws/config and credentials in ~/.aws/credentials on macOS/Linux, and C:\Users\<username>\.aws on Windows.
- Example configuration in config file:

```
1. [default]
2. region = us-west-2
3. output = json
```

3. Using Named Profiles:
- Create multiple profiles for different environments:

```
1. aws configure --profile dev
2. aws configure --profile prod
```

- Use a profile by specifying it in the command:

```
1. aws s3 ls --profile dev
```

Setting Up AWS SDKs
AWS SDK for Python (Boto3) on macOS and Windows
1. Installing Boto3:
- Install boto3 using pip:

```
1. pip install boto3
```

- Verify the installation:

```
1. python -c "import boto3; print(boto3.__version__)"
```

2. Example Usage:
- A simple script to list S3 buckets:

```
1. import boto3
2.
3. # Create a session using default profile
4. session = boto3.Session(profile_name='default')
5. s3 = session.resource('s3')
6.
7. # List all buckets
8. for bucket in s3.buckets.all():
9.     print(bucket.name)
10.
```

AWS SDK for JavaScript (Node.js) on macOS and Windows
1. Installing AWS SDK:
- Use npm to install the AWS SDK:

```
1. npm install aws-sdk
```

```
1. node -e "console.log(require('aws-sdk').VERSION)"
```

2. Example Usage:

A script to list S3 buckets:

```
 1. const AWS = require('aws-sdk');
 2.
 3. // Configure the region
 4. AWS.config.update({ region: 'us-west-2' });
 5.
 6. // Create S3 service object
 7. const s3 = new AWS.S3();
 8.
 9. // Call S3 to list current buckets
10. s3.listBuckets(function (err, data) {
11.   if (err) {
12.     console.log("Error", err);
13.   } else {
14.     console.log("Bucket List", data.Buckets);
15.   }
16. });
17.
```

AWS SDK for Java on macOS and Windows
1 Installing AWS SDK:
Add the following dependency in your pom.xml file for Maven:

```
<dependency>
<groupId>com.amazonaws</groupId>
<artifactId>aws-java-sdk</artifactId>
<version>1.12.15</version>
</dependency>
```

2. Example Usage:
Java program to list S3 buckets:

```
 1. import com.amazonaws.services.s3.AmazonS3;
 2. import com.amazonaws.services.s3.AmazonS3ClientBuilder;
 3. import com.amazonaws.services.s3.model.Bucket;
 4.
 5. public class S3ListBuckets {
 6.     public static void main(String[] args) {
 7.         AmazonS3 s3 = AmazonS3ClientBuilder.standard().build();
 8.         for (Bucket bucket : s3.listBuckets()) {
 9.             System.out.println(bucket.getName());
10.         }
11.     }
12. }
```

Best Practices
Managing Credentials:
- Use IAM roles and policies for permissions management instead of hardcoding access keys.
- Use AWS SSO for managing user access in multiple accounts.

Environment-Specific Configurations:

- Create separate profiles for development, staging, and production environments.
- Use environment variables to manage configuration dynamically.

Security:
- Regularly rotate access keys and use IAM policies with least privilege.
- Enable multi-factor authentication (MFA) for additional security.

Troubleshooting

AWS CLI Command Errors:
- Ensure that the correct profile is set and the credentials are correct.
- Verify that the region specified is available for the services being used.

SDK Connection Issues:
- Ensure that the SDK is properly configured with the correct region and credentials.
- Check network connectivity and firewall settings that may block requests.

Conclusion

Setting up the AWS CLI and SDKs on macOS and Windows environments is the first step toward effective management and automation of AWS resources. By understanding the installation process, configuration options, and best practices, you can ensure a secure and efficient workflow in your DevOps journey.

Further Reading and Resources:

AWS CLI User Guide: https://docs.aws.amazon.com/cli/
AWS SDK Documentation (Python) : https://docs.aws.amazon.com/pythonsdk/

Final Thoughts

Cloud computing has undeniably redefined the technological landscape, empowering businesses and individuals with scalable, flexible, and cost-effective solutions. This book has taken you on a journey that bridges foundational cloud concepts with practical expertise in Amazon Web Services (AWS), the industry leader in cloud services.

In the first section, we established a solid understanding of cloud computing fundamentals, including its evolution, core models, architecture principles, and essential security measures. These foundations are critical for grasping how the cloud operates and why it has become the backbone of modern IT infrastructure. We explored virtualization, service management, and cost optimization strategies that allow businesses to leverage the cloud effectively and efficiently.

The second section offered an in-depth exploration of AWS, providing step-by-step guidance on core AWS services, from compute and storage to networking, databases, and AI/ML capabilities. Each chapter combined theory with hands-on exercises to ensure a practical understanding of the tools and technologies AWS offers. Topics such as Identity and Access Management (IAM), VPC networking, security best practices, and DevOps tools prepared you to manage and optimize AWS cloud environments securely and confidently.

As we conclude this journey, it is clear that mastering cloud computing and AWS services is no longer optional but essential for modern businesses and IT professionals. Whether you're a beginner or a seasoned professional, this book equips you with the knowledge and skills needed to design, implement, and manage robust cloud solutions. Embracing the power of AWS will enable you to innovate faster, enhance operational efficiency, and drive business growth in an increasingly digital world.

With the cloud continuously evolving, the concepts and services discussed in this book lay a strong foundation to build upon. Keep exploring, experimenting, and refining your skills to stay ahead in the dynamic world of cloud technology.

References

1. https://docs.aws.amazon.com/AWSEC2/latest/UserGuide/concepts.html
2. https://aws.amazon.com/autoscaling/
3. https://aws.amazon.com/s3/
4. https://aws.amazon.com/ebs/
5. https://aws.amazon.com/iam/
6. https://docs.aws.amazon.com/vpc/latest/userguide/VPC_Internet_Gateway.html
7. https://aws.amazon.com/directconnect/
8. https://aws.amazon.com/rds/
9. https://aws.amazon.com/elasticache/
10. https://aws.amazon.com/redis/
11. https://aws.amazon.com/emr/
12. https://aws.amazon.com/kinesis/
13. https://aws.amazon.com/ses/
14. https://aws.amazon.com/sns
15. https://aws.amazon.com/ecs/
16. https://aws.amazon.com/location/
17. https://aws.amazon.com/api-gateway/
18. https://aws.amazon.com/amplify/
19. https://aws.amazon.com/sagemaker/
20. https://aws.amazon.com/workspaces/
21. https://aws.amazon.com/workmail/
22. https://aws.amazon.com/workdocs/
23. https://aws.amazon.com/about-aws/global-infrastructure/regions_az/
24. https://en.wikipedia.org/wiki/Cloud_computing
25. https://www.backblaze.com/blog/vm-vs-containers/
26. https://www.ibm.com/cloud/blog/containers-vs-vms
27. https://www.vxchnge.com/blog/different-types-of-cloud-computing
28. https://www.cloudflare.com/learning/serverless/what-is-serverless/
29. https://aws.amazon.com/serverless/
30. https://www.ibm.com/cloud/learn/serverless
31. https://dzone.com/articles/serverless-services-on-aws-an-overview
32. https://docs.docker.com/desktop/mac/install/
33. https://docs.docker.com/desktop/windows/install/

34. https://www.zdnet.com/article/using-google-authenticator-heres-why-you-should-get-rid-of-it/
35. https://hub.docker.com/
36. https://docs.docker.com/engine/reference/commandline/docker/
37. https://en.wikipedia.org/wiki/Multi-factor_authentication
38. https://www.aboutamazon.com/news/aws/partnering-with-the-nfl-to-transform-player-health-and-safety
39. https://www.contino.io/insights/whos-using-aws
40. https://press.aboutamazon.com/news-releases/news-release-details/twitter-selects-aws-strategic-provider-serve-timelines
41. https://docs.aws.amazon.com/whitepapers/latest/aws-overview/security-and-compliance.html
42. https://www.zdnet.com/article/using-google-authenticator-heres-why-you-should-get-rid-of-it/
43. https://www.youtube.com/watch?v=0R23JRR671I
44. https://www.reddit.com/r/askscience/comments/5imnis/how_do_gemalto_tokens_work_curious_how_the_system/

Thank you for taking the time to read *Cloud Computing and AWs Introduction*. I hope this book has provided you with a comprehensive understanding and practical, hands-on knowledge of cloud computing and AWS fundamentals.

Your feedback is incredibly important to me. If you found this book helpful, I would greatly appreciate it if you could leave a review or share your thoughts by emailing me at support@knodacx.com. Your suggestions not only help improve future editions but also guide other readers on their AWS cloud architecture journey.

Thank you once again for your support. I wish you great success in all your AWS cloud endeavors!